FACING THE WORLD

Facing the World

Defense Spending and International Trade
in the Pacific Northwest Since World War II

CHRISTOPHER P. FOSS

Oregon State University Press   Corvallis

Library of Congress Cataloging-in-Publication Data

Names: Foss, Christopher P., author.
Title: Facing the world : defense spending and international trade in the
  Pacific Northwest since World War II / Christopher P. Foss.
Description: Corvallis : Oregon State University Press, [2020] | Includes
  bibliographical references and index.
Identifiers: LCCN 2019055808 | ISBN 9780870719905 (paperback ; alk. paper)
  | ISBN 9780870719912
Subjects: LCSH: Economic development—Northwest, Pacific—History. |
  Northwest, Pacific—Commerce—History. | National security—Northwest,
  Pacific—History. | Defense industries—Northwest, Pacific—History. |
  Northwest, Pacific—Politics and government. | United States. Department
  of Defense—Appropriations and expenditures.
Classification: LCC HC107.A19 F67 2020 | DDC 338.4/735500979—dc23
LC record available at https://lccn.loc.gov/2019055808

♾This paper meets the requirements of ANSI/NISO Z39.48-1992
(Permanence of Paper).

First published in 2020 by Oregon State University Press
Printed in the United States of America

Oregon State University
OSU Press

Oregon State University Press
121 The Valley Library
Corvallis OR 97331-4501
541-737-3166 • fax 541-737-3170
www.osupress.oregonstate.edu

Contents

Contents

Acknowledgments

This book is a labor of love, but it was initially born out of the necessity that all who go into graduate school eventually face—to get out! I started my career wanting to do a project on US-Argentine relations during the Cold War. I got that out of my system, then decided I was interested in the history of bookstores, having worked in one for many years. The research paper that came out of that was a passion project, but it did not lend itself well to my primary field of US foreign relations. But in the summer of 2012, with only a few months to go until my comprehensive exams, the light bulb came on after I read former University of Nevada, Las Vegas, professor Andy Fry's *Diplomatic History* roundtable on domestic regionalism. Recalling that many prominent post–World War II politicians from Oregon and Washington were also strongly interested in US foreign relations, I got the idea of blending the histories of US politics and foreign relations in a work centered in my home region of the Pacific Northwest.

I want to thank the faculty at the University of Colorado Boulder, who supported me financially and provided mentorship before, during, and after this book was in the dissertation stage of my program in US history. Thomas Zeiler, my adviser for many of those years, kept me on track, patiently read and critiqued my work numerous times, and even kept me fed, thanks to numerous jobs he procured for me—including assistant editor of *Diplomatic History*, which allowed me to step away from teaching duties during a crucial year of dissertation research. My first adviser, Bob Schulzinger, was a key inspiration, even after illness forced him to retire in 2012. Graduate history secretary Scott Miller and dissertation committee members Paul Sutter, Thomas Andrews, Kenneth Bickers, and Kenneth Osgood were indispensable. The University of Colorado History Department, especially the members of the Graduate Studies Committee, provided travel and conference funding, as did the University of Colorado Graduate School. The Gerald R. Ford Presidential Library funded a major archival trip in the summer of 2015.

Archivists are the oft-unsung heroes of our discipline who make history possible by unearthing, organizing, and interpreting primary documents. I went to historical societies, university archives, presidential libraries, and other repositories throughout Oregon, Washington, Idaho, Wyoming, Colorado, Michigan, and Texas in support of this project. All the archivists I met were helpful, but I particularly appreciate Scott Daniels (Oregon Historical Society), Cheryl Gunselman (Washington State University), Mary McRobinson (Willamette University), and Paul Meuse (Willamette University). Beyond archives, I'm also extremely grateful to be able to forge links with those who helped shape the past I wrote about. Special thanks to Senator Slade Gorton for granting me a background interview that was helpful in crafting part of chapter 5, as well as former Senator Mark Hatfield staffers Gerry Frank, Gary Barbour, Wes Granberg-Michaelson, Tom Getman, Walt Evans, Jack Robertson, Steve Nousen, Carrie Klein, and Rick Rolf for their encouragement and their retrospectives on their old boss.

Conferences and workshops gave me forums at which to try out new ideas and make new acquaintances and friends who provided invaluable suggestions over the years. I particularly thank Andrew Johns and Mitchell Lerner for accepting me into the Society of Historians of American Foreign Relations (SHAFR) Summer Institute in June 2015 on the links between domestic politics and US foreign relations, where I presented part of my work and made friends with a great group of young historians, nearly all of whom work today in universities across the United States. The edited volume *The Cold War at Home and Abroad: Domestic Politics and US Foreign Policy Since 1945*, emerged from that workshop, published by the University Press of Kentucky. Beyond the SHAFR Summer Institute, I also was able to present parts of this work at other SHAFR conferences, as well as annual meetings of the Washington State Historical Society, the Western History Association, and the Pacific Coast Branch of the American Historical Association, between 2014 and 2019. I thank my fellow conference attendees and panelists at those events, who are too numerous to name here, for their help in making this a stronger book.

I appreciate the family and friends who provided me with lodging as I researched and presented my work at conferences. My parents, Judy and Lee Foss, were particularly patient and welcoming. Jared Prenguber, video producer for Washington State University Athletics and one of my best friends from a young age, put me up and put up with me while juggling Cougars football and baseball commitments. Dana Shaw, Naghme and Justus Morlock, and Carol and Danny Wells also hosted me at various spots around the Northwest, and Carol proofread an early draft of this book.

Beyond the dissertation stage, this book and the articles that came out of it have been in good hands. Special thanks to Mary Elizabeth Braun and Micki Reaman at Oregon State University Press for shepherding this project to completion, and for always enthusiastically believing in the work. I greatly appreciate their words of encouragement and positivity. Thank you also to the anonymous reviewers and the OSU Press Faculty Advisory Editorial Board for your critiques, suggestions, and support. Many thanks to Eliza Canty-Jones at *Oregon Historical Quarterly* and Bruce Hevly at *Pacific Northwest Quarterly* for permitting me to reprint slightly altered versions of articles that appeared in those journals here in chapters 1 and 6. Eliza, Bruce, the anonymous reviewers, and the copyeditors of those articles provided helpful guidance and suggestions.

Willamette University, the University of Portland, and Washington State University Vancouver provided me adjunct teaching positions and supportive communities as I completed the book. I particularly thank Ellen Eisenberg, Wendy Petersen Boring, Jennifer Jopp, Lora Yasen, Brian Els, Christin Hancock, Debbie MacKinnon, Blair Woodard, Laurie Mercier, and Sue Peabody for their much-needed moral and material support. I was also sustained financially through work at Powell's Books and the Franciscan Montessori Earth School. At the latter, where I was essentially raised for so many of my formative years (first grade into high school), Laurie Langevin, Heidi Walz, and Sister Therese Gutting deserve particular thanks for their mentorship and encouragement to stay on track with my work.

Big thanks also to my many friends who helped me get through the writing process. I especially appreciate grad school friends and fellow historians Doug Snyder, Dan DuBois, Keith Aksel, and Dave Varel. Outside of graduate school, Jeffrey Carlson and Matthew Micetic were especially great sources of support. Along with Doug, Dan, and Keith, they formed the groom's side of my wedding party; it's hard to find a better group of guys than that.

I again thank my parents for their ever-sustaining hospitality, advice, and love upon return visits to my home base in Portland, Oregon. My in-laws, MaryEllen and John Oilar, provided housing, many airport rides when I went on research trips, food, and good company. My beloved wife, Michelle Foss, made me take frequent breaks for exercise, put up with years of my sweating the small stuff, and endured my frequent trips away from her for research. Our son, Evan Caleb Foss, was born just as this book went to press. His imminent arrival inspired me through the hard work of finding illustrations, proofreading, and other finishing touches. I love you both forever: my heart always beats stronger when I know I have you to return home to.

I close by acknowledging lost friends and family, particularly my godmother, Patricia Steen Iverson, who passed away shortly before I submitted my final dissertation draft. The eastern Oregon-raised daughter of Republican state senator Lowell Steen, Pat interned for Senator Mark Hatfield in the early 1970s, and continued to hold great interest in Pacific Northwest politics even after her career took her to Oregon Health and Science University. Pat was a huge proponent of the project, and she pushed me to keep going with it even when I was discouraged. Thank you, Pat, for being an inspiration to work hard and persevere.

Major Ports of the Pacific Northwest

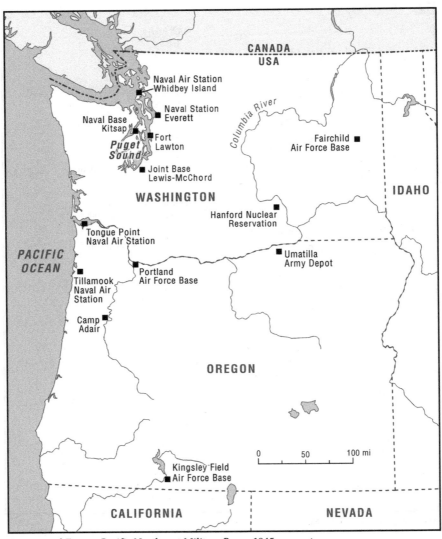

Current and Former Pacific Northwest Military Bases, 1945–present

Introduction

At the start of the 1940s, America was slowly emerging from the Great Depression, but not yet in the Second World War. Oregon's population at the time of the 1940 US census was 1,087,717, while Washington counted 1,721,376 residents. The region had four cities with a population of 100,000 or more, led by Seattle with 366,847, with Portland at 307,572, Spokane at 122,462, and Tacoma at 107,520. Slightly over 53 percent of Washington's population lived in urban areas, while just under 52 percent of Oregonians still lived in rural areas. Befitting its location on the Pacific Ocean, the Northwest states had a number of small military installations, led by the US Army post at Fort Lewis near Tacoma. Despite this coastal location, the Northwest states only exported $115 million in goods in 1940 and imported just $48 million. Many urbanites worked in factories or mills linked with the region's dominant extractive industry, timber. Many of those in rural areas felled trees for harvest; others farmed wheat or fished for salmon. Boeing was a relatively nascent airplane manufacturer, and Oregon's high-tech Silicon Forest at this time consisted merely of the US Forest Service Radio Lab.[1] The region had no microbreweries, future *Portlandia* stars Fred Armisen and Carrie Brownstein were decades from being born, and the coffee scene was dominated by the likes of Sanka and Maxwell House. Oregon Senator Charles McNary, the Senate minority leader and Republican vice presidential candidate in 1940, helped bring the area New Deal benefits by working across the aisle with the Democrats. McNary was the rare accomplished politician in a region better known for rightist reactionaries like former Oregon Representative Willis Hawley and Governor Charles "Iron Pants" Martin.

Flash forward to 2019. The United States was again emerging from economic calamity—the Great Recession—but this time the Pacific

Northwest was a leader in the recovery as an increasingly prosperous leader among US regions. Skyscrapers and construction cranes dominated the skylines of Seattle and Portland, which by 2016 boasted metropolitan area populations of 3,798,902 and 2,425,325 people, respectively. The Northwest's leading cities also had significantly below-average poverty rankings and above-average rankings in per capita income, home value, and educational attainment.[2] Listing "the 25 best cities to live in" based on data from the US Census Bureau, the Bureau of Labor Statistics, and recent Federal Bureau of Investigation (FBI) crime statistics, CBS News ranked Seattle 21st, while its suburb Bellevue ranked 10th. A *USA Today* report in late 2017 on what it considered to be the top 50 small cities in the United States—based on population, average home value, property rate, and the percentage of residents with a bachelor's degree—listed Bend, Oregon, at 43rd, Kirkland, Washington, 42nd, and Beaverton, Oregon, 37th.[3] The military stored and then incinerated much of its chemical weapons stock at Oregon's Umatilla Army Depot, sited plutonium production and nuclear waste storage and cleanup at Washington's Hanford Nuclear Reservation, and homeported nuclear submarines and aircraft carriers in Puget Sound. Washington also housed three major US Air Force, Army, and Navy bases: Joint Base Lewis-McChord, Fairchild Air Force Base, and Naval Station Everett, helping buttress the economies of Everett, Seattle, and Spokane. A host of recognizable global brand names—Microsoft, Amazon, Nintendo of America, Starbucks, Intel, Nike, Powell's Books, and Tektronix, to name a few— call the Northwest home and are among the region's chief employers. Major films and TV series, including *Animal House, The Goonies, Kindergarten Cop, Drugstore Cowboy, Northern Exposure, Sleepless in Seattle, Twilight, Fifty Shades of Grey,* and *Portlandia* were shot in the region. *Battlestar Galactica,* perhaps the most iconic TV series of the early 2000s, was filmed just across the border in Vancouver, British Columbia, taking advantage of the Northwest's natural environment for location shooting.

So, what changed? *Facing the World* is the story of how this modern, prosperous region came to be. For decades after Oregon and Washington joined the United States, the Pacific Northwest was a small outpost, dwarfed by California and larger, more powerful states in the East. By the time of World War II, and especially during the Cold War, the situation began to change. Led by progressive politicians and businesses at the federal and state level, and aided by the federal government, the military, and by foreign trade and direct investment, Oregon and Washington faced the nation at large—and the world—with peerless vigor in the late twentieth and early twenty-first centuries.

In 1993—three years before his retirement from the US Senate—Mark Hatfield of Oregon spoke to Chet Orloff of the Oregon Historical Society about the immense changes from the time of his small-town upbringing to the post–Cold War world. Over the course of Hatfield's long life—he was born in 1922 and died in 2011—the senator came of age during the Great Depression, fought in World War II, presided over the passage of Oregon's first civil rights law while in the state legislature, and worked for economic growth as governor. As US senator, Hatfield famously tried to end the Vietnam War, and brought federal riches to Oregon while helping to change the public perception of national security. In the beginning, however, Hatfield grew up in the small town of Dallas, Oregon, where community and region were bedrock principles. From an early age, learning about what life was like in the community going back several generations, Hatfield believed a strong sense of place played a role in the formation of his identity, as well as that of his community. "We belonged to something," he recalled. "We belonged first to our family, we belonged to our school and our classmates, we belonged to our church and its congregation, we belonged to the city . . . and it was a cohesive force."[4]

Hatfield was part of a generation of politicians in his home region—geographically described here as Washington and Oregon, but culturally as the Pacific Northwest—who felt much the same, and were important power brokers in the region, the nation, and the world in the years after the Second World War. Other politicians in other regions of the United States have often attributed their success to their local connections and have been able to bring home federal spending. Hatfield and his colleagues did likewise. They were unique, however, in being able to bring home a disproportionate number of federal dollars to a small, relatively unpopulated region. These federal and state officials brought the Pacific Northwest into the national mainstream, while maintaining the balance between growth and harmony with the natural environment on which the region has long prided itself. By using the post–World War II imperatives of national security and international trade, Pacific Northwest politicians used political power accrued during years of legislative experience and congressional seniority to economically transform Washington and Oregon.

The historical endurance of politicians like Wayne Morse, Henry Jackson, and Mark Hatfield; businesses like Boeing and Nike; and debates surrounding salmon, lumber, and hydroelectricity demonstrate that the Pacific Northwest obtained national and international influence despite its relatively small population vis-à-vis other regions of the United States. The region's politicians have effectively used their power to obtain federal dollars leading to the construction of military bases, dams, and other infrastructure projects. They also successfully garnered federal support for the expansion of international trade. In short, politicians in Washington and Oregon, via US foreign policy, played a crucial role in the economic growth and transformation of the United States, particularly in the Northwest, after World War II.

The Pacific Northwest was far from exceptional in its aims to attract more defense spending and more international trade in the postwar era—much of the rest of the United States was trying to do the same. Neither Oregon nor Washington ever ranked at the top of the nation in imports and exports, although they were two of the most trade-dependent states in the nation. Pacific Rim nations found ready and willing trade partners and homes for foreign subsidiaries in many other states in the United States, particularly in California and Texas, as they expanded to become the two biggest states in the country in terms of population during the Cold War. Japanese automakers Honda and Nissan, perhaps the most conspicuous of all foreign investors in the late twentieth century, based plants in Ohio and Tennessee in the 1970s and 1980s, taking advantage of historically low costs of labor , as the country as a whole became more dependent on foreign goods and international trade for its well-being.[5]

The unique story of the economic development of Washington and Oregon needs to be considered, however. It is, to some degree, an overlooked story because the Pacific Northwest states have often been considered the hinterland of the nation.[6] After the Oregon Trail, the

Northwest typically disappears from mainstream textbooks on US history and US diplomatic history. California has long fired the dreams of easterners who focused on gold, Hollywood, and eventually Silicon Valley, whereas boosters for transcontinental railroads and little hamlets in the Northwest were not quite as successful in luring people there. Still, the two world wars of the twentieth century brought increasing numbers of migrants to the region to take advantage of a unique geographical juxtaposition: the Columbia River and the hydroelectric power it generates alongside enormous stands of old-growth timber used to build planes for war. Even with the draw of its natural resources, the Northwest could have receded in the decades after World War II. It was largely because of the emergence of a liberal, activist political generation in the region, working in tandem with a variety of business and defense interests, that it did not.

There is a sense, however intangible but nonetheless prevalent, held by the residents of Washington and Oregon that they live in a unique place. The Pacific Northwest has been thought of as special, even Edenic, by the descendants of white settlers who began arriving there in the mid-nineteenth century, and even by the descendants of the various immigrants of color who followed in the late nineteenth and twentieth centuries. Many residents of Washington and Oregon feel that their home region is exceptional. Despite this perceived uniqueness, many often feel slighted, forgotten, and even disrespected by the rest of the nation.[7] When Mark Hatfield stated the belief that Oregonians were becoming disconnected from their sense of place, he may have been reflecting a sense of loss of exceptionalism. Over the course of the post–World War II era, foreign relations—broadly inclusive of national defense and international import and export trade—transformed the Pacific Northwest from an economic backwater dependent solely upon extractive industries to a more well-rounded economy driven by manufacturing, tourism, high-tech, and foreign direct investment from the Pacific Rim. At the same time, however, that the Pacific Northwest ceased to be the colonial hinterland of the United States, it lost the distance from the national mainstream which made it exceptional. The Northwest became just another part of the United States because of the efforts of its politicians and its people to economically grow and transform.

Foreign relations encompass not just the work of presidents, cabinets, and ambassadors, nor solely the engagement of the populace with policies imposed on them by a federal behemoth. Regional political power shaped the effects of foreign relations in Washington and Oregon during the postwar era. Coalitions of federal politicians, state politicians, lobbyists of various stripes, and businesspeople almost always agreed that the key to guaranteeing prosperity for the Pacific Northwest hinged on economic development predicated on increased defense spending (or, increasingly after Vietnam, redirected defense spending toward a new national security of education and health) and increased international trade links. Not all residents of the region benefited from the globally oriented development. As became increasingly clear near the end of the twentieth century, the region's poor, people of color, and even those concerned with the plight of the natural environment often found their voices silenced in the name of progress. Economic growth and diversification would have painful consequences, but these were unclear at the end of World War II. What we can say for certain is that the Pacific Northwest was transformed and internationalized thanks to the work of its most powerful and longest-tenured politicians during the postwar era.

Historian Richard White argues that for much of its history, the American West, more than any other region, has been a colonial appendage of the United States.[8] At the very least, the United States government traditionally saw the states of the far West as distant and incapable of influencing the decision-making powers that made national policy.[9] Events of the Great Depression and World War II tested the federal government's perception of the Pacific Northwest as colonial hinterland, however. The Grand Coulee and Bonneville Dams, constructed during the Depression, generated enough electricity to power the region's aluminum industry, shipyards, and the Hanford Nuclear Reservation, which produced the plutonium in the atomic bombs the US dropped on Japan in August 1945.[10] The population of Oregon and Washington dramatically increased during the war, thanks in large part to migrations of people looking for work in wartime industries. Oregon and Washington, then, played a major role in the Allied triumph in World War II.

In the wake of the vicissitudes of depression and war, a generation of liberal politicians in both major US political parties saw in new constituencies—many of whom depended on jobs provided by the federal government or in the region's nascent manufacturing sector—the opportunity to shake up the previously conservative politics of the Pacific Northwest and to chart a course toward lasting prosperity.[11] Because the Northwest was positioned geographically adjacent to the Pacific Ocean, many of these individuals saw foreign policies of national defense and international trade as vehicles through which to stimulate growth. The Cold War provided an opportunity for them to push the federal government for assistance in developing the region. The fight against communism provided a political opening for increased federal spending, even among fiscal conservatives, who now saw national security as overriding the need for tightening the nation's pocketbook. In sharp contrast to the laissez-faire attitude many Pacific Northwest residents took toward government prior to the New Deal, the residents of the region, like others in the nation, came to see the government as a welfare state that would help provide employment, education, infrastructure, and access to healthcare. They did not want to go back to the privations of the Great Depression, nor succumb to the Soviets, so government spending, obtained with the assistance of their representatives, became the regional path to prosperity for the residents of the Pacific Northwest.[12]

All regions of the United States benefited from the expansion of military bases and defense contractors that took place during World War II and the early years of the Cold War. But the Pacific Northwest had to fight hard to keep its bases and contractors. Because its geographic proximity to the Soviet Union made it a tempting target, from a strategic point of view, it might have been wiser to locate more of the national security state in the heartland of the country. Indeed, national defense facilities such as North American Aerospace Defense Command (NORAD), the Air Force Academy, and many Minuteman nuclear silos were positioned in the Rocky Mountains and the Midwest. Politics was another factor. The Pacific Northwest's population was small relative to California, the South, and the East Coast, areas that had stronger electoral influence, thereby making them more tempting areas for the federal government, whether controlled by Democrats or

Republicans, to offer defense dollars as patronage. As historians have repeatedly shown, the "Sun Belt" states of the South and Southwest particularly benefited from the military-industrial largesse of the Cold War years.[13] As more people were lured to defense-related jobs in those states, a circular logic developed that population growth would beget regional defense spending and vice versa. An increased population also meant more Electoral College votes for presidents, and more representatives lapping at the federal trough. In 1944, for example, Oregon had six Electoral College votes and Washington had eight; today, they have seven and twelve, respectively. Texas and California, by contrast, went from twenty-three and twenty-five votes to thirty-eight and fifty-five, respectively.

Certainly, the latter two states have benefited from their dramatically increased electoral power. Each has had two favorite sons win the presidency since World War II and gained tremendous amounts of military spending and several defense contractors, while experiencing dramatic gains in international trade. Washington and Oregon were lucky in the postwar years, however, because many of their congressional officials developed seniority that allowed them to have an outsized degree of influence.

In Washington, federal and state officials, especially Senators Henry Jackson and Warren Magnuson, worked assiduously to maintain defense installations and provide federal largesse to defense contractors. Oregon Senator Wayne Morse, by contrast, is perceived—somewhat unfairly—as fiercely independent of the military establishment because of his dissent against several major US foreign policy endeavors of the Cold War, most famously the Vietnam War. Morse could afford to be independent, however, because the military historically viewed Washington as a more strategically suitable for the development of military bases.[14] Oregon thus bred a number of politicians, most notably Senators Morse and Hatfield, who vigorously challenged US foreign and domestic policies they believed advanced US strategic interests, while generating deficit spending at home and anti-Americanism abroad. They did so not just because they believed those policies to be inherently wrong, but also because they believed Oregon did not benefit from those policies. Oregon politicians were not doves; in fact, they did try to maintain military bases and encourage defense contractors to come to their state. They had better luck, however, luring international trade.

As the Cold War national security threat began to decline in the era of US-Soviet détente starting in the mid-1960s, Northwest politicians pushed for greater growth in the region's foreign trade, particularly with Pacific Rim countries. Tom McCall, Oregon governor from 1967 to 1975, is ironically perhaps most famous for a 1971 speech in which he said that tourists were welcome to visit, but not to settle in the state. McCall, however, was mainly targeting the "Californication" he saw pervading the Northwest from the south; he joined Washington and other US states in adopting a welcoming international trade policy.[15] In the early 1970s, McCall enthusiastically welcomed Japanese business representatives to Oregon to strengthen business ties between Japan and Oregon, setting the stage for much greater growth in trade between the two which occurred during Victor Atiyeh's terms as governor a decade later. McCall's views highlight a major shift in the outlook of the Pacific Northwest toward the world, especially Pacific Rim peoples and nations, that economically and culturally transformed the Northwest during the latter decades of the twentieth century and into the twenty-first century.

This examination of the Pacific Northwest in relationship to the world discusses in detail the regional, domestic influences on US foreign policy that became increasingly commonplace during and after the Cold War. The region's federal politicians drove many of these influences. In the Pacific Northwest, politicians used traditional power politics—the power of their elected offices and/or the committees to which they were appointed—to balance economic prosperity achieved via federal government dollars targeted at improving regional defense and trade with other nations with the preservation of the states' natural beauty and civic values. In short, politicians from Washington and Oregon used not only federal largesse, but also foreign relations, to economically develop the Pacific Northwest parallel to a period of national economic transformation that followed World War II.

A few key political figures stood out in Washington and Oregon in this transformative context. Warren Magnuson, congressman from Washington's First District from 1937 to 1944, and one of its US senators from 1944 to 1980, is best known for his role in helping pass domestic legislation on civil rights and consumer issues. Magnuson also used his committee positions in Congress to ensure continued appropriations for Washington's military bases, to assist defense contractors like Boeing, and to further international trade to the region. Henry "Scoop" Jackson did much the same in his positions as Washington's Second District congressman from 1941 to 1953 and US senator from 1953 until his death in office on September 1, 1983. Arguably best appreciated as an authority on national security issues, Jackson used that authority to channel funds to Washington military installations, particularly the Hanford Nuclear Reservation and the naval bases of Puget Sound, while also serving as a key figure in the growth of the region's trade with the People's Republic of China during the 1970s and early 1980s. In 1961, Jackson hired a young counsel named Tom Foley, who went on to represent the state's Fifth Congressional District from 1965 until his 1994 reelection defeat. Foley is perhaps best remembered for expanding international trade between the state's wheat fields and Pacific Rim countries, particularly Japan and China, during his years as chair of the House Agriculture Committee from 1975 until 1981. Foley continued to exert considerable power to help his constituents in the succeeding years as he ascended the ladder of House leadership, all the way to a five-and-a-half-year stint as Speaker of the House at the end of his career. Foley also notably worked to maintain Fairchild Air Force Base near Spokane, as it became one of his major centers of support in a district which turned increasingly Republican and conservative in the late twentieth century.

Oregon, meanwhile, struggled to catch up to Washington in terms of population and key economic indicators related to defense and trade. Since Oregon became a state in 1859, the Republicans had traditionally been the stronger political party, but the post–World War II years saw the rise of a cohort of liberal Democrats. Like their Washington counterparts, Oregon Democrats sought to increase federal investment in the state for defense and trade purposes, thereby reducing the state's traditional dependence upon the timber industry. Senator Wayne Morse began his political career as a liberal Republican from 1945 to 1953, then served as a political independent from 1953 to 1954 before switching to the Democratic Party in 1955, where he remained until he

New Democratic members of Washington's congressional delegation look at the Congressional Directory in 1965. Seated are Senators Henry Jackson and Warren Magnuson. Standing, from left to right, are new Congressmen Floyd Hicks, Lloyd Meeds, Tom Foley, and Brock Adams. Jackson, Magnuson, and Foley in particular shaped Washington's international reach from the 1940s into the 1990s. Reprinted by permission from University of Washington Special Collections, Henry M. Jackson Photographic and Graphic Materials, Accession 3560-031, 7/10, 1126n; negative no. UW 27204.

was defeated for reelection in 1968. Morse is best known for his Vietnam War dissent, but also for his work locally to garner federal dollars for hydroelectric dams, military defense (especially prior to Vietnam), and international trade interests. In these efforts, he was also joined by Democratic Representatives Edith Green (who served Oregon's Third District from 1955 to 1974) and Congressman Al Ullman (Second District, 1957 to 1980).

Unlike in Washington, however, the Pentagon didn't benefit Oregon. From an economic and military standpoint, the state's most valuable asset was the mouth of the Columbia River as it spilled into the Pacific Ocean. But Oregon was cursed by the stormy Columbia River Bar at the river's juncture with the ocean, which made large-ship passage in and out of Oregon difficult at best. Thus, the state had only

Oregon Senator Wayne Morse, Representative Edith Green, and Senator Richard Neuberger, pictured in the late 1950s, were three forward-looking members of the state's Democratic delegation. Neuberger died following cancer treatment in 1960, but Green and Morse would continue to shape Oregon's responses to a globalizing society through the 1960s. Reprinted by permission from Oregon Historical Society, negative no. 37447.

small military outposts on the coast—Tillamook Naval Air Station, and Tongue Point Naval Station and Fort Stevens near Astoria, each of which closed early in the Cold War—while Washington saw the buildup of a huge naval presence in Puget Sound beginning in the late nineteenth century and lasting well into the twenty-first century. To the east, Oregon lacked Washington's combination of a flat, dusty desert juxtaposed with hydroelectric power and the intense local business boosterism that allowed the Hanford Nuclear Reservation to thrive decades after the bombings of Hiroshima and Nagasaki in Japan. Into the 1970s, Morse and the Oregon delegation were not as cohesive, nor consequently as effective, as the Washingtonians in getting federal spending to augment regional defense and trade interests. When the Republican Party made a national comeback in the late 1970s and early 1980s, Oregon Republicans, in particular Senator Mark Hatfield (1967 to 1997) and Governor Vic Atiyeh (1979 to 1987) found themselves in positions to take advantage and benefit their state.

Mark Hatfield never lost an election, despite often holding views that flew in the face of his constituents. Staffers and the regional press believed part of the reason why Hatfield stayed in power was because he was immensely admired for having an unusually strong moral compass for a politician. This quality translated into a perspective on foreign policy that led him to oppose the Vietnam War and buildups of nuclear and conventional arms. Perhaps because of his innate dovishness, and the lack of strong defense contractors in Oregon, Hatfield never embraced national defense in the same way as his Washington counterparts. He instead believed in refocusing military dollars to education and healthcare. An inscription on the clock tower at his alma mater, Willamette University in Salem, Oregon, reads in part, "Education is national security." In holding and acting upon these beliefs, Hatfield redefined the concept of national security relative to his counterparts in Washington. At the same time, however, like the Washington delegation, he strongly pushed for the expansion of the state's economic base, primarily through increased foreign trade. Hatfield established strong relations with Japan and poured money into infrastructure in Oregon that would aid greater commercial links with Pacific Rim and other nations.

Victor Atiyeh garnered the moniker "Trader Vic" during his eight years as governor, which coincided with the peak of Hatfield's power as, alternately, chair or ranking member of the Senate Appropriations Committee. As former head of the rug importer Atiyeh Bros. and the first Arab American governor in US history, Atiyeh touted his Arab ethnicity and business background to gain the state new trading partners abroad. Although Mark Hatfield and Tom McCall laid the groundwork for increased trade with Japan in the 1960s, Atiyeh made an even greater push, traveling to Japan, China, South Korea, and the Middle East on nearly two dozen occasions during his governorship to promote Oregon businesses and open new trade links between the state and Asian markets. The press was sometimes critical of what it referred to as overseas junkets at the taxpayer's expense, but Atiyeh was generally praised for his work: today the international terminal in Portland International Airport is named in his honor, and Oregon governors continue to regularly boost for the state abroad.[16] Atiyeh made international trade a centerpiece of his economic development agenda; thus, his significant work in the context of Oregon's economic evolution merits examination alongside better-known federal-level senators and representatives.

Statue of Oregon Governor Victor Atiyeh, dedicated in Portland International Airport's international concourse in 2007. As Oregon governor from 1979 to 1987, Atiyeh carried on the work of his predecessors to internationalize Oregon, most notably through trips abroad to Japan, China, Taiwan, the Middle East, and other nations. Photo by author.

Nonelite individuals and groups also worked to effect political and social change in the Pacific Northwest in the twentieth and twenty-first centuries. From radical unionists in Seattle to African Americans in Spokane to Latino migrants in Oregon's Washington County, throughout the Pacific Northwest, nonelite actors have decisively impacted the region's politics and its outlook toward the world.[17] They played a role in shaping the views of the politicians who increasingly oriented the Northwest toward the world, particularly in the ramping up of national defense and increasing trade links in Washington and Oregon. Politicians served as valuable go-betweens when businesses abroad wanted to make connections with other businesses and ordinary people in the Pacific Northwest, and vice versa, offering introductions and going through seemingly mundane and ceremonial acts of diplomacy that laid the groundwork for future business in their states. Prodded by avalanches of constituent mail and always reading the tea leaves of public opinion, politicians also used their power in Congress to bring in defense and trade-related federal funding through appropriations that brought thousands of jobs to the Pacific Northwest and diversified the region's demographics. These officials cajoled, bartered, and sometimes intimidated their way to get what they wanted for their home states. Because of the orientation of Washington and Oregon on the Pacific Ocean, foreign relations, broadly defined as inclusive of homeland defense and regional imports and exports, facilitated the economic transformation of the Pacific Northwest after World War II.

This economic transformation, for good and ill, is detailed in the context of national defense in part 1 (chapters 1, 2, and 3) and international trade in part 2 (chapters 4, 5, and 6). In the wake of World War II, Pacific Northwest politicians generally agreed with their national counterparts in the federal government that economic growth was achievable through expansion of the military presence in the US homeland, as well as through strengthening of international trade ties. The latter would come more slowly than the former, given the exigencies of the US-Soviet confrontation early in the Cold War. *Facing the World* shows how, through the actions and changing policies of Pacific Northwest politicians, the region transitioned from an orientation toward growing the economy through federal government spending—including on the military—to a more mixed economic portfolio that supplemented military and federal spending with an increased emphasis on trade, infrastructure, and healthcare. As congressional purse strings tightened during the late twentieth century, the Pacific Northwest had to do more with less, but still had strong political champions in the nation's capital, and also saw voters turn to more local leaders like governors as the region economically and culturally transformed. This is the story of how the Pacific Northwest evolved from a hinterland to become fully integrated into the United States' economy and society.

PART I

Globalizing the Pacific Northwest through National Defense

CHAPTER 1

Washington: The National Security State within a State[1]

In the wake of the unsettling geopolitical presence of the Soviet Union after World War II came an "ideological fervor" in the United States, one associated with anticommunist doctrine and nationwide public acceptance of the costs and dangers of the Cold War.[2] In this climate, the politics of national security was largely embraced by the residents of Washington and Oregon, but particularly in Washington. During the war, Washington had fifty US Army and Navy bases, and the state's major defense contractor, the Boeing Company, employed over 50,000 people.[3] The Cold War saw Boeing's employment swell to over 100,000 workers at times, and Washington maintained and expanded many of its armed forces bases despite occasional calls to curtail the defense presence in the state. Since 1945, various Washington politicians have worked to build up and maintain the state's defense establishments. To do so, they had to engage both the business community and the public at large, convincing them that national security was an issue that affected their lives personally, and that a defense buildup could improve their lives. For the most part, Washington politicians did so successfully, and national security politics played a large role in making the state a player on the national stage. As such, Washington was a national security state within a state throughout the Cold War.

Federal spending, particularly on defense, has been integral to the economy of Washington since the late nineteenth century.[4] Boeing, which was founded in 1916 and began selling "flying boats" to the US Navy as early as 1917, has particularly been synonymous with national defense efforts and the state economy. The *Washington State Atlas and Databook* for 1990 touted aerospace, a Boeing specialty, as "the most important manufacturing industry in the state" and highlighted

Boeing's history as a major defense contractor. With its employment rising to over 100,000 in 1988, Boeing was the most powerful engine in the economy of the Seattle metropolitan area, if not the entire state. In 2018, the company still employed over 65,000 people in Washington.[5]

The defense industry in Washington was more than just Boeing, however. As the Cold War ended in 1990, the state had twenty-eight National Guard facilities, including four Air National Guard bases. The US Navy was the largest federal employer in the state with numerous bases in Puget Sound near Seattle, and its Trident nuclear submarine base represented "one of the largest military projects in history." The state boasted thirteen US Coast Guard facilities, four Veterans Administration Medical Centers, Puget Sound Naval Shipyard near Bremerton, Fort Lewis Army Base near Tacoma, the Army Firing Center in Yakima, Madigan Army Medical Center near Tacoma, the Department of Energy Hanford Site, and air force bases at McChord near Tacoma and Fairchild near Spokane. For a state ranked nineteenth out of fifty in terms of population, this was an impressive haul.[6] Much of the credit belongs to the state's longtime giants in Congress: Senators Henry Jackson and Warren Magnuson, and Congressman Tom Foley.

"SCOOP AND MAGGIE" BUILD THE COLD WAR NATIONAL SECURITY CONSENSUS IN WASHINGTON STATE AFTER WORLD WAR II

An abundance of cheap electricity thanks to the construction of Grand Coulee Dam, Bonneville Dam, and other big and small hydroelectric projects in the Columbia Basin, and the establishment of businesses like Boeing which became major defense contractors, played a large role in the growth of national security as a major interest of Washingtonians. During and after World War II, Senators Warren Magnuson and Henry Jackson played increasingly bigger roles, flexing their muscles to get military contracts and to keep bases in Washington.

Warren Magnuson exerted immediate influence for Washington upon his arrival in the House of Representatives in 1937, when he was assigned to the Naval Affairs subcommittee of the Armed Services Committee. Despite his junior status, Magnuson was a Democrat at the height of the New Deal, as well as a charming, handsome politician.

He quickly built his list of political contacts, even procuring a meeting with President Franklin Roosevelt and British Prime Minister Winston Churchill during the latter's trip to the United States in the early days of World War II. At work, the young congressman used his growing power to gain millions of dollars in appropriations for Puget Sound Naval Shipyard, then Washington's largest employer. Magnuson also secured contracts for the shipyard to refit two aircraft carriers. Even before the outbreak of hostilities, he obtained federal funding for Boeing and for Forts Gordon and Lewis. Most notably, Magnuson obtained the B-17 "Flying Fortress" contract for Boeing.[7] Once the war began, Magnuson helped create the Alaska International Highway Commission, which expedited construction of a trans-Canadian highway that linked the US mainland with Alaska and promised to benefit his home state. Magnuson lobbied for the upgrading of the Naval Air Station on Lake Washington in Seattle, and unsuccessfully attempted to get all ship construction confined to naval shipyards, which would have benefited Puget Sound Naval Shipyard. As biographer Shelby Scates aptly put it, Magnuson "was persistent, if not a pest."[8]

After his election to the Senate in 1944, Magnuson continued to work for Washington to get more defense dollars. He played a key role in winning the B-52 contract for Boeing, perhaps becoming—per Scates—the "senator from Boeing" long before Henry Jackson earned that moniker.[9] Magnuson continued to aid local military installations as well. In 1955, he called for a $2 million appropriation to finance construction of a new dry dock at Puget Sound Naval Shipyard. In 1956, he argued for the relocation of a naval ammunition depot from Port Chicago near San Francisco to Bangor, Washington.[10] In 1957, he was unable to stop the closure of the Seattle Army Terminal, but as he told a Seattle constituent shortly before the shutdown, the Defense Department had been trying to shutter the terminal for over a year, and his "persistent efforts" did at least temporarily hold off the closure.[11]

By the mid-1950s, Magnuson's Democratic colleague, Henry Jackson, was a rising star in the Senate. As he built his congressional credentials as a national security hawk, gaining crucial assignments to the Senate Armed Services Committee and the Joint Committee on Atomic Energy, Jackson worked alongside Magnuson to keep military bases open in his home state and secure additional defense contracts.

In 1954, Jackson brought an Air Force Reserve training facility for Paine Air Force Base to his hometown of Everett. In 1956, he assured the enlargement of Whidbey Island Naval Air Station north of Seattle for an underwater weapons shop and test range. Later that year, his Military Construction Subcommittee of the Armed Services Committee approved new housing units for McChord Air Force Base.[12] Jackson was generally praised for his efforts, such as when *Seattle Times* reporter Marquis Childs applauded Jackson for resisting a push by the administration of President Dwight D. Eisenhower to balance the federal budget by lowering military expenditures.[13] There were a few dissenting voices: a church pastor slammed Jackson in 1956, arguing that Jackson's support of arms production in Washington in exchange for votes produced "machines of war." The pastor said he prayed these constituents would realize that "this road of living high on war industries is the road to ultimate ruin."[14] But letters like these were rare, as national security concerns combined with a strong desire for federal dollars to come into Washington, which Jackson was happy to oblige.

Jackson regularly ripped into any federal proposals for reduced defense spending. The senator called upon Eisenhower to increase the size of the army, pushed for the development of tactical nuclear weapons, and was an early advocate for the interstate highway system, which suited both national security interests and business interests at home by providing an easy system for conveying troops in time of war, and the means for the suburbanization and postwar expansion of the United States.[15] Jackson's support for federal spending also stemmed largely from his political need to obtain defense contracts for Boeing, the state's shipyards, and the Hanford Nuclear Reservation. In 1949, while Jackson was still in the US House of Representatives, Speaker of the House Sam Rayburn put Jackson on the Interior Subcommittee of the House Appropriations Committee, the first position from which Jackson proved effective at getting federal dollars for defense and public works. That year Jackson also joined the Joint Atomic Energy Committee, from which he spent decades promoting nuclear energy production, as well as the workers at Hanford and the economy of the nearby Tri-Cities—Richland, Pasco, and Kennewick—in southeast Washington.[16] In 1958, he co-sponsored the National Defense Education Act, which pumped millions of dollars into the region's schools. Ostensibly aimed at defense-related educational subjects, the act aided higher education overall, as did a succession of education legislation sponsored by Jackson and other Northwest senators in the coming years.

In the 1940s and 1950s, Jackson and Magnuson built the national security state-within-a-state in Washington. Magnuson continued to support Jackson's efforts, although he moderated his hawkishness somewhat later in his career. For Henry Jackson, however, his efforts on behalf of the national security constituency in Washington seemed to know no bounds.

SCOOP AND MAGGIE BATTLE FOR BOEING

Jackson and Magnuson are both similarly recognized for their efforts on behalf of Boeing, which was headquartered in Jackson's hometown of Everett throughout his career. This was more than just a case of a senator lobbying single-mindedly for his hometown. Historian Richard Kirkendall characterized the relationship that emerged in the 1950s between the senators, company officials, the air force, and Seattle city leaders as a "military-metropolitan-industrial complex" which would only deepen throughout the Cold War.[17]

Ironically, it did not initially seem apparent that Jackson would become the "senator from Boeing." During his first term, Boeing President William Allen referred to Jackson as "that goddamned socialist" for opposing an antilabor right-to-work law winding its way through the Washington State Legislature, and opposed his reelection campaign. Jackson countered, however, during his 1958 reelection battle with campaign literature touting that he "helped keep the B-52s [sic] and jet tankers rolling from Boeing plants by impressing the Defense Department with continuing need for long-range jet aircraft."[18] The relationship between Jackson and Allen was repaired because Jackson realized the effect Boeing's health had on his own chances of electoral survival. As historians William G. Robbins and Katrine Barber put it, "Seattle and Boeing's fortunes were closely linked to national and international events. . . . The ebb and flow of cold war anxieties contributed to cycles of boom and bust in Greater Seattle's economy."[19]

Jackson's commitment to Boeing even showed in times when he could not help the company. One of his most notable failures was his

1963 effort to obtain the Tactical Fighter Experimental (TFX) contract, which ended up going to Texas-based aircraft giant General Dynamics (GD). The Senate backed Boeing's bid for TFX against the Defense Department, which Jackson believed favored GD. The Pentagon thought Boeing's bid was "exceedingly optimistic" and rejected it even though it was $415 million lower than GD's winning bid. Jackson, in turn, called the final bid "an amazing operation in unrealism," sarcastically arguing that "as I understand the situation now, it is because Boeing didn't jack up their figures high enough that they are to be denied the contract."[20] An incensed Jackson told a constituent that the Department of Defense investigators of the Boeing and GD bids, "after 275,000 man hours, arrived at a decision that was arbitrarily changed by the highest authorities," and summarily launched an investigation in the Senate Government Operations Committee.[21]

Biographer Robert Kaufman believes that Defense Secretary Robert McNamara engineered GD's winning bid to appease Vice President Lyndon Johnson—from Texas, where General Dynamics was headquartered—and Southern Democrats distressed by President Kennedy's plan to submit a civil rights bill to Congress in the summer of 1963. When McNamara cried during a congressional hearing regarding the contract, supposedly because he was distraught that his son was being picked on in school about his role in the TFX controversy, "Jackson found McNamara's demeanor appalling, an unsavory mix of arrogance and weakness unacceptable for a secretary of defense."[22] Although the investigation failed to change the result, William Allen, now a Jackson defender, backed the senator against Republican critics during his 1964 reelection campaign. He said it would have been improper for the senator to use his influence to change the decision based on home-state bias, arguing that most TFX jobs would have ended up going to Boeing's Kansas plant even if it had gained the contract.[23]

Jackson and Magnuson steadily continued to rack up defense contracts for Boeing, and their next high-profile attempt to obtain government funding for the company came when it tried to develop a supersonic transport (SST) in the late 1960s and early 1970s. By 1968, the "Boeing effect" on Seattle's economy, stimulated in part by orders for commercial aircraft, but also by Cold War–related production contracts, caused the University of Washington's enrollment to grow to nearly 30,000—more than double its 1956 enrollment—as people flooded to the area seeking high-paying engineering jobs. But the next year Boeing started layoffs that triggered a significant economic recession in the Seattle metropolitan area, as employment plummeted from 105,000 to 38,000.[24] The pressure for Jackson to respond was high, and the SST seemed like the surest way to boost Boeing's fortunes.

The expensive project required government backing, however, and as early as 1967, President Lyndon Johnson warned Jackson in a recorded Oval Office phone call that support for SST funding was low in the Senate. "We've got the votes," Jackson told him. "I doubt it," Johnson cautioned, believing opponents included powerful Senators Robert and Ted Kennedy, Wayne Morse, and William Proxmire. Jackson himself speculated that Senator Stuart Symington, a key member of the Armed Services Committee, opposed the SST because of concerns about the US balance of payments deficit. "He thinks more people are going to travel," taking more currency out of the United States than would come in, which Jackson thought "doesn't make any sense. . . . We'll pick up anywhere from $20 to $40 billion."[25] Symington's opposition may have also stemmed from the fact that the aerospace manufacturer and Boeing competitor McDonnell-Douglas was headquartered in his home state of Missouri.

Although the SST fight continued into Richard Nixon's administration, and the project was supported by both Johnson and Nixon, Congress ultimately killed it. Growing constituent concerns about noise pollution, as well as the burgeoning federal budget deficit, doomed Boeing's hopes of producing the SST. Jackson fought on, however, listening to constituents like a thirty-year veteran of Boeing who pleaded to the senator that "the layoff at Boeing is drastic. It has never been like this. We need help!"[26] But by the end of 1969, the *Oregonian* commented that Jackson, "who last summer scorned opponents of the supersonic transport program as 'demagogues' and 'phony liberals,' is warning his constituents to be braced for the possibility that the SST may be shot down in Congress."[27]

Although Congress and President Nixon approved preliminary SST funding in 1969, future votes for the project failed. On December 3, 1970, the Senate voted down additional SST funding, representing "one of the few battles Maggie ever lost on the Senate floor" and contributing to a new round of Boeing layoffs to the tune of 7,500 workers.[28] The news was not all bad, however. Shelby Scates speculated that engineering problems doomed the SST, and that the program was a costly boondoggle, given concerns about rising oil prices and a lack of interest from fliers. By not winning the SST battle for Boeing, then, Jackson and Magnuson might have inadvertently dodged a bullet. The company's 700-series aircraft proved to be profitable in future decades and a major contributor to the company's later fiscal recovery and job expansion.[29]

Even as the SST controversy wound toward an unsatisfying conclusion, Jackson and Magnuson found other ways to aid in Boeing's recovery. When they obtained three parcels of land from the retired Larson Air Force Base near Moses Lake in 1968, the senators awarded the parcels to Boeing, after which the company announced it would employ 500 people, helping to alleviate the area's post-Larson economic depression. In President Johnson's 1969 budget, Boeing received $58 million for the Short-Range Attack Missile (SRAM), $664 million for two different kinds of Minuteman ICBMs, and various other defense-related projects. In 1982, Jackson and Slade Gorton, Magnuson's Republican successor in the Senate, pursued an amendment to sell the federal government surplus Boeing 747 jumbo jets, arguing it would save the Pentagon $6 billion over its plan to buy C-5 transports from Lockheed. The Jackson-Gorton plan passed the Senate 60–39 but died in a Senate-House conference. Pentagon interests successfully lobbied for the final defense appropriation bill to include the Lockheed transports, but bought three surplus 747s as compensation. At the time of Jackson's death in 1983, Boeing received $2.6 billion annually in defense contracts, and was the fifth most valuable prime-contracting firm in the United States.[30]

Contrary to the feelings of his critics in the Senate, and even jealous intraregional interests such as the *Oregonian*, Jackson, Magnuson, and Gorton were not invincible in their quest to obtain for Boeing all the federal investment and contracts it desired. Even if the senators were politically powerful enough to put their region above the national interest in terms of defense, others successfully did the same at times, too: SST critic Stuart Symington was a proponent of getting Minuteman missiles into Missouri, even though such missiles would neither be near the Soviet Union nor to the major population centers they would supposedly defend from attack.[31] There was widespread boosting for defense contracts, but ultimately, Jackson and Magnuson's work had a tremendous impact on the Pacific Northwest economy. By the 1980s, Boeing's employment had doubled even from World War II levels. The company remained an economic powerhouse in the region even as the Jackson/Magnuson era ended. Boeing expanded its operations into Spokane, and eventually moved across the state line into Oregon, buying one of its own parts supply businesses in Portland in 1974 and moving it to the nearby suburb of Gresham. By 1989, Boeing's Gresham plant employed 1,940 workers, eventually becoming one of Oregon's biggest employers, and remaining in operation in 2019.[32]

As the Cold War ended, Boeing mattered not just as a major national defense contractor, but as a source of livelihood for a large and increasing number of Pacific Northwesterners. Plants in and near Seattle, Spokane, and Portland showed that Boeing had significant reach. If one counts ancillary businesses that supplied Boeing and served its employees, hundreds of thousands of Washingtonians and Oregonians owed their livelihoods in great part to the decades of efforts by Jackson and Magnuson to aid Boeing throughout the latter half of the twentieth century.

HENRY JACKSON AND THE HANFORD NUCLEAR RESERVATION

By the 1970s, Henry Jackson was at the zenith of his influence. A survey by Ralph Nader's Capitol Hill News Service in 1970 ranked Jackson the most effective federal legislator in obtaining federal help for his constituents, and Warren Magnuson the second most effective. During the early 1970s, the senators successfully worked to increase the amount of federal outlays to Washington from $3.4 billion in 1970 to $5 billion in 1972. The state's rank in Defense Department spending went from eighteenth to twelfth, in National Aeronautics and Space Administration (NASA) spending from twenty-sixth to nineteenth, and in Interior Department spending from sixth to second. Jackson's ability to bring home federal bacon allowed him to stay in office as liberal Democrats were increasingly defeated amid a growing tide of conservatism nationwide.[33] One major reason for Jackson's staying power was his ability to aid one of his most conservative constituencies in eastern Washington via his strident support for the Hanford Nuclear Reservation.

Jackson particularly championed the work by Hanford to produce atomic-weapons-grade plutonium and electricity for the Pacific Northwest and the nation. Early in the Cold War, as Hanford expanded to meet growing plutonium demand for atomic and hydrogen bombs, Jackson told his congressional colleagues that the United States should, as quickly as possible, produce as many nuclear weapons as it could afford. Jackson was sufficiently enthusiastic about the possibilities of the atom that he sometimes handed out cans of irradiated bacon to nervous visitors to his office. His nuclear cheerleading can most clearly be seen in his lobbying for Hanford, beginning in the Truman years and continuing until his death, despite gradual cutbacks to the US nuclear program. The federal government eventually poured some $2 billion into Hanford, even as all but one of its nine reactors was shut down by the end of the decade, a tribute to Jackson's effectiveness in maintaining federal outlays for the reservation.[34] Many saw Hanford as a national security *and* an economic asset, and "nobody became more closely associated with Hanford's fortunes" than Jackson.[35]

After joining the Joint Atomic Energy Committee in 1949, Jackson supported nuclear industry in no small part because it benefited the workers at Hanford and the economy of the nearby Tri-Cities. As the Cold War heated up, Jackson announced a $25 million expansion of Hanford's plutonium production plant, in addition to $80 million already earmarked for construction by the Atomic Energy Commission (AEC), the federal agency in charge of administering the nation's nuclear arsenal and one with which Jackson would sometimes work closely and sometimes clash throughout his career.[36] Early in his career Jackson became "almost a faddist about the power of the atom," speaking, "nearly reverently, about a future of atomic cities, atomic farming, and atom-powered vehicles."[37] Historians John Findlay and Bruce Hevly contend that nobody surpassed Jackson in his advocacy for Hanford. As early as 1950, he made appearances in eastern Washington to announce "appropriations, construction, and jobs for Hanford." Looking ahead to his 1952 Senate campaign, Jackson was "already milking the Tri-Cities for votes." Findlay and Hevly argue that Jackson "could . . . well have been called the senator from Hanford, as local boosters marveled at his . . . abilities to advance or protect legislation favorable to Hanford."[38]

Over the years Jackson increasingly became a proponent of peaceful nuclear energy, in addition to defense purposes, to help strengthen the regional economy. As early as 1951, Jackson contended that Columbia River water that had been heated several degrees as a byproduct of its use to cool Hanford nuclear fission piles could be reused to generate steam to create electricity. Jackson told an audience that the plutonium used to produce nuclear bombs could also generate sufficient heat "to light cities, irrigate deserts, propel surface vehicles and commercial aircraft."[39] In 1958, the *Oregonian* endorsed Jackson's plan for a dual reactor at Hanford that would produce both plutonium and electricity for the Bonneville Power Administration, the government agency supervising the hydroelectric dams and other power facilities on the Columbia River. The Portland newspaper supported the proposal since, it argued, what would soon be called the N Reactor would put the United States on equal footing with the Soviet Union and Great Britain as they proceeded with their own dual reactors, and because "every addition of low-cost power to the federal system which can be offered to industrial customers on long-term contracts helps to bolster the Northwest's economy." The bottom line was that the N Reactor meant "jobs, profits, taxes and money in the bank."[40]

The late 1950s and 1960s saw Hanford become a statewide interest for the politicians and people of Washington, who wanted to make the reservation do more for the region beyond merely fueling the federal government's need for plutonium. On June 21, 1956, Jackson "helped Richland residents buy their houses from the AEC" following complaints that the commission set purchase prices "too high." Jackson and Magnuson called a Joint Committee on Atomic Energy hearing where Jackson criticized Federal Housing Authority procedures that had determined appraisals for the houses. New appraisals were ultimately set that cut the prices for "about half the homes in town." Also, that day, Jackson introduced legislation that would ultimately authorize construction on the N Reactor.[41]

The Eisenhower administration regularly discouraged public power projects as a result of its ideological orientation toward private development of infrastructure. After studies showed that the N Reactor would

Washington Governor Albert Rossellini, President John F. Kennedy, and Senators Henry Jackson and Warren Magnuson at the groundbreaking for a nuclear generating plant at Hanford, Washington, September 26, 1963. Kennedy's remarks culminated a long process by Jackson and residents of the nearby Tri-Cities to secure the peaceful use for nuclear energy initially meant solely for atomic bombs. In the background are Oregon Representative Al Ullman and Secretary of the Interior Stewart Udall. Reprinted by permission from University of Washington Special Collections, Henry M. Jackson Papers, Accession 3560-031, Box 6/38, negative no. UW 39876.

be cost-effective, however, it was funded for planning purposes in 1957 and construction in 1958. To secure funding, Jackson emphasized the project's necessity for national security and omitted overt references to its ability to produce public power and thus compete with private power interests. The AEC still resisted the dual-purpose nature of the reactor, however, so the fight for its funding continued into the 1960s.[42] In 1961, the House defeated an amendment for continuing appropriations for the project. President John F. Kennedy's administration had requested $95 million for N Reactor construction, but Republicans objected to the funding as a "public-power" encroachment on the free market. Jackson retorted that the vote was a "victory for the private utility and coal industry. The losers were the American people."[43] Jackson tried to restore funding in the Senate, but faced opposition from Iowa Republican Bourke Hickenlooper, who contended that "there has been not one argument advanced . . . that the operation of this electrical facility . . . will contribute a single provable benefit to the advancement of the art of atomic energy or to the art of the production of power." Jackson countered with a national security argument, stating that the N Reactor "will manufacture fissionable material urgently needed for the defense of the free world." Jackson also argued that "the new production reactor will generate enormous amounts of energy" which could be "transformed into steam, and thence into electricity for lighting homes and running factories." He noted that the project had the backing of the AEC, the Bureau of the Budget, General Electric (Hanford's main contracting company), the Federal Power Commission, and the Bonneville Power Administration.[44] Jackson's viewpoint ultimately carried the day, and much of the funding was restored by a Senate-House conference. Plutonium production started in 1964, while a steam generator operated by the Washington Public Power Supply System began operation in 1966.[45]

But by the early 1960s, government officials determined the United States had a sufficient existing stock of plutonium, and given the 24,000-year half-life of plutonium, the N Reactor was poised for a short period of usefulness. Hanford's plutonium-making piles were also dated in comparison to the government's nuclear facilities in Savannah River, South Carolina. From 1964 to 1971 the eight piles built at Hanford between 1943 and 1955 were shut down. Between 1971 and 1986, only the N Reactor remained operational at Hanford, and it produced mainly electricity instead of plutonium. Over time, this state of affairs generated fears for the economic health of the nearby Tri-Cities, sparking Jackson, regional boosters, and business leaders to lead a drive for regional economic diversification.[46]

As early as 1962, businessman Sam Volpentest and *Tri-City Herald* editor Glenn Lee proposed to privatize Hanford's operations, fearful that its AEC subsidy would eventually dry up along with America's need for plutonium. They went to Jackson with their concerns, and the senator responded by pushing for a congressional investigation. Jackson connected Volpentest and Lee with Washington, DC, lobbyist and attorney Fred Warren, who helped them form the Tri-City Nuclear Industrial Council (TCNIC), a lobby group designed to attract more atomic-related companies to the area that would generate business on the energy side of nuclear production as well as the weapons production side.[47] The senator organized a fact-finding trip with top officials from Hanford contractor General Electric, AEC officials, and John Pastore, chairman of the Joint Atomic Energy Committee in Congress. Jackson and AEC head Glenn Seaborg arranged for Volpentest to have top-level contacts with AEC and GE for the first time. Volpentest called Jackson the "father of diversification" in appreciation of his efforts. Volpentest's biographer, C. Mark Smith, argues that "the breakthroughs served as a major morale booster for a community that very badly needed one." Jackson spearheaded the creation of three task forces: one to ramp up private investment at Hanford, another to push NASA and the Defense Department to invest more heavily in existing facilities at Hanford, and a third to have the AEC review these facilities to see if they could be used by other public and private interests.[48]

In 1965, Jackson worked to ensure that the shutdown of aging Hanford reactors, which would save $13 million but cost 2,000 jobs, would be spread over several years to give economic diversification plans time to succeed. In one effective attempt to stem the pain of the shutdowns, Jackson got a post office mail-processing plant opened in Pasco. When General Electric pulled out of Hanford in 1965, Jackson helped recruit new contractors to take its place. His office put out press releases emphasizing that the Tri-Cities was a new frontier for private enterprise, being careful to gloss over the bad economic news caused by GE's departure. Volpentest, for his part, pushed the area's business-friendly climate, good weather, and his direct access to Jackson as selling points for new clients.[49]

As diversification ramped up, Jackson often visited Hanford and the Tri-Cities to boost locations he believed would be the pioneers in a new future for the region. On October 27, 1967, Jackson came to Richland to dedicate Battelle Pacific Northwest Laboratories. The senator touted its plan to manage a nascent Fast Flux Test Facility (FFTF), which he referred to as a "revolutionary device that could change the picture in the nuclear power field." Importantly for its role in an economically diversifying community, Battelle would not be a one-trick pony: Jackson promised it would lead the way in the cleanup of the nation's air and water supply as well.[50] Over the years, Jackson celebrated even the seemingly fringe benefits of diversification: on October 6, 1969, while dedicating the Hanford House Hotel in Richland, he acknowledged that while Hanford had lost most of its reactors and the closures had decreased Hanford's total employment, "completion of diversification commitments" would exceed job losses. He touted the role played by Atlantic Richfield, a new member of the diversification program, in committing funds to help build the hotel, a cattle feedlot, and a meat-packing plant. Jackson insisted that diversification was "more than a holding action" and that "a weapons economy has been partly replaced with an economy with a far greater potential for stability and expansion."[51]

When Jackson persuaded Jersey Nuclear Company to develop a nuclear fuel-rod reprocessing facility in a 160-acre complex which finished construction in 1970, Volpentest boasted that "it represents a breakthrough. . . . This is going to be the nuclear energy capital of the world."[52] It certainly seemed that way for a time. On September 24, Jackson came to Richland to dedicate a high-temperature sodium facility related to the development of the FFTF, which he hoped would generate a massive amount of clean nuclear power. Jackson argued at a speech he gave at the groundbreaking ceremony that "nuclear fission is a gift of nature so essential to the health and safety of people in every industrialized nation and indeed to the continued well-being of mankind."[53]

But diversification could not make up for years of poor prospects in terms of Hanford's production of plutonium and electricity. By 1971, all of the Hanford reactors were shuttered except for the N Reactor, which also was nearly shut down in February by the AEC in the midst of budget cuts by the Office of Management and Budget. The shutdown threatened 2,000 jobs, and was made by the Nixon administration without consulting the Washington congressional delegation.[54] Upon learning of the shutdown, Jackson is said to have turned white, started shaking, and to have asked, "What the hell have they done?"[55] A panicked Pacific Northwest was roused into action, as Jackson, Volpentest, Washington Governor Daniel Evans, and Oregon Governor Tom McCall petitioned for the reversal of the OMB decision. Jackson, warning that the closure of Hanford would cause the loss of 6,000 jobs, convened emergency hearings with AEC officials, ultimately working with the AEC and the Nixon administration to get the N Reactor back online. Just two days after the N Reactor shutdown was reversed, however, an anonymous Nixon administration official leaked to the *New York Times* that the plant was "unreliable and a possible safety hazard," as well as a "a sloppy engineering job" that would cost millions to bring up to modern safety standards. The official argued that the reactor was subject to frequent breakdowns and active less than half the year in 1970. The official also

noted that 80 million gallons of radioactive liquid waste stored underground needed to be managed. Despite these ominous portents, thanks
to Jackson's efforts the N Reactor stayed online until 1987.[56]

Despite the near-shutdown of the N Reactor, Jackson and Tri-
Cities boosters hoped that national energy supply woes in the 1970s
would work to Hanford's advantage. In the backdrop of brownouts that
plagued the Pacific Northwest following a severe drought affecting
hydroelectric capacity in 1972, Jackson argued that just as Hanford was
born in the crisis of World War II, it would help in the new energy
crisis. Nuclear energy had to be the new future of energy, he said, and
talk of new research and development suggested more federal funding
was on the way to assist the Tri-Cities at a time when the earlier reactor
shutdowns had lowered morale.[57] Years passed, however, and despite
months of electricity and gas rationing caused by an oil embargo by
Arab members of the Organization of Petroleum Exporting Countries
(OPEC) punishing Western countries' support for Israel in the Yom Kip-
pur War in October 1973, Hanford did not experience another boom.[58]
Meeting with the TCNIC in 1976, Jackson noted that "there has never
been a shortage of problems in the Tri-Cities . . . this is as true today
as it has ever been." He predicted, however, that the long-hyped FFTF
would soon "play a vital role in testing fuels and components needed
for the commercialization of the breeder-reactor concept." Jackson
showed he was not blind to environmental concerns brought up by the
Nixon administration earlier in the 1970s, emphasizing that Hanford's
volume of liquid high-level waste had been cut from 43 million gallons
in 1973 to 22 million gallons in 1976. He assured the TCNIC that the
federal government would help with environmental cleanup, noting
that an evaporator facility and four double-walled storage tanks had
received congressional authorization. In addition, an environmental
impact statement was underway to help plan Hanford's waste management operation, and Battelle's Pacific Northwest laboratory was study-
ing the problem of how to dispose of commercial radioactive waste.[59]

Nuclear energy production, however, continued to be at the forefront of Jackson's regional policy initiatives, as exemplified by a 1978
speech to TCNIC titled "Why Not the Best—Nuclear Energy." Jackson
argued that US nuclear power plants had been "extremely successful" and called on the federal government to streamline regulations

governing the building of new plants. He also advocated for the development of a plan to dispose of nuclear waste to reduce public ambivalence and concerns about the safety of nuclear waste, implying that nuclear waste could be safely stored at Hanford.[60] Unlike antinuclear activists or his future successors, Jackson envisioned nuclear cleanup that would strengthen, not reduce, the role of nuclear energy in regional and national energy policies.

It was not a coincidence that the last years of Jackson's life represented the last gasp of the nuclear energy drive in the Tri-Cities and Hanford. In 1981, Jackson and Representative Sid Morrison (R-WA) obtained congressional spending for research aimed at getting Hanford invested in fusion-power technology. In August 1983, Jackson, Senator Slade Gorton, and Morrison obtained $750 million in appropriations for the construction of an isotope separation and development facility that would employ 400 Washingtonians. "The announcement couldn't have come at a better time," Jackson said. "The Tri-Cities is going through a rough time economically and needed this boost."[61]

Indeed, the Tri-Cities was hit hard by a national recession in the early 1980s, but one of Jackson's final speeches in the Tri-Cities, in 1982, summed up his continued belief in the ability of nuclear energy and even plutonium production to carry the region economically. "Sure times are tough," Jackson admitted, but he was "getting just a little sick and tired of the doomsayers who are going around delivering eulogies on the Tri-Cities." With regard to federal funding, Jackson announced that "both the defense and nuclear energy programs are funded at levels to permit continued progress." In reference to plans by the Reagan administration to reorganize or eliminate the Department of Energy, which supplied much of the federal money coming into the region, Jackson called the administration's efforts to dismantle the department "a dead issue." In this Jackson was right, but with regard to other predictions, he was less clairvoyant. He believed that the energy crisis of the 1970s would return when the world economy recovered, requiring energy programs and Energy Department labs, such as those at Hanford. He also stated too optimistically that the N Reactor would continue in dual-purpose mode until "the mid-1990s" and that debate had started on a potential replacement reactor. As in the past, Jackson urged that the breeder reactor program should be pursued "without delay," noting the FFTF and its "huge energy potential" was now operational. Jackson also said Congress would increase funding for geothermal, solar, and synthetic fuel research and development.[62]

As late as three years after Jackson's death, the Hanford plant itself still employed 14,000 of the 100,000 workers in the Tri-Cities. The *New York Times* reported that Jackson "often told the voters of eastern Washington that as long as he lived, the Hanford nuclear reservation would never be closed." After Jackson's death in 1983, the declassification of government documents about nuclear contamination on and near Hanford and the end of the Cold War signaled a different fate for the nuclear reservation than the senator had in mind. Public opinion turned against nuclear energy in the wake of nuclear accidents in the United States and the Soviet Union. In this context, Washington public officials had to tread carefully. Slade Gorton narrowly lost his 1986 reelection bid to Brock Adams, who campaigned against Gorton's record of supporting, as Adams dubbed it, "the 'bomb factory.'" John Findlay and Bruce Hevly contend that "Hanford now tended to polarize rather than unify the electorate," but believe that Jackson, owing to the goodwill he had built up over decades with statewide voters, might have been able to still serve Hanford's interests in Washington, DC, while appeasing environmentalists. Indeed, it is a testament to the long shadow Jackson cast on the Tri-Cities that Sam Volpentest lamented, "Things don't operate like they used to, when you could just call up Scoop or Maggie."[63]

JACKSON AND THE NUCLEAR NAVY IN PUGET SOUND

In western Washington, Jackson and the region's US representatives worked to maintain and expand the US Navy installations in Puget Sound, including Puget Sound Naval Shipyard, Naval Station Bremerton, Naval Submarine Base Bangor in Kitsap County, and Naval Air Station Whidbey Island in Oak Harbor, near the San Juan Islands. At the time of Jackson's death in 1983, Naval Station Everett, designed as a homeport for a nuclear-powered aircraft carrier and other naval craft, was in the planning stages. At a celebration of Jackson's one-hundredth birthday in 2012, Everett Mayor Ray Stephanson praised Jackson for playing "an instrumental role" in laying the groundwork for the maintenance and

Senator Henry Jackson, pictured fourth from right, at the launch party for the hydrofoil USS *Gemini* at the Port of Seattle on February 17, 1980. Jackson worked throughout his career to bring US Navy bases and ship construction projects to the Puget Sound in western Washington. Reprinted by permission from University of Washington Special Collections, Henry M. Jackson Papers, Accession 3560-031, Box 16/40, negative no. UW 39875.

growth of regional naval bases.[64] Despite ongoing questioning of the military's presence in Washington by environmentalists and antinuclear activists, it remains appreciated as integral to the state's economy.

The presence of the US Navy and other branches of the US military, as well as the Washington National Guard, in Puget Sound predates Jackson. Beginning in the late nineteenth century, as the military projected its power into the Pacific amid a rising US presence in Hawaii, China, and the Philippines, growing Puget Sound cities "gained a measure of economic security from the military's presence." This arrangement remained strong through two world wars, but early in the Cold War the navy grew concerned that the new US Air Force, which initially held the monopoly on nuclear-weapons delivery among US armed forces, would supersede it in importance.[65] To keep up, the navy built larger aircraft carriers that could deploy nuclear-armed aircraft, and attached nuclear missiles to its new Polaris and Trident-class submarines. These moves were widely embraced by Puget Sound communities, especially smaller cities like Bremerton which relied on the navy as its economic lifeline. Jackson was cognizant of this constituent base as he became a major player in the maintenance and expansion of the navy's regional presence, and it did not hurt, either, that the navy's nuclear ambitions dovetailed with his own interest in keeping nuclear weapons at the forefront of American Cold War strategy.

Jackson assisted the navy-booster relationship in Puget Sound starting in his initial years in the Senate. His 1958 reelection campaign literature touted that, in his first term, he obtained appropriations for the construction of a dry dock for Bremerton. Jackson simultaneously pushed for the development of strategic nuclear submarines, calling for a fleet of at least 100 atomic submarines so that the United States would develop an undersea nuclear deterrent. By 1960, Jackson had convinced the navy and President Eisenhower to increase the number of submarine platforms slated for deployment.[66] In 1962, Jackson informed constituents that he would push for appropriations for the construction of a Polaris missile assembly center in Bangor.[67] The *Bremerton Sun* applauded the move, remarking that Jackson "won his battle despite severe pressure from the 'sunshine' boys who wanted this installation in California," noting that the move would boost the local economy by doubling employment at Bangor. Jackson said he did not "know of any area in the country that has a brighter potential in contributing to the national security as Kitsap county," citing the Polaris facility at Bangor, as well as the conversion of Puget Sound Naval Shipyard to refurbish nuclear-powered ships. The area's naval development was not just limited to military bases: in May 1963, Jackson announced the awarding of a $50.5 million naval contract to Puget Sound Bridge and Dry Dock Company to construct two amphibious assault vessels, a project that would employ up to 3,000 people.[68]

In the mid-1960s, Jackson obtained more federal funding for naval sites while resisting cutback attempts by the Pentagon. In fact, according to Jackson, only the Puget Sound and Pearl Harbor, Hawaii, naval shipyards escaped employment cutbacks.[69] He boasted of the enhanced importance that would come to Bangor once nuclear-powered submarines began ports of call there in 1965. Missile-loading and overhaul of ships would take place regularly out of Bangor, along with a doubling of its employment from 500 to 1,000. The senator claimed this would add "tens of thousands of square miles" to the range of US nuclear defenses, and that the resulting "fleet of Polaris missile ships, flying the American flag, is the equivalent of free world bases a few hundred miles from Moscow and Vladivostok."[70] When a Polaris missile assembly plant opened in Bangor in September 1964, Secretary of the Navy Paul Nitze credited Jackson for the plant's existence, asserting that "without his splendid efforts, it is doubtful that we would have reached this point in the development of the Polaris system so quickly and so successfully." Thanks to Jackson's work, in part, American nuclear defenses in the Pacific gained "credibility" with the Bangor plant.[71]

As the national political climate began to shift away from staunch support for the military and the construction of nuclear weapons in the late 1960s and early 1970s, Jackson's support for military installations near Puget Sound grew more tepid. This was a surprising development, considering his support for additions to the US deterrent against the Soviet Union. Throughout the late 1960s, Jackson was the strongest defender in the Senate of an anti-ballistic missile (ABM) system, seeing it as crucial for America to maintain a preponderance of power in the Cold War struggle. He clashed with the White House, however, which wanted ABMs to guard the nation's cities, including Seattle. Jackson preferred a limited ABM program that would defend the nation's intercontinental ballistic missiles (ICBMs), thus providing a counterstrike capability in case of attack by the Soviet Union or China. But on September 18, 1967, Defense Secretary Robert McNamara announced the ABM city defense plan. Staying loyal to the president, Jackson initially hailed the move, telling constituents that "the credibility of the system . . . will serve to deter an enemy nuclear attack."[72]

By the end of 1967, however, Jackson appeared to backtrack. The ABM plan included a missile site at Fort Lawton, an army post in the Magnolia neighborhood northwest of downtown Seattle. Antinuclear activists and even Seattle mayor Dorm Braman questioned the wisdom of placing ABMs in Seattle. Jackson defended the national ABM plan in the Senate, but perhaps sensing the shift in the political winds, ducked the official announcement that the ABMs were coming to Fort Lawton. The senator quietly worked behind the scenes to get the ABM site removed from Fort Lawton. In late 1968, Jackson arranged for the site to be shifted to Bainbridge Island and Port Gamble, both in Kitsap County. He reasoned that these areas would be more open to the missiles because of the county's history of support for navy bases. Over the Christmas holiday, however, Jackson received 600 letters of critical mail from Bainbridge residents who did not want to see the ABMs in their neighborhood. At the same time, new president Richard Nixon's incoming administration was under fire from Seattle and other cities to do away with the ABM plan entirely and thereby, they believed, lessen their susceptibility to a Soviet first strike. Seeing an opening, Jackson secured a meeting with Nixon, using the opportunity to press him to get rid of both the Seattle-area ABMs *and* reconsider his original plan to have ABMs protect Minuteman ICBM missile launch sites as opposed to cities. Nixon, who concurred with Jackson on national security to the extent that he tried to appoint him as his secretary of defense, agreed to the idea, and the greater Seattle area was spared the deployment of an ABM system.[73] Jackson retained his strong national security reputation, but his move to stop the deployment of ABMs to western Washington reflected an ability, ironically because of his well-earned bipartisan national security credentials, to respond to a key constituency that was drifting to the left, one which he needed to secure his next reelection victory in 1970.

Jackson's newfound ambivalence about the military—in the local context, at any rate—extended to his relationship with the region's nuclear navy. In 1973, Jackson provided only minimal support to efforts to make Bangor Naval Base the home of the Pacific Fleet's Trident nuclear missiles. Historian Brian Casserly credits the navy with much of the impetus behind making Bangor a support base for Trident submarines, contending that the decision to do so "was designed to increase the survivability of a major part of the US nuclear deterrent in the event of war with the Soviet Union by minimizing the time submarines based in the Pacific needed to visit shore facilities where they were most vulnerable to attack."[74] The navy had to contend with congressional opposition to funding the Trident submarine project. Peter Ognibene, who wrote a largely critical biography of Jackson prior to his 1976 presidential bid, believed that when the Senate vote arose on funding the Trident submarines in 1973, Jackson initially was against it, but changed his vote because he cut a deal with the Nixon administration to base the program out of Bangor. By this account, the arrangement would pump money into Washington's economy to the tune of $550 million for construction alone. The Trident vote carried the day in the Senate by a 49–47 count, and the interests of both the Pentagon and Puget Sound military boosters were served again. But with hindsight, it seems clear that Jackson, concerned about western Washington voters who were skeptical of military spending, actually *discouraged* the boosters from lobbying for the base. Worried about the voters but also concerned for national security, Jackson told naval officials that if they could convince him that Bangor was the best site for a Trident base, he would withdraw his opposition. Chief of naval operations Admiral Elmo Zumwalt and Admiral Kinnaird McKee convinced Jackson to back the Bangor site. But this incident, much like the ABM situation, showed that he was increasingly sensitive to the changing political climate and was no longer reflexively supportive of the military, especially in antimilitary parts of Washington.[75]

Jackson heard opposition to the Trident base from a variety of different sources. Some local residents worried about the prospect of their homes being acquired by the navy. One former naval officer and his wife wrote Jackson that they had retired to nearby Hood Canal to build their "dream home" and that they opposed the "desecrating" effects they thought the Trident facility would have on this area of "exceptional beauty." Other constituents, however, were not completely inflexible, arguing that the base could still be in Kitsap County as long as it did not encroach on their property. Many who feared losing their homes appreciated the economic boost they believed the base would provide and supported the naval installations, in general, which Jackson had helped build up over the years.[76]

Brian Casserly contends that "the most common basis for local antagonism to the Trident program was the adverse effects people felt the project would have on the local environment and quality of life." Even Kitsap County residents whose homes were not threatened by the base were ambivalent about an impending influx of workers, military officers, and their families who would degrade the environment. The State of Washington and governor Dan Evans fretted about the cost of new schools, roads, and public services required for the Trident base, as well as its environmental impacts. According to Casserly, "state officials regarded the Navy's assessment of the project's impact on the local community as detailed in its Environmental Impact Statement as inadequate" and estimated that it would result in $130 million in new costs to the state while bringing in only $26 million in new tax revenue. Ultimately Jackson, working with Warren Magnuson and Representative Floyd Hicks, secured federal support to assist Kitsap County "in dealing with some of the burdens created by Trident." In March 1974, the Associated Press reported that Jackson helped secure $103.8 million for the construction of the Trident base.[77]

The navy ultimately decided it would not buy additional property for the base, relieving Kitsap County residents worried about losing their homes. But as the ABM opposition in Seattle had shown, many in western Washington were skeptical about the benefits of military installations, and they were joined in the 1970s by critics of "the increased dependence on the federal government that the Bangor project would bring to Kitsap County." One Jackson constituent doubted whether Kitsap County had ever benefited from the navy, arguing that "the on-again, off-again employment of the navy oriented economic base works a hardship on everyone in the county." Other writers to Jackson attacked the federal government for its "bloated" spending on "unnecessary weaponry," argued that money for the base would be better spent on antipoverty programs, and called for the end of "welfare to the defense contractors and to the disadvantaged."[78] The navy also faced vocal and highly publicized opposition from peace and antinuclear activists, who believed the US nuclear deterrent—and, by extension, the Trident fleet—to be "unnecessary and even immoral." These activists "advanced the argument that security required disarmament of the US military's nuclear weapons, not just in the region but nationally."[79] Newspapers and local TV regularly covered the groups' efforts to disrupt construction of Trident support facilities in the mid-1970s, as well as the arrival of the first Trident submarines to Bangor in 1982.

Despite these dissenting voices, and his earlier ambivalence regarding the housing of the Trident base in Puget Sound, Jackson supported the new base once it was a *fait accompli*. In June 1975, Jackson helped secure $7 million in congressional funds for improvements to Kitsap County roads servicing the base.[80] On May 15, 1976, Jackson told the Puget Sound Naval Base Association in Bremerton that he could "think of no other city which has contributed more to our nation's military preparedness." Jackson vowed that the recent closure of a base in Boston would "never" be replicated in Puget Sound. He reassured his audience that Congress planned to invest $1 billion in the Puget Sound Naval Shipyard, the Trident base, and Keyport Naval Station, and that the Senate had recently restored $11 million in "Trident impact funds" to the defense budget to help the community pay for infrastructure to support the Trident base and its personnel. In an August 1976 speech to a Seattle gathering of AFL-CIO leaders, Jackson argued that "we have overcome much of the area's depression of the early 1970s," in part, by adding the Trident base. Referring to US Navy shipbuilding that had long been a feature of the Seattle economy, Jackson noted that "we now build Navy frigates in Seattle because the Senate restored the money, just as we kept the important Trident program alive."[81]

The Senate appropriated an additional $221 million for the Trident base in 1977, but voices of opposition continued to express their opinions to Jackson. "This massive spending of taxpayers' money not only inflates the economy and creates unemployment on a national level but may yet prove to be a boondoggle to the local area," one constituent wrote to the senator. The Trident buildup, the constituent argued, would be perceived by the Soviet Union as provocative. The constituent was sympathetic to anti-base protesters, who, he said, were being arrested for trying to give leaflets to construction workers in an area "which had until recently been deemed a 'public access area.'"[82] Of all the correspondence in one 1977 folder of Jackson's papers on Trident, about half the writers were for and half against the construction of the base to house the Trident submarines, showing continued polarization over the issue in the Puget Sound long after the matter had been officially settled.

By the early 1980s things appeared to be looking up for the regional defense establishment. Presidents Jimmy Carter and Ronald Reagan rolled out increased defense budgets to meet what seemed to be a renewed threat from the Soviet Union after its December 1979 invasion of Afghanistan. In December 1980, Jackson added $2.5 million to an already-appropriated $9.6 million to help cover project cost overruns on a new highway near the Trident base. Jackson was active beyond Trident as well: at the launching ceremony for a guided cruise missile in July 1981, he praised contractor Todd Pacific Shipyards Corps of Seattle, emphasizing the plant's role in job creation in noting that "the preachers of modern 'management' are mistaken to think that new computers and more paperwork systems can ever substitute for the individual worker doing his job correctly." The senator said that Puget Sound naval facilities would be critical to the rearmament authorized in the 1982 defense budget. In October 1982, as the nationwide recession of the early 1980s deepened, Jackson announced that the Navy would base part of the Pacific Fleet out of Puget Sound, creating 4,000 new civilian jobs and ultimately bringing 11,000 sailors and their families to invest in the region. The move represented "logical dispersal" for the navy to give more attention to the Japan-China area of the Pacific, according to Jackson. Perhaps to appease the local antinuclear movement as he approached election day in his reelection campaign, Jackson added that he did not believe the addition of the Pacific Fleet would make Puget Sound a bigger target for the Soviet Union.[83] Jackson would not live to see the fruits of his latest effort, but part of the fleet still remained based out of Everett in 2019.

Antinuclear activism in the months before Jackson's death served as a continual reminder of why the senator moderated his pronuclear stance locally in the latter part of his career. In 1982, dozens of protesters were arrested or "blasted with fire hoses" while attempting to disrupt the delivery of the first Trident-bearing submarine to Bangor.[84] These protests came amid the rise of the nuclear freeze movement, designed to force the United States to unilaterally halt construction of its nuclear arsenal and engage in unconditional talks with the Soviet Union.[85] One constituent stated her concern to Jackson that "one Trident submarine will carry TWO THOUSAND TIMES the destructive capability of the bomb dropped on Hiroshima." In February 1983, another constituent questioned the connection between military spending in Puget Sound and the Seattle economy, arguing that the increased military presence in the region had not led to the reduction of high unemployment. The constituent believed that development and deployment of Peacekeeper (MX) and Trident missiles were "dangerous steps" toward actual use of nuclear weapons. Furthermore, the constituent was concerned that military spending increased the federal deficit. "Have you any ideas about ways to help the unemployed in the Northwest by channeling defense money into more humane programs?" the constituent asked. Jackson gave no reply, but if he did, it seems unlikely he would have been sympathetic. The senator supported talks leading to mutual arms reduction with the Soviet Union but rejected a plan by Senators Mark Hatfield (R-OR) and Ted Kennedy (D-MA) to unilaterally halt nuclear weapons production.[86] Jackson remained a proponent of nuclear weapons production and a supporter of the Puget Sound nuclear navy until his death.

Jackson clearly left a mixed legacy in his support of the buildup of the Puget Sound nuclear navy. In 1984, an article in *Northwest Magazine* counted the costs of the naval buildup. By April 1986, the piece claimed, a typical Washington family of four would have $20,000 taken out of their paycheck by the taxes required to pay off a $1.5 trillion military buildup, only $6 billion of which would be reinvested in the state. The article took Jackson to task, contending that Northwest residents should be concerned about the "congressional-industrial complex" composed of Jackson and his successors in office. Kitsap County, meanwhile, was mostly reliant upon the US Navy, thanks to Jackson's boosterism for the Trident base. Forty percent of county residents were dependent upon federal employment. Of the county's top ten employers, only retailer JCPenney paid property taxes. The others were exempt because they were part of the naval base, leading to $33 million in lost taxes each year. The federal government provided just $55 million of an estimated $200 million needed for infrastructure improvements to house an influx of sailors and defense contractors, and their families. Washington compensated by taxing nonfederal parts of the county at the highest rate allowed by state law to make up for the shortfall, yet it still was inadequate because the county was next-to-last in the state in services per capita. For example, it was unable to hire enough police to deal with rising crime rates. University of Washington philosophy department chair Victor Hanzeli argued that Kitsap County citizens were becoming intellectually and economically impoverished by this state of affairs. "People are no longer taking the opportunity during their formative years to broaden themselves, to ask questions other than how to make a buck, to think about the main concerns of humanity in a disciplined way," Hanzeli contended.[87]

Despite this strong criticism, the Puget Sound naval establishment remained intact. Just as many, if not more, Washingtonians welcomed naval bases as shunned them. Given that Jackson had to balance liberal environmentalists and antinuclear activists, on the one hand, and armed forces boosters and conservatives, on the other hand, he was right to be

cautious with his actions on local military matters, especially after the
1960s. Once the Trident base was confirmed for Bangor, however, Jackson threw his support behind it, and his support for the Trident base and
the Puget Sound naval establishment in general critically shaped this part
of Washington, much the same as Hanford shaped the development of
the Tri-Cities and Boeing shaped various parts of the Pacific Northwest.

With Jackson's death on September 1, 1983, the Washington
congressional delegation lost much of its clout in the Senate. Oregon
Republicans Mark Hatfield and Bob Packwood had already surpassed
Jackson as regional leaders in senatorial clout and bringing home federal dollars, thanks to the Republican gain of the Senate in 1980 and
their resulting chairmanships of the Appropriations and Commerce
Committees, respectively. At the same time, the Reagan administration's defense initiatives came under criticism from the dovish Hatfield,
as well as from some congressional Democrats who viewed the defense
budget as driving up federal deficits and taking money from social
programs. The collapse of the Soviet Union ended the Cold War, and
Hanford came under increased scrutiny for the environmental damage
it caused to the nation and to southeast Washington in particular. Jackson's efforts helped the region economically during his lifetime but had
a mixed impact upon his constituents in the long term, some of whom
believed they fell ill because of Hanford's radioactive output. "In these
more recent contexts," according to historians John Findlay and Bruce
Hevly, "Cold War production of nuclear weapons represents not only a
crisis for American democracy but also the failure of it."[88]

After Jackson's death, the Hanford N Reactor was mothballed,
and a debate began regarding Hanford's potential new role as a federal
nuclear waste dump. In 1986, the removal of waste was a major point
of contention in the Washington US Senate campaign between Brock
Adams and incumbent Slade Gorton. "In the past our Northwest senators fought our tough battles in the Senate," Adams said. "But what do
we win now? The DOE . . . nuclear lottery?" referring to Hanford being
chosen as one of three possible sites for nuclear waste storage. Adams,
a former Jackson ally in Congress who sensed the shifting of political
winds in the wake of environmental concerns at Hanford, narrowly
defeated Gorton in the election. When Jackson's former Senate seat
opened in 1988, however, Gorton promised federal spending and jobs

for Hanford cleanup, thereby garnering crucial southeast Washington votes in a narrow election victory. These first two regular Senate elections after Jackson's death showed that while his legacy of federal assistance for Hanford remained intact, his nuclear ambitions for the region were now firmly buried amid a statewide rejection of nuclear energy. Such federal assistance was still needed: despite Jackson's efforts, the Tri-Cities' relative isolation, lack of a major college or university prior to the 1990s, and dearth of quality housing and retail centers hindered it from attracting a diverse industrial base. Even the much-touted Fast Flux Test Facility, though it went to full power in 1982, saw its fortunes decline after Jackson's death because it never was able to articulate a "strong defining mission."[89] Perhaps Jackson had been right that plutonium development at Hanford was needed to win the Cold War, but that era had passed. Now Washingtonians near and downwind from Hanford had to pay the environmental consequences of Cold War victory, while relying on fickle spending from the Department of Energy for their economic well-being in light of the twin failures of nuclear energy and economic diversification to completely end the regional economy's dependency on Washington, DC.[90]

In contrast to Hanford, the apparatus of Puget Sound naval installations stayed largely intact after Jackson's death, remaining a source of pride among the political and business establishment in the region. As Brian Casserly contends of Puget Sound cities that benefited from military spending, "Although their goals and motivations for the region were different from the military's, they were compatible enough to allow both the armed services and local cities to achieve a security consensus that has lasted down to the present."[91] Jackson and his successors in Congress played a major role as a caretaker for that consensus, ably balancing the needs of pro- and antimilitary constituents in helping increase the Puget Sound military presence.

Henry Jackson's legacy in the Pacific Northwest vis-à-vis nuclear weapons and energy, to say nothing of federal spending overall, is more mixed than his local defenders will admit. Jackson helped the region attain economic diversity and prosperity through his commitment to using the power of the federal government to foster economic development. In terms of the state's military establishment, one need only look to Washington's neighbor to the south to see what might have happened had Jackson and other members of the state congressional delegation not continued to boost for its bases and defense-related industries after World War II. Oregon lost nearly all of its military bases and defense contracts within a generation, and as the amount of money it received from the federal government diminished, the state suffered severely from national economic recessions in the late 1950s, early 1970s, and early 1980s from which Washington was somewhat cushioned, thanks to the presence of the military. Whether encouraged or tacitly tolerated by Jackson, depending on the whims of the prevailing political winds, nuclear weapons and nuclear energy development played a key role in the state's economic development until it diversified into greater international trade, tourism, and high-tech industrial growth.

Yet Jackson's focus on the military to achieve security both nationally and locally had costs and consequences. The buildup of Hanford and the nuclear weapon–based defense establishment in the Puget Sound created jobs which benefited hundreds of thousands of people. On the other hand, succeeding generations will continue to require federal help to clean up nuclear waste in Hanford. Puget Sound's economic development took place, meanwhile, in a distorted manner: those counties sustaining US Navy establishments footed the bill for its tax-exempt bases, while antinuclear activists feared—and continue to fear—that the region could be a target for America's enemies because of its nuclear arsenal, or that the arsenal itself could have a negative impact on the region's natural environment. Jackson's record on nuclear weapons and energy at home is a sobering reminder that the costs of the Cold War nuclear weapons buildup are paid not just in terms of the national debt or by a few people and hardened animals in the remotest deserts of the country. Those costs are also borne by the people of the Pacific Northwest, even as it is regarded as one of the most economically and culturally diverse and prosperous regions of the United States thanks to the work of Jackson and other gifted politicians of the Cold War era.

TOM FOLEY AND THE POLITICS OF NATIONAL SECURITY IN WASHINGTON'S HINTERLAND

In eastern Washington, meanwhile, a Jackson protégé, Democratic Representative Tom Foley, spent three decades working on behalf of national security and defense interests in the Fifth Congressional District, an area dubbed by locals as the Inland Northwest. In doing so, Foley economically benefited the region, especially constituents of Fairchild Air Force Base near Spokane, the district's biggest city. As Jackson's high-spending era of government ended, defense spending ironically became a liability for Foley, and he became the only Speaker of the House voted out of office in the twentieth century.

Foley was born March 6, 1929, in Spokane, the son of Spokane County deputy prosecutor Ralph Foley, who went on to become a respected superior court judge. The Foleys were Irish Catholics in a mainly Protestant, Republican part of the state, but father and son each gained respect for their ability to see many sides of every issue. This trait aided the younger Foley in understanding a diverse constituency which diverged from his own liberal beliefs on many issues, as well as from his relatively elite and privileged background. Interests in the plight of common people and fairness guided Foley forward as he earned a law degree at the University of Washington and entered private practice in the late 1950s. In 1961, he became Jackson's special counsel on the Senate Interior and Insular Affairs Committee, where he spent three years before being encouraged by Jackson to run for the Washington Fifth District seat in 1964. In a year that saw Democrats sweep Congress, Foley beat longtime incumbent Walt Horan to begin his thirty-year House career.[92]

The Fifth District is traditionally one of the most conservative and—outside of Spokane—rural parts of the Pacific Northwest. Spokane, which was Foley's hometown and the center of his political power, straddled the woody Okanogan Highlands and the fertile Columbia Basin, the latter of which contains the Palouse, "with its fertile wind-borne soils . . . the most productive wheat-growing region in the Northwest." The state produced over two million acres of wheat in 1990, 565,000 acres of which came from Whitman County in the Palouse. Despite being anchored by Washington's second-largest city in Spokane, the Fifth District was—and remains—generally white, rural, and conservative, particularly outside of the urban centers of Spokane, Pullman, and Walla Walla. Foley's successful reelection campaigns of 1972, 1980, and 1984 saw all the counties in his district swept by Republican presidential candidates: only in the year of Lyndon Johnson's landslide victory in 1964 did most of the Fifth District's counties go Democrat. In the 1988 presidential election, for example, out of all the counties in Foley's district, only sparsely popu-lated Pend Oreille County and Asotin County favored the Democrats. Even in Spokane County, 68,787 voters went for George H. W. Bush over 68,520 for Michael Dukakis; and Whitman County, with liberal Washington State University, went Republican by a margin of 7,680 votes to 7,403.[93] To win his own elections, as he did by a resounding majority in 1988, Foley had to court Republicans.[94]

Foley wooed conservative voters to be sure—particularly the small but vocal sliver that worked in the agricultural sector so crucial to exports out of the district and the state—but he mainly relied on a coalition that prominently featured government workers (including the military) and college and graduate students. Of the Fifth District's residents in 2016, 3,458 were employed by the military, mainly at Fair-child Air Force Base near Spokane. Just under 7,000 residents were employed in the agricultural sector, while over 55,000 worked for local, state, or federal government.[95] In 1989, the year Foley became Speaker of the House, Washington State enrolled 16,524 students, while East-ern Washington enrolled 8,098, Gonzaga 3,840, Walla Walla College 1,560, Whitman College 1,253, and Whitworth College had 1,788 students. In 1989, the area also had several community colleges, most notably Spokane and Spokane Falls Community Colleges, which had a combined enrollment of over 11,000 students, while Walla Walla Com-munity College had an enrollment of 2,705.[96] Foley thus had a large constituency dependent to some degree upon federal largesse, which only his ruling Democratic Party could proffer; but to win elections, he needed support from more conservative military-spending and trade-dependent voters.

During Foley's career, the district's per capita income was often the lowest in Washington. In the 1990 US Census, it was tallied at $31,073, a sharp contrast to the affluent Eighth District in the suburbs of Seattle, which came in at $50,601. The census furthermore revealed that 15.3 percent of Fifth District citizens lived below the poverty line. The Associated Press pointed out, however, that "large numbers" of college students had to be taken into account when considering the income, poverty, and unemployment figures. In short, the Fifth

District traditionally has had to rely on the largesse of government for economic sustenance, whether in terms of state or federal funding for education, unemployment and poverty reduction programs, proexport agricultural policies, or federal funds for military-related installations and services for veterans.[97]

Historian David Stratton credits Foley with keeping regional defense installations and other federal installations funded throughout his career. Fairchild Air Force Base was the Spokane metropolitan area's biggest employer, and it "added, with its diversified personnel and international mission, a significant cosmopolitan cultural influence to the region."[98] Not coincidentally, military issues played at least a tangential role in many of Foley's election campaigns. Foley's initial victory over incumbent Walt Horan in 1964 was a trend-setting example. As a Henry Jackson disciple, Foley knew that the Cold War climate "dictated that US political candidates routinely declare their opposition to communism." One of Foley's campaign fliers targeting rural voters declared that "Tom Foley and Senator Jackson believe US military superiority over any combination of communist countries [with] a strong national defense is our best weapon against communism." Foley routinely criticized Horan for voting against military and space appropriations, saying these votes would weaken US security. On this occasion, the popularity of his father, Ralph Foley, the broader popularity of President Johnson and Senator Jackson, campaign contributions from the AFL-CIO, and an ineffective campaign by an ill Horan were the primary factors in the victory.[99]

In relating to his conservative supporters, Foley could sound tough yet fiscally reasonable on national security, in part because he represented a district with just one major air force base. Thus, unlike other members of the Washington State delegation, Foley did not have to take into account the needs of multiple bases. For example, in 1982, Foley supported development of the B-1 bomber to replace the aging B-52 fleet, as well as research and development into the MX missile, but opposed construction of Nimitz-class aircraft carriers and battleship refitting because of cost concerns.[100]

On the other hand, Foley also had to appeal to more liberal anti-war university voters during close campaigns. Foley may have targeted this audience with antinuclear peace feelers he put out during his 1982 campaign. The *Seattle Times* noted that Foley blamed President Ronald Reagan for the continued nuclear weapons buildup. "The administration has made too many foolish proposals that only drive us apart from the Soviet Union," Foley said. "What are the Soviets supposed to think when the president talks about building backyard bomb shelters?"[101] Despite predictions of a tough campaign, Foley ultimately cruised to reelection, and was not seriously challenged again until his final defeat in 1994. The use of national security–based appeals to his advantage, some hawkish, some dovish, was a major part of Foley's campaign strategy throughout his career.

THE IMPORTANCE OF FAIRCHILD AIR FORCE BASE TO TOM FOLEY

Just as Hanford Nuclear Reservation and Puget Sound naval bases were important political considerations for Henry Jackson, Fairchild Air Force Base was critical to Tom Foley's political fortunes. The Spokane business community considered Fairchild their baby, and called on Foley to expand and defend the base against numerous attempts to declare it surplus to air force needs.[102] Even though Foley won one of his greatest political victories by keeping the base from being closed in 1993, it was ironically not enough to save him from losing his seat in the 1994 midterm election.

From the beginning of his time in Congress, Foley attached himself closely to Fairchild. In the summer of 1965, Foley joined Jackson and Warren Magnuson in announcing the establishment of an air force survival school at Fairchild, which would add 350 permanent military personnel and 4,800 annual students to the base's population. The congressional delegation also procured a $400,000 appropriation to modify existing Fairchild facilities to accommodate the school. In 1967, Foley helped secure a $1.4 million contract for Spokane construction company H. Halverson to build a Federal Regional Center for the Army. In January 1976, Foley's office announced it had secured a $1 million contract for an aircraft corrosion control facility. Later that year, Foley announced that Fairchild had secured a pair of modern B-52 bombers. Foley also managed to save three of the eight KC-135 tankers it was originally slated to shed via Defense Department cuts. The B-52 bombers would require the addition of 80 new jobs, cutting the net job loss expected from the KC-135 diversion from 350 down to 200. Foley also argued that the addition of Air National Guard personnel from Spokane International Airport would make up for the KC-135 losses over time.[103]

In 1985, Foley blocked a plan to move the air force survival school to Homestead Air Force Base near Miami, questioning an estimate that the move would save the Pentagon $2 million annually. Air Training Command (ATC), based at Randolph Air Force Base in Texas, recommended consolidating Fairchild's basic survival training school with water-survival training at Homestead. ATC argued the Air Force would save money from consolidation "because it no longer would send trainees from flight schools at Southern bases to Fairchild for survival training." Foley countered that the terrain and weather conditions at the current school were like conditions in Europe; thus, the Fairchild location helped the air force develop skills needed by flight crew members stationed at NATO bases overseas. He won the argument and the survival school remained at Fairchild.[104]

Foley pushed hard near the end of the Cold War not just to save Fairchild, but to upgrade and expand the base. In 1986, Foley supported five general military construction projects for Fairchild, on the grounds that they were all supported by Strategic Air Command and the Defense Department and already included in President Reagan's defense budget. Foley pushed for $1.95 million for renovation of Fairchild's central personnel support office, $1.35 million for aircraft nose dock weatherization, security improvements, and a "noise suppressor support facility." In May 1987, Foley asked for similar upgrades, plus new tanker squadron buildings, replacement of asbestos insulation in the central steam plant, renovation of family housing units, improvements to the alert aircraft parking area, a new dining hall and physical training areas, and a new KC-135 training facility. By then Foley managed to secure $6 million in a defense authorization amendment for a mission operations facility and asbestos removal.[105]

As the Cold War ended, Foley had to balance the desires of constituents who wanted to turn military spending toward domestic programs with those who wanted funding for Fairchild. This balancing act was exemplified in the debate over whether to place MX missiles at

Fairchild in 1989, after the fall of communist governments in Eastern Europe, but before the collapse of the Soviet Union. In one letter, Foley told a constituent that he wanted to see the differences between the House and the Senate on a conference bill which would decide on the deployment of a missile garrison but was noncommittal on whether he wanted Fairchild to get the missiles. Another constituent pled with Foley to "have the courage" to oppose the MX because of the potential environmental hazards the project would pose, as well as its cost. "America has been a junkie for too long, addicted to economic quick-fixes," wrote the constituent. "Please help her kick her military dependency before it's too late." Another constituent wrote Foley in April 1990, concerned about an unspecified, but "direct" and detrimental "impact" if the missiles were to be sited in Fairchild. "With the reduction in international tensions, this is an excellent time to take a positive step for the nation by getting rid of a weapons system the country does not need and channeling those funds toward our domestic needs," the constituent contended.[106] Ultimately, the MX was never deployed to Fairchild.

Even after the MX fight, Foley still saw evidence of the economic necessity of Fairchild to many other constituents. In 1991, he asked for funds for Fairchild to receive a state-of-the-art fuel storage tank, a parachute training facility, and a child-care center. In 1993, Foley requested three new construction projects for Fairchild, including an intelligence training facility, new quarters for general officers, and a hospital upgrade to meet fire and safety codes. It looked like Foley's efforts would go for naught, however, as Fairchild was targeted for closure by the Department of Defense Base Closure and Realignment Commission. In May 1993, he went on the offensive, noting that despite the commission's plan to close Fairchild, the air force had decided to create and deploy a large wing of KC-135 tanker refuelers to Fairchild. "The Air Force is demonstrating very clearly its desire to keep Fairchild as an important element of its overall force structure well into the next century," Foley argued in a press release. He said he believed the deployment would show the commission the continued economic viability of Fairchild, and that it would be supported by the greater Spokane community.[107]

On June 4, 1993, Foley testified to that effect before the commission, supported by testimony or personal appearances by a bipartisan group of politicians, including Spokane's mayor and city council, and Senators Patty Murray (D-WA) and Slade Gorton. Foley argued that not only was Fairchild one of just three bases nationwide that supported KC-135 tankers, but it also formed a vital part of a US strategic air bridge to the Pacific because of its mild climate (only 1 percent of its yearly sorties were canceled due to inclement weather) and high fuel storage capacity. He noted that the base's satellite control element, air force survival school, and physical plant had just been renovated. Because it was the most northern and western Air Force base for tankers, Foley contended that its closure would negatively impact deployments to and from McChord Air Force Base and Fort Lewis Army Base, located near the Seattle metropolitan area. Foley warned, furthermore, that unemployment, then at 6.3 percent in Spokane and 14 percent in surrounding counties, would worsen if Fairchild closed. The base employed 6,000 people, or 3.5 percent of the workforce in the Spokane area. If it and the Kaiser Aluminum plant in the nearby community of Trentwood were to close, he argued, regional unemployment could double. Pointing out the relationship between the base and area hospitals and educational facilities, Foley said Spokane and Fairchild had "worked together to produce a thoroughly harmonious relationship. The Air Force is welcome here and they know it." He also played up the "diverse educational, cultural and recreational opportunities" Spokane offered to Fairchild in return, all with a "moderate" cost of living.[108]

In follow-up testimony on June 16, Foley added that a proposed compromise to move the base's Air National Guard unit to Spokane International Airport was impractical; and, taking a page from his playbook of the mid-1980s, touted the usefulness of the air force survival school. "Fairchild's military value is high because of its extensive and excellently maintained facilities," he said. Foley argued that the federal government would spend $400 to $450 million to replace the base's functions if it closed. At one of many times in the late twentieth century of US tensions with North Korea, he reminded the closure committee that "Fairchild has the ideal Northwest location to support a major contingency response in the Pacific region—to build an air bridge to support our forces in Korea, for instance."[109]

Foley's testimony was steeped with both national security and local concerns. He highlighted the symbiosis between the greater Spokane community and its military installation that influenced the thinking of many congressmen and senators during the twentieth century. The *Spokane Spokesman-Review* backstopped Foley during his testimony, strongly supporting the base in an editorial. "During Desert Storm and in other times of trial," the paper noted, in reference to the base's support of US military efforts during the then-recently concluded Gulf War, "Spokane's large community of military retirees and its promilitary climate brought a deluge of personal help and support to military families." Although it is unclear whether Foley directly saved Fairchild from closure, his efforts seem to have made a difference. The base closure commission determined, in conjunction with Foley's contentions, that taxpayers would not "break even on the deal for 17 years" if the base closed, a closure it determined would cost $379 million. By a unanimous vote, the commission voted to keep the base open. A triumphant Foley exulted that the decision "ought to give us every confidence (the base) will stand any test in the future."[110]

News from Fairchild throughout the remainder of Foley's tenure in Congress seemed to back up his confidence. In the summer of 1993, KC-135 tankers from Fairchild deployed to Bosnia for United Nations peacekeeping support, on a mission to refuel US and European warplanes operating in support of a no-fly zone there. In early 1994, the US Air Force removed its aging B-52 fleet from Fairchild and replaced it with more KC-135s. Foley hailed this development, stating that "by establishing Fairchild as the nation's largest tanker base, the Air Force once again demonstrates its long-term commitment to and investment in our air base. The entire Spokane community and the civilian and military personnel at Fairchild should view this announcement as a big vote of confidence."[111]

Foley and other Fifth District boosters had saved Fairchild, and the base remained open as of 2019. Foley did not benefit electorally from this triumph, however. His use of political power to aid in the upkeep and restoration of Fairchild ironically played a role in his ultimate *loss* of political power during the 1994 Republican insurgency against Democrats and what the increasingly conservative Republican Party saw as federal government overreach, including by Foley.

NATIONAL SECURITY AND FOLEY'S 1994 DEFEAT

Pundits periodically penned Tom Foley's political obituary during his years in office. Strong challengers gave Foley close calls in 1966, 1976, 1978, and 1980. The notion that he would lose became farther-fetched as he romped to victory against token opposition through the 1980s, but the eventual erosion of Foley's political base and his reelection defeat in 1994 came in large part due to the loss of faith in the federal government in the wake of recessions, scandals, and the end of the Cold War. National security issues played a role in the erosion of Foley's base on both the left and the right of the political spectrum. From the left, concerns about military spending and the impact of the military on the natural environment that impacted Henry Jackson's later career also began to affect Foley in the 1980s and 1990s. From the right, the concern was less that Foley was in favor of the national security state-within-a-state, but that he was seen as symbolic of the overreach of the federal government, even on issues which positively impacted national defense.

Foley's politics were generally moderate throughout his career. His middle-of-the-road position began to infuriate dovish liberals in the mid-1980s, portending trouble for Foley in his most reliable constituency. Arms control negotiations with the Soviet Union, for example, became a major issue on which constituents diverged with him, whether for or against. Peace activists questioned his initial support for the MX missile. When a student at Washington State University asked Foley in 1984 how he could be for both a nuclear freeze and a buildup, Foley said "a vote for the nuclear freeze is not a vote against new weapons," adding that he wanted to see Soviet MX missiles "eliminated," and that he valued "stability" of the American nuclear arsenal over quibbling with the Reagan administration about its size. Peace activist Al Mangen of Spokane resignedly said that "it's just a question of who his constituency is. It's the establishment."[112]

The end of the Cold War meant the nuclear arsenal was no longer a damaging issue to Foley's left flank, but students and liberal activists remained dissatisfied with some of their congressman's foreign policy stances. A visit to Pullman, Washington, shortly after the Gulf War in 1991 showed how foreign policy would play a role in Foley's impending electoral defeat. The crowd at Pullman High School, near the Washington State University campus, was "overflowing" with liberals angry that Foley did not do enough to stop the war, even though he had voted against its authorization. One told Foley outright that "you don't have my vote." Another said that "one of the problems we have are smart bombs and dumb politicians." The *Tacoma News Tribune* reflected that "it was a tough crowd for Foley."[113] Although the Gulf War was a significant issue to many, biographer Kenton Bird argues that Foley was actually less criticized for his vote against authorization for the war than for not having been in his home district enough in recent times. Noting that he spent just three days in the district before heading back to Barbados to finish a vacation that was interrupted by the Gulf War, Bird criticizes him for this neglect of his constituents, saying he tended to "view interactions with constituents as intellectual exercises rather than opportunities to learn his constituents' views" at this point in his career, and that while he liked the give-and-take, he did not take the protesters' views seriously.[114] Foley won reelection in 1992, but his margin of victory was smaller than it had been at any time since 1980.

As Foley began his fifteenth term in the House, he came under increasing fire for federal appropriations, which were once considered a positive for Democratic lawmakers, but were now often seen as unnecessary pork-barrel spending. Such a viewpoint hurt Foley in a largely conservative district, even when discussing national security-related accomplishments. For example, a Walla Walla constituent railed against the US Army Corps of Engineers headquarters and the city's VA hospital as examples of wasteful spending.[115] If Foley's district had been in urban western Washington, he might have garnered more support for his work on behalf of federal installations, but donations from corporate contributors there could not outweigh the work of right-wing political action committees and grassroots opposition at home. Foley now constantly had to defend himself from charges that he was out of touch with the Fifth District.

The midterm election of 1994 was an uphill climb for Foley, as his Democratic Party reeled from charges of big-government malfeasance by eager Republicans. His support for the North American Free Trade Agreement (NAFTA) and the World Trade Organization (WTO) came despite a split in his party—and even with some Republicans—on the merits of free trade. Closer to home, Foley's endorsement of President Bill Clinton's unpopular universal healthcare plan proved to be an albatross; in addition, the speaker was beleaguered by a scandal in which many House members were implicated in overdrawing their checking accounts, culminating in the imprisonment of longtime Foley ally and chairman of the House Ways and Means Committee Dan Rostenkowski on corruption charges. Public opinion turned against the Democrats, who were broadly blamed for the scandal dubbed "Rubbergate." Foley escaped direct implication, but his leadership came under increased scrutiny from the GOP, as it galvanized its ranks under the campaign banner of "Contract with America" led in 1994 by Georgia Representative Newt Gingrich. That year, fifty-four House Democrats and eight Senate Democrats lost their seats, flipping Congress to Republican control for the first time in forty years.[116]

Foley had little margin for error in this political climate, despite his advantages as an incumbent. A major, tragic opportunity for Foley to connect with his district *and* national security interests came about on June 20, when ex–Air Force service member Dean Mellberg, who had recently been discharged after a history of mental problems, opened fire with a MAK-90 assault rifle at Fairchild, killing four people and injuring twenty-two others. Long an opponent of gun control and a staunch supporter of the National Rifle Association, Foley was nonetheless shaken by the mass shooting. In an era before political gridlock over the response to shootings paralyzed any chance of federal action, the speaker now backed an assault weapons ban that had been working its way through Congress. The ban passed the largely Democratic Congress, but it infuriated many of his constituents, who saw him as betraying one of his few bedrock conservative credentials by backing gun control. Although Foley couched his support for the ban in terms of taking a tough stance on crime, and even though Foley's move arguably showed support for the military community at Fairchild after the tragedy there, pro-gun constituents did not see it that way, and the NRA put Foley on its list of congressional targets for defeat in the fall election. In September 1994, physician-turned-politician George Nethercutt cruised to victory in the Republican primary and surged to a huge early lead over Foley in the polls. The Foley campaign ran ads attacking Nethercutt for opposing the assault weapons ban, but local pro-gun advocates proved more persuasive to voters in attacking Foley for pushing the ban through Congress.[117]

Nothing seemed to stand in Nethercutt's way, not even Foley's return home to campaign and his announcement of new jobs at Fairchild. Foley held a press conference to announce the air force survival school there would get additional instructors and students under an agreement with the Pentagon to bring 2,500 Navy and Marine aviators to Fairchild for training, along with $5 million in payroll. Nethercutt argued that the announcement smacked of election-year politics: "I didn't think it was appropriate to exploit it for political purposes," he told the *Spokane Spokesman-Review*. Foley acknowledged using his pull by writing to Chairman of the Joint Chiefs of Staff John Shalikashvili on behalf of the survival school, but added that "Congress does not micromanage these things," while denying "any suggestion that the consolidation represents 'pork.'" Foley contended that the move would, in fact, reduce overall air force operating expenses. "Pork is the unjust spending of money for political purposes," he said. "There's no way that saving money is pork." While Foley denied playing politics, he said he "had no apologies" for the announcement. "Because I'm a candidate doesn't mean I stop being a member of Congress," he said. "I'm not going to stop working for something because of someone's charges that it shouldn't happen in an election year."[118]

One of the big questions of the race, however, was whether Fifth District voters wanted their government to work for them at all anymore. The *Spokesman Review* interviewed a man named Michael Chappell who said he was "so fed up with government—with the spending, the bureaucracy, the lies—he wants to throw the bums out," starting with Foley. On the other hand, the paper reported that Chappell owned land near Fairchild and worried that "without the House speaker's influence, the base might close and the value of his land drop." The anti-incumbent mood in the piece nonetheless reflected broader feelings across the nation, spelling trouble for the speaker. In the face of criticism, Foley went on the offensive, launching negative campaign ads and debating Nethercutt numerous times, including a memorable encounter in Walla Walla during which he received numerous standing ovations. By the end of the passionate debate, Foley was shouting into the microphone to exhort the support of the audience. He had, at

Washington Representative Tom Foley at a campaign rally at Fairchild Air Force Base in Spokane during his 1994 run for reelection. When Foley was defeated by Republican challenger George Nethercutt, he lost his powerful position as US Speaker of the House. Reprinted by permission from Washington State University Manuscripts, Archives, & Special Collections; Thomas S. Foley Papers.

least for that night, seemingly gained the upper hand. The *Walla Walla Union Bulletin* subsequently endorsed Foley, reminding residents that if not for him the city would lack its VA hospital and Army Corps of Engineers center, causing the loss of jobs, and that Foley would have been "vilified" if that had happened.[119] The speaker nevertheless lost his 1994 reelection bid. His vote share dropped precipitously outside of Spokane, and he was not able to corral enough urban voters to overcome this shortfall.

Jim Camden of the *Spokesman-Review* argued that Foley failed to correctly gauge his district, including its national defense interests. "Out at Fairchild," Camden noted, "while the top brass was glad to appear at press conferences with the speaker, sergeants were given to grouse about Foley's ads on saving the base or his stance on restricting guns—a strange position indeed, considering the one gun Foley ever voted to ban was the kind used to kill four people at their hospital complex."[120] It was ironic that officers at an installation Foley had worked so hard to boost and to save from closure much of his career voted for his opponent in 1994. In running through the official tally of votes in the race, Camden noted that "Foley's claim that he worked to help keep Fairchild Air Force Base off a hit list for closure apparently carried little weight with the military. Nethercutt beat him nearly 2–1 in the base's single precinct, and won in nearby Airway Heights."[121] Jess Walter of the *Spokesman-Review* similarly concluded that Foley had lost in part by making the race a referendum on his work for Fairchild, where he was apparently unappreciated by the voters on and near the base.[122]

In the end, Foley's mainline Democratic Party political stance doomed what had been a remarkable career, leading him to be largely remembered as the first ousted incumbent Speaker of the House since the Civil War. He had gradually eroded his liberal support by not being strong enough against military spending over the years, and his consistent support for Fairchild may thus have hurt him with this bloc, while conservatives who may have supported him because of his boosting for Fairchild and national security bolted after he backed the assault weapons ban. Taking their cues from broader anti–big government sentiment across the nation in 1994, eastern Washington voters took for granted—and may have even resented—the federal largesse he brought to the region. Foley was ultimately ineffective at demonstrating how that largesse, including Fairchild, benefited the Fifth District.[123]

CONCLUSION

For most of the twentieth century, Washingtonians—aided by their federal representatives—ate at the national security trough. Political campaigns crackled with ominous Cold War warnings, combined with promises by incumbents and challengers alike that they would strengthen Washington's defense apparatus. Naval and army bases, Fairchild Air Force Base, and Hanford Nuclear Reservation, as well as the communities around them, by and large benefited from the national Cold War consensus and the apparent threat of the Soviet Union.

The limitations of the Cold War consensus were evident, however, as early as the late 1960s, as the nation showed its growing disapproval of the Vietnam War. Henry Jackson, the most ardent Cold Warrior of all, showed no sign of ebbing popularity, as he was reelected by landslide margins in his campaigns of 1970, 1976, and 1982. Tom Foley's gradually declining political fortunes, however, as well as the dissent against Jackson's Puget Sound naval buildup, showed that the Washington national security state-within-a-state, as it became associated with growing antigovernment sentiment, was increasingly unpopular on both the left and the right late in the twentieth century. While bases and defense contractors clearly benefited Washington, those benefits were distributed unevenly among its people. As shown in the case of Fairchild, furthermore, recipients of defense spending increasingly shunned government largesse even when it appeared to be in their economic interest.

An examination of the politics of national security in Washington dramatically illustrates both the benefits those politics had upon this specific region of the United States, as well as the consequences of over-reliance on local defense spending and contractors. In some cases, the consequences consisted of environmental degradation, as at Hanford; in others, like Fairchild, the changing geopolitical paradigm caused a more critical examination of the benefits of federal defense spending on the region. Washington nonetheless, as of 2019, remained home to Fairchild, many Puget Sound naval bases, and Joint Base Lewis-McChord. Although Boeing's headquarters have moved to Chicago, the company is still a major regional employer and defense contractor. Despite criticism from antigovernment conservatives on the right and environmentalists on the left, the state continues to benefit from defense spending, showing the clear impact of a strident national foreign policy posture toward China, North Korea, and Russia.

Washington is hardly unique in its ability to obtain federal defense spending. From California to Massachusetts, most states at one time or another have successfully jockeyed for defense spending and military bases. Few congressmen or senators ever wanted their base to end up on a closure list. The Washington story, however, is one of uncommon political power and force of will to obtain a continued military presence for a state which even today is home to just 2.2 percent of the nation's people.[124] Henry Jackson, Warren Magnuson, and Tom Foley continuously got reelected, and they climbed the rungs of congressional power, meaning that they could deliver federal military largesse to a region starving for it during World War II, the Cold War, and beyond. To the south in Oregon, meanwhile, a very different narrative was taking place with regard to national security during the Cold War. Washington's less-populous neighbor was left searching for scraps at the trough of defense appropriations after World War II. Senators Wayne Morse and Mark Hatfield were hardly the equal of Jackson and Magnuson in their ability to obtain federal largesse, meaning they would need to look in another direction in order to move Oregon beyond its pre–World War II timber economy.

CHAPTER 2

The Evolving Politics of Defense and National Security in Oregon

Unlike its West Coast neighbors, Oregon did not receive a huge influx of Pentagon investment after World War II. Most of the state's military bases were built before or during the war and were either shuttered or turned over from federal to National Guard control during the intervening years. Some Oregonians were dismayed at the ability of Washington and California to secure military largesse and federal investment. As the Cold War progressed, Oregon adapted, as it evolved from pursuing military spending to a more diversified approach to economic development. By the end of the twentieth century, many Oregonians went from backing the national security state to supporting a broadening of the definition of national security to include infrastructure, trade, education, and healthcare.

This transformation can be vividly seen through Oregon's representation by Senators Wayne Morse from 1945 to 1968, and Mark Hatfield from 1967 to 1996. Neither Morse nor Hatfield rejected outright the idea that the United States had to defend itself against the Soviet threat, but they criticized predominant thinking about how to wage the Cold War, culminating in their passionate dissent against the Vietnam War. Morse seemingly offered little more to Oregonians than his Vietnam dissent, a perception that factored into his 1968 reelection loss.[1] Hatfield, by contrast, is remembered as arguably the greatest politician in Oregon's history. He earned an exalted status among Oregonians because he redirected national security dollars beyond the diplomatic and military spheres. Hatfield argued that regional and national spending on education, health, and infrastructure represented paramount investments in national security. Oregon thus received plenty of federal dollars, particularly in the Hatfield years, and even Morse was more effective at making deals than many historians and contemporaries believed. The upshot overall for Oregon was that while its economy never became as dependent as Washington's upon the vagaries of the Pentagon, it also did not get the boost from military spending that its northern neighbor enjoyed thanks to its powerful politicians.

THE HAWKISH EARLY COLD WAR POLITICS OF NATIONAL SECURITY IN OREGON

At the height of World War II, Oregon's major military establishments were the US Army's Fort Stevens, Camp Adair, and Umatilla Depot; Tongue Point Naval Station, Naval Air Station Tillamook, and the US Navy shipyards in Portland; and the US Army Air Force bases at Kingsley Air Field and Portland International Airport. These facilities were shuttered during the Cold War, except Umatilla Depot, which closed in 2012. Defense contractors, such as Willamette Iron and Steel Works in Portland, fared somewhat better. But defense spending in Oregon was overall much lower than in Washington. In 1967, at the height of the Vietnam War, Oregon received $185 million in federal outlays for defense purposes. That number represented an increase from $156 million in 1966, and the state's prime contracts went up from $90 million to $118 million in the same period, yet Washington's haul of $1.37 billion from the Pentagon dwarfed that of its neighbor to the south.[2]

Several historians have considered why Oregon was less endowed by the Pentagon than its western neighbors. Carlos Schwantes suggests that it was because Boeing happened to be based in nearby Seattle that Oregon did not become as fully vested in defense industries as its northern neighbor.[3] Bruce Cumings pins most of the blame on Wayne Morse, whom he argues "was better known for hammering the Pentagon than sticking his palm out."[4] During Morse's years in the Senate, military expenditures to Oregon fell precipitously: by 1969, Oregon's "prime defense contracts numbered but 0.3 percent of the national total." Historian Gordon Dodds argues that while Oregon avoided becoming dependent upon military spending, its congressional delegation was not aggressive enough in pursuing defense contracts for some economic benefit.[5] Lack of harmony among the delegation may have played a role. Maurine Neuberger, Morse's Oregon colleague in the Senate from 1961 to 1966, called him an "uncouth person," noting that, on the rare occasions the Oregon delegation would meet in the nation's capital, "it was so futile because Morse ran the whole thing and he didn't want to hear what anybody else had to say." Morse, she charged, "was never good for Oregon," and in a jab representative of Morse critics, alleged that "to this day nobody can find a bill or a piece of legislation that passed that had his name on it."[6] Historian Eckard V. Toy more charitably contends that Morse demurred from pursuing military dollars because he believed that "Oregon would be less dependent upon the vagaries of Congressional politics" as a result, and not because he was an ineffective senator or poor colleague.[7]

While Morse was not as able as Henry Jackson in pursuing large-scale military installations and contracts, he was not uninterested in getting defense dollars to Oregon. Morse is nonetheless best remembered as casting one of two votes in Congress against the Gulf of Tonkin Resolution authorizing the use of US military force in Vietnam in August 1964. Already viewed by many colleagues and constituents—many of whom nonetheless loved him for it—as a difficult crank, Morse was stuck with a dove label that he was unable to shake for the remainder of his career. Though his critics painted him far outside the mainstream, Morse believed in spending at home and abroad to ensure the security and prosperity of Americans, and like most politicians nationally, he was not allergic to the national security ethos. This made electoral sense for Morse, because Oregonians were as swept up as the rest of the nation in the move toward constructing the Cold War national security state. By the end of Morse's tenure in office, in 1969, the total defense budget amounted to 42.9 percent of federal expenditures, with defense funds going to every state, 363 out of 435 congressional districts, and to over 5,000 communities nationwide, with defense workers making up 10 percent of the country's labor force.[8] Morse could not ignore this reality any more than his counterparts in Washington state. Over the decades he and Hatfield focused on building up what Jack Robertson, one of Hatfield's aides, characterized as the homeland defensive. This euphemism characterizes the senators' balancing of their relatively less hawkish foreign policy inclinations with a posture that favored limited military spending in Oregon, albeit not on the massive scale engendered by the Washington congressional delegation.

As the Cold War heated up in the late 1940s, Morse supported universal military training and air power for both defensive and offensive purposes. It would be surprising to Morse's later, dovish, supporters that, in 1950, he was privy to meetings regarding the potential siting of the Air Force Academy in the Portland suburb of Canby, and apparently did not object to the idea of having the academy in the Portland metropolitan area. In 1952, Morse lobbied the army to support a Portland Chamber of Commerce proposal to install a chemical plant in the city. In 1957, he joined the Oregon congressional delegation in protesting the air force's cancellation of plans for a semi-automatic ground environment (SAGE) near Pendleton which would have provided 700 local jobs.[9] In 1958, Morse co-sponsored the National Defense Education Act, telling Oregonians in a radio address that the bill would "strengthen the intellectual training of our youth, particularly in the fields directly associated with national defense." He offered an amendment to the bill to provide federal funds for school construction, but it received insufficient support from the Senate Labor Committee to be adopted before the bill went to the Senate for a full vote. Dismayed at the outcome, Morse warned that unless it matched Russian education spending, the United States "will simply end up being Russia's richest satellite."[10] In doing so, while he foreshadowed Hatfield's later campaign to reorient defense spending toward educational purposes, it is clear Morse was not a military dove.

Other Oregonians questioned the power of the military to operate in Oregon. Edith Green, who represented much of Portland in the US House from 1955 to 1974, was ambivalent at best about defense spending. In 1957, the chamber of commerce in the Portland suburb of Newberg wrote to Green to protest the rumored loss of a mental institution. Believing the facility was to be replaced by a US Air Force base, the chamber asked Green to intervene and see if the base could be moved to Woodburn, farther south of Portland. Green wrote USAF legislative liaison Major General Joe Kelley, who assured her there would be no development near Newberg. But the Air Force did plan to expand activities at its Portland International Airport base and to build an ammunition dump site at Vanport, destroyed by flooding a decade earlier. Both sites were near population centers in Portland. Oregon Governor Robert Holmes and Portland Mayor Terry Schrunk wrote Green to protest the move. The congresswoman concurred with their opinion, but House Armed Services Committee chair Carl Vinson warned Green that to interfere with the military's legal rights governing an airport it developed—Portland International Airport began as an air force base during World War II—would set a precedent that other cities might follow, potentially disrupting military operations nationwide. Green nonetheless announced that she opposed further air force development near the Portland airport because of safety concerns. In the end, Kelley argued that budget cuts, not the politicians' protestations, forced the cancellation of the air force's expansion of its Portland operations.[11] Green pushed for defense dollars to go south of the city, but the near-simultaneous closure of Camp Adair near Corvallis showed that the Defense Department did not wish to expand its operations in that region.

Morse, meanwhile, was not interested in turning Oregon into a national security state-within-a-state like Washington, but he did not obstruct the defense establishment as did Edith Green. Like Green, however, he recognized that expanding the military in more rural parts of Oregon might pay political dividends and boost the state economically. Even into his supposedly more dovish years in the 1960s, Morse pushed for a Pentagon presence in Oregon.

NOT A DOVE? TONGUE POINT, BEAVER ARMY TERMINAL, AND WAYNE MORSE'S OTHER MILITARY ADVENTURES IN THE 1960S

On March 31, 1961, the *Oregonian* reported that the Defense Department ordered the Pacific Reserve Fleet site at Tongue Point, near Astoria, "inactivated." As late as 1958, over 1,000 naval personnel and 360 civilians had worked at the station, not an unsubstantial economic impact to a city that had a population of 11,239 at the 1960 census.[12] Thus began a multiyear odyssey by Morse to determine what to do about the economic spiral that would be coming to one of Oregon's most economically challenged areas. Morse first approached the task with a determination to keep Tongue Point operational. In March 1961, Morse wrote Secretary of Defense Robert McNamara, urging that the Defense Department find some use for the base. He pointed out that it was ready for immediate use for defense purposes, contending that it could serve as an air force training base, house submarines or nuclear missiles, or become a hub for oceanographic research. The geographic location of nearby Astoria meant the base was "in a position to supply all of the requirements of a major defense installation."[13] The West German, Japanese, and Indonesian navies all used the base as a port of call, and 430 US Navy enlisted men, 40 officers, and 241 civilians worked there. Morse said he was "far from convinced" the action to close Tongue Point was justified, even though only 100 ships homeported at Tongue Point, down from 550 during World War II.[14]

In July 1961, Morse requested that federal agencies inspect Tongue Point and discuss alternative uses for the base. He feared that if the General Services Administration, the federal agency tasked with disposing of the base, sold off Tongue Point to private interests, the buyer might not reinvest the land in the community, thus sinking one of Oregon's largest ports into economic recession. To that end, Morse brought representatives from the Departments of Defense, Navy, Labor, Commerce, Health, and Interior, along with the Small Business Administration and the GSA, to visit Tongue Point.[15] Meanwhile, he helped secure a $2.4 million contract for Willamette Iron & Steel to convert a military transport into a satellite communications ship, a project that would temporarily employ between 300 and 450 workers. While this contract coincided with the reactivation of dormant ships to active duty up and down the Pacific coast, Tongue Point was left off the list of ports of call for those ships.[16]

The *Daily Astorian* newspaper wrote in early 1962 that Morse's actions stood "in sharp contrast with what appears to be lack of action by other members of the Oregon congressional delegation," also criticizing them for not fighting harder when Tongue Point lost a federal contract for an oceanography research lab to Seattle. The newspaper saw the situation at Tongue Point as symptomatic of a larger problem afflicting the whole state, namely the relative lack of federal largesse in contrast to Washington: "We Oregonians should be more than a little tired of paying enormous federal taxes which help build up a federal empire in the Puget Sound region and make Seattle a sort of federal branch capital in the Northwest," the paper argued.[17]

Despite the support of the *Daily Astorian*, Morse faced an uphill climb to return to the Senate in 1962 and continue the fight for

Tongue Point. In March 1962, Oregon labor unionist Charles E. Gilbert announced that he would challenge Morse in the Democratic primary, partly with the goal of bringing more defense contracts to Oregon.[18] Morse was able to turn back this insurgent threat, but the *Oregonian,* then Oregon's leading Republican newspaper, criticized the senator for being an ineffective representative of the state's interests in Washington, DC, suggesting that this could make him vulnerable in the fall campaign against Republican nominee Sig Unander. The paper charged Morse was ineffective in attracting defense dollars to the state while Washington and California had received huge amounts of federal money for new bases.[19]

Morse took a position of strength on national security issues. In a Senate floor speech on September 23 that seemed pointed at Unander's assertion (similar to others Republican candidates routinely leveled against Democrats during the Cold War) that he was soft on the Soviet Union, Morse, who chaired the Latin American subcommittee of the Senate Foreign Relations Committee, called for resolve against communism in the Americas in the face of the Soviet buildup of nuclear weapons in Cuba that would precipitate the Cuban Missile Crisis later that fall. Morse touted a recent conference in Punta del Este, Uruguay, which resulted in Latin American republics proclaiming a "unanimous commitment" to stop the spread of communism in the hemisphere. He advocated for a meeting between the United States and the Organization of American States to decide what to do about the Soviet placement of missiles in Cuba. Soviet leader Nikita Khrushchev and Cuban president Fidel Castro, he argued, "had better take note of the fact that we will not be bluffed by any course of action of theirs nor by their threats," Morse warned. "If they proceed with any program for aggression in Cuba, such as ground-to-ground missiles, or launching installations, that would endanger Miami, New York, Chicago, or any other part of the United States, let them understand that we have no intention of waiting for them to fire the first missile."[20]

Returning to Oregon to campaign, Morse touted not only his national security credentials, but also his role in making more federal dollars come to Oregon than in almost any other year. The *Oregonian,* meanwhile, praised Sig Unander on Cuba, arguing that he had called for prevention of a communist military buildup in Cuba as early as the

summer of 1961, while Morse called for a more cautious approach and
had recently opposed President John F. Kennedy's blockade of Soviet
ships as being too provocative.[21] In a speech to the Portland Chamber
of Commerce on October 30, Unander characterized Morse as "the
voice of appeasement and double-talk" and said the senator was trying to capitalize on Cuba "with the footwork of a ballerina," accusing
Morse of initially being soft on Cuba and then taking a more hardline
approach only as the election drew near. Unander believed Morse had
been soft on communism since he opposed the Formosa Resolution
to defend Taiwan against the communist People's Republic of China
in 1955. This was hardly a fair characterization: Morse was generally
anticommunist, and he had opposed the resolution because he feared
handing over power to President Eisenhower to launch a preemptive
nuclear strike.[22] Unander also attacked Morse for refusing to support
more fully the failed "Bay of Pigs" covert invasion by the CIA and
Cuban exiles in 1961. The challenger argued that Kennedy feared repri-
sals from "senators like Wayne Morse" if he had been more vigorous,
and that if Kennedy had stayed the course in the invasion, Cuba would
be free from Castro's rule.[23]

Despite Unander's attacks, Morse won reelection in 1962. A post-
election analysis by political scientist Donald G. Balmer argued that the
senator's foreign policy stances played a positive role in the outcome.
Balmer believed that the Cuban Missile Crisis may have played a piv-
otal role, highlighting a Republican poll that decreased Morse's lead
over Unander to 1.1 percent on October 22, before bumping it back
to 5 percent on November 5, after the crisis had passed. Balmer also
argued that Morse's campaign staff succeeded at depicting him as a
national and global force as well as an effective senator by playing up
his service in the Senate Foreign Relations Committee and his close ties
with President Kennedy.[24]

After winning reelection, Morse resumed his efforts to bring new
life to Tongue Point. It appeared that his work had paid off on September 27, 1963, when President Kennedy joined Edith Green and
Morse in visiting the former naval station. Kennedy announced that
reactivation of Tongue Point had been approved for training Defense
Department employees in weapons system management. In his address
to a crowd in Astoria, Kennedy said, "I came here as a result of—I will

Oregon's congressional delegation with President John F. Kennedy upon his visit to the site of the former Tongue Point Naval Station near Astoria on September 27, 1963. Though Kennedy announced plans by the Defense Department and the Coast Guard to use Tongue Point, the station would eventually be converted into a facility for the Job Corps. Surrounding Kennedy are Senator Maurine Neuberger, Senator Wayne Morse, and Secretary of the Interior Stewart Udall. Reprinted by permission from University of Oregon Special Collections, Wayne L. Morse Papers, Coll001_014.

not say consistent prodding, but I will say that on every occasion I have seen Senator Morse this matter has come up in one way or another, and, therefore, I felt it incumbent upon me" to visit the city, adding with no small amount of exaggeration, "We are here to take a look at what is a great national asset."[25] To get Kennedy to make a stop in Astoria and to place such importance on Tongue Point during a trip better remembered for his dedication of the N Reactor nuclear plant at Hanford in southeast Washington was a major victory for Morse and the Oregon congressional delegation.

Tongue Point was also proposed as the site for a Native American school but was ultimately rejected for this purpose. Julia Butler Hansen, who represented the congressional district across the Columbia River from the base in Washington, reportedly rejected the proposal in her House Appropriations subcommittee because she thought it unwise to

try to acculturate Native Americans through federal education based
on the historic failure of past efforts.[26] The Kennedy plan for a Defense
Department ordnance plant was also reversed, and plans for a $50 mil-
lion NASA electronics research center that Morse had pushed came to
naught.[27] The senator berated Hansen, telling the *Oregonian* that "her
arguments are thoroughly unsound," and that "she was . . . abetted by
certain Republican newspapers in Oregon who have bitterly opposed
my attempt to save the taxpayers of the country millions of dollars by
preventing the junking of the fine Tongue Point facility."[28] Morse also
attacked Hansen in a telephone call with Bill Moyers, aide to President
Lyndon Johnson. In a memo to congressional aide Lawrence O'Brien,
Moyers reported that Morse was "to put it mildly, 'agitated.'" Morse told
Moyers that "President Kennedy had helped him get the program reactivated and now Julia Hansen and Edith Green were trying to scuttle
him. . . . He said, and I quote directly, 'I will not take this. I want the
President to know that if I do not get help on this program, I intend to
do everything in my power to fight,'" Moyers reported.[29]

That same day, Morse wrote Moyers and shared with him that he
had recently gone before a Senate Interior and Insular Affairs subcommittee to make the case for Tongue Point.[30] "I have yet to vote in the
Senate . . . to keep a Federal installation going for a purpose that has
become obsolete," Morse told the subcommittee. He also argued that
the closure "pulled the economic rug out from under Astoria and
Clatsop County, Oregon, and put it at the bottom of the totem pole as
far as depressed areas in the United States are concerned." The senator
estimated that three to four thousand people were employed at Tongue
Point during its operation, meaning that its shutdown represented
a major economic loss to the region. "There must be some Federal
use for Tongue Point," claimed Morse, to help revive economically
depressed Astoria's downtown. Morse argued that Oregon had already
been unduly passed over by Congress when its delegation tried to have
Tongue Point turned over to the Coast and Geodetic Survey installation
programs, only to have those programs end up in Puget Sound instead,
for which he said the Secretary of Commerce apologized personally:
"President Kennedy said, 'Wayne, I think you are the only Senator who
ever got a letter of apology from a Cabinet officer,'" Morse related. He
added that discussions were ongoing about developing a vocational

training school at Tongue Point in connection with the Peace Corps, one that would bring in youth from Asia, Latin America and Africa "whom we want to train to be community leaders with . . . tractor skills and machinery skills, and carpentry skills." Morse tried to keep alive the possibility of a federally funded school for Native Americans, arguing also that refurbishing part of the base for this purpose would cost $3 million less than building a brand-new school elsewhere: "If they can't go out and hold jobs, if they aren't trained to hold jobs, forget about them being economically integrated into our society; they never will be, and they will continue to be the problems many of them are now," he said. Even though Oregon had only 8,000 Native Americans, Morse pointed out, this facility would be open to tribespeople nationwide.[31]

The Native American school never came to be, but Morse did help make Tongue Point a Job Corps site under President Johnson's Great Society program for poverty relief. The *Oregonian* wrote that "the Oregon senator has at last 'saved Tongue Point'" noting that the Job Corps site "will funnel some of [the Great Society] into a section of Oregon that has been economically depressed for many years." The paper believed that while Astoria Chamber of Commerce members might never vote for Morse, they could no longer say he did nothing for Oregon after "the dollars begin to jingle their cash registers."[32] The Pacific Reserve Fleet also maintained a small presence at Tongue Point, and as Morse geared up for reelection in 1968, he negotiated with the Johnson administration to retain it in the face of additional defense cuts. According to his campaign literature that year, "Senator Morse has cooperated with Oregon ship alteration, conversion and repair firms to bring major contracts to Oregon" to bring jobs for workers and business for local companies.[33] As of 2019, Tongue Point continued in its role as a Job Corps center, an undeniable legacy of Morse's battle to keep the base open, although it no longer is used for defense purposes. In all, the Tongue Point fight goes against the notion that Morse was utterly ineffective or uninterested in Oregon issues. Tongue Point was a small, but prime example showing that when regional politicians combined their foreign and domestic affairs interests, their efforts furthered the economic transformation of the Pacific Northwest.

Meanwhile, in rural eastern Oregon, Morse adopted colleague Henry Jackson's tone, noting as early as 1955 that water heated for plutonium production at the Hanford Nuclear Reservation could be used to generate electric power. Morse helped pass legislation in 1962 enabling the first kilowatts from Hanford's N Reactor to be introduced into the Pacific Northwest's power supply by 1966, thereby using this defense establishment to generate 800,000 kilowatts of electricity annually for the region.[34] In line with his regional colleagues who favored major federal investments in electrical infrastructure during the mid-twentieth century, Morse admittedly acted more in the role of supporter of public power than as a backer of the defense establishment in the Hanford case. If he was as against the Pentagon as his detractors claim, however, it seems unlikely that he would have supported the Hanford project at all. Perhaps his opinion would have changed had he lived to see the day when the environmental consequences of Hanford became apparent in terms of cancer cases among residents of Oregon and southeast Washington who lived downwind of the reservation, as well as the diminishing fish population in the Columbia River.

Further evidence of Morse's efforts to support military establishments in Oregon can be seen in his unsuccessful struggle to stop the closure of the Beaver Army Terminal near Clatskanie in 1964, as well as his effort to keep the US Air Force from leaving Portland International Airport. Beaver Army Terminal served as a depot for shipment of ammunition during World War II and the Korean War, then prepared shipments of equipment and spare parts for the US Army Supply and Material Command, while still maintaining the ability to convert to an ammunition depot in case of war. But an army information sheet released on April 24, 1964, slated the terminal, also used by the army for "wet storage of marine equipment," for closure and the dismissal of all 113 of its civilian and military personnel by July 1965.[35] Morse protested the closure of the terminal, while attempting to find a government agency that would take possession of the land and either preserve jobs or create new ones. On April 28, Morse and Senator Maurine Neuberger wrote to Secretary of the Army Stephen Allen that "a strong case can be made for expanding use of the Terminal by bringing in functions now performed at the Army Rio Vista Storage Site" in California as part of a Defense Department consolidation process. They recognized that government termination of the army site was inevitable, but noted that the process of disposal, unless drawn out, would hurt the regional economy.[36] The Port of St. Helens ultimately purchased the terminal, operating part of it, while leasing out parcels of the land to other business interests. There is little evidence, however, to suggest that the loss of the terminal was helpful to Oregonians, who are still dealing with environmental cleanup of the site stemming from the army's use of the land, as well as contamination from the Trojan Nuclear Power Plant, which operated a few miles upstream along the Columbia River from 1976 to 1993.

In December 1965, Morse wrote President Johnson to protest the transfer of the US Air Force base there to the Oregon Air National Guard. Morse expressed particular concern regarding the inactivation of the 460th Fighter-Interceptor Squadron from the base. Because he was not informed in advance, Morse said that the action left an "adverse impression" upon Portlanders angry either at him or the Johnson administration. The senator vowed to protest the action until he received a "full explanation," demanding to know how Portlanders who feared Soviet attack would be defended if the squadron was deactivated, and how defense of Hanford and the region's hydroelectric dams would be affected. He also asked how the federal government planned to assist the 1,500 Portlanders he believed would lose their jobs as a result of the base closure, and if it would truly save the Pentagon money when taking into account the cost of relocating families and personnel, the transfer of base functions to the Oregon Air National Guard, and the cost of dealing with retired military personnel dependent upon the base's medical and post exchange benefits.[37] Morse was apparently somewhat placated by the answer he ultimately received. As he told a Portland constituent in February 1966, the Office of the Secretary of the Air Force assured him that a reduced force of fighter squadrons from across the Northwest would be deployed more widely and the Oregon Army National Guard base at the airport would be beefed up with modern F-102 fighters. Morse noted at end of the letter, however, that he would have preferred the air force base at Portland to remain open.[38]

Morse also did extensive work throughout the decade on behalf of Oregonians who served in the military, despite his misgivings about the Vietnam War. In 1965, Morse received numerous letters from constituents across the region and the country complaining that servicemen received low pay. On February 18, he wrote to an airman at Portland International Airport, expressing his belief that a recent bill passed by Congress increasing pay for servicemen was "hardly sufficient" and vowing to support another bill increasing pay in the future.[39] He also received many letters on behalf of Oregon service members deployed to Vietnam. In 1967, he sympathized with a woman from Cottage Grove whose son had told her that his weapon often jammed, without apparent prospect for being replaced. Morse said he had spoken with Defense Department officials about similar problems numerous times following complaints from other constituents and that he would take up this case with the appropriate officials.[40] Later Morse received a letter from the Office of Legislative Liaison, stating that the army was dealing with the problem through retraining officers and developing "product improvements."[41] Morse told his constituent that he hoped her son had received assistance in his particular situation, while encouraging her to be in touch if this was not the case.[42] Morse was clearly able to separate his personal feelings about Vietnam from his professional obligation to assist Oregon constituents who were serving in combat. Such assistance arguably constituted aiding the war effort, but it seems unlikely that Morse would leave an Oregonian in a situation where he would be unable to defend himself should he come under enemy fire.

Overall, Morse was not the raving antimilitarist his critics believed him to be. Indeed, as he geared up for his 1968 reelection campaign, the senator reminded his campaign workers and Oregon voters of his work *for* the military establishment. He argued that he had sponsored GI Bills for home loans and educational financing for Korean War, Cold War, and Vietnam War veterans. He also said he sponsored a bill that opened a house for "febrile" vets near Grants Pass in 1948, and that he stopped a Johnson administration attempt to close the house in 1965.[43] Morse was clearly trying to balance his overall record against charges of his dovishness stemming from his opposition to the Vietnam War. While he may not have succeeded in fully doing so with Oregon voters, his record on Oregon defense establishments complicates his dovish historical legacy.

THE VIETNAM WAR AND THE 1966 AND 1968
US SENATE ELECTIONS IN OREGON

The saga of Wayne Morse's 1968 US Senate reelection run begins with the 1966 midterm election. Morse's role in the contest for Oregon's junior US Senate seat, which was vacated by the retiring Maurine Neuberger, showed the extent to which the Vietnam War was beginning to affect the state's politics. Mark Hatfield's victory and subsequent lengthy tenure in the Senate, moreover, showed that Oregonians were divided, at best, on the merits of high levels of traditional defense spending and the national security state.

Bob Duncan, US representative for Oregon's Fourth Congressional District (including the cities of Eugene and Medford), began 1966 as the favorite for the Democratic nomination for Neuberger's Senate seat over Morse's preferred candidate, the dovish longtime state party operative Howard Morgan. Morse angered party leaders by threatening to cross party lines and support the Republican Hatfield if Duncan defeated Morgan in the Democratic primary.[44] Morse issued a press release accusing Duncan of "echoing . . . shop worn political slogans," and arousing anticommunist sentiment instead of seeking fresh solutions in Vietnam.[45] Duncan defeated Morgan for the nomination, and Morse kept his word, breaking with state Democrats to back Hatfield's candidacy. The senator contended that the primary election results showed that voters were skeptical about the war, citing the case of dove Charles Porter's winning the Democratic primary for Duncan's soon-to-be-vacant congressional seat. Morse predicted the Democrats could lose to Hatfield in the general election because of Vietnam.[46] Although this may have been a case of Morse exaggerating for political effect, historian William Robbins argues that there were more than just a handful of doves in Oregon. Prominent among them was Arthur H. Bone, head of the Oregon-Washington Farmers' Union, who told Duncan "he would 'either go fishing or support Hatfield, rather than vote for a Democrat who supports our immoral Vietnam policy'" and predicted a Hatfield victory because of Duncan's hawkishness.[47]

Hatfield had been popular while serving in the Oregon legislature and as secretary of state and governor of Oregon for fifteen years, while Duncan had never won a statewide election. Political scientist Donald Balmer believed Hatfield's support stemmed from the war, but not because of Morse swinging antiwar voters his way. Balmer argued that voters may have been pulled away from the Democrats because the US Federal Reserve had raised interest rates to dampen an economy that was overheating due to war production. A tighter money supply resulted, leading to diminished capacity for the home-construction industry to get loans, turning into subsequent closings or cutbacks at lumber mills in traditionally Democratic constituencies in western Oregon.[48]

President Lyndon Johnson, Vice President Hubert Humphrey, and Senators Robert and Ted Kennedy all supported Duncan not only out of partisanship, but because they recoiled at the thought of Oregon having two dove senators. Some saw this as a proxy race between the Johnson and Morse positions on Vietnam, but it was not that simple. Hatfield was not running a single-issue campaign, and he even fudged his Vietnam position during the general election campaign against Duncan, at one point showing "willingness" to mine Haiphong Harbor in North Vietnam. This position did not cost Hatfield with "Democratic intellectuals," who definitively knew Duncan was a hawk and calculated it was better to vote for Hatfield, whose position was murky, than Duncan, whose stance was clear. Duncan tried to play up his hawkishness as an advantage: in addition to Vietnam, he attacked the presence of Russian trawlers off the Oregon Coast, leading to "swift" congressional action to extend US territorial waters up to twelve miles offshore. Throughout the campaign, Duncan played up his "manliness" and his image as a rugged outdoorsman, in contrast to the perception of Hatfield as a "reserved, stiff" churchgoing teetotaler. But Hatfield refused to debate Duncan, thus denying the Democrat an opportunity to directly challenge Hatfield on his Vietnam stance. Hatfield thought a Robert Kennedy rally in the state stirred up the dove vote and helped him more than Duncan, since Kennedy was showing outward signs of turning against Johnson's war policy.[49]

With Hatfield's win, Morse had a new ally on Vietnam. Because he crossed party lines to support Hatfield and opposed the war, however, many Oregon Democrats turned against Morse when it was his turn for an election battle. In November 1967, Democrats in Josephine County, one of many rural counties that was more hawkish than Oregon's urban centers, called for Morse's defeat in the 1968 Democratic primary, citing his war opposition. By now, however, the war was a personal issue to Morse, one which he felt negatively affected Oregonians, even if they did not see it that way. Historian Lillian Wilkins argues that Morse turned his 1968 Senate contest into a debate on Vietnam, despite the electoral disadvantage of this strategy. As public condemnation of Morse increased in 1967 and 1968, his dissent was seen by angry Oregonians as demonstrating a lack of caring for the troops, who falsely equated it with a lack of patriotism.[50]

Bob Duncan challenged Morse for the Democratic primary, and early polls gave him a huge advantage in the run-up to the vote. The bitterness of the campaign can be seen in the editorial pages of the *Oregonian*. Letter-to-the-editor writer Kenneth Stullerly supported Morse for reelection mostly because of Vietnam. He said it was to Congress's "everlasting shame" that no one but Morse and Alaska Senator Ernest Gruening voted against the Gulf of Tonkin Resolution, and believed that the Soviet Union could win the Cold War without any of its soldiers dying if the United States were to continue waging wars like Vietnam.[51] Richard Washburn, meanwhile, suggested that if Morse quit the race, "some of the color will have gone out of the cheeks of Oregonians who have been blushing with shame" because Morse, he believed, "has denounced his own country as a war criminal." Washburn accused Morse of giving aid and comfort to North Vietnam through "loud-mouthed free-spouting."[52] Mack Jacobs, meanwhile, accused the *Oregonian* of deceit when it said it was untrue that the Vietnam War had been started during the Eisenhower administration. This "slander" caused Jacobs, a "lifelong Republican" who had never voted for Morse, to change his vote.[53]

Meanwhile, consistent with his previous non-Vietnam foreign policy stances, national security was foremost on Morse's mind at a fundraising dinner in Portland on January 25, where the senator discussed the recent seizure of the Navy ship USS *Pueblo* by North Korea. Not generally given to supporting the Johnson administration on foreign policy, Morse credited Johnson for a cool approach and for calling up armed forces reserves in response to the crisis. Morse called for UN intervention to resolve the dispute but said Johnson's restrained course prevented the United States from going to war with North Korea and China over the incident. Officials claimed the dinner netted $10,000 for Morse's reelection campaign.[54] Campaigning in Eugene, Duncan derided Morse as a "senior showman instead of a senior senator."[55] But the *New York Times* praised Morse for his public policy work, including his "constant communication" with the State Department during the *Pueblo* crisis as part of the Senate Foreign Relations Committee. The *Times* believed this tactic would replicate Morse's 1962 reelection campaign, in which he successfully touted his foreign policy credentials during the Cuban Missile Crisis.[56]

On the Republican side, Robert Packwood cruised to a relatively easy primary victory. Packwood became infamous in the mid-1990s when he was forced to resign from the US Senate after damning allegations of sexual misconduct, including by some of his own female aides. In 1968, however, Packwood was a relatively young state legislator from Portland who had made a name for himself by founding the Dorchester Conference, an annual gathering designed to recruit more moderate Oregon Republicans to positions of political power, including the Senate.[57] While he addressed the Vietnam issue, Packwood tried to downplay it in the campaign, arguing on the one hand, "I don't think the war is unconstitutional as Senator Morse claims," but telling the press that while the United States had a "legal and moral obligation" to Vietnam, it should eventually leave the country.[58]

Mark Kirchmeier argues that Packwood determined it was in his best political interest to remain "nonideological" to avoid being on the wrong side of an increasingly polarized debate. Rather than confront Vietnam head-on as Duncan had unsuccessfully done in 1966, Kirchmeier contends Packwood's solution was to "obfuscate" the issue. His "vague" proposal calling for land reform to aid South Vietnamese peasants "had no mechanism, no time line, and no cost controls, and no one in Congress or in academia took it seriously," Kirchmeier argues. "But it worked for the voters, and Packwood spread the land reform line with a well-heeled campaign largely financed by manufacturing and banking interests."[59]

While Packwood cruised to the Republican nomination, Morse fought in the spring of 1968 to get renominated by the Democrats. Clackamas County Representative Dale M. Harlan complained after a Morse speech to the county's Democrats that "much of the audience . . . found his remarks so boring and egotistical that they went to sleep."[60]

Morse also got bad press in the aftermath of Senate Foreign Relations Committee hearings on the Vietnam War in early March. The *Oregonian* editorialized that the hearings "added not one iota of new information on the conduct of the war," calling them "a spectacle no one should have enjoyed." The paper thought the hearing was political theater, with Morse seeking face time as he waged his reelection campaign.[61] The *New York Times* reported that the Oregon Democratic State Convention adopted a Morse-friendly plank favoring a negotiated settlement to the war and United Nations involvement.[62] The *Oregonian* endorsed Bob Duncan, however, favoring him because of his antagonism to the "cut-and-run" wing of the Democrats the paper charged with running President Johnson out of office (on March 31, Johnson had decided not to seek reelection). Duncan, the paper argued, "does not believe in handing South Vietnam over to Ho Chi Minh."[63]

As the primary fight ended, the *Oregonian* argued that Duncan, not Morse, was the true peace candidate. A vociferously anti-Morse editorial denounced the senator's "abusive and irrational attacks" against the Johnson administration on Vietnam, claiming that despite these efforts, the United States pulled South Vietnam back from the brink of destruction in 1965. The piece argued Duncan was right to assert that only force could bring Hanoi to the peace table on terms other than outright surrender, which, it alleged, Morse called for. The editorial said that Duncan should "take a share of the credit for the beginning of peace talks in Paris" and accused Morse of "isolationism and near-hysteria in the field of foreign affairs." The *Oregonian* was off base in its partisan attacks on the senator at least in one aspect. To accuse a subcommittee chairman on the Foreign Relations Committee of being "isolationist" was a partisan attack that, worse, displayed a lack of understanding of the senator's responsibilities. In any case, the paper endorsed the "common sense, courage, and stability" of Duncan.[64] But hawkish Democrat Phil McAlmond served as spoiler in the primary campaign, siphoning enough pro-war votes to deny Duncan a majority and handing Morse a plurality victory.[65]

As Morse concentrated on the general election, Vietnam continued to be a campaign issue amid the turbulent summer and fall of 1968. Urban rioting, the assassinations of Martin Luther King Jr. and Senator Robert F. Kennedy, and the antiwar demonstrations at the Democratic

National Convention in Chicago weighed heavily on Morse and Packwood, whose Senate race was overshadowed by Lyndon Johnson's
withdrawal from the presidential campaign and the highly contested
nomination of Vice President Hubert Humphrey at the convention
to challenge Republican nominee Richard Nixon. Many of Morse's
most fervent supporters were, by this point, protesters of the Vietnam
War. Morse did not endorse many of their radical views, however, and
approved only of nonviolent, nondisruptive protest. When Humphrey,
who championed a continuation of Johnson's war policy, made a campaign stop at the University of Oregon that many feared would turn
violent, Morse successfully convinced the gathered crowd that the vice
president deserved to have his point of view heard even though it was
one with which the senator admitted he personally disagreed.[66] During
the general election campaign, Morse projected himself as a moderate conciliator, discussing Vietnam but attempting not to let his dovish
feelings about the war become a liability.

Late in the campaign, however, Morse blundered when he agreed to
debate Robert Packwood at the City Club in Portland. Mary Courtney,
a student at nearby Linfield College, studied the debate, and much of
what follows relies on her analysis. Courtney concluded that Packwood
believed that "if a nation had pride in its leaders, it should not ridicule
them in the eyes of other nations. He believed this was what the Senator
had done" and sought to expose that as well as other perceived Morse
liabilities in the debate.[67]

According to Courtney, Packwood's debate style was "middle-class,"
while Morse's was "academic," a difference in style which played into
the hands of the challenger.[68] For example, when asked a question about
Vietnam War protesters, the candidates agreed that dissent should be
legally undertaken. Morse, however, gave a rambling response, posed
in legalistic terms, in which he concluded that "the right to dissent
doesn't carry with it the right to violate the laws."[69] Packwood's colorful
response, however, was more eye-catching:

> I am not going to stop them from protesting the war or the draft
> or anything else that they want to do, but when they cross that
> line and when they start to say that this society is so rotten that
> it's got to be destroyed in order to save it, then I say stop. When I

see a guy like that crazy kid at Columbia University sitting in the president's chair with his feet on the desk and smoking a cigar I get mad, and I'd put that kook in the pokey until he's learned to live by the laws that the rest of us have to live by.[70]

Morse, for the most part, tried to avoid discussion of the war, however. The senator began the debate not by addressing Vietnam or national security, but by talking extensively about the domestic benefits that he would secure for Oregonians after the election, pointing out that he would assume the chairmanship of the Senate Labor and Public Welfare Committee if he was reelected. Near the end of his opening statement, he called for a truce in Vietnam based on multilateral negotiations, citing the extensive loss of life and treasure in the region. He also pointed out that even popular Korean War General Matthew Ridgway had advocated negotiation over continued warfare.[71]

In his opening remarks, Packwood pushed his idea for land reform before withdrawal from Vietnam, and in doing so, generated more memorable sound bites. "The Communists, of course, promise land reform," he said at one point. "That's a phony—you know it and I know it."[72] He later added, "you're not going to find me, as you have Senator Morse, calling my President drunk with military power." Finally, he criticized Morse's comparison of the Soviet occupation of Czechoslovakia to American activity in South Vietnam, saying that "anybody who confuses those two policies, to me, has forfeited any right he has to remain in the United States Senate."[73] Packwood was in attack mode, but the question-and-answer period to follow would be even more decisive in giving him an advantage over Morse.

The turning point of the debate came when a questioner asked Morse to discuss the federal expenditures he had brought to Oregon. Morse conceded that the state received far fewer defense dollars than other western states but argued that if one were to subtract defense dollars from the equation, Oregon ranked second in the nation in spending originating from the Interior Department, as well as third in Army Corps of Engineers spending. But Packwood countered by dramatically showing the crowd and the television audience a copy of the book Morse's campaign staff had issued to reelection workers, arguing that it revealed that in other categories of federal spending, Oregon lagged far behind other states in dollar-for-dollar terms. The debate format precluded Morse from immediate rebuttal, and he appeared to suffer a devastating blow, torpedoed by his own campaign literature.[74]

Morse later received another question about how Oregon had economically benefited from his public service. Given an opportunity to repair the damage Packwood had inflicted upon him earlier, Morse argued that Oregon had become a diverse "private enterprise economy" as opposed to a "defense economy" that he said existed in the states Packwood had cited, which received more dollars per capita from the federal government. Morse claimed Oregon's per capita income was higher than those of other western states, accounting for the fact that Oregonians paid more taxes and thus only appeared on the surface to have fallen behind in terms of ratio of benefits. The problem with this answer was that it allowed Packwood to repeat his simplistic attack that Oregon received fewer federal dollars per capita. The charge stuck and was repeated in numerous press and historical accounts of the debate, while Morse's more complex arguments were largely forgotten.[75]

Mark Hatfield retrospectively argued that at the City Club that day, "Packwood was seen as a fresh, young face, [with] snappy answers," while Morse "hadn't even gotten to the *core* of his argument in two minutes."[76] Packwood made the senator look ineffective in the bigger picture of achieving federal defense dollars for the state, as well as for having a weaker foreign policy stance vis-à-vis communist countries. On Election Day, Morse went down to the first electoral defeat of his career, ultimately conceding to Packwood after a protracted recount showed that the senator lost by approximately 3,000 votes. His loss was part of a gut-wrenching Election Day for Democrats and doves, who also saw Richard Nixon narrowly triumph over Hubert Humphrey in the presidential contest. In Morse's case, the City Club debate was widely seen, in hindsight, as sealing his fate.[77]

DID VIETNAM AND DEFENSE ISSUES CAUSE MORSE TO LOSE IN 1968?

In the immediate days after the election, a wide variety of rationales were given by pundits trying to understand Morse's loss. Packwood credited his victory not to foreign policy differences, but rather his aggressive campaign of relying on door-to-door volunteers to get out the word as opposed to Morse's reliance on mailing campaign literature to his constituents. *Oregonian* reporter Harold Hughes, meanwhile, did think Vietnam played a role: he surmised that if a write-in campaign had been mounted by supporters for Bob Duncan to run in the general election as an independent, he would have siphoned off hawkish Packwood voters and given Morse a victory by plurality. According to Hughes, Morse knew in October about a proposed write-in effort, but blundered by failing to encourage it.[78]

Foreign affairs figured in many Oregonians' opinions about the immediate aftermath of the campaign. The *Oregonian* editorialized that voters tired, in part, of Morse because of foreign policy, saying his move to cross party lines and support Hatfield against Duncan in 1966 cost him with the Democrats.[79] Several letters to the editor defended Morse, however, against the paper's assertion that he was a divisive figure in Oregon politics because of Vietnam. Joann Burton called Morse "one of the most compassionate leaders of our time" and praised his "work for the rapid end of the Vietnam war, because like many of us he is sorrowed by the suffering of others."[80] Gerald Cogan lamented that "the nation lost a rare asset in Washington—an advocate for justice and human rights."[81] In a 1969 election postmortem for the *Western Historical Quarterly*, Joseph Allman argued that Bob Duncan's primary campaign had played down Vietnam as an issue, focusing on Morse's age and eccentric political "style" as his liabilities. But Allman did note that Packwood received campaign contributions from people outside Oregon who were "concerned" about Morse's antiwar position.[82]

Lillian Wilkins, meanwhile, asserted that one of the major causes of Morse's defeat was the fracturing of the Oregon Democratic Party into hawk and dove factions, which, combined with Morse's outspoken anti–Vietnam War stance, turned Democrats who supported Duncan in the primary toward Packwood in the general election. Rank-and-file Democrats and liberal Republicans deserted Morse in the general election. Rural and eastern Oregon constituted Morse's biggest losses, and across the state, his numbers declined in comparison to his 1962 reelection in all but one county. This was a recipe for disaster given that Oregonians, like voters in other states, turned out in greater numbers for presidential elections as opposed to midterm elections. Each of the

Democratic-leaning counties outside of the more liberal Willamette Valley voted strongly for Duncan in the primary, and Morse failed to carry them in the general election even though Democrats generally held a registration advantage over Republicans.[83] In opposing the Vietnam War, Wilkins concluded, Morse challenged "the innocence of the American enterprise and of those who supported it. . . . It was a direct confrontation with one of the country's most sustaining myths," one which led to his downfall.[84]

Some liberals believed that President Johnson aided in bringing down Morse because he was angry that the senator broke with him over Vietnam. Senator Ernest Gruening (D-AK), who joined Morse in voting against the original congressional authorization (the so-called Gulf of Tonkin Resolution) for military force in Vietnam in 1964, claimed that a "man of unimpeachable repute" told Gruening that Johnson told him, after a series of congressional debates on Vietnam in 1966 that were damaging to his administration's narrative of the war, "I'm going to get Wayne Morse. I'm going to offer him an assignment which he won't refuse. It'll ruin him." Gruening claimed the assignment was to settle a dispute between airlines and their machinists' union in 1966. Morse accepted the offer, but Gruening believed it caused Oregon machinists, "a substantial segment of organized labor in Oregon," to come out against him, enough to hand Morse defeat in 1968.[85] Morse biographer Mason Drukman thought Johnson intentionally assigned Morse labor cases to adjudicate, cutting into his support from Oregon labor and taking time and attention away from his reelection campaign. Drukman also believed Morse lost because Packwood, unlike Duncan, could command both hawk and dove votes with his moderate foreign policy platform.[86]

A more recent memoir by Oregon journalist Ron Abell details his experience working on Morse's reelection staff and contends Vietnam was only one of many issues that negatively affected his campaign. Beginning in June 1967, Abell was among the workers who mailed letters soliciting campaign contributions: among the first to get sent out were "thousands" that went to Morse's out-of-state Vietnam supporters. According to Abell, "modest" contributions that came in from supporters involved in the peace movement helped finance the campaign during its early stages.[87]

Oregon Senator Wayne Morse, seated third from the right, rides Air Force One with President Lyndon B. Johnson on May 4, 1966. Morse's opposition to the Vietnam War incurred Johnson's wrath and cost the senator dearly in his reelection bid in 1968. Reprinted by permission from University of Oregon Special Collections, Wayne L. Morse Papers, Coll001_013.

Abell believed that the seeds of Morse's defeat were sowed when he abruptly changed his campaign strategy after narrowly beating Bob Duncan in the May 1968 primary. Had Morse returned to Washington, DC, after the primary and remained at work, Abell believed, he probably would have been reelected "without breaking a sweat because Packwood wouldn't have had an in-person target to shoot at," referring to Packwood's later attacks on Morse in which he directly referenced the campaign literature. Democratic Party blundering played a role too. Abell thought Morse almost lost to Duncan because he shed "thousands" of votes when Robert F. Kennedy's presidential campaign incorrectly announced that Morse would support Kennedy at the Democratic National Convention. This outraged supporters of left-wing candidate Eugene McCarthy, who flooded Morse's office in Portland with angry phone calls, threatening to split the dove vote in Morse's primary race. At another point, Morse's friend Henry Carey suggested to Abell that Morse could support land reform in South Vietnam as a pet cause that would moderate his antiwar position. Morse rejected the idea, however, and Packwood poached the idea, using it against him in the City Club debate.[88]

In addition to foreign policy and national security issues, Abell said the anti-Morse bias in the Oregon press and incompetence in Morse's campaign staff played major roles in his downfall. A reporter for the *Oregon Journal*, then the state's Democratic-leaning newspaper, told Abell the day shift crew nevertheless hated Morse, and Abell himself noted at the time, "When Bill Knight (publisher of the *Journal*) sees Morse's picture in the paper, he gets physically ill."[89] Morse's prospects were little better with the *Oregonian*, where publisher Mike Frey reportedly told Mark Hatfield, "If Morse is for heaven . . . I'm for hell."[90] Morse, meanwhile, lost his chief aides in mid-1968: Bill Berg, his administrative assistant in Washington, DC, died of cancer, while Oregon aide Charlie Brooks's wife was diagnosed with brain cancer, forcing him to resign. By mid-September 1968, Morse was seemingly unwilling to listen to anyone in lieu of his top aides, and when Abell nonetheless tried to convince him not to debate Packwood, Morse "blew up" and overruled him.[91] Because Morse made the decision to debate Packwood on the same day that Berg died, Morse's emotional state, Abell speculated, was irrational, and "he retreated to the comfort zone" of oratory and debate which had worked in the past but was ill-suited to combat Packwood's modern campaign. By this point, Abell recalled, the campaign staff included a man named Don Rothenberg "who had to work sub rosa because, as I got the story, he was or, had been a known communist." Rothenburg had the "bizarre" notion to load a caravan of Bay Area buses with college students "and bring them up I-5 flaunting banners that said, 'Berkeley Students for Morse.'" When Morse got wind of the plan, he reportedly referred to the students as "mercenaries" and said that "Packwood ought to pay for their transportation." Morse killed the idea, but the damage was done: his train-wreck campaign combined with damaging public perceptions about his foreign policy and national security ideology to sink his reelection hopes.[92]

CONCLUSION

Wayne Morse refused to rest after losing to Robert Packwood in 1968. National security issues, particularly the Vietnam War, were the main foci of his two Senate comeback attempts. In 1972, Morse decisively lost to Mark Hatfield, the latter focusing successfully in his campaign on his accomplishments for the people of Oregon (discussed in chapter 3). In 1974, Morse defeated Oregon State Senate President Jason Boe in the Democratic primary in May, setting him up to challenge Packwood once again in the general election that coming fall, but he went into the hospital two months later and died on July 22. The man known as the tiger of the Senate went down clawing, savaging President Richard Nixon just before his death: he warned that the United States was turning into a police state because of the abuses of power being uncovered daily in Congress's investigation of the Watergate burglary that would force Nixon to resign just weeks after Morse's death.[93]

In the end it was not opposition to the military or defense contractors, but a combination of poor campaigning, Vietnam War opposition, and a lack of attention to Oregon that caused Morse's downfall. Ron Abell concluded that the campaign bungling of Morse and his staff in the fall of 1968 was the main factor in the failure of his reelection bid. Abell believed that Vietnam hurt Morse because "it reinforced his image as a cantankerous individual always spoiling for a fight," but that he had always managed to play "the flip side of the image, presenting himself as the lonely, independent champion of Everyman." He recalled that an ABC News reporter once asked the senator, "Isn't Wayne Morse the issue (in the campaign)?" Morse replied, "I'm always the issue. That's why I win." When Packwood made Morse the issue of the 1968 campaign on his own terms, however, he painted an unflattering portrait of the senator: thus, Abell concluded, "Vietnam didn't beat him."[94]

Or did it? Given how the election was defined by negative perceptions of Morse's anti-Vietnam crusade, the war and the lack of federal defense spending in Oregon slayed the tiger of the Senate. Morse's opposition to the war and fixation on national issues such as the labor disputes of 1966 distracted him from Oregon issues and served as bait to be feasted upon by his political opponents. The perception that Oregon didn't get enough federal bacon because of Morse provided the final straw. Moreover, although Morse was not against defense spending, and far from the extremist on foreign policy that his foes painted him to be, when it comes to his legacy, there is a lack of nuance, as those who remember Morse tend either to love or revile the senator. Perhaps his real legacy, however, is not through his boisterous rhetoric or debates about what he did or did not accomplish, but his moderate public policy on defense and federal spending in a state that was not well endowed by the federal government. Through Morse's efforts to channel lost defense dollars and jobs in other directions that aided Oregonians, he pointed toward a strategy that Mark Hatfield would utilize more effectively as he gained political power in subsequent years. Hatfield would avoid the widespread perception that attention to national and international affairs kept him from paying attention to constituents at home. In doing so, he would eclipse Morse as Oregon's best-known national political figure.

CHAPTER 3

Mark Hatfield and the New National Security

In 1987, Senator Mark Hatfield of Oregon sat down for an interview with *Arms Control Today*, the monthly magazine of the Arms Control Association, and recalled his arrival in Hiroshima after Japan surrendered to the United States at the end of World War II. Viewing the devastation of the first atomic bombing, Hatfield said he wondered, "What happens to the world? Where do we go from here?" In starkly critical terms, Hatfield said the aftermath of the bombing revealed "the real evil side of war, what it does to strip people of their sophistication, of facades of education, and culture, because here were American service personnel looking for gold teeth out of bodies to make a little earring. The bomb itself didn't create that. It was a manifestation of what war in general does to reduce the culture of human life to animalistic tendencies." He wondered, "Is this not the ultimate obscenity, and the ultimate arrogation of power when the creation can say to the creator, 'I have a right to divest you of the creation.'" The bomb, according to Hatfield, forced a sharp reevaluation of society's priorities. "The fundamental question to me is what *is* national defense?" he said. "As long as we look at national defense in a narrow perspective of military weaponry, then we are never going to have enough money in the military budget. Until you look at national defense in the broader context of the infrastructure, a healthy well-nourished people, a well-housed people, careful monitoring and stewardship of natural resources—these are all part of our national defense." The question of what constituted national security should be the "great debate" of American society, Hatfield concluded. "To the average American, this is still an esoteric discussion," he acknowledged. "Until we can tie the political policy of this arms race to the local job opportunities, the local educational quality, to the health, to the housing, to the resource problems, until we broaden that to show the implication and interrelatedness, we are never going to win this battle."[1]

Hatfield fought this battle throughout his career by generally opposing the Cold War national security paradigm that had dominated the thinking of his counterparts in Washington state, and had even guided much of the foreign policy positions of the ostensibly-dovish Senator Wayne Morse. Hatfield reframed national security to reprioritize infrastructure, education, health, and homeland defense over offensive weaponry. He did so in a particularly effective manner in the 1980s and 1990s through his position as chair or ranking member of the Senate Appropriations Committee. Much of Hatfield's largesse and attention in this matter was devoted to his home state, which received billions of dollars in federal grants during his Senate tenure. The money proved vital to Oregon's economic recovery after a disastrous recession in the early 1980s and set the stage for the state's economic and cultural renaissance that began in the 1990s.

Through it all, it is important to recognize that, like Morse, Hatfield did not completely ignore or avoid the benefits that the traditional national security paradigm could bring to Oregon. Though not pushing to attract new weapons or defense industries to Oregon as did his Washingtonian counterparts, Hatfield did not completely spurn the Oregon defense establishment, and he made a case for keeping bases open in Oregon when closures were threatened. Local constituencies for the homeland defensive included the Oregon National Guard and the Umatilla Army Depot, where hundreds of underground storage bunkers were once used to store military munitions and supplies during and after World War II. The depot became a storage facility for chemical weapons as well, making it a lightning rod for environmental activists during the Cold War whenever the federal government would propose shipping new weapons to the depot. Jack Robertson, one of Hatfield's aides, notified the senator that the metal casing on some of the nerve gas weapons was corroding, meaning the weapons could break and release deadly nerve agents. Hatfield was roused to action, not to get the weapons removed from Oregon, but to destroy them, by obtaining federal funding for an incineration system.[2] When Hatfield did support the defense establishment, it tended to be in cases such as these, where he favored federal outlays to reduce offensive armaments.

Hatfield believed his reputation as a dove was overblown, but that since Oregon's geography placed it at a relative disadvantage compared to Washington in terms of obtaining military bases, he encouraged the federal government to invest in medical research and education in Oregon. Hatfield believed directing federal money to healthcare, like Oregon Health and Science University (OHSU) or beefing up the non-military federal presence in Oregon, such as the state's National Oceanic and Atmospheric Administration (NOAA) office, were better investments than trying to direct any of the Department of Defense budget to the state. Hatfield admired the power of Henry Jackson and Warren Magnuson to direct federal money to Washington, but believed it was overreliant on the military.[3] In the end, Hatfield's approach was clearly successful in utilizing political power to complete the transformation of Oregon from hinterland to active player in the globalizing economy.

Hatfield was not the only Cold War politician to challenge the national security state paradigm, but he may have been the most effective. Warren Magnuson championed health and infrastructure projects and distanced himself from promilitary positions later in his career, but he never openly criticized the Pentagon in a notable way. The long-serving Senator William Proxmire of Wisconsin, a sometimes foil of Hatfield's as ranking minority member of the Senate Appropriations Committee, played a key role in the early 1970s in killing Boeing's Supersonic Transport, championed by Henry Jackson and Warren Magnuson. A longtime critic of military procurement procedures, Proxmire was unsuccessful, however, in his recommendation that an independent civilian agency, not the Pentagon, be in charge of making purchases for the armed forces.[4] By contrast, Hatfield stood out as both thoughtful maverick on defense policy and skilled Washington, DC, political insider at playing the spending game on behalf of Oregon.

ROOTS AND RACE FOR THE SENATE

At times throughout his career, Hatfield was charged with cowardice or deceit by his political foes, particularly when it came to his most famous policy position: his opposition to the conduct of the Vietnam War. This moral opposition was linked with his religious views. Hatfield grew up as a Baptist in Dallas, Oregon, and his faith played a role in his dovishness and in his policy preference to redirect military funds. Robert Eells and Bartell Nyberg argue that Hatfield's shift from concern over the conduct of the Vietnam War to outright criticism was the result of Christian moral objection. In a speech to the American Legion of Oregon in 1965, Hatfield said he did not believe that within "the ideals of both our Judeo-Christian faith and our great political idealism" that the bombing of nonmilitary targets resulting in the deaths of noncombatants, as was taking place in Vietnam under President Lyndon Johnson's Operation Rolling Thunder, could ever be condoned in US foreign policy. Hatfield believed someone could not be a true, faithful Christian, yet still condone the mass aerial bombing associated with the conduct of the war.[5] By taking this stance, Hatfield was hardly alone: he fit in with a broad, left-leaning, evangelical antiwar movement, with leading figures such as the Presbyterian minister William Sloane Coffin, who appeared with the senator at antiwar demonstrations and would later side with Hatfield's position against the construction of new nuclear weapons during the early 1980s.[6] Nevertheless, his position was an uncomfortable one for him politically throughout his career.

Despite the political risk, Hatfield often used religious appeals with constituents. When he spoke in Oregon churches, Hatfield mixed biblical parables with warnings against military growth and the size of the nation's atomic arsenal, while also urging parishioners to confront the great problems of the world. To Hatfield, the church was not a comfortable club, but a base of operations. Contending that an amoral national security was a false doctrine, Hatfield believed true national security could only be determined by the strength of one's spirit. Hatfield's religious beliefs not only gave him moral clarity but helped make his political positions on a variety of issues palatable to Oregonians. One author claims that although he confounded critics with his combination of fiscal and moral conservatism, "progressive politics and evangelical piety," Hatfield's "emphasis on decentralization, voluntarism, compassionate globalism, political localism, and populist electoral measures such as the recall, initiative, and referendum in fact dovetailed nicely with Oregon tradition," also boosting his appeal to home-state voters.[7] Even constituents who disagreed with Hatfield's policies supported him and may have even voted for him in many cases because they believed that his basic religious morality gave him an aura of integrity that they respected. This aura would help Hatfield win elections, even in adverse circumstances where his unpopular beliefs, often on matters of national security, hurt his chances for electoral success.

Hatfield served in the Oregon state legislature from 1950 to 1956, as secretary of state from 1957 to 1958, and then as governor from 1959 to 1967. After winning a second term as governor in 1962, Hatfield began to eye higher office. At the forefront of his public policy throughout his career was a desire to modernize and grow Oregon's economy, and he often tried to win constituents over with probusiness appeals. In doing so, Hatfield emphasized his desire to diversify the economy vis-à-vis Washington state, particularly appealing to Oregonians to look beyond military spending as a source of federal income. Speaking on Oregon's industrial development at a 1963 meeting of Portland's East Side Commercial Club, an organization dedicated to commercial development and civic improvement in the city, Hatfield noted that "we have some military bases . . . and we're proud of those we have. But they have not been a large part of our economy." Noting the national push for base closures by the Johnson administration, Hatfield contended, "we must look to an economy based on peace."[8] Hatfield's speech reflected an audience not as concerned with defense industry as a comparable group in Seattle would have been. Given Oregon's relative paucity of defense contracts and military bases it was easy for Hatfield to retain a pro-peace posture during his career in public office.

In the ensuing years, Hatfield never tried to wind down Oregon's limited defense contracts and military bases, but he ratcheted up the pressure on the Johnson administration regarding the Vietnam War, despite poll numbers showing the conflict was popular among Oregonians. A November 1965 *Oregonian* poll concluded that even 75 percent of surveyed college students in the state supported continuation or even escalation of the war while only 3 percent argued for withdrawal.[9] Hatfield later recalled, "I had a number of friends say to me, 'Mark, you're committing political suicide—I agree with your view, but I would be eaten alive by my constituents.'" Hatfield aide Martin Gold recalled that "coming out against the war seemed unpatriotic." But Hatfield argued that Oregonians "were willing to tolerate dissent with which they disagreed on the basis that they wanted to exercise that same dissent at any other time." He maintained that "the people of Oregon *are* unique, in their high tolerance of diversity [and] pluralism of thinking."[10] The *Oregonian* poll, despite its contention at the surface that Oregon college students were hawks, backs Hatfield up to some degree upon closer inspection. Over 20 percent of those polled called for immediate withdrawal or a ceasefire to give negotiations a chance to get underway. The article showed that women tended to be more dovish than men and concluded that "many of those" surveyed who wished to continue or even to escalate the conflict agreed that the fighting was "morally wrong."[11] Hatfield may have found a window within this context to justify further pursuit of his anti-Vietnam viewpoint. In a February 1966 *Oregonian* editorial, Hatfield explained that his Vietnam stance was meant to open debate on the war, in contrast to what he considered the Johnson administration position of stifling it shut. Continuation of the status quo, he argued, threatened World War III, while eroding world confidence in US leadership.[12]

Despite popular and media perception, Hatfield contended that his 1966 US Senate run was not a one-issue campaign. The candidate preferred to run on issues important to Oregonians, such as economic growth, as well as his Vietnam opposition. As he later recalled, "President Johnson twisted the arm of one of our outstanding political leaders of our state [Oregon congressman Bob Duncan] and persuaded him, as I understand, to come home and become the Democratic candidate and make a referendum on the war."[13] To Hatfield, the war was important, but not all-consuming: indeed, "Hatfield would prefer to campaign on other issues," the *Washington Star* contended. "Hatfield reflects more of a man-in-the-street attitude. He simply asks 'Why?' His interest in Viet-Nam is not obsessive or even profound. But it is genuine," emanating from his brief World War II service in Southeast Asia. The piece warned Republicans that "if the campaign turns on one issue he could be in trouble because, he says, 'the right to dissent is questioned today and dissenters are said to be unpatriotic or soft on communism.'"[14]

Duncan seemed to have hit on a winning strategy by taking advantage of Hatfield's Vietnam position to turn the race into a referendum on the war. In a letter to President Johnson, Palmer Hoyt, publisher of the *Denver Post* and former *Oregonian* publisher, said Hatfield's campaign staff was "worried" that he and Vietnam dove Wayne Morse shared similar foreign policy views. "It looks possible to me that Hatfield just might get himself knocked off," Hoyt told the president. "The people, I believe, are likely to equate Hatfield's 'dove' position, which is mild, with Morse's, which is extreme."[15] Hoyt urged Johnson to watch the race carefully, and some of his staffers clearly did so. In an April 1966 memo to Johnson aide Marvin Watson, William Connell, an aide to Vice President Hubert Humphrey, called Duncan a "key figure in terms of the vindication of the President's policy, and I should think we would want to give him every bit of help that we can possibly muster." Connell noted that "Morse has Hatfield squirming over his remark that he will vote for him if Duncan is the candidate against him," and contended that "in the fall if [Morse] keeps his love fest with Hatfield, this too, will help Duncan."[16]

Appearing before the Portland Rotary Club after Duncan won the Democratic primary, Morse argued that the statewide election results showed skepticism about the war, given that dovish ex-US Representative Charles Porter won the Democratic primary in Duncan's own congressional district. Morse predicted the Democrats could get beaten by Hatfield in the general election.[17] Although his view would ultimately be vindicated, it did not appear in the spring of 1966 as though this would be the case. A Portland-based research firm told Hatfield campaign manager Travis Cross that "Hatfield seems to be having some troubles." In the populous congressional district spanning much of Northwest Oregon and including part of Portland, "a tremendous majority oppose[d] his Viet Nam policy." According to the firm's poll, 80 percent of the district believed the United States should stay or escalate in Vietnam.[18]

In October, the *Oregon Journal* contended that a "strong majority" in a poll of "civic and church groups" still favored escalation of the Vietnam War, while 65 percent opposed a halt in the bombing campaign against North Vietnam. Duncan was making inroads in the upper Willamette Valley: Hatfield led in polls by 4 percent throughout the rest of state, but Duncan was up by 2 percent in the upper valley, which was crucial because it was home to Portland, by far the biggest city in the state.[19] *Time* dubbed it the "Viet Nam race," arguing that Hatfield was uncontested and sure to win until his antiwar stance drew the hawkish Duncan into the election. "I am morally certain that if we withdraw, we will be involved in a third world war," said Duncan. "I'm convinced that if we stand firm, we'll bring to Southeast Asia a new experience of freedom without a gun at people's heads."[20]

In response to increasing concern that Vietnam was dominating his candidacy, Hatfield went on Portland's KGW-TV to further elaborate his position. Asked why he spoke out on Vietnam during the campaign when it would have been easier for him to remain silent, Hatfield responded that he believed individuals seeking office should be willing to face up to and render an opinion on controversial issues. He criticized President Johnson for not keeping his 1964 campaign pledge that Vietnam would only be fought by "Asian boys." At the national governors' conferences of 1965–66, Hatfield claimed he had asked Johnson administration officials "for identification of our global commitments that could lead us into other Vietnams in the world," yet "no one could give us a list of what those global commitments were." Under such circumstances, he said it was undemocratic to give Johnson "blank-check power" with so many lives at stake. Hatfield also gave viewers a history lesson about Vietnam, arguing that its leader, Ho Chi Minh, would not surrender, even if the United States increased troop levels. When asked if it was inconsistent for him to give US troops full support yet advocate for a pause in the bombing of North Vietnam or for the United States to slow down its attacks, Hatfield said he thought there was a difference between supporting troops and opposing policy, and that on both counts he had been consistent. He said not all diplomatic channels were being pursued and called for more "Asian manpower" and fewer US troops.[21]

Hatfield made the case that while he was a dove on Vietnam, he was reasonable. He won endorsements from over thirty major Oregon newspapers, as well as the *New York Times,* which editorialized that it believed Hatfield's emphasis on searching for peaceful solutions in Vietnam through negotiation deserved support.[22] William Sanderson of the *Oregonian* said that although Hatfield's Vietnam opposition made the contest close, "he did not become—nor did he seek to become—a spokesman for antiwar extremists."[23] Hatfield himself believed the outcome of the election showed it was not all about Vietnam, since 56 percent of Oregonians wanted the United States to stay in the country, and

20 percent even wanted additional forces sent there. Hatfield aimed, however, to show voters how Vietnam broadly affected their lives, while avoiding narrower and more emotional issues, such as whether it was unpatriotic to question the war. He argued that national concerns about inflation, linked to the expanded war budget of the Johnson administration, hurt the home-building industry vital to Oregon's economic well-being. As lumber mills closed statewide, he said, "each day added to the mounting list of unemployed." Hatfield said he tried to keep these issues in the news, but Duncan "was too busy pursuing the emotional advantage of supporting the war in Vietnam."[24] A full-page ad taken out by the Hatfield campaign in the *Oregonian* the day before the election de-emphasized Vietnam and other foreign affairs issues, listing them toward the bottom of a 16-point "plan for Oregon." The ad did not even discuss his anti-Vietnam stance in discussing his record while governor, highlighting instead his work to build Oregon's economy, improve the state's infrastructure and education system, increase environmental conservation, and make progress in social benefits and on civil rights.[25]

Historian Andrew Johns argues that Hatfield's "slim" 24,000-vote margin of victory reflected the fact that "his outspoken antiwar views made the race closer than it should have been."[26] This may have been true, but Hatfield argued that it was because of all the other things he had done right as governor, not Vietnam—where he was self-admittedly vulnerable—that he had won the Senate.[27] In this way, he simultaneously took on the traditional national security state and its war in Vietnam, pushing instead for new pathways to economic prosperity for Oregonians. As the KGW interview shows, Hatfield still took the Vietnam issue head-on at times. Unlike Wayne Morse, though, Hatfield was effective at showing his constituents how the war negatively affected them through higher interest rates and the consequent decline of the timber industry. Hatfield also largely kept out of the fray of divisive partisan politics, unlike the oft-curmudgeonly Morse. The governor had a strong economic record to run on, as he attempted to diversify the state away from traditional extractive industries into more manufacturing, and to increase state financing for high-tech, education, and transportation investments. Hatfield demonstrated a road map he would follow to future success, convincing Oregonians that channeling energy and federal dollars away from war and toward domestic prosperity was in their best personal and economic interest.

PURSUING SECURITY THROUGH PEACE: HATFIELD'S FIRST TERM IN OFFICE

Once he took office, Hatfield became an increasingly ardent critic of the Vietnam War, arguing that the Republicans should be the "peace party" vis-à-vis Lyndon Johnson's Democratic Party.[28] But as the Republicans coalesced around the decidedly pro-war Richard Nixon prior to the 1968 election, Hatfield found himself drawing generally unfavorable comparisons to the similarly intractable antiwar positions of Wayne Morse. This stance hurt Hatfield with many Oregon constituents. In 1967, Hatfield said, he received an average of 400 letters daily on Vietnam.[29] While he received some support, many were angry at his opposition to the war's conduct. "I had people who would come up to me and shake their fist in my eyes and say, 'My son has given his life for his country, why are you supporting Ho Chi Minh?'" Hatfield later reflected. "It wasn't a very pretty picture, and I could only say, 'I can understand how you feel, even though that is not accurate.'"[30] A writer to the *Oregon Journal* said it was "unbelievable" Hatfield had been elected because of his "neo-isolationism" which, she argued, was forty years behind the times regarding Vietnam. Because Hatfield's most recent visit to Vietnam was twenty years earlier, she believed he was unqualified to speak with authority about the war. Questioning Hatfield's loyalty, the author added, "It is a pity he doesn't feel a little of the nationalism for his own country that he so much admires in Ho Chi Minh. If he does, he has yet to reveal it."[31] In April 1967, Hatfield received a dire warning from William Rusher, publisher of the influential conservative magazine *National Review*, stating that he had a "very dim" future because of his Vietnam stance.[32] The senator pressed on, however, gaining ground as the war became more unpopular.

Throughout his first term, one of Hatfield's major policy initiatives was a plan to end the military draft and institute an all-volunteer force. In 1967, Hatfield was virtually alone in his quest to end the draft, joined in testimony before the Senate Armed Services Committee only by the young Illinois congressman and future Secretary of Defense, Donald

Rumsfeld. The two argued unsuccessfully before committee chairman Richard Russell that a smaller, better paid, all-volunteer force would provide greater national security because it would be more motivated to do so than a conscripted force. But Hatfield kept up the fight, gradually getting more support at home in Oregon. Bruce Chasan, a chemistry graduate student at the University of Oregon, was summoned by Hatfield to testify before a congressional committee in early 1969 to show how the threat of government-imposed hardship via the draft adversely affected students.[33] The University of Oregon student newspaper editorialized shortly thereafter urging the "speedy enactment" of Hatfield's bill.[34] The *Oregonian* called for the adoption of a volunteer army in 1971, arguing that although it would not be easy to end the draft, the federal government needed to lay the groundwork to do so, because "it is in the national interest that the inequities of conscription be ended and that a sincere trial be given the concept of a career army in a free nation."[35] Anecdotal evidence from the papers of Bob Packwood, Hatfield's Senate colleague from Oregon, suggests that many Oregonians, along with Packwood himself, favored the creation of an all-volunteer force.[36] As the Vietnam War dragged on and support for the conflict faded throughout the country, Congress and the Nixon administration finally crafted legislation ending the draft in 1973 and establishing the all-volunteer army.

Regional considerations also factored into Hatfield's attempt in 1970 to establish a timetable to cut off funding for the Vietnam War via an amendment to a military spending bill. After Nixon announced that the United States had invaded Cambodia in April, thereby expanding the war, Hatfield ended his support of Nixon's "Vietnamization" policy of gradual troop withdrawal, and co-sponsored the so-called McGovern-Hatfield Amendment with South Dakota Senator George McGovern. If passed, the amendment would have forced the withdrawal of US troops from Cambodia within thirty days, and from Vietnam by June 30, 1971, while limiting taxpayer dollars spent on the war to covering the costs for troop removal.[37] The amendment struggled to gain support either in the Senate or at home in Oregon. A poll conducted by Senator Packwood showed that Oregon voters only narrowly supported the legislation: approximately 49.5 percent of those polled favored McGovern-Hatfield, while 45.7 percent opposed it, and almost

5 percent were undecided. After the first version of the amendment failed to pass, Packwood told a constituent that he believed it "was not the proper course of action for the Congress to take" and that he instead supported President Richard Nixon's efforts to withdraw troops in phases from Vietnam.[38] Most Republicans were loath to oppose Nixon in a midterm election year and feared being considered anti-American by their patriotic constituents.[39]

Hatfield claimed that his main objective in pursuing the McGovern-Hatfield amendment was to force Congress to vote to fund the war, thereby asserting some of the responsibility over the conduct of the war, rather than lying prostrate before the Nixon administration.[40] But the amendment was perceived as blatantly antiwar and thereby provoked strong dissent among Oregon hawks, threatening Hatfield's position among his political allies and endangering his 1972 reelection campaign. One constituent told Hatfield that "should the amendment pass, it may be the very instrument that will spell defeat for our side." Noting that he donated to and supported Hatfield in his 1966 Senate run, the constituent nonetheless threatened to abandon Hatfield at the next election.[41] US Representative Edith Green, an early Vietnam War opponent and a Hatfield supporter throughout his career, told a constituent the amendment was a "naïve and simplistic" panacea that she could not back because it was so unpopular among her colleagues that she would lose credibility with them if she did so. Green claimed to have recently cast at least five antiwar votes in Congress, but that she could not waste political capital by continually voting for such legislation.[42] Green's concern was reflected in the opposition to the amendment unleashed by the *Oregonian*. The paper editorialized that congressional adoption of a timetable to cut off funding "would surely preclude any chance that North Vietnam will agree to a negotiated peace." The paper said the amendment was "an uncalled for effort to rebuke a President who is getting us out of a mess he inherited as quickly as possible," concluding that "it would serve the purposes of aggressive Communist imperialism by weakening countries fighting to defend themselves." In another anti-amendment piece, the *Oregonian* called on the Senate to "bury . . . this spineless, peace-at-any-price, harmful proposal under an avalanche of 'No' votes."[43]

The *Oregonian* editorial board rejoiced at the rejection of the amendment, which garnered 39 yes votes against 55 no votes, equating

Oregon Senator Mark Hatfield joined fellow Senators Frank Church, Charles Goodall, George McGovern, and Harold Hughes in this May 11, 1970 national television appearance, urging for an end to the Vietnam War. Later that year Hatfield and McGovern would unsuccessfully support an amendment in the Senate to defund the war. Reprinted by permission from Boise State University Digital Collections, Frank Church Papers, MSS 056 POR_305.

it to harassment of the Nixon administration's withdrawal policies.[44] A modified version, the Vietnam Disengagement Act of 1971, also was defeated in the Senate, 42 yes votes to 55 no votes. Despite these defeats, Hatfield's actions, along with those of like-minded Senate doves, arguably helped restrain Nixon and played a critical role in moving opposition of the war from the left-wing fringe to the mainstream throughout the country.[45] This did not mean, however, that Hatfield was out of the woods at home. Bob Packwood told a constituent that while he now favored McGovern-Hatfield, he believed Nixon's own plan was still the best course of action. One *Oregonian* reader accused Hatfield and his supporters of proposing a withdrawal plan that would lead to American surrender and humiliation and suggested they should instead "shut up and help the President with his plan."[46] Hatfield's popularity plunged by the end of his first term as even supporters questioned his policymaking priorities: former Hatfield aide Lon Fendall recalled that even "state party leaders responded with tepid support" when the senator geared up for reelection.[47] By 1972, he faced the possibility he would not even be renominated for a second term in office. A poll in the summer of

1971 put Hatfield's approval rating at just 24 percent, and an October poll showed he would lose a theoretical reelection matchup with Edith Green by a margin of 51 percent to 37 percent.[48] In order to survive politically, Hatfield had to back up his rhetorical commitment to redefine national security in a way that would clearly materially benefit his constituents.

MEETING MARK: REDEFINING NATIONAL SECURITY FOR THE VOTERS IN THE 1972 REELECTION CAMPAIGN

The years 1971–72 were a key turning point in Hatfield's career and played a major role in shaping his legacy at home and in terms of US national security policy. *Oregonian* political reporter Jeff Mapes later reflected that for years the congressional debate over the war "consumed" Hatfield, and that while his popularity rose with students and the antiwar left, many Oregonians believed he neglected his home state. As Hatfield considered leaving the Senate in 1971 amid sagging poll numbers, he promoted longtime friend and advisor Gerry Frank to be his chief of staff. Frank, who became known as "Oregon's third senator" for his work on behalf of the state, streamlined what Mapes described as "the office's chaotic operations" and reoriented Hatfield toward constituent services. Frank also convinced Hatfield to pass up a seat on the Senate Foreign Relations Committee: he instead took a spot on the more prominent Appropriations Committee. From there, Hatfield could continue to be an influential figure on national security and related global issues that he cared about, while simultaneously being in a better position to funnel federal dollars to Oregon. Frank also made sure that Hatfield regularly toured the state and listened personally to constituents' concerns. Now "Oregonians lined up for the free bacon breakfasts that Hatfield served and were quite willing to listen to his high-minded sermons in exchange."[49] There were many facets of Hatfield's relationship with constituents that needed attention, but after promoting Frank, the senator visited Oregon at least once a month and gave speeches across the state. Frank decreed that a staff member or Hatfield himself had to respond to constituent letters within forty-eight hours of receipt. During the 1972 reelection campaign, in part because of the greater speed and efficiency of his office in answering his constituent mail, Hatfield became a very popular regional figure after years of decline in his stature since he had been Oregon's governor during the early to mid-1960s.

Hatfield still faced a challenge, however, in selling his antiwar position to voters in a way that would make for good local public policy. Despite the growth of antiwar sentiment in the early 1970s, Hatfield's anti-Vietnam stance was still difficult to sell to Oregonians. But Hatfield could maintain his political base largely because Oregon was a sufficiently small state where personal contact and retail politics could make a difference. Many Oregonians disagreed with Hatfield about Vietnam but came to feel they nonetheless personally knew the senator and could trust him to have integrity and be consistent in his political positions. But because of his opposition to the war as well as much of the Nixon administration's legislative program, Hatfield was in political trouble. He had to persuade Republican voters and more Oregonians in general than just the antiwar left that Vietnam was the wrong war, and not just for moral reasons. The senator's staff responded by compiling a report showing how much per capita Oregonians were spending on Vietnam and demonstrating the domestic benefits of that money. "Just in Oregon taxpayers had spent nearly a billion [dollars] on Vietnam—$364 for each and every resident," Hatfield claimed.[50] Working down to the county level, staffers analyzed what could be done in Oregon if the government redirected military funding into public works, infrastructure, and healthcare. This was an unusual undertaking for a US senator, arguably one that aided his reelection and brought home to the people of Oregon the true cost of national defense.

Walter Evans, a lawyer who worked for Hatfield during his early years in the Senate, recalled that Hatfield saw his job as being like the college professor he had once been at Willamette University. In that vein, his mission was to instruct Oregonians so that they could have a basis to evaluate the issues. In early 1972, Hatfield told his staff that while he was a hero to antiwar voters, he needed to broaden his message to a greater cross-section of Oregonians. His staff thus worked to extrapolate the costs of the infrastructure projects that Hatfield was fighting for to aid all Oregonians. One particularly effective exchange with voters about the relationship between Vietnam and local spending took place in the coastal city of Newport. After discussing local economic development, Hatfield received a question about Vietnam. Acknowledging the legitimate differences of opinion among the crowd, he recalled that a local education bond issue was coming up, and pointed out to voters that two years of war-related taxes would have paid for a new high school. He challenged the audience, warning voters about war costs and the minimal benefits being obtained. After this exchange, Hatfield's mail referenced his statements about the domestic costs of the war. As the campaign progressed, staffers put out fact sheets at the county, city, and state levels, showing the financial impact of redirecting military spending toward domestic needs. Evans believed that voters increasingly began to realize that the war was a never-ending drain on the taxpayer, and that the United States needed to reorganize its military priorities.[51]

Hatfield had a great deal of success in combining Gerry Frank's campaign strategy and the staff's Vietnam research to engage in an educational campaign across Oregon. These events, dubbed by Frank as opportunities to "Meet Mark" at meals or coffees in churches, school auditoriums, or civic centers, were highly popular and were duplicated in Hatfield's future trips to Oregon throughout his career. At one of these events, a man stood up and said he was a conservative who supported Richard Nixon's Vietnam policy over Hatfield's. But the man went on to say that when nobody else in the Oregon congressional delegation would help his father deal with the Veterans' Affairs bureaucracy, Hatfield made phone calls and visited with VA officials until they made changes that helped the man's father get the service he needed. The man finished by adding that Hatfield had his vote whenever he ran for office.[52]

Events like these arguably demonstrated that, to Hatfield, the welfare of people mattered more than policies when it came to national security. Hatfield faced Wayne Morse, himself still running against the Vietnam War, in the 1972 general election. One incident that threatened to hurt the Hatfield campaign came when Democratic presidential nominee (and Hatfield's anti–Vietnam War ally) George McGovern held a post-nomination breakfast attended by Morse, and McGovern, not realizing that Morse was running against his friend Hatfield, issued a statement endorsing Morse. The endorsement deflated Hatfield's campaign staff. Morse believed the best way he could get leverage against Hatfield was to siphon off left-wing peace votes by obtaining McGovern's endorsement.[53] Ultimately, however, Hatfield's record of opposition to Vietnam cut into support Morse hoped to get from independent voters and prevented him from going over the top. Hatfield's "Meet Mark" strategy also worked to shore up center and right-leaning voters who would never go for Morse, and the senator ended up winning reelection with 54 percent of the vote.[54]

NATIONAL SECURITY POLITICS DURING HATFIELD'S SECOND TERM, 1973–78

Mark Hatfield's reelection cemented the "Meet Mark" strategy, a political approach designed to reconcile the senator's moral and ideological positions—particularly in the realm of foreign relations—with pragmatic domestic considerations. With his second term secured and the Vietnam War ending, Hatfield could rekindle his interest in global affairs. Hatfield believed that national security also extended to using the power of the United States to secure the peace and prosperity of the developing world. The senator's name increasingly carried weight globally as well as locally through the 1970s. When Gerald R. Ford assumed the presidency upon Richard Nixon's resignation, he received letters asking him to consider Hatfield as his vice presidential nominee, even from as remote a writer as Jakarta, Indonesia, member of Parliament Darius Marpaung. It could be expected that Hatfield would have foreign admirers in the wake of his dissent against the Vietnam War, but Hatfield also received an endorsement for the vice presidency from Oregon House Republican leader Ron MacPherson, showing that he had mended fences with the state's GOP establishment.[55]

US foreign relations continued to be a strong interest for Hatfield, albeit one coupled with domestic considerations. An example of this was Hatfield's interest in alleviating global hunger. Early in the Ford administration, Hatfield urged the new president to use the presidential bully pulpit to draw the American people's attention to global hunger. Not only was inaction endangering American efforts at world peace, Hatfield said, "it is crushing the dignity and hopes of those millions and millions who must dream and work and cooperate with us if we are to accomplish the worthiest of our goals." To Hatfield, the crisis represented "one of the

greatest moral challenges in decades."[56] His efforts followed closely on
the heels of the United Nations World Food Conference held in Rome
during the fall of 1974, which was organized after acute food shortages
struck South Asia and sub-Saharan Africa during the early 1970s. During the conference, several US senators, including Hatfield and George
McGovern, called for the Ford administration to make an increased
commitment in food aid. Hatfield argued before the Senate that his own
constituent mail showed that "the American people were ahead of their
leaders," before at one point reading a letter from a child in rural Yamhill
who wrote the senator, "They are starving to death. If we was [sic] them
they would send food to us. Why don't you do something."[57]

On January 8, 1975, Hatfield received a letter from William T. Kendall, Ford's deputy assistant, saying he thought Ford "will give careful
consideration to your suggestion that he appoint a Food Administrator to direct programs of conservation, production, and distribution
of food to the needy people around the world."[58] Ford later thanked
Hatfield for his suggestion, saying he agreed on the need for a larger
US grain reserve, and pledged he would increase the part of the foreign
aid budget dedicated to help needy countries develop their agriculture.
Hatfield and his staff subsequently worked with the Ford administration
to revamp the federal government's Food for Peace program designed
to provide humanitarian food assistance around the world. The president eventually told Hatfield he had decided to double Food for Peace
funds to $1.4 billion over the previous year, to a level higher even than
Hatfield had asked. The senator pressured the administration to reallo-
cate $118 million in humanitarian food aid to needy countries because,
he believed, Secretary of State Henry Kissinger was using much of it
for political purposes. Hatfield was among the congressional leaders
who restricted Food for Peace funds dedicated to political allies to 30
percent of overall levels.[59] This was another example of Hatfield seeing
national security as encompassing matters beyond Cold War concerns:
in this case, keeping immediate American allies happy through politically motivated food aid.

Sometimes Hatfield's commitment to national security as inclusive
of aid for the underdeveloped world extended to the realm of punitive
sanctions. In Uganda, the genocidal actions of dictator Idi Amin—
reputed to have caused the deaths of 300,000 of his nation's 12 million

people—constituted a bigger threat than poverty and hunger in the late 1970s.[60] Hatfield heard of the plight of the Ugandan people through Festo Kivingiri, the archbishop of the Ugandan Anglican Church, who fled to the United States upon learning Amin had targeted him for assassination. Hatfield and his intern—later aide—Rick Rolf were instrumental in obtaining congressional support for sanctions banning the import of Ugandan coffee, despite counterpressure from US importing company Procter & Gamble. The senator recalled that after the US Senate food service started returning Ugandan coffee to distributors, a boycott of Ugandan coffee spread along with the import ban. Amin's government fell in April 1979, shortly after the sanctions took effect, although internal civil strife and an invasion by Tanzanian troops backed up by Ugandan rebels also played a major role in the demise of Amin's regime.[61]

The need for Hatfield to consider domestic considerations remained, even when considering the world hunger problem. On February 15, 1980, the senator and other chairmen of the lobby group Northwest Response to World Hunger asked timber kingpin Hillman Lueddemann to join them for a luncheon in Portland to help organize an antihunger telethon they hoped to host that spring on Portland television station KOIN-TV. Hatfield and the others believed that "announcements during the telethon that the Portland business community was picking up the tab for the program costs could aid materially in increasing total contributions from the general public."[62] While it is unclear if Lueddemann aided Hatfield, it does show the senator engaging with his constituents to help him in his major foreign policy initiatives. On February 17, Hatfield spoke to approximately 200 religious leaders at a Northwest Response to World Hunger luncheon, urging them to support the telethon.[63] Dubbed "Portland With a Heart for the World," the telethon featured "stories filmed on location in Africa, Asia, Latin America and right here in Portland," and advertising for the event argued that "this is Portland's unique opportunity to show the world what it means to care." The telethon aired on April 17 and was co-hosted by Hatfield and well-known regional newscaster Mike Donahue.[64] More than sixty Portland business and civic leaders contributed to the event, including rabbis, ministers, doctors, City Commissioner Charles Jordan, and Multnomah County Commissioner Gladys McCoy.[65]

Overall, during the 1970s, Hatfield changed his perception from Vietnam War dove to deliverer of federal bacon for Oregon, and consequently cruised to renomination on the Republican ticket in 1978.[66] Concerns about Oregon's lack of Pentagon dollars had drastically declined, and Hatfield mostly fought to limit dangerous Pentagon activities in Oregon. *Willamette Week* journalist A. Robert Smith reported that in November 1976, when Hatfield received a tip from a government worker that there were enough surplus World War II–era chemicals buried beneath the tiny Oregon town of Arlington to kill hundreds of thousands of people, the senator hoped to remove the chemicals "before some crackpot got hold of them and threatened to defoliate . . . Portland." Hatfield convinced the *Oregon Journal* not to publish the scoop they had on the existence of the chemicals so that they could be expeditiously removed from the region without any pushback.[67] In August 1978, Hatfield fought the army's planned transport of chemicals to Denver via a route that would take them through Pendleton before picking up nerve and mustard gas from Umatilla Army Depot.[68]

On another occasion in this reelection year, Hatfield was more prodefense, probably because Oregon jobs were at stake. In May, Hatfield protested the decision to close Kingsley Air Force Base near Klamath Falls. The senator protested a lack of public involvement in the decision, which would ultimately cost 310 civilian jobs, along with the transfer of 325 military personnel and the loss of $7 million in military payroll. The air force countered that Kingsley was only involved in two interceptions in the previous two years, had only two jets, and was part of a broader plan to reorganize the Defense Department and close bases in thirty-one states.[69] While a setback for Hatfield, the base closure did not make or break his reelection bid. The fact that Kingsley was not a big issue in the 1978 campaign showed how different the politics of national security were in Oregon in contrast to its West Coast neighbors, highlighting his continued success in diversifying the state's economy and broadening the definition of national security to his constituents.

Although state senator Vern Cook, Hatfield's Democratic challenger in 1978, was a far lesser-known opponent than he, Hatfield nonetheless had to sweat a bit during the campaign because of his unpopular vote in favor of the Panama Canal Treaties. Supporters argued the treaties restored full sovereignty to Panama at a time when the United States needed to improve its relationship with Latin America. Conservatives, however, believed the treaties were a giveaway of US property that would weaken national security.[70] Hatfield once again had to argue that his position, although perhaps counterintuitive to the majority of voters, actually made the United States more secure in the long run. As early as the summer of 1977, the treaty caused Hatfield to face tough questions from voters. Hatfield answered one protester in the coastal town of Waldport by asserting that he thought "many people are thinking with their glands rather than their heads." His response generally was to teach people about the issue and not to fan the flames. He challenged one gathering, however, asking audience members if they knew better on national security than President Ford, Secretary of State Kissinger, and the Joint Chiefs of Staff, who all supported the treaty even before the unpopular Carter administration did. On this issue, Hatfield, normally a maverick challenger of presidents, supported the executive branch's national security argument. The senator told the gathering that if the United States continued to hold the canal, Cuban Communist leader Fidel Castro—ever an unpopular figure with conservatives—would hold up the issue as one more example of US imperialism in Latin America, one that could fuel communism in the region.[71] Given that Chile elected a socialist government in 1970 and Nicaragua would experience a Marxist revolution in 1979, this was no idle threat.

Biographers Robert Eells and Bartell Nyberg believe Hatfield saw the canal issue in moral terms, arguing it was against the senator's moral and religious beliefs to support what amounted to American colonialism.[72] But despite Hatfield's attempts to educate voters and the moral consistency of his position compared to other national security issues, Cook, a conservative Democrat, followed the lead of other treaty opponents and hammered Hatfield with the issue in the fall of 1978. A pro-Cook ad accused Hatfield of going against the will of the people—two out of three Oregonians, the ad claimed—by voting for the treaty. "I opposed the Panama Canal giveaway which jeopardizes our defense" was a standard line in Cook's ad. The challenger accused Hatfield of supporting "unilateral disarmament" and argued that "Hatfield places his faith in the UN and the peaceful intentions of others, a stance which has brought disaster to civilizations throughout history."[73]

Cook distorted Oregonians' feelings on the Panama Canal, however. A March 1978 poll showed that Oregon residents rejected the treaties by a "more than 3-to-2 margin," not quite two out of three as Cook asserted. The *Oregonian* editorialized, furthermore, that the poll was unfairly biased because its language reflected that Congress was "considering the advisability of turning the Panama Canal over to Panama by the year 2000" when, in fact, the Senate had recently approved an amendment permitting the United States to militarily intervene if any nation sought to block the canal *after* 2000. The editorial argued that "the real issues are more profound" and complex than a stark choice between the United States giving away and keeping the canal.[74]

Hatfield may have lost some rural, conservative voters with his Panama stance, but unlike Wayne Morse, he successfully emphasized his ability to obtain federal spending for Oregon. In the campaign literature for his reelection bid, Hatfield noted that he had obtained funds for Columbia River dams and powerhouses, particularly at the key Bonneville Dam near Portland. The literature also noted that Hatfield "authored amendments which provided funds for construction of hopper dredges for coastal and Columbia River ports," that he obtained design and construction funds for a deep draft channel to ease shipping out of Coos Bay, and that he sponsored legislation to cut off funding for a proposed neutron bomb, an important issue to more liberal constituents in the most populous parts of Oregon.[75] Accomplishments like these likely strongly appealed to the senator's urban Republican-Democratic coalition, which carried him to an easy reelection victory by a margin of 62 to 38 percent of the vote.[76]

WITH SOME OF OUR FRIENDS, WE DON'T NEED ENEMIES: HATFIELD'S THIRD TERM AND REELECTION BID, 1979–1984

Hatfield's third term in the Senate overlapped with a period of time in which international arms control efforts were frustrated by the failure of strategic arms limitation talks with the Soviet Union. As the Reagan administration failed to pursue further nuclear accords and beefed up the arms budget, traditional national security a la Henry Jackson enjoyed a resurgence. But Hatfield nevertheless continued to work for arms reduction as a national security imperative. In March 1982, Hatfield introduced a resolution in the Senate calling for a unilateral halt in nuclear weapons tests, production, and development, and warned it might not be possible to verify and control the next generation of nuclear weapons. Hatfield urged the United States and the Soviets to decrease their current warhead deployments by a fixed annual percentage. Hatfield also regularly opposed the Reagan administration's military budget proposals, and his unorthodox arms control position flummoxed Reagan. In an entry in his diary, angry at what he perceived as Democrats trying to blame him for budget deficits, Reagan expressed frustration that his own camp could not agree on a defense budget, writing that some senators "like Hatfield & Domenici want to cut it too much." The president believed Hatfield "engineered the defeat" of his preferred defense bill. "I'm frustrated as [hell]," he said. "With some of our friends we don't need enemies."[77]

Reagan failed to appreciate, however, that Hatfield's position on the defense budget was consistent with ones the senator had held throughout his career on national security and defense. Many urban voters supported Hatfield, while hawks and rural voters admired his morality and evangelical religiosity and found other issues on which to agree with him, such as his advocacy for increased exports of timber and wheat, and his strident opposition to abortion. Hatfield also brought home more congressional bacon than ever, as he had assumed the chairmanship of the Senate Appropriations Committee in 1981. The senator could thus afford to play up his antinuclear position when announcing his intention to run for a fourth term. "We in Oregon live and breathe the polar opposite of the apocalypse which lies at the end of this obscene race toward Armageddon," Hatfield said in his October 1983 reelection announcement speech. Pointing out what he believed to be Oregon's unique natural environment, Hatfield argued that "no people on earth can better appreciate the tragedy of creation destroyed, because no people on earth have been as blessed with the glory of creation." He called for a "spiritual renaissance" among the people to "catapult us into a struggle for the cause of peace."[78]

Oregon Democrats, having failed to defeat Hatfield with a national security right-winger in 1978, moved to the left in 1984 with their nomination of Margie Hendriksen, a state senator from liberal Eugene.

Hendriksen mainly attacked Hatfield for his anti-abortion position, but also asserted that the senator was not quite as dovish as he seemed on national security. The Hendriksen camp charged that Hatfield received campaign contributions from defense contractors Lockheed, Grumman, Rockwell International, Boeing, Northrup, Martin Marietta, GE, and GM in 1984.[79] A letter to the *Oregonian* from Hendriksen supporter Robert O'Brien, moreover, launched numerous unflattering attacks on Hatfield's national security record. O'Brien criticized Hatfield's vote for Kenneth Adelman, "who, in 1981, called arms control 'a sham'" to head the Arms Control and Disarmament Agency. In addition, O'Brien contended that on April 5, 1984, Hatfield voted to spend $21 million to aid the insurgent contra force attempting to overthrow Nicaragua's government, and that on May 10 Hatfield voted against an amendment to reduce military spending. O'Brien also pointed out that Hatfield was serving as Reagan's reelection committee chair for Oregon, even though he supposedly disagreed with many of the president's policies. Noting that Hatfield refused to debate Hendriksen, O'Brien concluded that "clearly, Hatfield's image as an advocate of peace would crumble if he were forced into a debate with Hendriksen."[80]

Hatfield responded to Hendriksen's challenge, however, by continuing to emphasize his position as a warrior for security through peace. In a June 1984 newsletter to constituents, the senator reiterated his call for a nuclear weapons freeze because of the inherent danger and expense. Tying in his national concern to local interests, he called for a reduction in defense spending so that interest rates could be lowered, thereby triggering new construction starts and higher timber sales to boost Oregon's economy, which struggled in recession during the early 1980s. The senator also proudly played up the ways in which Oregonians, he argued, were engaged in national and international affairs. "I recall open meetings during the darkest days of the recession in which the main topic of concern was the Lebanon crisis, and town hall meetings in predominantly agricultural areas of Oregon in which the principal topics of discussion . . . involved deficit spending or the nuclear freeze," he said. "In an era in which blatant self-interest has become the basis for political advocacy, Oregon has emerged as a state which recognizes that state concerns and national concerns are inextricably bound."[81]

Hatfield's campaign literature touted the senator's support for his positions. One pamphlet cheered Hatfield for standing up to the Reagan military buildup, and claimed the senator originated the concept of a nuclear freeze as early as 1979. The pamphlet noted that Hatfield chaired a Senate subcommittee in 1983 that funded Department of Energy warhead production and, in that position, killed a plan to build neutron bomb artillery shells. "His positions on foreign policy . . . and on nuclear issues are popular in Oregon," the pamphlet argued, claiming that Hatfield ran for another term partly because of pressure from the antinuclear lobby.[82] All of this seemed to hold water with the voters: not even the discovery by the news media that Hatfield's wife, Antoinette, who worked as a real estate agent in Washington, DC, had received money from Greek businessman Basil Tsakos, who was simultaneously lobbying the senator for his support for a trans-African oil pipeline, could derail his campaign. Critics argued that the scandal seemed to suggest that Hatfield could be bought by private interests in his quest to secure lower energy costs—and perhaps greater national security—for Americans weary of high energy prices because of political turmoil in the Middle East, the source of much of the world's crude oil. After a period of antagonism between the Hatfields and the press as well as heightened calls from Margie Hendriksen's campaign for the senator to reveal his connections with Tsakos, Hatfield apologized and his wife donated the money to Shriners Hospitals for Crippled Children's branch in Portland.[83] On September 9, a month after the scandal broke, the *Oregonian* released a poll nonetheless showing Hatfield with a margin of 64 percent over Hendriksen's 28 percent. "Two-thirds of the voters who were aware of the Hatfield-Tsakos links said the controversy had no effect on their views of Hatfield" and 65 percent of those polled were "satisfied" with his explanation of and apology for his role in the affair.[84] The senator easily won reelection in November.

NO MORE NUKES: HATFIELD'S FOURTH TERM, 1985–1990

In the late 1980s, as the Cold War loosened its grip on the world amid the rise of a new détente between Ronald Reagan and Soviet leader Mikhail Gorbachev, Hatfield continued to challenge the idea that the force of arms could ensure security. His October 1985 constituent newsletter criticized Pentagon waste, noting that despite major increases in US Air Force and Navy aircraft procurement budgets, "11 percent fewer airplanes were obtained" between 1982 and 1985 than in the Carter administration. The letter went on to explain US and Soviet defense expenditures, how Congress put together the defense budget, what Hatfield alleged to be "hidden costs" in the budget, and finished with Hatfield's opinion, which was stridently in favor of cutting the budget. In a familiar refrain, Hatfield contended that "if we are to provide for an adequate defense based on conventional strength and strategic deterrence, we must not ignore important long-term investments in the country's infrastructure and human resources." Domestic needs must come before foreign policy to have national security, Hatfield said, while railing against decreased funding for low-income housing, education, medical care, and infrastructure.[85]

The homeland defensive did not lose out entirely, however. In 1986 Hatfield convinced the US Navy to base four merchant marine vessels out of Portland as part of its ready-reserve fleet after presenting a General Accounting Office report contending that the government unduly favored southern California for ship-repair contracts.[86] In 1987, Hatfield worked with Les AuCoin, who represented a large part of Portland in Congress and served on the House subcommittee on defense appropriations, to draw more US Navy business to Portland's dry dock. AuCoin gave House Appropriations Committee Chair Les Aspin a tour of Portland's dry dock, touting its importance to naval repair work. The congressmen toured the docked USS *Paul F. Foster*, which AuCoin argued represented "a complicated job" highlighting "the sophistication of the Portland yard." The *Oregonian* reported that AuCoin and Hatfield were working to stave off efforts to cut the amount of naval repair work in Portland.[87] Aside from the Navy yard effort, Hatfield, AuCoin, and Governor Neil Goldschmidt sponsored the formation of the Oregon Institute for Advanced Computing, which was partially funded through a $5 million Pentagon grant.[88]

Hatfield was not utterly allergic to defense spending, despite his moral qualms against war and nuclear weapons. The senator did, however, continue his antinuclear crusade in the late 1980s, particularly by pushing for the deactivation and cleanup of the Hanford Nuclear

Reservation. After Henry Jackson died in 1983, Hanford came under Hatfield's powerful eyes as a prime target for shutdown. Mindful of the need to ameliorate allies in the Senate who were national security hawks, Hatfield argued that Hanford's shutdown would not hurt the US capacity to produce plutonium, which, he said, could be recovered from scrap, or taken from nuclear generators in South Carolina. Hatfield argued that a report conducted by his staff on US plutonium needs would result in "the meltdown of public confidence" against plants specifically geared to produce plutonium.[89] In November 1987, Hatfield sponsored an amendment to an appropriations bill for energy and water that put Hanford's N Reactor in cold standby, meaning that it could only be reactivated in case of national emergency.[90] Ultimately, the N Reactor was shut down completely, never to be reactivated. Environmentalist and Hanford-watcher Robert J. Alvarez noted that the shutdown might not have occurred had Jackson and Warren Magnuson remained in the Senate: "Now that they aren't, and you have such a powerful political opponent as Mark Hatfield, it would be impossible for [the US Department of Energy] to keep that reactor running."[91]

On the other hand, in the aftermath of the shutdown, Hatfield pushed for economic recovery for the nearby Tri-Cities. This move was consistent with his political ideology that a replacement for traditional national security should not only help improve the world, but bring home political bacon as well, in this case for residents of southeast Washington. An *Oregonian* editorial—parroting the earlier public policy goals of Jackson and Sam Volpentest—argued that "any decision to close a large government-operated facility in a small community carries with it the obligation by Congress to help the community diversify its economy, to retrain the displaced workers and to help stimulate recovery in the area," and noted approvingly that Hatfield proposed to do just that. The senator pushed for the DOE to accelerate the cleanup of defense-related waste at Hanford, a project that even in the late 1980s was estimated to cost at least $2 billion and employ 3,500 workers. The *Oregonian* also contended that because "Hanford's future lies in scientific research," replacements for the loss of N Reactor jobs should help the Tri-Cities retain a workforce trained in science and high technology.[92] Indeed, thanks in part to the efforts of Hatfield and other members of the congressional delegation, the Hanford site has continued to receive a great deal of federal and private investment, both despite and because of the scrutiny surrounding the revelations about the level of its Cold War–era environmental waste.

Hatfield's national security position earned him increasing amounts of praise in these years. In 1988, the *Salem Statesman Journal* praised the senator for challenging the Reagan administration's attempt to renew military aid to the Nicaraguan contras. "The word for this ploy is extortion," the editorial argued. "Hatfield stopped short of using the word, but he exposed the administration's methods in a courageous speech on the floor of the Senate." While Reagan, the *Statesman Journal* argued, "coldly attempted to use the lives of American soldiers as an emotional substitute for a genuine, popularly supported foreign policy," Hatfield, by contrast, "has the courage to boldly challenge the leader of his own party. The senator has done his state proud. Again."[93] Meanwhile, *Oregonian* columnist Steve Duin, a frequent Hatfield critic, did ask quizzically if "in an age where all of Hatfield's seniority may be required to preserve the state's interests, is Oregon best served by a successful senator or a faithful one?" He noted, however, that the question "clearly amused" a "high-ranking energy official" who credited Hatfield with shutting down the N Reactor at Hanford. The official told Duin that "when it comes to issues of war and peace, issues that are extremely important to him, Hatfield has established himself at the rampart of one point of view. . . . It is not a political position he's taking. It is the antithesis of a political position. He wants to establish a moral point. He will not compromise. He is rock solid."[94]

Such principles continued to form the bedrock of Hatfield's approach to national security as he geared up for his final Senate run. In a 1989 commencement speech for Portland State University graduates, he invoked Christopher Wren, the eighteenth-century architect of St. Paul's Cathedral in London, in creating a metaphor for a new kind of national security in a post–Cold War world. "I came here to enlist the energy and the enthusiasm of the cathedral builder in each of you," Hatfield told the graduates. "Think of our world as a cathedral: a cathedral in progress." He argued that the developing world was like the scaffolding and the framework of the future, but questioned its strength in the light of American failures abroad. He also contended that "if the developing world is the scaffolding . . . the developed world is the foundation: and cracks have begun to appear throughout the foundation—even here at home." Referring to a Portland street plagued by a large homeless population as well as the recent crackdown on student protests in Tiananmen Square in China, Hatfield argued that "as tied as we are to the students in China, we are also tied to the homeless person huddled in the doorway down on Burnside." He urged students to work close to home to address the root human causes of pain, thus strengthening the scaffolding and repairing cracks in the foundation of the home cathedral: only then, he said, should they reach further outside themselves to the world.[95] The speech demonstrated Hatfield's increasingly regional policy commitments in the name of national security.

To fulfill these commitments and to keep bringing federal dollars to Oregon, however, he had to overcome a tough reelection campaign against Democratic challenger Harry Lonsdale in 1990. In September, Lonsdale, a high-tech tycoon and a political newcomer from the growing central part of Oregon, took a page from Margie Hendriksen's playbook, airing campaign ads attacking Hatfield's campaign contributions from big national defense interests. "Two new spots . . . say Hatfield has changed during his years in the Senate," said the *Oregonian*. "In both spots, a list of Hatfield's campaign contributors scrolls across the screen. The list includes Atlantic Richfield, Exxon, the Benj. Franklin Savings and Loan Association, Dow Chemical, Chevron, Shell, Chevy Chase Savings, General Mills and others."[96] Lonsdale later charged in his autobiography that Hatfield received $64,000 total in contributions from "defense"-related political action committees.[97]

Just as he had done in past election cycles, however, Hatfield strove to make his campaign message more about economic growth for Oregon and achieving a new kind of national security for the region and the nation. He looked forward to one final term of attempting to mothball weapons programs and reprioritize health and education spending. Speaking before a group of healthcare professionals at a campaign rally, Hatfield said that his top priority in his final term would be to improve the quality of human life. "It bleeds my heart, it grieves me to think, that with just a snap of the fingers, we could find $15 to $20 billion to embark on a chemical weapons program, and then at the same time, when we talk about the 37 million Americans who have no access to medical care, we say, 'We can't afford it,'" he said. The senator announced he and Senator Ted Kennedy were co-sponsoring legislation to encourage teacher training in mathematics and science at the elementary school level, along with linkages to private-sector science interests like the Oregon Museum for Science and Industry. Understanding the diversity of a growing and changing economy in the Northwest, Hatfield also argued that the program could not just rely on young white males: "We have to reach out to the women, we have to reach out to the minorities," he exhorted. Hatfield also announced that he had introduced legislation to establish an assistant secretary position for community colleges within the Department of Education. Education, thus, would be the new national security after the end of the Cold War.[98]

But Lonsdale led in the polls late in the campaign, forcing Hatfield to respond by engaging in attack ads, something he claimed he had never had to do before. In doing so, he ironically portrayed Lonsdale as weak on national security, in the context of the homeland defensive. Hatfield assailed Lonsdale's mid-1980s support of Bhagwan Shree Rajneesh, the leader of a religious group then embroiled in a bitter land dispute with the state government. Rajneesh, a spiritual guru from India, had imported his following to the former Big Muddy Ranch in central Oregon during the summer of 1981. As the ranch was transformed into Rajneeshpuram, it counted thousands of sannyasins, or followers, from around the world among its ranks. When the expanding complex encountered resistance from nearby ranchers in its attempt to incorporate as a city in order to receive state services, sannyasins moved into nearby Antelope and seized control of its city council, sparking conflicts with its neighbors that escalated over the years and eventually captivated the entire state of Oregon. By 1984, a number of Rajneeshpuram's residents, led by Ma Anand Sheela—whose fiery and occasionally vulgar public appearances offended many Oregonians—set out to seize control of the Wasco County board of commissioners in that fall's elections. Investigations by the state and the Federal Bureau of Investigation later determined that sannyasins under Sheela's command undertook an unsuccessful effort to poison residents of The Dalles, the county's biggest city. Sheela and her closest advisers had hoped to keep enough residents away from polling stations on Election

Day to get sannyasins elected to the county commission, in effect taking over the county, in an apparent bid to preserve Rajneeshpuram from state and federal scrutiny. Sheela and Rajneesh were eventually arrested, and the latter was deported back to India after a controversial series of detentions and interrogations by federal officials.[99] Hatfield, Governor Vic Atiyeh, and James Weaver, representative from Oregon's Fourth District in Congress, were part of the political effort to expose Rajneeshpuram's illegal transgressions and to shut down its central Oregon operations.

As subsequent studies of Rajneeshpuram—leading up to and including the celebrated 2018 Netflix documentary *Wild Wild Country*—have shown, Rajneeshpuram was neither a simple story of good overcoming evil, nor was it easily forgotten. During the controversy over the commune, Harry Lonsdale emerged as one of its strongest defenders from the perspective of freedom of religious expression. Although Lonsdale criticized Sheela's extremism, his support for the peaceful coexistence of Rajneeshpuram with the rest of central Oregon came back to haunt him in his Senate campaign years later. Hatfield's campaign seized on the issue: Oregon Republican Party chair Craig Berkman presented a letter written by Lonsdale in 1984 to then-Oregon Attorney General David Frohnmayer "that asked for understanding treatment of Rajneeshpuram residents," as well as an advertisement Lonsdale took out in the *Bend Bulletin* "bidding a fond farewell" to Bhagwan Shree Rajneesh after he pled guilty to two federal felonies upon leaving the United States in 1985. The candidate responded that he wrote the letter in support of Rajneeshpuram's rights under the First Amendment of the US Constitution protecting freedom of religion, not as an endorsement of the criminal activities carried out by "wrongdoers." Lonsdale said he thought Rajneesh "was tried, found guilty, and sentenced to the electric chair by the press," and criticized Berkman's attack as a "political smear."[100]

Hatfield himself argued that if Lonsdale had been in charge of determining the fate of Rajneeshpuram, "that sad chapter in Oregon's history might never have been closed."[101] He got help from Vic Atiyeh, who asked, "How could someone who wants to be one of 100 US Senators be so blind and naïve to be drawn in by the followers of Rajneesh?"[102] At a campaign press conference, Hatfield charged that "Lonsdale's claim that he was merely defending religious freedom doesn't wash. . . . The issue isn't religious freedom, it's a question of judgment." Lonsdale, who routinely criticized Hatfield for refusing to face him in a public debate, "crashed" the press conference and attempted to get the senator to answer questions while the senator's aides led him away. In response to this political stunt, Hatfield said, "I'm conducting a press conference, not a circus" and derided Lonsdale's tactic as an uncivil "act of political desperation."[103]

Hatfield's overall national security strategy was consistent with past campaigns, but his adoption of Rajneeshpuram as a wedge issue was atypically aggressive. Reviving memories of the criminal activities of some Rajneeshpuram residents undoubtedly resonated with voters who associated Sheela's criminal activities and Rajneesh's perplexing behavior with the commune as a whole. The senator's assault on Lonsdale's support for the commune highlighted the divisions between Oregonians who feared Rajneeshpuram as a sex cult, a socialistic Soviet-like utopian society, and an overall menace seeking to take over Oregon; and those, like Lonsdale, who contended that, however repugnant the actions of individuals such as those who poisoned the residents of The Dalles, the commune as a whole still had a legal right to exist. Rajneeshpuram also represented a rare use of a national security-like issue by Hatfield in election-year politics: like Henry Jackson stirring up fears of the Soviet Union to get more defense dollars to Washington, Hatfield reignited the Rajneeshpuram controversy, apparently to get votes. In the end, after running essentially neck-and-neck in the polls with Lonsdale in October 1990, Hatfield's campaign spent over $1 million on television attack ads, also an atypical tactic for him, in an effort to regain voter support and return him to the Senate for a fifth term. For his part, Hatfield claimed his use of television ads was in order to "correct the record" as opposed to going after Lonsdale, and vowed never to use such ads again.[104]

DEFENSE THROUGH HEALTH AND EDUCATION

With his final bruising campaign behind him, Hatfield returned to Capitol Hill in January 1991 and immediately had a chance to back up his rhetoric against military spending. The Senate debated a resolution on whether to support the US-led coalition of armed forces in the forthcoming Gulf War to force Iraq's Republican Guard from Kuwait, which Iraq had invaded the previous summer. The George H. W. Bush administration sold the war to the American public on the principle of defending a sovereign nation against attack from an aggressive neighbor, but Hatfield voted against the Senate resolution and attacked it in a floor speech, issuing warnings to the American people that would be prescient: "What happens when domestic public opinion, which even now is sharply divided over whether or not the United States should go to war with Iraq, begins to plummet?" Hatfield asked. "What happens when a tidal wave of anti-Americanism sweeps across the Arab world?"[105] Hatfield was ahead of his time in predicting future complications of US involvement in the Middle East. The senator fought for defense cuts right to the end of his career. *Oregonian* columnist David Reinhard reflected in 1996 that Hatfield's "belief that national defense encompasses more than megatons and military hardware—education and research spending, for example—comes straight from Dwight Eisenhower." Reinhard argued that "today's young conservatives ought to give Hatfield credit for the work he has done to cut spending and balance the budget."[106]

The Hatfield of the 1980s and 1990s was more than just a military budget slasher: Steve Nousen, who succeeded Gerry Frank as Hatfield's chief of staff, recalled that late in his career, Hatfield saw Oregon Health & Science University (OHSU) as his legacy. In tackling transnational diseases that could threaten the Northwest, OHSU was perhaps the clearest example of Hatfield's redefinition of national security, and also an area in which he used his political power to serve both regional and national interests. Because Hatfield "didn't want an [Oregon] economy based off war," he increasingly pushed for funding for the healthcare industry in Oregon late in his career.[107]

This was not just a parochial pork-barrel interest: the senator also pushed for money for the National Institutes of Health (NIH), even during the political pressure to cut spending which characterized many of Hatfield's final Senate years. In May 1995, Hatfield saved the NIH from funding cuts, arguing that it was as important as appropriating money for a military threat. He remarked on the Senate floor that the United States had saved "billions of dollars per year" fighting diseases like tuberculosis, which he warned was "having a revival" in Africa, along with Ebola, a warning that turned out to be prescient when an outbreak reached the United States in 2014. During the Cold War, Hat-field argued, "anybody who wanted to cut military spending, we'd tell them, the Russians are coming. And then, boy, everybody would jack up another billion dollars. Well I want to tell you, viruses are coming. And they're here, and we'd had better get ready for that warfare because we need this kind of weaponry to fight it."[108] In gratitude for Hatfield's work, the NIH named part of its complex after him, and he received care there before he passed away in 2011.

If the NIH was the biggest nationwide beneficiary of Hatfield's conception of health as integral to national security, OHSU benefited the most in regional terms. The *Oregonian* wrote in 1990 that without Hatfield's help, OHSU might have been nothing more than "a mediocre medical limb" of its parent institution, the University of Oregon. The article related that in 1978, the future of "Pill Hill" was grim. Faculty and staff suffered from low morale, and the university medical school "lacked cohesion and direction." It turned to Leonard Laster, its new president, who sought to boost the school's reputation as a research institution. At that time, the university needed new scientists and state-of-the-art facilities to compete against top institutions for research grants. Hatfield was, as always, looking for ways to diversify Oregon's economy, so Laster turned to him for help to obtain federal funding for new infrastructure on campus.[109]

In a 1998 interview conducted for OHSU's oral history program, Hatfield played up the connections between health and international affairs that drove his interest in improving healthcare. The senator spoke of his 1945 visit to Vietnam while in the US Navy, "seeing the utter squalor of the people, the starvation." Hatfield wrote home that he "had gained an idea about the hunger and the poverty of people being a destabilizing political force." During his graduate work at Stanford University years later, Hatfield recalled that in his Latin American government class, the professor "began to recite to us the health statistics of Latin Americans. . . . He then proceeded to instruct that until you understand the health problems of Latin America, you'll never under-stand their politics, because you cannot build stable government on unhealthy people." Hatfield's professor held a simplistic, even paternal-istic, point of view that emphasized the superiority of US society and technical know-how in solving Latin American problems, but Hatfield took a different lesson from the class altogether: he considered it to have been what led him to connect health to successful governance at home, as well as with national and international security.[110]

In 1955, Hatfield was on the Oregon State Senate Health Committee, which was holding hearings on a bill to create a teaching hospital at what was then known as the University of Oregon Medical School (UOMS). He remembered being charmed by UOMS booster and future dean David Baird, but he was also lobbied by representatives of the Oregon Medical Association, who opposed the bill. Hatfield subsequently believed that the OMA lobbyists tried to argue that a bill supporting UOMS "would be the first step toward socialized medicine" because "it was competition; it would be competing with existing hospitals." But Baird, he said, always had "a very strong rebuttal to those opposition voices." The bill passed and UOMS got underway with its physical presence shifted from the University of Oregon's main campus in Eugene to a new campus in Portland where OHSU now stands. In 1956, Hatfield also secured state funds for the university dental school to move to a new campus near UOMS.[111]

After Hatfield was elected to the US Senate, he "went back to Washington and got disconnected" from the situation at UOMS. But in the late 1970s he read that the Oregon legislature "was debating a resolution to close medical education, health education, for budgetary purposes. In other words, the whole Hill was going to be shut down by this resolution." The resolution stunned Hatfield. "It was like a cold shower," he remembered. "I'd been in a coma, so to speak, in my loss of connection and knowledge of what was going on." Hatfield met soon after with incoming university president Leonard Laster. "He wanted to share his vision of what could be up there on that Hill, but he said that I would have to play a very vital partnership role in terms of getting federal support," Hatfield recalled. "And he explained to me a great deal of background that I didn't know about how certain of the eastern universities had received a great deal of support from the federal government, and telling me that support produced benefits, of course, for the whole nation and the whole world in the field of research."[112]

Hatfield recalled that a significant part of Laster's vision involved strengthening the university's research wing. University Hospital "was doing well" and the faculty were "adequate," Hatfield recalled. "But to fill out that third part of a medical center, research, they really needed some significant support." Laster sent Hatfield studies showing him that federal research funds were going to "the old-boys' club, the network on the East Coast," but also sometimes to Seattle, because Warren Magnuson chaired the Senate Appropriations Committee. After Hatfield replaced Magnuson as committee chair, he found himself able to send money to UOMS (known as OHSU starting in 1981), just as his predecessor had done for Seattle-area hospitals. One of his first projects succeeded in obtaining $25 million for the Vollum Institute, a scientific research facility on the university campus; Howard Vollum, founder of high-tech giant Tektronix, contributed $30 million to the project. To Hatfield, although federal funding was important, people mattered just as much as money. "It was not just federal money, but we were triggering and leveraging that money to double the money," Hatfield recalled. "And I saw the tremendous change that took place on that campus with the faculty, and then immediately the kind of people they attracted to that center. . . . It was very obvious that that could help leverage the values of people in attracting them."[113] Thus, as the University of Oregon Medical School became Oregon Health Sciences University, then Oregon Health & Science University, a regional powerhouse was taking shape in Portland's West Hills thanks to Hatfield.

A major part of Hatfield's OHSU work that *was* tied to the traditional national security state—or at least those under medical treatment after combat—was his effort in the late 1970s to obtain funding for a new Veterans Administration hospital near the OHSU campus. Hatfield's old adversary, Bob Duncan, had returned to Congress; as a member of the House Appropriations Committee, he potentially held enough sway to locate the VA in his district in urban Northeast Portland near Emanuel Hospital, a major health and research complex in its own right. Under Hatfield's plan, the VA would have 600 hospital beds in the West Hills, while Vancouver, Washington, would get 250 beds to satisfy Senate Appropriations Committee chair Magnuson. "I don't want to get down to a situation where a limited amount of money is available and one facility is built," Hatfield said, in a warning to Duncan about Magnuson's power to steer the entire project to Vancouver if only the Northeast Portland site was ultimately recommended to the Appropriations Committee. "I don't have to tell you who would win that battle."[114]

OHSU officials later recalled Hatfield's work to save the VA for OHSU. Leonard Laster believed "it took great political courage on Hatfield's part to be standing up for keeping the VA on the Hill when so many influential individuals . . . were really pushing to move it off the Hill," Laster recalled. "That was a really mean, vicious fight."[115] Regarding that fight, OHSU Dean of the School of Medicine John Kendall believed "the community in general and certainly community forces would have voted for it to go over to Emanuel." Yet Hatfield contended that it would be better off near OHSU because the strongest VA hospitals "are the ones that [are] physically linked with a medical school or university." Kendall also remembered that the senator later fought successfully to link the VA to the rest of OHSU through a federally funded sky bridge. "He stayed behind it for about five or six, seven years, while multiple antagonists had their run at killing it," Kendall said.[116] Hatfield and his allies likely feared an outcome similar to what had nearly happened when city leaders tried to force the city's branch of Shriners Hospitals for Crippled Children (later renamed Shriners Hospitals for Children) to relocate to Emanuel: the Imperial Potentate, or president, of the entire Shriners organization told Portland mayor Neil Goldschmidt he would move the hospital to Los Angeles if he did not get permits to build a new Shriners near OHSU. Goldschmidt backed down, and the Shriners, a major civic force in Portland, remained in the city.[117]

OHSU faculty member Stanley Jacob argued that Bob Duncan's acquiescence played a critical role in resolving the impasse over the VA site. "Len Laster was president at that juncture, and Len knew about my association with both Mark and Bob, and he called me down to his office, and he said, 'Stanley . . . do you think you could talk Bob Duncan into allowing us to have the Veterans Hospital at our school?'" Jacob said he would be willing to try and arranged for Duncan to have dinner with the two of them. "I explained to Bob why the veterans would be better off," Jacob said, appealing to Duncan's affinity for the military and his prior service. He explained that Oregon's best doctors and newest medical advances were coming from OHSU. When Duncan tried to push for the Emanuel site, Jacob said that "around the country veterans hospitals are situated as peas in a pod with university centers." Duncan, realizing how strongly Jacob felt, asked for some time to think over the situation. "About a week or two later he backed away from pushing for

View of the skybridge connecting Oregon Health and Science University with the Portland Veterans Affairs Medical Center. As chair of the US Senate Appropriations Committee, Senator Mark Hatfield directed federal funds to build a new hospital and the skybridge during the 1980s. The bridge dramatically cut transit times between the hospitals and allowed for greater collaboration among patients, staff, and researchers on what is colloquially known as "Pill Hill." Photo by author.

the Veterans Hospital at Emanuel," said Jacob. Whether it was because of Jacob's appeal or the political calculation that Oregon might lose the VA to Warren Magnuson's Washington, Jacob, Laster, and OHSU got their hoped-for result.[118]

Jacob and Hatfield developed a close reciprocal relationship because of the success of the VA battle. Jacob recalled that "when Mark got into a little [financial] difficulty . . . one of the friends he had was me, and he called me on the phone, and I got a lot of people together; and I was instrumental in raising a defense fund for him." As Hatfield remained in office, Jacob remembered that the senator made the cash registers ring in OHSU's favor. "He . . . made it possible for the school to get a half a billion dollars, [and] he raised the credibility level of the university around the country," Jacob argued. "Everyone . . . whether it was the president of Duke University or president of Harvard, would go to Mark's office and they wanted Mark's help." Jacob believed Hatfield "did more than any other outside person to change" the university's reputation.[119]

Hatfield's work on behalf of OHSU was challenged in 1991, when the *Oregonian* alleged that the senator's daughter, Elizabeth Hatfield Keller, benefited from a special admissions policy allowing Keller and three other applicants to the university to receive preferential consideration outside of OHSU's normal admissions process. Admissions committee members William K. Riker and Judith Ray resigned in protest, believing Keller's admission was the result of a quid pro quo in exchange for Hatfield assisting OHSU in obtaining federal grants. Hatfield countered that he told OHSU he did not want his daughter to receive special consideration. The story noted that Keller had years of experience as an emergency medical technician and an emergency room nurse before applying to OHSU, and Ray admitted that Keller might in fact have been qualified for admission. To some, Hatfield's reputation was further tarnished, years after the Tsakos controversy of the mid-1980s seemed to have faded into memory. Others, however, argued Hatfield's private business dealings were not the business of the general public, contending that if he was able to cut good deals in private, that translated into an ability to do the same for Oregon.[120]

In later years, however, the *New York Times* also went after Hatfield, alleging that his work for OHSU amounted to a misuse of federal funds, and that the supposedly high-minded senator was a pork-barrel politician, much like Warren Magnuson, the Northwesterner he had succeeded as chair of the Senate Appropriations Committee. In 1994, Hatfield came under fire for using a process called earmarking, designed to circumvent traditional merit-based allocations for federal funding bills, to bring the submarine *USS Blueback* to the Oregon Museum of Science and Industry. California Representative George E. Brown Jr., chairman of the House Committee on Science, Space, and Technology, was angered by Hatfield's use of earmarking. He alleged the process "relegates about 90 percent of the House and 80 percent of the Senate, who are not on the appropriations committees, to a nonparticipatory role, and that is not healthy for the institution." In 1992, Brown had tried to block earmarks for science projects, including a building at OHSU. Though Brown got the projects cut from one appropriations bill, supporters reinserted them during a closed committee meeting. The omnibus bill then went to House members just two hours before a vote. Not wanting to quibble over minor details, the House approved the whole bill. Earmarking did not seem to bother the voters in Oregon, and Hatfield shrugged off Brown's charges. "I'm very proud of earmarking for the state of Oregon," he said. "One man's pork is another man's bacon." Aide Bill Calder argued that "this is part of Sen. Hatfield's vision for Oregon, and it means access to healthcare, quality medical research,

improving the quality of life for Oregonians. . . . And if it means taking criticism for building a medical research infrastructure, then he's
happy to take the criticism." OHSU spokeswoman Julie Remington
made the case that earmarks were fair, because they leveled the playing field for the university in its competition for grants with big-name
medical schools. "Medical research is a field where those who have, get,
like Harvard and Columbia," she said. "Thanks to earmarks, OHSU now
is a world-class academic health center."[121]

Clearly this was the case. There is no doubting that his final decade
in office saw OHSU, along with the rest of Oregon, tremendously benefit
from his work to divert national security resources toward healthcare.
By 1987, the senator had obtained $20 million in federal appropriations
for the Vollum Institute for Advanced Biomedical Research.[122] The
Oregonian reported in 1988 that "over the last three years, he pressed
for $10 million for renovation of the OHSU hospital, $5 million for the
Oregon Hearing Center and $10 million for a five-floor extension to the
Basic Sciences building at OHSU."[123] In 1989, Hatfield arranged financing for the construction of a new critical care unit for OHSU. He also
helped finance a $14.5 million Biomedical Information Communica-
tions Center that he touted as representing a "new generation in access
to medical information," one that "will have unparalleled potential to
foster world peace by eventually making medical information available
worldwide," because, he believed, "as world health improves so will the
chances for global peace."[124] In September 1989, the Senate approved
$10 million to build the Neurosensory Research Center to replace the
outdated Oregon Hearing Research Center at OHSU. At that point, a
Hatfield aide estimated OHSU had received $74 million in federal funds
since 1980. The senator also obtained $131 million for construction of
the VA, $37.4 million for the Biomedical Information Communications
Center, $22 million for the Neurosensory Research Center, $20 million
for the OHSU Ambulatory Research Center, $16 million for the VA's
expansion in 1997, $12 million for the OHSU School of Nursing build-
ing, and $6.7 million for OHSU's skybridge to the VA.[125]

After Hatfield retired from the Senate, he joined OHSU's board of
trustees and continued to lobby on behalf of the hospital–university.
In 1998, OHSU announced a $60 million research building named for
Hatfield, "built largely with federal money secured through Hatfield's

Bust of US Senator Mark Hatfield in the Mark O. Hatfield Research Center at Oregon Health and Science University. The Hatfield quote below it reads, "True national security begins within our borders—in the health and education of our people." Photo by author.

Entrance to the Mark O. Hatfield Research Center at Oregon Health and Science University. OHSU named the center after Hatfield upon its opening in 1998, in tribute to the federal funding Hatfield brought to "Pill Hill" during his time in the Senate. Photo by author.

efforts and gifts from friends of the university." By this point, years of Hatfield largesse, "together with research grants OHSU scientists obtained, ha[d] catapulted the university into the top 100 schools in federal financing."[126] OHSU has continued to expand in the intervening years, adding a new campus in the Portland suburb of Hillsboro, and building along Portland's south waterfront. There, a major new hospital complex is connected with the main OHSU campus via a tram that has become a major feature in the Portland skyline, perhaps the most visible testament to Mark Hatfield's years of work to make a nontraditional form of national security ideology work for Oregonians.

CONCLUSION

Throughout the Cold War, the Pacific Northwest ran the gamut in terms of public opinion and public policy in the pursuit of attracting federal dollars that would defend the region and the United States. By the time of the post–Cold War, pre-9/11 moment of May 2001, it seemed as though Mark Hatfield's policy position—in favor of redefining national security as broadly linked to infrastructure, education, and healthcare—had become preeminent, at least in Oregon. Hatfield found a receptive audience when he expounded upon his commitment to global health in a discussion of his memoir at Willamette University. Drawing in the friendly crowd at his alma mater, Hatfield argued that "we can talk about issues like military-industrial complex, we can count the tanks, we can count the planes, we can count the bombs, but when we talk about health and disease, we're talking about you." No longer could Americans isolate themselves, Hatfield warned, "because with international trade, international commerce, international travel, the world has now become truly one, and a threat in any one part of the world becomes a threat to all of us in disease." He lamented, meanwhile, that "we find ourselves thinking of national security strictly in how much military hardware we have." Referring to one of his heroes' warnings about excessive military weaponry, Hatfield contended that "President Eisenhower said that's not really national security. . . . That becomes a theft to scientists, to those who are hungry and not fed, and to those who are cold and not clothed." National security, Hatfield contended, was too complex to be reduced to weaponry. He worried that "every president—Democrat, Republican—bought in on the old idea that the bigger the bombs, the more bombs we have, the more security we buy." As a result, he said, "we neglect the human needs of this country. We are weakening national security, we are not strengthening it."[127] Within a few short months, however, Hatfield's words would be even harder to sell outside of Oregon when terrorists from the Al-Qaeda network destroyed the World Trade Center in New York City and attacked the Pentagon in Washington, DC. Over the years, the presence of the national security state grew as some of Washington State's military bases added personnel: Puget Sound Naval Shipyard added 1,000 new civilian positions, and US Army Fort Lewis (now Joint Base Lewis-McChord) received 5,500 new troops, serving as a major jumping-off point for troops and armored tanks during the US invasion and occupation of Iraq which began in 2003.[128]

Hatfield did everything he could to strengthen the security of Oregonians during his years in public life. But the Pacific Northwest in the post–World War II period saw a complex mixture of sentiments about national security. Whether a more traditional approach was followed— as with Henry Jackson and Tom Foley in Washington—or redefined gradually by Wayne Morse and Mark Hatfield in Oregon, the politics of national security played a crucial role in the economic transformation of the region. Thanks to the international outlook of these individuals, national security politics helped globalize the Pacific Northwest. Defense contractors with foreign clients increasingly populated the region, particularly in Washington. Debates about major foreign policy issues such as the Vietnam War played a major role in elections in the Pacific Northwest and in the balance of power in the US Senate. Finally, as questions about the nature of national security itself proliferated in the post-Vietnam era and especially after the Cold War, increasing attention to regional and global health further integrated the Pacific Northwest into the modern healthcare apparatus, as Warren Magnuson and especially Mark Hatfield broadly redefined national security to include more than just military hardware.

In all, national defense, whether conceived in traditional terms by Washington politicians, or in less conventional ones by Oregon politicians, played a key role in the region's economic development and fuller integration into national and global marketplaces. As they worked to increase federal investment in the Northwest, however, the region's congressional delegation also worked to stimulate global trade to further interconnect Oregon and Washington with the world, fuel regional economic growth, and make the Northwest and the world a safer place through freer exchanges of goods, information, and technology. As with national security, this was not always a clear or simple process, but it was an ongoing project and concern of regional politicians that dovetailed nicely with security concerns. If the Pacific Northwest could build a national security state-within-a-state, it could also build bridges to neighbors eager to cash in on what Oregon and Washington had to offer.

PART II

Globalizing the Pacific Northwest through Trade

CHAPTER 4

The Opportunities and Perils of Postwar International Trade

Washington US Representative Tom Foley often regaled visitors with a story about building bridges between the United States and Japan. In 1967, a Japanese delegation came to the US Capitol to thank the Agriculture Committee of the US House of Representatives for its role in providing food aid to Japan. But at the end of the meeting, committee chair Bob Poage berated the group, which was having trouble understanding his directions, for not leaving the committee hearing in a timely manner. Foley, then a young member of the committee in just his second term as representative from Washington's Fifth District, said that he helped smooth things over behind the scenes by making dinner for the delegation at his home. "Should I go out and buy some saki?[*sic*]" he asked an intern in his office who was of Japanese descent. "No," she replied, "scotch." This dinner led directly to visits by Foley to Japan which, over time, did increase US-Japan trade ties generally, and likely later led to Foley's appointment as US Ambassador to Japan after his congressional career ended. But Foley also had an eye on improving the trade relationship between Japan and his home district. As Foley built relationships such as this, constituents increasingly sought him out for his foreign affairs views and his ability to get things done. "In both Washingtons," Press Secretary Jeffrey Biggs explained, "foreign affairs wasn't simply one more arrow in his political quiver, it was a deeply rooted interest."[1]

This was clearly the case for many of Foley's fellow federal-level politicians from Washington and Oregon. In May 1965, he joined Senators Henry Jackson and Warren Magnuson in inviting President Lyndon Johnson to dedicate a new international terminal at Spokane International Airport. "Spokane's strikingly new Northwest gateway is visible evidence of a forward-looking people keeping pace with the jet age," Johnson later commented to Magnuson. "I congratulate Spokanians on constructing an edifice they can be proud of."[2] Throughout his career, Foley insinuated himself into as many international trade-related projects in his district as he could, particularly relating to wheat, his district's primary export crop. The entire Pacific Northwest congressional delegation joined Foley, Jackson, and Magnuson in broadly supporting international trade.

Foley's opinions and policies were representative of a wider consensus by Northwest politicians to increase economic security and growth, not just in the oft-contentious realm of the national security paradigm of seeking defense dollars, but through trade between the region and other parts of the world. Politicians and their business constituents particularly understood that the region's proximity to growing Pacific Rim economies such as China, Japan, and South Korea was advantageous. Both on their own and with the support and lobbying of the private sector, Northwest politicians seized the initiative to increase trade ties during these years. During the post–World War II decades, raw agricultural goods, along with manufactured goods produced by the aerospace industry centered around Boeing, were the region's key commodity exports. International trade was hardly unquestioned during these years, however. Depending on whether a particular industry or constituency fared better from tariffs or export expansion, Northwest politicians had to act like representatives and senators from other parts of the country, walking a delicate tightrope between advocating for freer trade they believed would benefit the region and more protectionist measures. In the end, however, the Northwest was hardly a backwater of a globalizing United States, but rather on equal footing with other American regions or states better known for their international trade, such as California and Texas.

In this regard, the Pacific Northwest can also be compared to the US South in its emergence from cultural and economic backwater to globalized place. As sociologist Wanda Rushing points out in her study of Memphis, anyone worldwide who listens to Johnny Cash or Elvis Presley, shops in a supermarket, goes to St. Jude Children's Research Hospital, or stays at a Holiday Inn utilizes a product or innovation from Memphis. As a professor at the University of Memphis, Rushing notes the partnership between her employer and Hubei University in

China to promote greater intercultural ties.[3] In addition, because it is home to Federal Express's global headquarters, Memphis is a center of global trade, roughly equidistant to Vancouver, British Columbia, to the northwest and London, Amsterdam, and Paris to the east. The Memphis airport has a major economic impact on the South, driving $20 billion in activity, which Rushing contends makes it an even greater economic engine than the better-known Hartsfield-Jackson International Airport in Atlanta.[4] In reconciling modern Memphis with its image as disease-ridden, racially segregated, and the site of the assassination of Martin Luther King Jr., Rushing contends that "attitudes about some things have not changed very much, but Memphis has proved that it can learn from its mistakes."[5] Although Memphis has changed because of globalization, she asserts that "the city embedded in its own accumulated local history, and subjected to global flows of commerce and communication, continues to shape and be shaped by the people who live and work there."[6] Beyond Memphis, other Southern cities like Atlanta, Charlotte, and New Orleans became connected to the global economy and helped to complicate, if not eradicate, old negative traits and stereotypes about the South.[7]

As in the South, trade to and from the Pacific Northwest and the resulting international connections helped bolster the region's identity as a cosmopolitan, socially and culturally diverse attraction. As a result of the decades of work done by Northwest politicians and export-minded businesspeople to open up and diversify its economy, the region came to attract brand names, high-tech businesses, tourists, outdoors people, the environmentally conscious, and the food and beer snobs from around the world for which it is now well known. Such connections also helped the region start to shake its exclusionary past, born of the white supremacist racial attitudes common to many of those of European descent who traveled west to settle the region during the nineteenth century.

THE PACIFIC NORTHWEST JOINS THE PACIFIC RIM

Oregon and Washington were beneficiaries of a post–World War II foreign policy by the United States that saw international trade as key to maintaining the peace and prosperity of an atomic world. For much of its history, the United States focused on developing its own homegrown industries: consequently, Congress erected high tariff walls, raising taxes on imports of goods or products that challenged core domestic industries, including steel and textiles. By the time of the Great Depression, however, the consensus about the utility of tariffs eroded. Some economists and Democratic Party politicians and strategists believed that the Smoot-Hawley Tariff Act, passed by Congress and signed by Republican president Herbert Hoover in 1930, worsened the Depression; so, as part of the response of the administration of Democratic president Franklin D. Roosevelt, his congressional allies passed the Reciprocal Trade Agreements Act (RTAA) in 1934. The act empowered the president to pursue trade agreements with other nations that agreed to mutually reduce tariffs, thereby allowing them to receive more US exports. This modest New Deal reform was strengthened by the postwar adoption of the General Agreement on Tariffs and Trade (GATT), which spread the principle of reciprocal tariff reduction throughout the world. Over time, most nations came to join the agreement, which served as a precursor to the World Trade Organization (WTO). The RTAA and GATT inaugurated what economic historian Douglas Irwin dubbed the "era of reciprocity" in US trade relations.[8] As the United States came to more bilateral and multilateral agreements by using legislation that extended RTAA powers, as well as through periodic GATT negotiations, the nation's import tariffs dropped from approximately 20 percent during the Great Depression to well under 10 percent by the end of the twentieth century.[9] As for fears that reducing tariffs would harm US businesses, those were swept aside by the economic reality of the postwar period: much of the non-US industrial world was so devastated by wartime destruction that it would take decades for it to compete.

The Pacific Northwest benefited immensely from this dramatic change in US trade policy. Already a largely export-dependent region, shipping out the timber, salmon, wheat, and other bounties of its nature-extractive industries, the Northwest saw its opportunities and partners expand as more trade agreements were signed in the mid-twentieth century and as more nations rebuilt after World War II. Academics and journalists of the Pacific Northwest have focused, rightly, on the massive postwar growth in trade between the region and the East Asian countries of China and

Japan. The immediate postwar years saw major obstacles to a strategy of increasing trade with these countries, however. Mainland China succumbed to communist rule in 1949 and was summarily expelled from the United Nations, and any hope for rapprochement vanished when China intervened on behalf of North Korea in the Korean War late in 1950. This combined with pressure from right-wing "Asia Firsters", who supported nationalist Chinese leader Chiang Kai-shek and denounced the Democratic administration of Harry Truman for having "lost" China to Communists under Mao Zedong, and led to the cutoff of nearly all contact between the countries for two decades.[10] Japan, meanwhile, was emerging from the devastation it suffered during the war at the hands of the Allies. Feeding the Japanese people proved to be the biggest priority in US-Japan relations under the Government and Relief in Occupied Areas assistance package that began coming to Japan in the summer of 1946. Indeed, in the early postwar years, according to Michael A. Barnhart, "Japan's chief problem was a chronic inability to pay for the imports necessary to sustain basic economic recovery."[11] Despite these obstacles, Pacific Northwest politicians and businesses made gradually more successful and lucrative inroads with these two nations, aiding the cause of bilateral economic and cultural relations along the way.

Senator Warren Magnuson was an early proponent of maintaining friendly relations with Taiwan, the remaining non-Communist portion of China and increasingly a Northwest trade partner, while simultaneously pushing for the United States to resume trade relations with the mainland. In 1950, he called for Washington to join the other nations of the world in recognizing the government of the People's Republic of China (PRC). Magnuson found little support for his efforts among his constituents, however, so he downplayed China relations during election years.[12] In 1957, immediately after his most recent election, Magnuson told *Business Week* that US passenger and mail flights to Beijing would be discussed at hearings on US trade policies, arguing that the United States could not keep the Chinese "behind an economic bamboo curtain forever just because we don't like the policies of their government."[13] In 1959, the senator said he opposed diplomatic recognition of the PRC or its admission to the United Nations, but he supported lifting the ban on American travel and resuming trade of nonstrategic goods "to give us some entree to 600 million people, as distinct from their ruthless government."[14] As part of a congressional subcommittee to study Asian trade, Magnuson contended that Chinese trade would benefit Pacific Northwest businessmen, while also providing the United States with intelligence on conditions within China that the US government could use to its advantage in future diplomatic negotiations.[15]

The rhetoric of Senator Henry Jackson, meanwhile, closely hewed to the anticommunist hardline opposing China's Maoist regime. When nationalist Chinese premier Chiang Kai-shek fled to Taiwan in 1949, Jackson, like many other Americans, saw his regime as representing the real China, and opposed recognition of Communist China for decades. In 1956, Jackson joined a group of senators—including the demagogic Joseph McCarthy—opposed to loosening of trade restrictions to the PRC.[16] He was pressured, however, by Northwest constituents aware of the market potential on the Chinese mainland. In 1957, Thomas Kerr, the president of Kerr Grain Corporation in Portland, Oregon, wrote Jackson and Senator Wayne Morse, urging resumption of flour and wheat exports to China and asking for protection of regional exporters. Kerr complained that the administration of President Eisenhower paid little attention to Northwest exporters when they asked for relief in circumstances like the embargo on trade with China, telling Jackson the United States needed a more "realistic" policy on China trade.[17] A perceptive Jackson constituent argued the United States should play a constructive role in the evolution of China. The constituent contended that industrial development was taking place in China, and that, whether Americans liked it or not, Beijing was gaining acceptance from European and Asian nations. If the US-China trade embargo ended, the constituent contended, "the results, in years to come, might well be a volume of commerce between the United States and China the like of which we have never before known with any other nation."[18] On the other hand, Jackson paid heed to his anti-PRC mail as well: for example, the pro-Taiwan China Club of Seattle made sure the senator knew that it opposed activity in 1957 by the Senate Interstate and Foreign Commerce Committee to explore ending the embargo.[19]

As local and national opinion was influenced by the standoffs in 1955 and 1958 between the United States and China over the disputed islands of Quemoy and Matsu that were claimed by both the PRC and Taiwanese governments, as well as China's testing of a nuclear weapon in 1964, Jackson remained hawkish toward the Communist regime. In a July 1963 speech, he warned that "Red" China would soon have a full arsenal of nuclear weapons and join the arms race.[20] In 1969, Jackson gave a speech to Seattle-area Democrats in which "he got carried away" talking about China's military and the need for the United States to maintain its defenses in the Pacific: "Reaching for a metaphor to emphasize his point, he raised his voice and loudly declaimed, 'We can't afford to have any *chinks* in our armor!'" Some of those in attendance reportedly "doubled over to keep from laughing but with little success." Jackson, meanwhile, "peered over his glasses like a schoolmaster who had just been hit by a spitball, glowered at his naughty class, rustled his notes, and continued to lecture."[21] Jackson's *faux pas* and the reprehensible response of some in his audience, arguably, just served to underline the lack of gravity with which many still took the idea of improving relations with China even at this point in time.

Meanwhile, as the Johnson and Nixon administrations searched for solutions to the Vietnam War and pursued relaxation of Cold War tensions in the late 1960s, one tactic they pursued was to improve relations with Beijing. This gave the Pacific Northwest delegation an opening to push for increased US-China trade. In a November 1969 speech to the Seattle Rotary Club, Jackson argued that a new US policy could, while respecting US treaty obligations to its allies, "open the way for a positive Chinese response [and] should increase the chances of more normal relations."[22] As the United States permitted China to join the United Nations in 1971, and Nixon visited China in 1972, the Northwest delegation rode the resulting wave of US-China relations toward enhanced trade and cultural openings. In July 1974, Jackson traveled to China for the first of four visits, commencing a warm relationship with the leadership that lasted the rest of his life. After talks with Chinese premier Zhou Enlai, Jackson called for "more openness and a gradual lowering of old barriers between the United States and China that still stand in the way of human contact." The senator argued for exchanges of journalistic correspondents and scholars, increased mobility for US diplomats in Beijing, arms control talks, and moving the US embassy in China from Taipei, Taiwan, to Beijing, which it would do in 1979, when the United States and China officially finished the process of normalizing their diplomatic relations.[23]

Jackson's reversal on Sino-American relations came about not just because of pressure from constituents who wanted to trade with China—that pressure had persisted throughout the 1950s and 1960s, and it had not moved Jackson before. Geopolitical changes in the late 1960s and early 1970s, however, made it easier for the senator to support an opening with China. The dissolution of the alliance between the Soviet Union and China—and the threat of warfare between the two countries—led Jackson to believe that the Communist Chinese no longer saw the Americans as their greatest enemy. He started calling for normalizing US-China relations as early as February 1969, and he supported the PRC's readmission to the United Nations in 1971, as well as the opening of a China liaison office in Washington, DC, in 1973 that predated the opening of the Chinese embassy upon the normalization of relations in 1979.[24]

Jackson's reversal in the early 1970s was only the precursor to a strengthening of his relationship with Beijing in the late 1970s and early 1980s, in the early years of normalized relations. Oil was important to both the US and Chinese economies, and because Beijing needed foreign currency to finance economic modernization, Jackson urged China in 1974 to develop its reserves, and for the United States to help China develop its offshore oil exploration. Jackson told the *New York Times* that "a strong China, able and determined to assure its own security, is an asset to the United States in helping maintain the strategic balance."[25] Although his 1974 and 1978 visits were largely focused on US foreign policy aims, Jackson hardly neglected his home region on these trips. In 1978, he urged Chinese leaders to visit the Pacific Northwest to analyze its dams and bring home ideas on how to develop China's hydroelectric capacity. He also persuaded then-Vice Premier Deng Xiaoping to come to Seattle during a state visit to the United States in early 1979 that bolstered bilateral relations and helped Northwest and Chinese statesmen and businessmen build new trade relationships.[26]

As US-Soviet tensions ratcheted up in the late 1970s and early 1980s in the wake of the breakdown of arms control talks and the Soviet invasion of Afghanistan in 1979, Jackson worked to ensure that the US-Chinese relationship was solidified as a counterweight to Moscow. Upon the beginning of an eighteen-day visit to China in August 1979, Jackson said China should be granted most-favored-nation (MFN)

Senator Henry Jackson and Communist Chinese leader Deng Xiaoping embrace during Jackson's final trip to China, shortly before his death in 1983. Jackson visited China several times in the 1970s and early 1980s and hosted Deng in Seattle in 1979 in efforts to spark more trade between Washington state and China. Reprinted by permission from University of Washington Special Collections, Henry M. Jackson Photographic and Graphic Materials, Accession 3560-031, Box 19/9, 3082n, negative no. UW 27284.

trade status through Senate approval of a US-China trade treaty already signed by President Jimmy Carter, meaning China would experience only minimal US trade tariffs.[27] This showed the growth of Jackson's commitment to China as a national partner of the US and a regional partner of the Pacific Northwest. That commitment strengthened in Jackson's final years, even as the administration of President Ronald Reagan threatened to upset US-China relations by making new overtures to Taiwan. In July 1982, Jackson told *Face the Nation* that the administration "would be making a serious mistake" if it made arms sales to Taiwan: he warned that Beijing might be compelled to retaliate by making an arms deal with the Soviet Union, "and we could wake up one morning and find another 1939 Hitler-Stalin pact with a new group in power in China."[28] Jackson thereafter took credit for helping the Reagan administration engage on friendlier terms with Beijing. In August 1983, Jackson greeted Deng Xiaoping "with a bear hug" upon arriving once again in China and met with the premier for two hours, one of the results of which was to get Deng to commit to a meeting with Reagan in 1984. Jackson also engaged in extensive talks with Chinese officials, largely on trade issues, in what proved to be the senator's final visit to China prior to his death.[29]

While Jackson was nationally oriented in his attempts to strengthen US-China relations, Tom Foley was more focused on strengthening ties between China and grassroots interests in the Pacific Northwest, particularly as he rose in the House of Representatives leadership ranks in the late 1970s. As East Asian nations became more integral in the export trade of the Pacific Northwest, interests in Foley's district lobbied him to get involved in raising their international trade hopes. In March 1979, the president of Eastern Washington University asked if Foley could contact the Chinese Ministry of Education to expedite the start of an exchange program in business management between EWU and two Chinese universities. A few weeks later, a Seattle businessman urged Foley to support negotiations in the Tokyo Round of the General Agreement on Tariffs and Trade talks to help out US workers and businessmen involved in industries handling imported cars.[30] Foley had the confidence of national as well as local leaders on trade matters: on May 10, 1979, Speaker of the House Tip O'Neill appointed him to serve as a member of President Jimmy Carter's Export Council. Foley told the press that he was pleased to be named to the council because he believed agricultural exports could help the nation reduce its trade deficit while easing farm income problems. Championing his home state, Foley announced that "the council is expected to recommend specific ways to boost exports and that is good news for growers in Eastern Washington."[31]

By 1980, trade and immigration ties between Washington and China were booming relative to just a decade earlier. The Washington State China Relations Council made up of political and business interests came into existence with a business membership of seventeen, increasing to one hundred by 1984. US Census data showed that Seattle's Asian and Pacific Islanders made up 7.4 percent of the city's total population in 1980, up from 4.2 percent in 1970. In Tacoma, the figure was 3 percent, up from less than 1 percent in 1970. Immigration to Oregon occurred at a slower rate, but of the approximately one million Chinese who came to the United States between 1968 and 1980, many came to the state after initially settling elsewhere in the United States.[32] On July 29, 1980, new West Coast consul general Hu Dingyi told business leaders at the Portland Chamber of Commerce that "our trade policy has changed. . . . China no longer follows a policy of strict self-reliance and is trying to increase its trade relations abroad."[33] Relations between the Northwest and China had grown remarkably close relative to the 1950s, and it was clear that continued good relations would be paramount for the region's economic prosperity.

Even more important for Northwest politicians and businessmen during the post–World War II years, however, was the bilateral relationship between the United States and Japan, one of the region's top trading partners. Just as the relationship between Japan and the United States was contentious at times, so were the interactions between the Japanese and Pacific Northwesterners. Politicians from the region aside from Tom Foley played a major role in improving this relationship, too.

In the fall of 1960, Albert Naito, a descendant of Japanese immigrants and head of the Portland company Import Export Consultants, asked Senator Wayne Morse to intercede with the Japanese ambassador to the United States to urge visiting Crown Prince Akihito to see a display set up by the city's Chamber of Commerce showing "many of the fine things we grow, manufacture, and produce in Oregon." Morse was apparently able to convince the ambassador: just two days after Naito's original contact with Morse, he wrote the senator thanking him for making the Portland event for the visiting Japanese delegation a success.[34] In April 1961, Morse told Portland Mayor Terry Schrunk he would attempt to get Secretary of State Dean Rusk to speak at the conference of Japanese and US mayors to be held in Portland that September. While Morse was unsuccessful in that endeavor, he obtained an extension of diplomatic immunity for Japanese visitors who came to Portland for the conference, an act that contributed to the success of the event.[35]

Occasionally, Northwest politicians went to Japan in efforts to achieve better trade deals for exporters, and Morse's spot on the Senate Foreign Relations Committee ensured he would undertake regular congressional delegations abroad. In a November 1965 visit to Japan, Morse pushed an agenda that would positively impact his constituents. Addressing a joint luncheon of the Japan-America Society and the American Chamber of Commerce in Japan, Morse praised United States chambers of commerce for "exporting economic freedom of choice for the individual for the benefit of the indigenous population in the many countries in which Americans maintain their investments and operate their businesses." Morse called for additional ties between the United States and Japan and expressed his hope for Japan to send a parliamentary delegation to the United States in 1966.[36] Such delegations would follow. In 1968, the US-Japan Parliamentary Exchange program inaugurated with the first delegation of American congressional officials to Tokyo, and included Wendell Wyatt, Republican Congressman from Oregon's First District. Japan began sending Diet members in 1974, and the exchange program continues to this day: a congressional delegation went to Tokyo in 2017, while a Diet delegation visited the United States in 2015.[37]

Morse believed that the United States and Japan needed more political ties to follow the trail blazed by businessmen from the two countries to strengthen their bilateral relations. In a speech at the University of Oregon, Morse praised the work of the Oregon Wheat League in Japan, arguing that the Japanese food market was being successfully penetrated by Northwest wheat producers to the tune of $120 million annually in sales, well over the $22 million tally for 1955. Morse called for additional exports, touting the OWL as an example for the Northwest—and the nation—to follow. On Japan, Morse expressed that "there can be no doubt that Japan is ready to take her place as a leader of Asia." Yet he contended that "the United States has nothing to fear from the emergence of Japan . . . in fact, we should welcome it." Noting presciently that Americans might not approve of many Japanese policies, Morse nonetheless contended that "we have more to gain from the emergence of strong, non-communist Asian nations than we could possibly lose from having them independent of American dictates."[38]

As Morse predicted, the Pacific Northwest gained a great deal from improving trade ties with Pacific Rim countries of all political persuasions in the decades to come. As with China, US-Japan trade came about largely as a Cold War imperative, not from an idealistic notion that it could be a way to improve bilateral relations. Nonetheless, ties between the Pacific Northwest and Japan improved in a wide variety of ways in the immediate postwar decades. The Northwest states most notably increased their exports of agricultural goods. Timber, wheat, and fruit, for example, had all been exported from Washington and Oregon to other states and throughout the world since European settlement; however, the pace of this trade increased dramatically after World War II.

THE NORTHWEST TIMBER INDUSTRY AND INTERNATIONAL TRADE

Debates among Pacific Northwest congressional and business leaders about timber exports have characterized the region's iconic industry since World War II. In the early postwar years, with high supply and a booming domestic industry, it was easier for small timber interests to favor, or at least not stand in the way of, increased exports. Politicians worked to assure steady export flows in the initial postwar decades and did not concern themselves with protectionists seeking shelter from foreign buyers. As the global economy expanded and more nations sought to purchase US logs, some in the Northwest thought all of the region's timber supply should be open to export. Others favored a more selective approach, pushing exports of lumber products finished in the region by local workers as opposed to raw logs that could just be shipped to foreign countries, which would, in essence, outsource Northwest timber manufacturing and processing jobs abroad. Another problem with raw log exports was that they would increase the price of timber, making it harder for American homebuilders, the main customers of US timber mills, to make purchases, especially from smaller lumber mills operating on a relatively narrow margin. These mills thus generally favored lower timber prices and resources to assist in the sale of finished products that they could then sell in the domestic market. However, as bigger operations, such as Georgia Pacific and Weyerhaeuser, increased their market share amid a rise in timber prices in the 1960s and 1970s, sales of raw logs abroad became more desirable to bigger firms. These sales enriched big lumber companies and shipping interests, providing jobs to dockworkers and others who lived in port cities, but contributing to the decline of smaller inland timber firms. Politicians had to balance the pro-trade demands of major timber companies and the typically more protectionist leanings of smaller mills.

In 1953, Henry Jackson represented Pacific Coast Lumber and Shingles in Portland in a successful protest against duties on timber imports imposed by the Netherlands and Belgium. In 1955, Jackson helped Walton Lumber Company in Everett obtain funding from the US Export-Import Bank for operations in Chile. By the late 1950s, however, a national recession slowed the industry, leading to the first drive for protectionism among some timber interests. On the one hand, Jackson charged that tight money policies—encouraging high interest rates—by the Eisenhower administration did damage by limiting borrowing and hurting the housing industry. On the other hand, in March 1958, Jackson testified to the House Ways and Means Committee that Congress needed to increase its authority relative to the executive branch over trade agreements, particularly when tariffs caused injury to timber workers.[39] A complication with increased log exports had shown its face for the first time in the postwar period: as major countries recovered from World War II, trade began to have winners and losers in certain US industries, even as the executive branch favored increased international trade at the macro level to bolster the world economy and challenge closed communist economic systems. In the case of the Northwest timber industry, exports tended to favor port and large timber-company interests over small mill workers. Many Japanese companies, for example, preferred to purchase cheaper raw logs over the finished manufactured products that small and medium-sized Northwest mills specialized in. This began to hurt mill workers as early as the 1950s. One exasperated constituent used racist overtones in a complaint to Jackson in 1958: "If you want to subsidize the Japs why don't you do it with cash. Why take the jobs away from the poor old plywood worker."[40] The beginning of a timber slump that would result in the near-collapse of the industry by the end of the twentieth century had—in part—to do with an increase in exports. Attitudes like those held by this Jackson constituent toward Japan would continue, even as the US and Japan continued to move on from World War II and build a postwar alliance.

Washington politicians were less affected by the difficulties of the timber industry than their Oregon counterparts. With its lack of military bases and major manufacturers like Boeing, Oregon was more dependent upon the health of both trade and protectionist interests in timber. In the early 1960s, Wayne Morse was caught between these interests, and somewhat hemmed in by his personal proclivity toward increased exports despite growing concern about high quantities of log exports to Japan. A major Kennedy administration policy aim was to pass the Trade Expansion Act and increase the president's power to negotiate reciprocal trade agreements. Historian Thomas Zeiler contends that many protectionists did not generally oppose trade but desired aid for industries suffering from imports. The administration thus needed to placate congressional delegations attuned to industries under stress from trade, as was the case with Morse vis-à-vis timber. Kennedy reminded Japan that the United States paid for its defense and felt wronged by tight controls on foreign exchange, but also promised Tokyo trade expansion, telling Americans they had to be importers. The president worried, as Japan sought foreign markets with which to obtain raw goods to grow its economy, that if Tokyo were discouraged by protectionist interests in the United States, it might trade with communist nations, like China and the Soviet Union. As the situation with Morse demonstrates, however, Kennedy still had to consider import protections for lumber producers, especially in Northwest states that he had lost to Republican Richard Nixon in the 1960 election.[41]

Indeed, even before Kennedy took office, Wayne Morse asked Secretary of State Christian Herter to find out why Georgia-Pacific, a large producer of paper products in Oregon and other timber-rich states in the US West and South, bid for a contract for a Korean housing project, yet lost to a lower bid by a Japanese firm amid allegations that South Korea offered Japan bribes and kickbacks. The International Cooperation Agency, a US government agency tasked with dispensing foreign aid, failed to give Morse an adequate answer, even though the US Embassy in Seoul had recommended against the Japanese firm getting the bid. Morse announced he would call for hearings in the Senate Foreign Relations Committee.[42] The Korean incident foreshadowed more troubles for the Northwest logging industry to come vis-à-vis East Asia.

In July 1961, A. Robert Smith of the *Oregonian* reported that Northwest politicians complained about Japanese competition in log exports, particularly on behalf of labor unions. Governor Mark Hatfield, Smith said, contacted Morse, who in turn met with Kennedy congressional liaison Larry O'Brien to discuss the possibility of finding a solution in the next round of US-Japan trade talks. While Northwest senators called for a task force to keep an eye on this dispute, the US government, according to Smith, denied organized labor's accusations that Japan was getting timber at premium rates. Meanwhile, Morse, at the behest of the Western Council of the Lumber and Sawmill Workers Union, requested congressional hearings. The union's executive secretary, Earl Hartley, said that Japanese exports were slowly strangling the region's lumber supply. In August, the House Labor Subcommittee agreed to hearings in the Northwest to investigate the effects that imports of plywood from Japan and log exports to Japan had on unemployment.[43] While airing the grievances of protectionist loggers, the hearings did little to assuage their fears about Japan. In October, Morse wrote W. J. Runckel, general manager of the Dee Division of the Edward Hines Lumber Company in Hood River, assuring him that the Northwest delegation understood complaints that log exports hurt the domestic industry. Morse testified at a hearing of the House Agriculture Committee in Portland, making known his awareness of possible harm caused by excessive exports, and suggested Japan should look elsewhere in Asia for a source of logs if the export situation excessively injured Oregon interests.[44]

Speaking in Bend, Morse told concerned timber workers that "the distinction between international problems and local issues is smaller than at any time in our history, and the American people know it." He contended that "because we are the richest and the most powerful nation in the world we also have the most interest in world affairs, and because we are a self-governing people, our individual citizens *must* have an interest in world affairs." For this audience, he said, international trade was the best example of the need for Oregonians to take an interest in world affairs. Turning specifically to timber, Morse said he had met with local industry leaders about the problem of the log trade to Japan. He reiterated the need to encourage Japan to buy logs from other locales, in addition to Washington and Oregon, to relieve the strain on the region's timber supply. At the same time, Morse reminded his audience that Japan overall was buying far more from the United States than it was selling, and that Japan was buying finished lumber from Oregon as well as raw logs.[45] Hardly a protectionist, Morse was pushing for fair trade with the Pacific Rim.

Morse was clearly trying to heed his constituents at home, and support the Kennedy administration, as he headed into a reelection year with the Trade Expansion Act still hanging in the balance. In January 1962, Morse co-sponsored Senate Bill 2663, an early version of the act.[46] Howard Petersen, Kennedy's main aide in charge of getting the TEA passed, argued with Morse that the timber industry needed to learn to compete better with foreign competition. But Oregonians in the timber industry were disenchanted with the TEA, and Morse pushed the president for compromises in the act. Morse worried about a handbill circulating in

Oregon mills asking foreign workers to apply to his office for jobs lost by Americans if the TEA were to pass. At one point, Morse pledged to oppose the TEA on behalf of lumber producers, demanding trade concessions like those which textile producers in the South, hurt by increased clothing imports from Japan, had negotiated with the Kennedy administration. Pressure from Morse and others in the Northwest delegation forced Kennedy to act. On July 26, 1962, the president issued a six-point program of assistance for lumber, including new loans and depreciation schedules for mill upgrades and productivity promotion, more access roads, an Agriculture Department study on timber cuts, and an increase in timber cuts on land controlled by the Bureau of Land Management, while also ordering the federal government to buy more US lumber. The TEA passed with the entire Northwest lumber bloc voting for it.[47]

Domestic political considerations clearly played into Morse's ambivalence on the TEA in 1962. Opponent Sig Unander was from a wealthy timber family, thus threatening the senator's long-standing support among big industry interests. But Morse tended to support small operators who bought local timber, altogether making up most of the one in ten Oregon workers who were in the industry. Timber worker lobbies like the Western Forest Industries Association who favored keeping lumber prices low were inclined to side with Morse over Unander in 1962 because they felt it was in their best interest. Morse could hardly lose the support of timber workers over the TEA, hence his need to work for a compromise to smooth out the ways in which it hurt smaller operators.[48] But the TEA also had strong support in Oregon outside of the lumber industry which Morse had to consider as well. When Deputy Assistant Secretary of Commerce Peter T. Jones addressed the Junior Chamber of Commerce world trade luncheon in Portland in May 1962, he argued that unless the United States passed the TEA, it risked being shut out of trade with the European Common Market, which would have a negative ripple effect in many Oregon industries. Jones pointed out that not only would big regional lumber companies like Weyerhaeuser be hurt by a loss of access to the ECM, but smaller local businesses trading with Europe would suffer too. One such business was Key Equipment Co. of Milton-Freewater, which, it was announced at the luncheon, had been selected for a presidential award for excellence because it increased its export business from 5 percent to 23 percent of its total volume over three years. The company manufactured foam and air flotation cleaners which had been sold in Europe, Israel, and Australia, while employing "60 to 70" workers and doing $1 million in annual volume in this small city of just over 4,000 residents.[49]

In August 1962, Morse sent a letter to constituents justifying his support of the TEA. Avoiding mention of Japan, Morse argued that the United States could not afford to lose its trade advantage over the European Common Market, the maintenance of which was a key aim of the TEA. He pointed out that Oregon ran a trade surplus and contended that it risked retaliation against its exports if the TEA did not pass.[50] In the end, according to Zeiler, "Congress and the administration laid their demands on the table and reached an accommodation that addressed constituent interests, but ultimately maintained the president's drive for liberal trade."[51] The final bill passed in October, with Morse hailing a section giving the president authority "to raise tariffs or quotas on any product if he found it to be in the national interest," along with provisions to give domestic lumber preference when government agencies needed to make purchases and "expansion of forestry research at state universities."[52] The national security provision was largely ignored until it was cited by President Donald Trump in raising a variety of tariffs on China and the European Union in 2018 and 2019, a deeply unpopular move across the political and business spectrum meant to appeal to his base of voters that, like some of Morse's 1962 constituents, were hurt by international trade.

Upon entering the Senate in 1967, Mark Hatfield faced the same problem as Wayne Morse: namely, that increasing demand for logs from federal lands for domestic and foreign use led to increased prices, making it harder for small mills to buy logs to convert into finished products. In particular, Hatfield believed, prices went up because Japanese lumber firms outbid the small Oregon mills, increasing log exports to Japan. In a recollection of his early years in office, Hatfield noted that in 1966 Northwest log exports to Japan increased by one-third over 1965 levels. The logs would be shipped across the Pacific, processed in Japan, and returned to the United States as low-cost veneer, undercutting firms trying to sell locally made veneer either domestically or internationally.[53]

Like Morse, Hatfield believed the solution was to decrease—but not halt—exports of unfinished logs, encouraging the Japanese to buy more finished lumber and thereby increasing the domestic availability of raw logs. But complicating Hatfield's timber policy was the change in Oregon's timber industry as it went from being based on small firms to relying on big logging companies. Historian David Peterson del Mar relates that while the flush years immediately after World War II saw the rise of independent loggers, the 1960s and 1970s was a time of consolidation under the control of big operators like Weyerhaeuser and Georgia-Pacific. By this time independent loggers had exhausted "just about all the small stands on local farms and ranches" and did not have enough capital to bid for lumber on federal land, unlike the big operators.[54] According to Hatfield, small mills, which had no private log supplies and had to depend upon government-controlled logs, were being outbid by Japanese buyers. Yet consumers of veneer unquestionably benefited from cheaper prices, while dock workers and shipping interests in Portland handled more exports of logs to Japan and imports of finished products. While acknowledging that consumers and port workers benefited from Japanese log buyers, Hatfield sympathized with the small mill workers. One possible solution, he said, was to increase available timber from federal lands by building more access roads so small workers could penetrate even further into western forests. He called for a conference on exports involving the United States, Japan, and the state governments of Alaska, Oregon, and Washington, with timber and maritime interests represented. He argued for the US government to compel Alaska to export logs cut on public land to Japan, thereby driving prices down and making smaller timber interests more competitive.[55]

The State Department held a preliminary conference in December 1967, but Hatfield criticized the department for performing "the bare minimum of their duty." Accusing department officials of playing wartime politics, Hatfield said the department was "disposed to accede to Japanese demands on the export problem in order to buy a little support from Japan on our Vietnam policy." In response, he and Morse collaborated to bring department officials before the Small Business Committee to "force them to divulge whatever secret cartel agreements they had made with Japan that precluded giving assistance to the Oregon timber industry, or just what it was that tied their hands."[56] The end result was the Morse amendment that limited log exports off federal land.

The Morse amendment came about because it was clear by late 1967 that the stopgap measures in the TEA were failing in the face of increased lumber exports. Morse, again up for reelection, had to face the issue anew. In September, Cone Lumber Company urged Morse to halt exports of hemlock, white fir, and noble logs so that Willamette Valley mills would get relief in the face of the loss of their domestic supplies. Morse replied that he would take up their grievance with the appropriate federal officials, adding that because of his insistence, a debate on log exports was on the agenda of a US-Japan committee on trade and economics.[57] In October, Assistant Secretary of State for Congressional Relations William B. Macomber told Morse that Japanese officials had agreed to an intergovernmental meeting to look into reconciling the two nations' trade disputes, including consideration of lumber interests.[58]

Although Morse seemed to be making headway in a modest attempt to address the interests of the protectionists, he was under pressure from big lumber companies as well as small ones to obtain an actual quota on log exports. John B. Crowell Jr. of Georgia-Pacific's Portland office expressed outrage to Morse at the "apparent unpreparedness of the State Department to deal effectively with the Japanese negotiators" on log exports, saying it was important to establish quotas on Japanese log exports from the Northwest, while getting Tokyo to accept exports of manufactured wood products. Morse replied that he generally agreed with Crowell, but also thought that future bilateral negotiations needed a greater element of give-and-take than Crowell suggested. But Crowell insisted restrictions be placed on Japan's ability to buy Northwest logs, arguing that export limits would strengthen the State Department's bargaining position with Tokyo. Ultimately, Morse concluded that the department's initial talks with Japan were unproductive, leading him to push for unilateral action on export limitations along the lines Crowell suggested.[59]

In January 1968, Morse called for hearings on the impact of log exports on the Northwest economy in the subcommittee on small business retailing, distribution, and marketing, which he chaired in the Senate. The senator called for a new trade policy wherein the Japanese would take finished US lumber and not unfinished logs, but said he would settle for the immediate cessation of log exports from federal land.[60] Journalist A. Robert Smith dubbed Morse the "lumberman's pal," duly noting that no other Northwest senator had held hearings into the plight of timber workers who felt injured by timber exports, but also opining that this was an election-year ploy because timber workers were big Morse campaign contributors. Noting that Morse got the endorsement of the Industrial Forestry Association during the hearings, Smith nonetheless said the senator had reverted to "classic maverick" form, "taking up the cudgels for the wounded underdog against the bureaucratic monolith."[61] State legislator Sidney Leiken of Roseburg saw a cynical motive in Morse's maneuvering, however, claiming the senator thought big timber companies were little more than "forest raiders" and "tree burners" until election time. Leiken, a mill operator and chair of the campaign of Morse's Democratic primary challenger, Bob Duncan, said Morse once held the opposite position in the export debate. To be sure, Morse had favored increased exports from federal lands when times had been good for the timber industry. Leiken called it a "callous politically cynical appeal," adding that "Morse has played a role of absolute duplicity. He's for one thing one day, and for another the next. No one can really be sure what he stands for."[62]

Morse also faced opposition in the hearings themselves, as one federal agency after another testified in favor of expanding log exports. Deputy Assistant Secretary of State Joseph A. Greenwald repeated the old claim that the United States had to keep Japan free from dependence on the Soviet Union and thus needed to avoid any "unnecessary action which might work against amicable relations." Morse reputedly yelled "Hogwash!" in response to Greenwald's comment, retorting that the United States needed to make it clear to Tokyo that it would not be able to buy as many logs as in the past.[63] But the *Oregonian* opposed Morse in a subsequent editorial, contending the US position was understandable because of the national security concern of not wanting Japan to turn to the Soviet Union, and because the United States needed exports to alleviate growing concerns about the balance of trade. Morse needed to consider the position of Oregon exporters and ports, which were thriving at this time of increased trade.[64]

Despite these criticisms, Morse rallied popular and congressional support to his position. In his February 1968 constituent newsletter, Morse told readers that "for the first time, Japan has come to realize that her log purchases are causing a problem in the Pacific Northwest, and that she cannot expect to increase her log purchases indefinitely," crediting his hearings in the Senate Small Business Committee for pointing out to US officials the seriousness of the log export issue. Morse said that "considerable progress" was made in the talks toward getting Japan to purchase finished wood products in lieu of raw logs, and in getting US industry to pursue finished lumber purchases in the Japanese market. He reported that the talks would run for years to come and ensure both increased overall log exports, mostly of finished products, and the stabilization of Oregon's timber industry.[65] Later in the year, the "Morse amendment" to a foreign aid bill was passed, but it was far shy of the quota demanded by protectionist Oregon timber interests. This more modest measure instead merely barred Japanese raw lumber purchases of more than 350 million board feet per year from public lands. This nevertheless placated the Oregon lumber industry, and Morse even earned an election-year endorsement from the Willamina Lumber Company, which claimed the amendment would save up to 10,000 Oregon jobs.[66]

Once the 1968 general election came around, Morse won back most of the unions that had gone for primary opponent Bob Duncan or remained neutral, and even maintained crucial timber support in the primary itself, such as from the building trades and the sawmill workers.[67] Neither this support nor the foreign aid amendment was enough to save Morse in his reelection campaign, but it did create another stopgap for Oregon's timber industry in its battle for survival. It also showed Morse balancing trade and protectionist interests, negotiating a foreign aid bill amendment that limited, but did not completely bar, timber sales to Japan off federal lands.

Overall, the timber export trade grew and enriched the Northwest during the postwar years. By 1977, even with the Morse amendment restriction on federal log exports, the Port of Portland exported 275 million feet of logs and lumber, worth over $600 million in exports, and exported an additional $971.6 million in woodchips; this total of just under $1.5 billion was greater than any other product except the state's wheat exports for the year, which totaled over $3.4 billion. Other ports handled more combined logs, woodchips, lumber, wood pulp, plywood, and other wood products than wheat that year, and Japan was by far Oregon's biggest buyer of all exports, propelling the state toward a trade surplus, with nearly $1.8 billion in exports versus $1.5 billion in imports.[68] Oregon's economy seemed to benefit from the timber trade at the macro level, even though there were clearly losers at the local level.

This trend continued into the 1980s and 1990s, even as the timber industry declined relative to Oregon's economy as a whole. After Wayne Morse's 1968 reelection defeat, Bob Packwood and Mark Hatfield recognized the continued, often conjoined, importance of timber and international trade to Oregon's economy. As the timber industry slumped domestically while struggling to adjust to foreign nontariff barriers, Hatfield particularly admired individuals who cut lumber specifically tailored to the Japanese market, and encouraged businesses engaged in foreign trade to adapt to international tastes.

Instead of forcing US products abroad, Hatfield believed businesses had to determine other countries' needs and then design products for those markets. Rather than merely fighting the old Morse battle of trying to restrict unfinished lumber exports, Hatfield and his staff tried to educate the Oregon timber industry to be smarter exporters. To do business overseas, Hatfield's office urged businesses to put customers first, ahead of their product; and not to complain that the door was closed to doing business in Japan unless they were prepared to listen to what the Japanese needed first.

But did the Hatfield vision for international trade help the typical Oregonian? Democrat Harry Lonsdale challenged this notion when he ran against Hatfield in the 1990 US Senate race. Lonsdale zeroed in on Hatfield's increased support for timber exports to Japan, appealing, on the one hand, to environmentalists by saying that the state should stop clear-cutting what he called "ancient forests," and, on the other hand, to small firms by contending that, even where logging was permitted, Oregon should stop exporting unprocessed lumber to Japan. He later argued that an anti-export TV ad was decisive in making the race as close as it was. In the ad, Lonsdale said, "If the Japanese want our trees, they'll have to buy our furniture, and plywood, and finished wood products to get them."[69] Hatfield might have agreed with the sentiment, if not the stridency, of Lonsdale's message, but nuance was in short supply during a campaign in which the Democratic challenger regularly attacked many of Hatfield's policies and succeeded in making the Senate race competitive.

Logs cut by Pacific Northwest timber giant Weyerhaeuser near North Bend, Oregon, being loaded for shipment to Japan in 1990. Large logging companies like Weyerhaeuser lobbied Pacific Northwest politicians to improve US trade relations with Japan throughout the latter half of the twentieth century. Reprinted by permission from University of Oregon Special Collections, Oregon Digital, identifier OIMB_4938.

Lonsdale relentlessly pressured Hatfield on the timber issue during the campaign. In an appearance at the Portland City Club, Lonsdale spoke about wanting to change "a system where [timber company] George Weyerhaeuser exports our raw logs, and we pay for it with our jobs." The challenger argued Hatfield's timber policy hurt the state's environment and cost loggers' jobs, charging the senator was too cozy with special timber interests who wanted to export at all costs. Going even further, Lonsdale argued that "we've got to have an all-out ban on log exports now—no loopholes and no exceptions." He contended that "quick profits made by selling logs to Japan are costing us jobs. We want a total export ban, and we mean it. Not one more log and not one more job lost." Lonsdale asserted that economic inequality—wherein, he argued, one percent of the populace had more wealth than the bottom 100 million people—had much to do with unfettered free trade. He said that a Hatfield proposal to limit the export of raw Oregon logs that was similar to the Morse amendment would provide an unfair tax incentive to big timber interests like Weyerhaeuser. "It doesn't work," Lonsdale charged. "He would just give more money to George Weyerhaeuser to

keep the logs here that he's already keeping here." Noting that Weyerhaeuser made $700 million the prior year, Lonsdale noted, "That com-
pany's doing just fine, thank you. They don't need any more help from
us." He proffered that Oregon instead needed to export more "value-
added" lumber products.[70]

Lonsdale campaigned for middle- and working-class loggers and
exporters of finished lumber products. In 1988, 3.7 billion board feet of
raw logs were exported from Oregon and Washington, or 25 percent of
the total cut. A Clinton administration official noted several years later
that it was a paradox for the region's lumber supply to be dwindling, "and
at the same time you can go out to Port Angeles and see logs stacked to
the sky, as far as the eye can see, destined for mills and jobs in Japan." Yet
132 sawmills and plywood mills closed between 1990 and 1993, but not
just because jobs and mills were going to Japan: also to blame were dwindling supply and increased environmental activism, in particular, to get
forest habitat preserved for a species of spotted owl.[71] Lonsdale's attacks
on Hatfield, while not without merit, tended to simplify the timber issue
by blaming the industry's struggles on increased exports.

Hatfield battled back with spirited counterattacks to regain the
edge and, ultimately, his Senate seat. On matters of economic growth
including international trade, he emphasized personal contact with
Oregonians, avoiding partisanship, finding solutions to common problems, and trying new approaches at diversification. "Establishing and
maintaining a diversified economy will take time and a lot of just plain
hard work," Hatfield said in an *Oregonian* op-ed late in the campaign.
"Oregon's economy has been and will continue to be based on natural
resources." Hatfield slammed environmentalists who threatened log
exports, remarking, "I cannot—and will not—buy into their dream of
a utopia built on the backs of Oregon's families." In a strikingly sharp
rebuke of environmentalists, the senator accused them of being "no
more interested" in addressing difficult questions of Oregon's economic future than Congress was in accepting responsibility for the
lives of soldiers about to be deployed in the Middle East in the Gulf
War against Iraq.[72] Thanks in part to the efforts of Hatfield and Bob
Packwood to limit federal land-based exports while helping private
exports, the overall industry—if not its smallest operators—continued
to be strong into Hatfield's final term in office. As late as 1990, timber

constituted 44 percent of Oregon's manufacturing base and 28 percent of Washington's.[73]

TRADING PACIFIC NORTHWEST AGRICULTURAL GOODS

As the example of timber shows, the economic health of the Pacific Northwest was closely linked to extractive industries in the postwar years, just as it had been before World War II. High-quality agricultural commodities remained important to the region's economy as exports to the East Coast and other parts of the United States were now joined by international exports. East of the Cascade Mountains, water impounded by Grand Coulee Dam after its construction in the 1930s turned the semiarid, sagebrush plains of eastern Washington and Oregon into fields of sugar beets, potatoes, and other crops. East and west of the mountains, apple growers first planted Red and Golden Delicious trees, then switched to Granny Smith in the mid-1970s as consumer tastes changed. As American food culture expanded abroad, so did Pacific Northwest foodstuffs, as evidenced by the growing outflow of frozen French fries on Columbia River barges bound from Umatilla, Oregon, to Hong Kong and other Asian destinations.[74] Wheat was the mainstay of the extractive economy east of the Cascades, however.

During the Cold War, wheat was second to timber in rank of importance of agricultural commodities in the Pacific Northwest. Industry groups such as the Oregon Wheat Growers League led the way in rallying politicians and wheat growers to the needs of the industry, including exports. Based in the state's wheat-rich eastern side but also composed of members from the wheat-fertile Willamette Valley, the OWGL was founded in 1926 as "the first commodity organization formed in the United States for wheat."[75] The OWGL had a strong reputation for international wheat marketing, and in the 1950s it regularly visited Asia to promote Oregon wheat, pursuing congressional foreign aid legislation that favored wheat exports in exchange for currency and other imported goods. These exports played a major role in ensuring the financial prosperity of OWGL members. As executive secretary Richard K. Baum put it to Wayne Morse in 1954, "We feel this offers great possibilities for moving surplus wheat into foreign markets."[76] The efforts of the OWGL were often fruitful. Morse wrote one OWGL leader in 1958 that he learned upon a visit to Japan that many children preferred bread to the traditional Japanese staple of rice. In 1959 Morse wrote the vice president of the league to assure his continued support.[77]

Agricultural constituents in wheat and fruit were keen to get Morse and other congressional officials to support their efforts to sell their goods more widely abroad. By the 1960s, apples were becoming a particularly important export crop: according to the *Oregonian*, Oregon produced 2.6 million bushels of apples in 1963, while Washington's yield was a massive 29.2 million bushels, an increase of eight million over 1962.[78] On July 13, 1962, Morse announced that he had joined with seventeen other senators in urging the State Department to take steps to open foreign markets to US fruit exports, especially advocating for the removal of nontariff barriers on fruit exports to Europe. Morse assailed seasonal restrictions, quotas, and licensing, and what he called "unreasonable" packaging requirements. He noted that his constituents were particularly concerned that Great Britain was about to join the European Common Market, since Britain was a major consumer of US fruit, and the ECM had strong tariffs on fruit.[79] On January 23, 1963, senators from Oregon and Washington wrote to Undersecretary of State George Ball, complaining that apple growers had poor access to the French market. They charged that France prohibited imports of US apples, unless they were of "Extra" or "Fancy" quality, a determination the growers believed was meant to exclude all imports outside of the European Economic Community (the forerunner organization to the European Union). Ball replied that the US Embassy in Paris was already negotiating with France about lessening this restriction. The undersecretary said France claimed that lessening their standards for the United States would open their market to a glut of Italian apples, and in any case, they had no need for imports because of sufficient domestic supply. Ball said he would work with the embassy and through GATT to get the apple import quota lowered or removed.[80]

Henry Jackson would not let the issue drop, given that apples were one of Washington's major exports. On April 8, 1963, Jackson wrote to Ernest Falk of the Northwest Horticultural Council, indicating his strong desire for GATT to act on apple quotas after Falk had lobbied Jackson on the issue. On April 16, Jackson and Warren Magnuson wrote Special Representative for Trade Negotiations Christian Herter, urging him to act much as they had urged Ball in January. Herter responded that he shared the senators' frustration. To Herter, the French were intransigent on this issue. He promised that the US Embassy would continue to negotiate with Paris, and that the United States would also file a complaint with the Organization for Economic Cooperation and Development complaining that West Germany and Belgium were engaging in unfair trade practice to keep out Washington pears. Herter also wrote a confidential letter to Jackson saying he would recommend President Kennedy initiate trade retaliation against the French if Paris failed to take action. Even if this move were to fail, Herter assured Jackson it would show France and other countries that the United States took firm positions in trade disputes. Ultimately, the correspondence on this matter ended with a letter from Herter merely indicating that the State Department had made some headway in the negotiations with the French.[81] The exchange does show personal doggedness on the issue by Jackson; unlike with timber, there were no competing anti-export lobbies forcing Jackson to take a stand that would be unpopular to either free traders or protectionists.

These apple export negotiations with Europe were disappointing, but in 1966–67 Jackson successfully represented Washington business interests seeking to overturn a long-standing ban on the importation of Unshu oranges from Japan. On August 22, 1966, Jackson and Magnuson wrote to Secretary of Agriculture Orville Freeman, urging the easing of the restrictions by pointing out the trade and cultural benefits with Japan which could result. A letter to Jackson from a constituent who wanted the Unshu import restriction to end contended that if Canada had no import restriction of its own and its citizens had suffered no ill effects, there was no reason why Americans could not eat Unshus. Jackson was also pressured by businessman L. F. Whiteley, president of Watton Distributing Inc. in Seattle, who asked Jackson to sponsor a USDA proposal to permit imports to Washington, Idaho, and Montana.[82] On March 29, 1967, Jackson received a letter from F. A. Johnston, the director of the US Agriculture Department's Plant Quarantine Division, saying that domestic concerns about citrus canker disease in Unshus could be dealt with via a bacteriophage test, and thus affirmed that the oranges could be imported into nearly all western states.[83] On April 19, Jackson spoke at USDA hearings in Portland to recommend the easing of the Unshu ban, saying that it "seems clearly inconsistent with our national policy to encourage international trade."[84] The *Seattle Times* endorsed the end of the import ban in an editorial two days later, and the ban was finally lifted later in the year. Jackson got much of the credit, receiving personal thank you letters from exporters such as R. B. McCleary and Company Food Brokers, as well as prospective domestic Unshu dealers such as the Ken Grimes Produce Company.[85]

With regard to some Northwest agricultural products, regional politicians were aggressively pro-trade. In relationship to others, as with timber, they had to temper their free-trade enthusiasm, out of consideration for constituents looking to safeguard favored domestic industries. During the mid-1960s, Wayne Morse backed cattle interests in Oregon who perceived that they needed quota-based protection against imports, particularly from Australia and New Zealand. The *Oregonian* reported that Oregon cattle ranchers and feeders blamed imports for the sharp decline of prices for some of their animals: at the livestock yards in North Portland, prices for choice beef in December 1963 fell to a nearly seven-year low of $22.50 per steer, down from $28 a year earlier. In response, on March 6, 1964, Morse backed a Senate bill to impose beef quotas. His correspondence later that spring with the Chamber of Commerce of Milton-Freewater, a hub for cattle ranchers in eastern Oregon and southeastern Washington, indicated that the city's business leaders strongly backed quotas. Morse promised Chamber President Ray Powell that he would work with fellow Oregon Senator Maurine Neuberger and Representative Al Ullman, in whose district Milton-Freewater lay, to support additional quotas proposed by Ullman in the House. Morse even raised the issue on the Senate floor with the protectionist-sounding speech, "The Time Has Come to Protect the Interests of the American People with a Quota on Beef Imports." Morse claimed that US trading partners had failed to abide by agreed-upon stipulations when it came to beef and other agricultural products; nevertheless, he clarified that he was still in favor of reciprocal trade acts and agreements.[86]

Morse's efforts bore fruit when an import quota bill passed the Senate in the summer of 1964. Rural Oregonians were particularly thankful for his support, as expressed in letters the senator received from the head of the Morrow County Livestock Growers Association and the Baker County Livestock Association. However, the chapter of the League of Women Voters in Salem objected to the bill, arguing that it went against US free-trade ideology and would negatively affect the State Department at upcoming GATT negotiations with the European Common Market.[87] Voices like those of the LWV reflected a more pro-trade climate nationally which saw the bill get watered down by the time it got to a Senate-House conference in August. In a Senate floor speech, Morse said he would still support the final bill because he believed it was the best alternative to unfettered trade but added that he had "no tears to weep over Australia, New Zealand, and the other countries which want to flood the American market." To foreign beef exporters, Morse said, "I have one simple solution for them. It is about time we tell them to sell their beef elsewhere." He criticized the import quota bill as "by and large . . . a surface protection, and no protection in depth," calling the State Department's export policy "sordid" and a "giveaway," while railing against Australia and New Zealand, calling them "alleged allies" of the United States.[88] Congress passed the Meat Import Quota Act of 1964, which set limits on imports of unprocessed beef and veal to 15 percent below 1963 levels. A *New York Times* article criticized the move, warning that if farmers "persuade Congress to erect new discriminatory trade barriers, they will be the recipients of unjustified relief that will have to be paid by consumers." The article noted that Latin American countries, as opposed to Australia and New Zealand, suffered more from the import quotas, threatening the Kennedy-Johnson Alliance for Peace program to strengthen joint US–Latin American efforts against domestic conditions which could lead to the spread of communism.[89]

Morse nevertheless kept up the fight in 1965, supporting a Senate resolution expressing concern over the danger of hoof-and-mouth disease resulting from imports of tainted cattle. In an address to a meeting of the Red Angus Association of America in Portland that summer titled "The Peril at Our Gates," Morse argued that Canada's relaxation of import restrictions on cattle could cause hoof-and-mouth disease to spread across the continent. "The safeguards that North American cattlemen—Mexican, Canadian and American alike—are entitled to have against this ravaging plague have yet to be provided," Morse said, calling for a ban on imports of Canadian cattle during times of year in which Canada imported cows from countries with hoof-and-mouth outbreaks. The legislation died in committee, however, after objections by the State and Agriculture Departments.[90]

The senator's push for import restrictions was not just limited to beef. In 1967, Morse supported a Senate bill calling for limitations on imports of prepared or preserved strawberries. The bill stalled in the House, but Morse told a concerned constituent in June 1968 that he still hoped for consideration of the bill in Representative Al Ullman's House Ways and Means Committee, which he promised would include friendly testimony from the Oregon Strawberry Commission. The bill ultimately passed and was signed in October 1968. Morse also joined in support of a Senate bill in 1967 to ensure that the amount of ground fish imports would not exceed the average amount exported in 1963 and 1964. Morse's correspondence indicates that this was a popular, bipartisan effort also joined by Republicans like Senator Mark Hatfield, Representative Wendell Wyatt, and Governor Tom McCall. Correspondence between Morse and the administrator of the Otter Trawl Commission of Oregon in Astoria indicated Oregon fishing industry support for the bill.[91] This effort was unsuccessful, but it further depicts Morse as interested in seeking what he perceived to be reasonable limits on trade, while still upholding the ideal of commercial exchange between the Pacific Northwest and the world.

In the rural Fifth District of eastern Washington, a big concern of Tom Foley was to ensure that his district's export-dependent farmers were happy. He did this so well that during a visit to Spokane, Tsutomu Hata, a former prime minister of Japan, referred to Foley as "Mr. Wheat."[92] The farm vote was critical to tilting conservative constituents in the district toward the liberal Foley and to building his electoral base of support as he ascended the leadership ladder in Washington, DC. His position on the House Agriculture Committee and his chairmanship of the full committee from 1975 to 1980, as well as of its subcommittee dealing with grains and soybeans from 1981 to 1986, stemmed from his strategic need to keep his constituents happy and from his desire to put his interest in foreign affairs to work for his district.

The context for Foley's export-minded agriculture policy stance was the postwar national shift from production controls to export expansion to solve the problem of low commodity prices that had typically plagued US agriculture since the late nineteenth century. Historian Baodi Zhou contends that "Foley's political style of gentle persuasion and compromise, combined later with his leadership position in the Democratic Party and Congress, made him a forceful advocate of trade relations that benefited his constituents, many of whom were wheat farmers who depended heavily on exports."[93] By 1985, all of Washington's wheat was exported to Asia, a status quo that fluctuated little during Foley's years in Congress. Unlike red wheat produced by Midwestern states, Eastern Washington's soft white wheat was normally used in noodles and pastries consumed by Asians, and there was traditionally little domestic demand. Foley thus had a natural interest in expanding wheat exports: Zhou contends that Foley's policy position favoring trade over production control reflected his constituents' dependence on foreign markets, and that the congressman believed that agricultural exports trickled down to benefit the national economy as well as farmers.[94]

Recognizing the importance of wheat to his district early in his career, Foley worked in 1965 with Al Ullman, the Northwest's senior representative on the House Ways and Means Committee—which then had authority over freshmen representatives' committee assignments—to get placed on the Agriculture Committee. From there, Foley landed a spot on the Wheat Subcommittee, where he would remain for the next 22 years. One of Foley's first acts was to support the Food and Agriculture Act of 1965, which aimed in part to increase exports by reducing export bureaucracy. Foley was instrumental in enabling farmers to go longer without needing so-called export certificates, allowing them more time to plan and increase the stability of agricultural programs. This reform especially helped Northwest farmers who raised only one major crop every two years. The legislation, which had as one of its goals to increase US farm exports by 50 percent within a decade, was signed into law by President Lyndon Johnson on November 4, 1965.[95]

Foley's work saw immediate regional dividends, as there was a large increase in wheat sales from the Pacific Northwest to East and South Asia during the late 1960s and early 1970s. In January 1968, Foley announced that $7 million in Northwest white wheat would be shipped to Pakistan through local ports, a week after the US Department of Agriculture approved a $16 million, 200,000-ton shipment to India. In January 1969, Foley secured $6 million in Northwest wheat purchases for India by the USDA, shortly after Western Wheat Associates informed Foley that Japan would buy 55,000 tons of Northwest wheat for $3.5 million. A month later, Foley announced that South Korea had signed an agreement with the Commodity Credit Corporation of the USDA to buy $17 million in wheat. Foley continued to help consummate similar agreements in the years ahead, also including expanded sales to Indonesia and Iran.[96] In 1972, the guide to Congress put out by consumer advocate Ralph Nader described Foley as a "Hero on Agriculture," noting the House Agriculture Committee staff considered him "one of the most effective and able members of Congress on the committee" because of his work on behalf of farmers, which increased after redistricting ensured that he would be the representative of a greater number of farmers needing government subsidies.[97]

Foley's trade policy became more complex, however, once he assumed chairmanship of the House Agriculture Committee in 1975. In the coming decades before he lost his final bid for reelection as Speaker of the House in 1994, Foley had to balance the needs of his constituents with those of Democrats with more protectionist constituencies. During the economic recession of the mid-1970s, Zhou argues Foley had a "practical, flexible approach" toward agriculture, arguing that "when free trade would benefit the farmers, he advocated it and criticized the [Ford] administration's control policy. But he was at the same time against completely free international trade and wanted government controls when international prices were not good."[98] As Foley moved into a position of national leadership, "he increasingly felt the tension between the interests of his constituents and the demands that national leadership imposed."[99]

World food aid, a popular cause among many on Capitol Hill seeking to increase US exports of foodstuffs under the guise of foreign aid, also brought out tensions between free traders and protectionists and caused Foley some difficulty in the mid-1970s. After attending the World Food Conference in Rome in the fall of 1974, Foley reported to his constituents that actions discussed at the conference were unlikely to affect the Pacific Northwest. But Washington State Agriculture Director Stewart Bledsoe, in a speech to the Walla Walla County Association of Wheat Growers, "blasted the Rome conference," criticizing the "posturing role played by second-rate international politicians." Foley argued that the battle against world hunger would rely more on increasing output from developing countries than from the United States.[100] Eugene Moos, a farmer from Edwall, Washington, and the international trade affairs representative for the Association of Wheat Growers, also criticized the conference's aims, arguing that an increase in exports would eventually lead to the rise of food prices at home. Appearing before the Spokane Press Club in February 1975, however, Foley announced he was looking into ways to give foreign buyers credit with which to purchase food from the United States, and that he did not favor export controls. In March, Secretary of Agriculture Earl Butz allied himself with Foley and said he also favored doing away with export/import restrictions on agriculture, saying controls would harm US credibility with trade partners and damage the economies of Washington and Oregon.[101]

This balancing act worked for a time, but when Foley supported the Food and Agriculture Act of 1977, many Fifth District farmers were angry at him because they thought he had not done a good enough job in terms of keeping wheat price supports high at a time when their exports had leveled off from their high point in the early 1970s.[102] At an April 1978 town hall meeting in the Tri-Cities, Foley encountered farmers who were irate about commodity price turmoil. One farmer raged that "we hold over 50 per cent of the exportable wheat market. Dammit, we should be the cartel. WE should set the world price!" Foley responded that he theoretically favored congressional support of the cost of production for wheat farmers but warned that he did not think Congress would enact such a program because it would cause an increase in food prices. Foley said his constituents had to understand that two-thirds of House members were from urban or suburban districts sensitive to supermarket food prices and would thus reject such a plan. Overall, he said, price supports would also constitute more government intrusion into agriculture than these conservative farmers could stomach.[103]

Despite nearly losing his 1978 reelection bid in part because of the farmers' dissatisfaction, Foley continued to view export expansion as the best balance between regional and national interests. His years as House Agriculture Committee chairman saw a major increase in Pacific Northwest grain exports to China and the Soviet Union. As early as 1966, despite their strident anticommunism, Foley's constituents supported increased trade with the Soviets and the Chinese. When the United States normalized relations with China in 1979, Foley argued that Washington was well positioned to benefit from increased agricultural trade with the East Asian power. When Chinese Vice Premier Deng Xiaoping visited Washington in early 1979, Foley toured grain storage and shipping facilities in Puget Sound with him and promised that Washington would especially benefit from the opening of trade with China. Foley praised China's plans for development, noting while planning an April 1979 trip to China that Beijing wanted agricultural modernization. Other interests in the state concurred. In April 1979, Foley received a letter from Crane & Crane Growers, Packers, Shippers (of apples and pears) in the rural town of Brewster, Washington, thanking Foley for helping his company obtain visas to travel to China for business. That fall he received a letter from Cathay Imports in Spokane, thanking him for his efforts to lift restrictions on the export of Washington apples to China. During the summer of 1979, Foley met with top Chinese officials in Beijing, and upon returning home, he reported progress in trade talks he said were of vital interest to the Pacific Northwest. The congressman said he was particularly pleased with efforts by Western Wheat Associates and the US Department of Agriculture to set up a pilot bakery project in Beijing to grow China's demand for wheat, as had been accomplished with Japan in the 1960s. Although Foley warned that exporters should not expect miracles in the short term, he (correctly) predicted that exports would grow over the long run.[104]

TRADE PROMOTION

The Northwest congressional delegation also tried to increase exports and attract new foreign trade clients by boosting regional trade fairs. A few notable early examples included the Japan Trade Fair in Seattle in 1951, the Centennial Exposition in Portland in 1959, and the Seattle World's Fair in 1962. Warren Magnuson was instrumental in supporting the Japan Trade Fair, even traveling to Japan as a goodwill ambassador to drum up interest in the fair. Though unsuccessful in getting top State Department officials to attend, he was praised by fair organizers for pushing a bill through Congress allowing fair-related materiel to be shipped from Japan to Seattle duty-free, contributing to the fair's success. Twenty-two foreign countries were represented at the Centennial Exposition eight years later, which featured an international garden that included a Japanese tea house. Despite Governor Mark Hatfield's efforts, however, the fair drew only 1.5 million visitors; hoping for a bigger turnout, Magnuson netted a $10 million appropriation for federal support for the 1962 Century 21 World's Fair. The funding, which matched bonds and funds raised by the city of Seattle and the Washington State Legislature, was crucial, according to biographer Shelby Scates, who argues the exhibition would have failed otherwise. In the end, the fair dwarfed Portland's effort, drawing 9.6 million visitors and 35 countries as exhibitors, although the Soviet Union declined to participate amid poor US-Soviet relations just after the construction of the Berlin Wall and leading up to the Cuban Missile Crisis.[105] These efforts did help, however, to put the Northwest on the map as a major international trade destination.

Even amid growing concerns about the effects of global trade on some industries in the United States, the Washington delegation worked in the early 1970s to obtain funding for relatively small Spokane to host a world's fair of its own. On September 22, 1972, Jackson and Magnuson put forth a bill to provide $11.5 million in appropriations for the fair, arguing it would "encourage tourist travel in and to the United States, stimulate foreign trade, and promote cultural exchanges."[106] Senator J. William Fulbright of Arkansas, the chair of the Senate Foreign Relations Committee and a frequent Jackson opponent on foreign policy issues—especially the Vietnam War—wrote in an SFRC report that most of the committee favored the bill, but he charged the Washington senators with "underwriting civic improvements under the guise of participating in international expositions," calling the bill "an insult to the taxpayer." Fulbright argued that $11.5 million was "a great sum which could be better utilized in more ways than I have time to list" and sarcastically suggested that "if, indeed, the Federal Government needs more office space in Spokane, it can go through the proper channels in Congress and justify its request." Fulbright called the Spokane project an "alleged fair," arguing near the end of his report that "this proposal is not even 'international' in the true sense of the word. Only four countries to date have been willing to commit themselves to participate." Jackson retorted that since the United States had "recently concluded certain agreements with the Soviet Union on the environment" it could use the Spokane exposition to hold Moscow's feet to the fire on their

Visitors peruse Expo '74, the first environmentally-themed world's fair, in Spokane, Washington, in 1974. Senator Henry Jackson and Representative Tom Foley successfully pursued federal funding to help bring the fair to Spokane. Reprinted by permission from Washington State University Manuscripts, Archives, & Special Collections; Thomas S. Foley Papers.

promises. Only by supporting the Spokane world's fair, Jackson said, "can we demonstrate our deep commitment to make this country and the world a better place in which to live."[107] In the end, the Northwest delegation carried the day, and President Nixon signed the bill into law on October 27, 1972, with the $11.5 million appropriation intact.[108]

Perhaps no regional politician had a bigger stake in the success of the Spokane world's fair than Tom Foley, in whose district the fair would take place. Spokane businesses pushed Foley to support the fair, and he worked hard not to disappoint them. Foley took part in the contentious hearings on funding for the fair and increased his reputation for statesmanship as he rose above the feud between Jackson and Fulbright. The congressman testified before the SFRC that "there appears to be no doubt that Expo-74 will attract the participation of both our major trading partners and those with whom we are especially hopeful of establishing such a relationship."[109] On the House side, Foley showed that Spokane was all-in on the fair, testifying to the Foreign Affairs Subcommittee on International Organizations and Movements that the city had raised $5.7 million in local taxes, received $6.8 million in business contributions, and obtained millions more dollars in donations from local railroad interests. Impressed by Foley's performance and by the commitment of the people of Spokane, the bill passed the House by unanimous consent on its way to Nixon's desk.[110]

Foley's vision and passion for the Spokane exposition drew praise as the fair approached. Local journalist Dorothy Powers—ironically a former Foley foe as his Republican opponent for Congress in 1966—glowed about the fair in United Airlines' official magazine distributed to advertise the fair to international travelers. Fair general manager Petr L. Spurney told Powers's readers that "for 180 days, Spokane will be the entertainment capital of the world," with Czechoslovakian live actors, Taiwanese musicians, "folklore" groups from Brazil and the Soviet Union, along with French, German, and Russian food vendors. Spurney promised "international pavilions" by the Soviet Union, Japan, Taiwan, South Korea, Canada, Mexico, France, Australia, Iran, West Germany, and the Philippines. Powers reported that two hundred Russians would live in Spokane during the fair and would be accessible to Americans who wished to meet them. Referring to the fair's major theme of environmentalism, she noted that a proposed environmental symposium series was expected to attract world leaders for a multinational discussion of environmental matters. The fair's architect, furthermore, had "given the city a legacy of incredible beauty" with new trees and "rechanneled water" from the Spokane River that would outlast the fair. Addressing concerns that Spokane was the smallest city to ever host a world's fair, Powers contended that Spokane countered its small size with its geographic location, arguing that it looked "north to the grandeur of Canada's British Columbia and Alberta, and west to the Pacific Ocean."[111] Foley himself worked extensively to promote the fair both internationally and at home. In March 1974 he issued a press release inviting the media to a cocktail reception hosted by the Washington congressional delegation and fair organizers to a kickoff event to acquaint them with the exposition. A major selling point in the release touted that Spokane would mark the first Soviet participation in a world's fair since 1939, a feat not even achieved by Seattle's 1962 fair. As late as April, Foley continued to try to woo countries to participate in the exposition, writing to the Norwegian Secretary of Commerce, the Norwegian ambassador to the United Nations, and its ambassador to the United States, urging them to attend.[112]

The fair, known popularly as Expo '74, ran from May 4 to November 3, 1974, and was ultimately attended by ten countries, including Japan and the Soviet Union. Once it was underway, reviews were often critical, mirroring the dim mood of a country in the midst of an energy crisis and the Watergate scandal engulfing President Richard Nixon's administration. The conservative *Washington Star*, perhaps predisposed to be critical of a fair that was heavily subsidized by the government, reported that a Washington state official reputedly said of Expo '74 that "the whole thing's embarrassing." The *Star* said fair organizers were only anticipating five million visitors in six months, while the most recent world's fair in Osaka, Japan, had aimed for a million visitors *per day*. Despite poor initial public response to the announcement of the fair, new city taxes and "the local wealth chipped in" to get it off the ground. But, the *Star* reported, it would only have twenty exhibitors, "half of them domestic," and much of it second-rate in the eyes of the paper. "Thrown into the entertainment galaxy," the *Star* noted caustically, "along with the likes of Bob Hope and Ella Fitzgerald, is a, gulp, 'Junior League Rummage Sale.'" Echoing J. William Fulbright's criticism, the piece cynically concluded that "even if the fair flops, Spokane profits" because of major new investment into the city's downtown, railroad terminal, and hospital.[113]

On the left side of the political spectrum, civil rights activists also disapproved of the Spokane world's fair effort. Some in the city's black community believed none of the fair-related infrastructural investments would directly benefit them. Between two and three thousand blacks called Spokane home, and this small community suffered decades of job and housing discrimination and segregation from the white community. By the time of the fair, blacks had made some progress toward better jobs and equality under the law thanks to court challenges led by the local NAACP branch. Lawyer Carl Maxey headed a coalition named Concerned Black Citizens which challenged Expo '74 organizers and the Spokane City Council to also support a housing authority, reasoning that funding should be diverted to improving the city's housing situation for black and poor community members. This was not the first time Carl Maxey had challenged the aims of liberal Pacific Northwest politicians: in 1970, he ran a quixotic campaign for the Democratic nomination for the Senate against Henry Jackson. Maxey challenged Jackson's record on civil rights and his support for the Vietnam War, but earned a meager 13 percent of the vote against the hugely popular senator. Once again, Maxey's efforts came to naught in the world's fair conflict. City officials shrugged off the concerns of the black community, arguing that the urban renewal would remove a blighted train yard and create a riverfront park in its place. An opera house and convention center were also constructed that lasted beyond the exposition, but there were no improvements in housing for poor blacks. In the end, however, historian Dwayne Mack argues that "Maxey's misgivings about funding the Expo in lieu of the city's housing crisis were valid because the city failed to turn a profit and instead accrued a deficit."[114]

Expo '74 not only disappointed some residents, but apparently some visitors as well. The *International Herald Tribune* noted that the fair attracted what the paper considered a tepid 20,000 visitors per day in its opening week, even reporting that some conservationists called the environmentally minded fair "a disgraceful commercial sellout." The *Tribune* argued that visitors interviewed at random appeared to agree with a Beaverton, Oregon, man named Oscar Indal that "there's not too much here about the environment I didn't know before, but it's a real nice fair." The article noted that "visitors find displays that range from sobering messages on man's mutilation of nature to sales pitches for recreational vehicles." In the end, most of the visitors interviewed said they were impressed by the Soviet exhibition, despite it conspicuously lacking a major contribution to the environmental movement. While the Soviet Union claimed it started thinking about environmental conservation from the time of the Bolshevik Revolution, the *Tribune* noted that a pavilion on alternative energy omitted the environmental problems of the strip mining prevalent in the country, adding that "no major environmental protection groups have exhibits." Attending Soviets took time to chastise American hypocrisy on the environment as well: amid the roar of B-52s taking off and landing at nearby Fairchild Air Force Base, a Soviet journalist quipped that "it is a great irony . . . an environmental fair down here and that thing that destroyed the environment of Vietnam up there."[115]

In all, Expo '74 dissenters raised good points, but the fair did nothing to harm the Pacific Northwest delegation and remained a particularly popular aspect of the legacy of Tom Foley. Dorothy Powers declared the day of the opening of the fair to be "the greatest day in Spokane's history."[116] The *Spokane Spokesman-Review* reported that "a palpable feeling of cynicism and criticism" among reporters was replaced by praise once the media was let into the fair for the first time.[117] Despite the fact that it did end up in a budget deficit, exposition general manager Petr Spurney said that nearly 5.2 million people visited in all, more than the five million he was hoping for.[118] After the fair closed down, the grounds, which had once consisted of railroad tracks and warehouses, were converted into Riverfront Park, arguably accomplishing the fair's main task of cleaning up Spokane and making it a more cosmopolitan, vibrant city. In terms of its economics, the fair made up its deficit when the corporation that organized Expo '74 called in the pledges made by local donors earlier in the decade. The donors were happy to pay up, since they ended up collecting interest on the bonds they paid to help finance the fair.[119] In the end, Expo '74 was clearly a success, if not an unqualified triumph, and it exposed more Pacific Northwesterners to the world—and vice versa.

CONCLUSION

Pacific Northwest senators and representatives between 1945 and 1981 were, in a general sense, in favor of increasing the region's relationship with the world, whether via projecting American hard power by expanding the region's military bases, or soft power, through pushing regional exports. They joined most of their counterparts in Congress in this attitude. The internationalization of the Pacific Northwest did not, of course, work out for the benefit of all. Constituent pressure made the delegation consider the needs of protectionists in some notable cases, particularly those of small timber operators and cattle ranchers, as world prices for their products dropped in the midst of the global economic recovery from World War II. These constituents were susceptible to foreign competition and were not shy about soliciting help from their elected officials when they felt it was in their best interest. The pro-international trade paradigm was thus generally accepted, yet circumstantially embattled in the Pacific Northwest, as throughout the United States, even before the poor economic climate of the 1970s and the early 1980s. Those who helped elect Ronald Reagan in 1980 pushed for a more belligerent foreign economic policy. Angry at foreigners who they perceived as taking their jobs and outsourcing longtime American staple industries like textiles, cars, and timber, Americans in the 1980s increasingly challenged the post–World War II international order that

Wayne Morse, Henry Jackson, and Warren Magnuson among others had done so much to build, one that had encouraged the growing of ties among the countries of the free world to bolster global security against communism. Despite the passage of these congressional leaders from the political arena, the reality remained that the majority of those living in Oregon and Washington relied on international trade to one degree or another for economic sustenance. The following decades would not only see a growth in trade under the leadership of a younger generation of politicians, but the rise of a new internationalism in the Pacific Northwest.

CHAPTER 5

Nintendo Power: The Growth of Foreign Direct Investment and International Trade in the Pacific Northwest Since 1981

By the time Ronald Reagan was inaugurated president of the United States on January 20, 1981, Wayne Morse was dead, Edith Green and Warren Magnuson were out of office, and Henry Jackson—just two years away from his own death—was in the minority as Republicans took control of the Senate. The power of Pacific Northwest politicians to help their region appeared badly eroded. These politicians had understood that, despite some exceptions, encouraging foreign trade and cultural exchange would improve the region, as Oregon and Washington joined other parts of the United States in starting to see tangible results from global outreach in the postwar decades. In the Reagan years and beyond, however, a few Northwest politicians were able to build an increasing base of local support for increasing global links while battling growing anti-trade sentiment among the American public at large. Three members of the Northwest delegation—Senators Slade Gorton and Mark Hatfield, and Representative Tom Foley—were particularly successful in revitalizing the region's economy through improving its trade links, especially with Pacific nations like Japan.

FIGHTING THE TIDE? THE NORTHWEST VS. AMERICA ON TRADE IN THE 1980S

The context for the growth of international trade between the Pacific Northwest and the world in the late twentieth century was the development of a Janus-faced mentality on the part of Americans regarding foreign relations. On the one hand, state governments and businesses were increasingly keen to grow both trade and foreign investment. On the other hand, however, many Americans saw danger in the growth of foreign trade, which accelerated in the 1960s not only thanks to the Trade Expansion Act, but the success of the Kennedy round of negotiations among the signatories to the General Agreement on Tariffs and Trade. Western European nations and Japan had not only found their footing, but had started to take off, now that World War II was far in the rearview mirror, and they were increasingly making products that Americans wanted. Economic historian Douglas Irwin argues that "this was simply a return to normal conditions of competition. The immediate postwar position of the US economy as the world's sole industrial power was unsustainable." Of course, the fact that "the growing economic strength of Europe and Asia was not only inevitable but desirable did not make the experience any less painful for some domestic producers," especially in the US automobile and textile industries, which came under the heaviest siege from foreign imports. "Having grown accustomed to operating in a world without serious foreign competition," Irwin contends, "many industries and their workers were now forced to adapt to a new situation."[1]

As exports picked up from Europe and Asia, the United States started to run trade deficits in the early 1970s for the first time since the Great Depression. President Richard Nixon's administration in particular took notice when the Williams Commission on International Trade & Investment Policy concluded in July 1971 that the United States needed to push Europe and Japan to accept more American exports. Nixon's Secretary of the Treasury, John Connally, apparently urged a more belligerent approach. "My philosophy is that the foreigners are out to screw us," Connally told Nixon. "Our job is to screw them first."[2] In particular, Connally went after Japan, arguing that "they have built up tariff arrangements, they have built up trade restrictions against US goods," that the Japanese people were more industrious than Americans, and that "many other nations" were "out-producing us, out-thinking us and out-trading us." The president's response was classic Nixon: "We'll fix those bastards." He went on to impose a temporary 10 percent "border tax" on US imports. Upon reflection, ever mindful of his place and that of the nation in history, the president concluded that "the US cannot build a fence around itself and expect to survive as a great nation" and later supported the Trade Act of 1974, which passed Congress after his resignation from office.[3] Despite rumblings of discontent from members of Congress affected by imports of textiles, shoes, and televisions, among other heavily consumed products that were being made more cheaply overseas in these years, presidents after Nixon mainly resorted to voluntary export restraint agreements with individual nations whose products were adversely affecting American producers.

When the US economy went into recession from 1979 to 1982, however, calls grew nationally for import restrictions. As a result, the Reagan administration imposed a variety of nontariff trade restrictions on imports. By 1984, the share of US imports affected by some sort of trade restriction rose to 21 percent from just 8 percent in 1975.[4] Senator John Danforth of Missouri was especially keen to impose restrictions on Japanese automobile imports, a national symbol of American economic turmoil in the early 1980s, as this iconic sector shed thousands of jobs. In lieu of an import restriction bill introduced by Danforth, the Reagan administration got Japan to voluntarily agree to limit its vehicle exports for much of the 1980s.[5] This was not enough for many in Congress. In 1983, Speaker of the House Tip O'Neill declared, "President Reagan seems willing to preside over the de-industrialization of America. We in Congress are not." The next year, 600 bills relating to international trade were introduced, including a radical proposal by Congressman Richard Gephardt to put a 25 percent surcharge on imports from Japan, Taiwan, South Korea, and Brazil.[6]

None of these bills went anywhere in Congress, but restrictionist pressure continued and became more widespread as the decade went on. Analysts outside of government, including journalist Theodore White and economists Chalmers Johnson and Pat Choate, warned Americans about the rise of Japan, by now the second-largest economy in the world and a heavy purchaser of American dollars and market share in the 1980s in industries from film to video games to real estate. Their views ranged from Johnson's laudatory take on the connections between Japanese industry and government to Choate's worries about the supposed dangers of links between US lobbyists for Japan and supposedly devious Japanese businessmen.[7] New York hotel magnate Donald Trump, then just emerging onto the national scene, got attention with an antiforeigner speech to the Portsmouth, New Hampshire, Rotary Club in October 1987 during the run-up to the Republican presidential primary. In September Trump had spent nearly $100,000 on a full-page ad featured in the *New York Times, Washington Post,* and *Boston Globe* declaring that "for decades, Japan and other nations have been taking advantage of the United States." Thrilled by Trump's get-tough rhetoric, the conservative organizers of the Rotary event hoped he would run for president, and while Trump declined, he still gave a stem-winding speech to a cheering crowd. "It makes me sick," Trump said, as he bemoaned that the United States was "being kicked around" by countries like Japan, Saudi Arabia, and Kuwait. Calling for them to pay back America's entire trade deficit, Trump warned, "I'm tired of nice people already in Washington. . . . I want someone who is tough and knows how to negotiate. If not, our country faces disaster." He warned the gathering, "If the right man doesn't get into office, you're going to see a catastrophe in this country in the next four years like you're never going to believe. And then you'll be begging for the right man." The gathering packed the restaurant where the Rotary held its meetings to the tune of 500 people, far exceeding the local organization's total membership of 300 members. The crowd enthusiastically cheered Trump on numerous occasions, showing the strength of belligerent words and ideas about international trade that would resonate not merely among conservatives, but across the political spectrum in the United States for decades to come.[8]

By the 1980s, the Pacific Northwest stood to lose from import restrictions and belligerence toward American allies and trading partners. Forty percent of US imports came in from Asia by that point, up from 17 percent in the 1950s, and much of the cargo was handled in West Coast ports like Portland, Seattle, Tacoma, and other smaller regional points of entry. As textiles, footwear, and steel were increasingly imported, growing exports of electrical machinery, aerospace equipment, and semiconductors came from the US West, including Pacific Northwest cities. By 1990, 32 percent of workers in the West worked in industries sensitive to exports, the highest share of any region in the United States. The country's grain belt, meanwhile, which included eastern Washington and Oregon, feared retaliation against their exports if the United States continued down the road of import restrictions.[9] Both exporters and foreign companies investing in the Northwest—employing thousands of local residents—counted on their political representatives to improve or at least maintain the status quo, despite occasionally fierce opposition to pro-trade policies.

FOREIGN DIRECT INVESTMENT: SENATOR SLADE GORTON HELPS NINTENDO OF AMERICA

In the early 1980s, Japanese entrepreneur Minoru Arakawa arrived in the Pacific Northwest, settling initially in Vancouver, British Columbia, before moving to Seattle. Arakawa was the first president of Nintendo of America (NOA), a video game distribution company striving to compete in the US market. The fledgling company's New York warehouse was unsuccessful because Nintendo headquarters in Kyoto, Japan, was a fourteen-hour time difference from Manhattan, meaning any conversation with the home office required either headquarters or the American distributor to work outside of normal business hours. Arakawa determined, however, that moving to a new warehouse in the Seattle suburb of Tukwila would not only enable more convenient long-distance business meetings, but also speed up shipment times of Nintendo games, while allowing his family to be closer to Japan via a nonstop flight. Arakawa started by employing two truckers, Al Stone and Ron Judy, who were importing and reselling wooden cabinets from Hawaii housing Nintendo arcade games.[10] Stone and Judy were beneficiaries of the expansion of international trade in the region: tired of their earlier work for large companies, the two men started a trucking company in Seattle. Seeing the growth in the video game industry in the 1970s and 1980s, they formed Far East Video to sell Nintendo games, which were making "obscene profits," when they joined up with Arakawa.[11]

Arakawa chose Seattle not just because it was near Japan: the Seattle area was also attractive because it could draw from a labor pool—much of it educated at the University of Washington—from nearby Boeing and other high-technology companies. Don James, a UW graduate with a degree in industrial design, was hired to manage the first NOA warehouse in Tukwila. Howard Phillips, who carpooled during elementary school with Microsoft co-founder Bill Gates, was James's first employee, initially hired to uncrate Nintendo games shipped from Kyoto to Tukwila. When NOA installed a game called Donkey Kong in a local bar, the Spot Tavern, it quickly became a huge hit, as people lined up to play the game locally and eventually across the country. While the games' motherboards, power supply, and unassembled cabinets came from Japan, the American workers at NOA assembled the consoles, re-crated and loaded the games onto trucks, and sent them to distributors throughout the country. In 1982, Arakawa bought sixty acres of land in the suburb of Redmond and moved NOA there. Once a timber town, Redmond's logs were clear-cut in the 1920s, but it enjoyed a revival in the late twentieth century as home to NOA, Microsoft, and other high-tech companies.[12]

With Nintendo's move to home entertainment with the Nintendo Entertainment System in 1985 and Super Nintendo in 1991, NOA dominated the US video game market and was a major part of a high-tech boom in the Pacific Northwest. But when it joined a venture to purchase the Seattle Mariners, the city's Major League Baseball fran-chise, in 1992, Nintendo encountered scrutiny, despite the success of its American distributor, whose Redmond presence nominally made the Mariners' purchase a homegrown effort. In an era when Japan was considered by some a feared competitor of the United States in the global economy, Nintendo became "a tennis ball in the election-year face-off between the United States and Japan, with epithets volleying back and forth." Focusing on Nintendo's Kyoto headquarters and ignor-ing NOA, MLB Commissioner Fay Vincent argued, "We had to keep *something* sacred, out of the grips of Japan," stating that no non–North American interest should control a major league team.[13]

Nintendo president Hiroshi Yamauchi agreed to share the Mari-ners with local backers, including Microsoft executive Chris Larson, chairman of Puget Power John Ellis, and Boeing CEO Frank Shrontz. But Vincent remained stubborn despite Yamauchi's offer to give his voting interest in Nintendo to Arakawa, by then a longtime resident of the Seattle area (in sharp contrast with then-Mariners owner Jeff Smu-lyan, who had never lived in the Northwest). Many citizens, politicians, and businessmen in Seattle and throughout the state were outraged at Vincent's intransigence. The Japanese press believed Nintendo was the victim of Japan-bashing in America.[14] *New York Times* Seattle corre-spondent Timothy Egan wrote that angry fans pointed out the hypoc-risy, even racism, of MLB's policy allowing Canadians, but not Japanese, to own a team. According to Egan, "a majority" of television and sports radio call-ins supported the Mariners' proposed sale to Yamauchi and his co-investors, but Vincent nonetheless contended baseball had "a strong policy against approving investors from outside the United States and Canada."[15] The commissioner defended himself by arguing that "people equate baseball policy with my personal view . . . it is my job to articulate baseball's policy."[16]

The situation seemed dire for NOA until Senator Slade Gorton stepped into the fray. During the mid-1980s, Gorton chaired the Merchant Marine Subcommittee, firmly aligning himself with the pro-trade bloc in Congress. In 1983, he was upset with Washington congressional delegation members who voted for a bill that would require US-made parts in foreign cars. "For every two jobs it might save it would cost three jobs elsewhere, many of them in the West," Gorton argued. Nearly 25 percent of the state's jobs were considered export-dependent, the highest in the United States at that point. Imports to the Seattle customs district had increased from under $1 billion in 1970 to $10 billion in 1981, while exports went from just under $2 billion in 1970 to $13 billion in 1981.[17]

Gorton thus had a lot riding on Pacific Rim businesses like Nintendo of America. In 1983, the senator, with the support of the Port of Seattle and the Washington State Horticultural Association, pushed an Ocean Shipping Act through the Senate Commerce Committee that deregulated the ocean shipping industry. Opposing Democrats warned that consumers would pay higher prices by having the fleet more Americanized. Gorton's biographer John Hughes argues, however, that the Shipping Act of 1984 ultimately helped the overall shipping industry and Washington interests, representing a major triumph for the senator. During his Senate career Gorton also supported permanent most-favored-nation trade status for China—which later surpassed Japan as the Pacific Northwest's top trading partner—seeing it ultimately approved by Congress just before he left office in 2000. Gorton also favored the North American Free Trade Agreement, strengthening US trade ties with Canada and Mexico. Like his predecessors Warren Magnuson and Henry Jackson, Gorton also helped Boeing make deals with foreign customers for its aircraft, working "hard for the almost 100,000 Washington state families who work at Boeing and rely on aircraft sales."[18]

Washington Senators Slade Gorton and Henry Jackson, seated and flanked by their wives Sally Clark Gorton and Helen Hardin Jackson, while signing a document in the Senate Office Building in Washington, DC, on April 21, 1982. After Jackson's death, Gorton followed in his predecessor's steps in aiding congressional efforts to secure more international trade opportunities for Washington. Reprinted by permission from University of Washington Special Collections, Henry M. Jackson Papers, Accession 3560, negative no. UW 28890.

It was natural that Gorton would aid Nintendo's effort to purchase the Mariners. By 1992, Nintendo of America was a major local employer, providing 1,400 jobs in the Redmond area. During Gorton's first term, he helped Nintendo protect its intellectual property rights, at one point pushing US Customs and the Federal Bureau of Investigation to crack down on counterfeiters of its popular Donkey Kong game. Gorton had sought Japanese investment in the Mariners as early as 1987, and when the prospect of Smulyan moving the Mariners arose, Gorton met with NOA chief Minoru Arakawa about the possibility of Nintendo purchasing a stake in the team. Arakawa was initially uninterested, believing the Mariners were a bad investment, but nonetheless met with Nintendo's top political ally for nearly two hours. Nintendo president Hiroshi Yamauchi ultimately overruled Arakawa, acknowledging that Gorton had long been a friend of Nintendo and believing that even if the Mariners proved to be a bad investment, he had to help his Senate ally. Yamauchi ultimately offered $100 million toward the purchase price for the Mariners. Gorton knew he had to work against anti-Japanese sentiment in the United States, and he was instrumental in cobbling together the mostly American Mariners ownership group announced on January 23, 1992. When Fay Vincent made clear his complaints about Yamauchi, the Nintendo chief offered to reduce his stake in the team to mollify the MLB commissioner. Gorton was ashamed at the thinly guised anti-Japanese veneer put on by Vincent, while Howard Lincoln, Arakawa's top US deputy at NOA, said he was "pissed off" at the disrespect shown to his boss. In addition to Gorton, the Washington State Senate, Governor Booth Gardner, and Seattle Mayor Norm Rice all supported the Nintendo-led bid.[19]

Local public opinion also defended the sale to the coalition of investors, now called the Baseball Club of Seattle. The *Oregonian* endorsed the sale in a January 26 editorial, noting the number of local jobs provided by NOA, Arakawa's local residency, and the diversity in the Baseball Club. The paper noted that the ownership group would terminate the team's escape clause in its lease with the Kingdome, the Mariners' home stadium, and give local buyers the first opportunity to purchase the team should the group ever decide to sell. The paper chided Vincent's North American–only ownership policy as outdated, and hinted that Gorton might launch an investigation into whether Vincent's attempts to block the sale constituted a violation of Major League Baseball's exemption from federal antitrust laws giving it a monopoly over professional baseball in the United States. The editorial concluded that not only would Nintendo-led ownership be good for Seattle baseball fans, it would help the game, too, by stimulating Japanese market interest in the game that could benefit other teams as well as the Mariners.[20] In a similar vein, Seattle resident Steven Kendall wrote to the *New York Times* arguing that Vincent should "quit his public, crypto-racist posturing about the inclusion of Japanese money . . . and present the plan to owners for approval, without public or private interference" or face a lawsuit in federal district court "for discrimination based on color and national origin."[21]

Gorton, meanwhile, worked to save the deal. The senator told the *Seattle Times* that if Texas Rangers owner George W. Bush did not back the purchase, he would be reluctant to help President George H. W. Bush during his reelection campaign. The younger Bush ultimately convinced MLB that the purchase was good for the game, while his father, President Bush, sought good US-Japan relations despite continued worries by some Americans.[22] On January 30, 1992, Bush met with Japanese Prime Minister Kiichi Miyazawa and reassured him that "US-Japan relations are in good shape." They discussed a return visit for Miyazawa in May, regarding which Bush said, "The more the American people see you and hear from you the better. I want to keep on track. Please do not get discouraged by election year politics. . . . The relationship is important and we want to keep it on track."[23] On May 1, Bush had a friendly meeting with Japanese Minister of Trade and Industry Kozo Watanabe about sustaining the Uruguay Round of the General Agreement on Tariffs and Trade talks.[24] The week before, Bush had signed the Paper Market Access Agreement designed to "increase opportunities and sales for foreign firms exporting paper products into Japan," including US firms. The treaty, Bush argued, represented a "step toward our two countries becoming equal partners in trade."[25]

Gorton told George W. Bush that the sale was not part of a Japanese plot to take over baseball, and later believed that this was a decisive factor in gaining the support of both Bushes. To sell the deal to a still-skeptical Fay Vincent, however, Yamauchi's ownership stake was reduced to 49 percent, making Americans the majority controlling share. On June 11, 1992, MLB owners voted overwhelmingly in favor of the deal.[26] Seeking to save face and seeing few suitors for the Mariners, Vincent claimed he needed to push the sale forward for the good of professional baseball. Vincent pointed out that the mostly US composition of the Baseball Club prevented this from being a sale to a non-US entity. "When the Japanese bought Columbia Pictures, a company I used to work for, they bought it all," he said. "Here, the non–North American investment is less than control. The control remains solidly in Seattle."[27] In the end, former Puget Power CEO John Ellis became chairman of the Mariners, leading the *New York Times* to sarcastically note that "baseball has shown uncommon statesmanship in permitting a Japanese millionaire to invest a considerable amount of money but apparently none of his expertise in the ailing Seattle franchise."[28]

Despite the contentious nature of the deal, when the Mariners' sale went through, "Nintendo was viewed as a savior in a town that had been frustrated by the large company's lack of involvement in local society and philanthropy" up to that point.[29] The sale also represented positive relations between Nintendo and a respected US senator in an era when Congress regularly questioned both video game violence and trade with Japan. The Mariners, meanwhile, had their most on-field success in franchise history over the next decade, with American stars like Ken Griffey Jr., as well as Japanese imports Kazahiro Sasaki and Ichiro Suzuki, helping to power the regional economy. In large part due to Gorton's intervention, Nintendo and the Mariners remain mainstays of the Pacific Northwest and brand names worldwide. The Nintendo battle is emblematic of work Northwest politicians undertook during the late twentieth century to strengthen international trade through the region, despite increasing public skepticism about the benefits of both the federal government and the worldwide movement toward a freer flow of peoples and goods that was by now known as globalization.

TOM FOLEY FACES CONSERVATIVE CHALLENGES TO FREE TRADE

In 1988, Marlyn Derby was the latest Republican challenger to try to unseat Congressman Tom Foley, who was by that time the House Majority Leader and perhaps the most influential federal voice on behalf of Washington State. In what was becoming a familiar attack upon Democratic incumbents, Derby went after Foley for sponsoring wasteful federal spending. While the congressman did tout the ways in which federal spending aided the Washington Fifth District, press secretary Jeffrey Biggs argued that another key in the campaign—which ended with a blowout reelection victory—was that Foley "emerged as the one Northwest leader capable of putting in a plug for agricultural products with Japanese Prime Minister Noboru Takeshita" at a time when support for protectionist measures against Japanese trade was at its peak among Congress and the US public.[30] During the 1980s and 1990s, Foley was perhaps the most prominent pro-trade congressman in an era where protectionist voices were particularly loud within his Democratic Party.

As the Northwest's economy slumped along with the rest of the nation during the 1980s, Foley pushed for the expansion of trade into and out of Washington as a compensatory measure. In April 1982, Foley unveiled a plaque at the new Spokane administration building for Cominco Electronics, whose parent company was a Canadian mining company. The electronics division produced gold and aluminum wires for microchips and would employ 700 Spokane residents.[31] In 1985, Foley plugged a proposed Washington International Agricultural Trade Center for Spokane, telling Mayor James Chase that it would be "enormously helpful" in deepening export trade out of the region, noting that "aggressive export" had already met with success. "Given our current national trade deficit, the growth of foreign competitors, and the increased aggressiveness of other nations in invading markets traditionally viewed as our own, the establishment of the proposed center would give our region a much-needed new instrument to develop new markets and expand those that have been so hard won in past years," said Foley.[32] Thanks in part to Foley's efforts, the trade center ultimately opened in 1989.[33]

Cultural exchange was also an important element in the expansion of ties between Foley's district and the world. In September, Robert Allen Skotheim, the president of Whitman College in Walla Walla, urged Foley to write to the Toyota Corporation in Japan to thank them for donating $50,000 to the Japanese Studies program at Whitman. Skotheim relayed the benefits the donation had on Foley's district in terms of cultural exchange. "It is very important that young people of our area with leadership potential be educated about Japan, its culture, history and economy, as well as its language," Skotheim said. "Your continuing support of this new program serves many interests well." Foley apparently agreed, for he promptly forwarded the letter to Toyota president Eiji Toyoda.[34]

As he ascended the ranks of leadership in the House in the mid-1980s, Foley tried to balance protectionist impulses in Congress with his own pro-trade ideology and generally pro-trade constituency in eastern Washington. But federal lawmakers also faced pressure to combat growing US trade and budget deficits. In the Midwest, meanwhile, where layoffs hit the automobile industry and red wheat farmers (as opposed to the white wheat exporters common in the Northwest) suffered from falling commodity prices, support grew for a new US trade policy that would pressure foreign markets to end their own discriminatory trade practices, as well as for more dramatic measures like retaliatory tariffs or quotas that Foley feared would start a trade war. In May 1986, the House passed a bill with an amendment by Missouri Representative Richard Gephardt, a longtime adversary of Foley within the Democratic Party on trade, to retaliate against Japan, West Germany, and Taiwan if they did not reduce their trade surpluses with the United States by 10 percent within six months; the bill passed with 234 Democrats in favor and only six opposed. Speaker of the House Tip O'Neill said in response to critics, "We don't believe we are protectionists. We believe we are patsies for the rest of the world, and we want to be fair traders."[35] Although President Reagan opposed the Gephardt amendment, he authorized the US Trade Representative to investigate the foreign trade practices of Japan and South Korea. Reagan went so far as to declare in a September 23, 1985, speech, "I will not stand by and watch American businesses fail because of unfair trading practices abroad. I will not stand by and watch American workers lose their jobs because other nations do not play by the rules."[36]

The reaction of Washingtonians to the possibility of protectionist legislation was almost universally condemnatory. On September 17, 1985, Jim Langlois, executive director of Washington Citizens for World Trade, wrote to thank Foley for his "ongoing efforts" to prevent the passage of the Textile and Apparel Trade Enforcement Act of 1985. Langlois acknowledged that efforts needed to be made to increase US markets abroad, but that the Reagan administration could best do that by putting pressure on foreign governments "to set realistic targets and timetables for our trading partners to correct their trade imbalances with us."[37] Washington Governor Booth Gardner wrote Foley a similar message, also urging him to work for the defeat of the import restriction bill. "Curtailed textile exports by China, Japan, Korea and other nations would translate quickly into reduced purchasing power—and thus reduced imports of Washington agricultural, wood, and other products," argued Gardner. Perhaps trying to keep in mind Foley's position of national leadership in the House, the governor argued that the bill would hurt the nation, not just Washington state. Gardner also asserted that the US government and businesses needed to work to make their products internationally competitive instead of shielding whole industries.[38] Other opponents of the textile bill included the Port of Seattle, an economics professor at Washington State University, Washington State Korean-Americans for Political Action, and the Washington State Retail Council.[39]

On October 4, 1985, T. A. Wilson, chairman and CEO of Boeing, also wrote Foley in opposition to the textile bill. While acknowledging that the bill would help the domestic textile industry, he worried that retaliatory tariffs would endanger jobs in industries heavily dependent on exports like aircraft and aerospace. As with Gardner, Wilson tried to appeal to Foley as a national leader by arguing that he was worried about the national aircraft industry, not just Boeing or Washington.[40] Foley faced pressure from congressional colleagues, however, to support either a textile bill or an omnibus trade bill with protectionist features. On November 14, Foley received a letter from Senate President Pro Tempore Strom Thurmond from South Carolina, a textile-heavy state, urging him to support the Textile and Apparel Trade Enforcement Act. The following May, House Majority Leader Jim Wright pressured Foley to support a bill whose framers argued it would, rather than encourage protectionism, have the goal "to open up markets" abroad, while punishing countries that violated trade agreements.[41]

Even the seemingly laudable goal of opening markets was not so simple for Foley to accomplish. On December 26, 1985, Tsutomu Hota, a member of the Japanese Diet and the chairman of the Liberal Democratic Party of Japan's Research Commission on Forestry, wrote Foley that attempts to open Japan's timber industry to additional imports would go nowhere due to a depression in that industry. He did promise, Foley, however, that "we will earnestly carry out . . . demand expansion measures to encourage the improvement of circumstances where importation is further accelerated."[42] When Congress moved closer to passage of a trade bill in May 1986, Minister of Ports and Telecommunications Bunsai Sato wrote Foley that he was concerned about congressional actions to try to force open Japanese markets to trade in the telecommunications sector, when, he believed, Japan was already working unilaterally toward this aim. Sato worried that if President Reagan signed the bill, it would "undermine the confidence of the people of Japan in the possibility of solving problems with the United States through constructive engagement."[43]

Faced with pressure from the Japanese as well as from constituents who were dependent upon trade with Japan, Foley sided with these pressure groups over congressional leadership during the 99th (1985–86) Congress. On October 11, 1985, he sent a letter to constituents warning that protectionism endangered Washington's economy. Instead of erecting trade barriers against countries who dealt unfairly with the United States, Foley insisted the way forward was for the Reagan administration "to negotiate firmly and decisively" against violators of trade agreements.[44] While he believed Japan's trading practices were "highly" restrictive, Foley thought recent moves by the US Federal Reserve to lower interest rates, as well as the Plaza Accord agreement between the United States, Great Britain, France, West Germany, and Japan weakening the value of the dollar against the Japanese yen and the West German mark would encourage exports and ease the US trade deficit.[45] Under no circumstances would Foley entertain protectionism, as he reiterated in a letter to a Spokane constituent in November. "Washington is a major exporting state with real promise for even greater growth in future years," Foley wrote. "Protectionist legislation potentially poses a grave threat to this important area of the economy by inviting foreign retaliation against Washington State products that are successfully competing in foreign markets."[46]

The 99th Congress ultimately failed to produce a restrictive trade bill, but the threat of new legislation with retaliatory features resurfaced in the 100th Congress (1987–88) because Democrats, the more protectionist of the two parties, regained control of the Senate and picked up more House seats in the 1986 midterm elections. Foley was elected House Majority Leader, meaning that he had to weigh regional and national concerns even more than before, but he was still essentially pro-trade. In February 1987, Foley warned farmers in Spokane about the dangers of trade wars that could be sparked by increased protectionism. He cautioned farmers, for example, who were interested in banning foreign products that contained steroids they could not use in their own goods that because of protectionist interests elsewhere in the United States, foreign countries could retaliate against Pacific Northwest products.[47]

As Foley tried to plot a middle course between his constituents and Congress, Japanese Consul General Shigenobu Nakai turned up the pressure during a visit to Spokane in which he reminded eastern Washingtonians of the benefits of US-Japan ties. Nakai warned Foley about the perils of going against his constituents by allying with protectionist Democrats, reminding those gathered at a town hall meeting that 25 percent of Washington workers depended to some extent on trade for their livelihood.[48] On the other hand, Bill Salquist of the *Spokane*

Spokesman-Review reported that Spokane businessmen he spoke to said they did not expect Tokyo to retaliate by reducing its imports of Northwest wheat.[49]

Other pro-trade interests in Foley's district and throughout Washington were concerned, however, about the potential consequences of a new trade bill. Robert Baker, a Reebok sales representative based out of Spokane, complained of a feature of the bill which would place a quota on imports of foreign footwear at 1986 levels. Fearing protectionism would do more harm than good to the economy, Baker pointed out to Foley that there were many in his district whose livelihoods depended on trade. Other constituents opposed an amendment to the bill proposed by Majority Whip Richard Gephardt to cut trade on countries running trade surpluses with the United States, a measure clearly aimed at Japan. William Whitaker, vice president and manager of the international division of First Interstate Bank of Washington in Seattle, told Foley that although in his heart he favored a harsh trading bill, he believed in negotiation. While approving of the motivation behind the Gephardt amendment, Whitaker feared it would hurt, not help, global trade expansion. A Spokane IBM worker, meanwhile, fretted that the bill would undermine pending GATT negotiations, and in doing so, lead to less international trade and closed markets. The president of a Mazda dealership in Spokane urged Foley to support a compromise bill by Dan Rostenkowski that would only punish countries that violated trade agreements instead of all that ran a trade surplus with the United States. The only Northwest opposition in Foley's Ways and Means Committee file on international trade during the 100th Congress came, not surprisingly, from a Spokane representative from textile company Jockey International.[50]

Foley tried to play peacemaker among his various constituencies. The *Seattle Times* praised his efforts, arguing that "the Japanese could scarcely find anyone better qualified . . . to warn them of the peril in which their own protectionist policies have placed them." Despite Foley's placement as one of the country's most powerful politicians and Washington state's economic interests in international trade, he represented "an increasingly unrepresentative point of view within Congress and his party." The *Times* warned of "ample signs of what Foley calls 'a strain of developing American militant nationalism.'"[51] Meanwhile a Port of Seattle official warned that the Gephardt amendment to tax American allies carrying a trade surplus with the United States would endanger Pacific Rim trade, "reduce local employment by several thousand jobs and eliminate millions of dollars in revenue from the King County and Washington state economies." Foley again warned that "the position of the Seattle port director . . . is not reflected in the general attitude of the United States," which he argued supported protectionism. While saying he disagreed with protectionist "militancy," Foley did sympathize with it, arguing "Japan practices a cutthroat competition internally—sometimes anything seems justified to win," he said.[52] In the end, however, the best result possible for Foley occurred, as the Gephardt amendment was stripped out of the bill before it passed Congress in 1988. The weakening of the US dollar encouraged more countries to buy US goods in the late 1980s, and that coupled with the recovery of the economy lessened protectionist pressures as the decade went on.[53]

Foley continued his work with Japan on behalf of the Northwest. When Japanese Prime Minister Noboru Takeshita came to the United States in January 1988 for a summit at the White House, he also met with Foley, who said he "stressed the importance of agricultural trade to the Northwest" and left the meeting with "no doubt he [Takeshita] understands that for us in the Northwest and on the West Coast, Japan is our most important trading partner."[54] Foley downplayed conflict among the various parties. A February 1988 article in the *Seattle Times* described Foley as an "advocate of a measured approach to problems with Japan" who argued that "singling out one country in trade relations is a poor way to set policy." The *Times* quoted Foley as contending that there had always existed "an imbalance in our knowledge about Japan" and arguing that "Japan gets blamed for events after it has made alterations and corrections."[55] Contending Japan received insufficient credit for correcting its mistakes, Foley related an incident where the Toshiba Corporation sold the Soviet Union technology for their nuclear submarines. On January 11, 1988, Foley told his constituents that a Toshiba subsidiary sold the Soviets equipment to make their submarines quieter. He said it would cost the Department of Defense $30 billion to reconfigure its submarine detection devices, but that the United States would not retaliate with broad trade restrictions on Japan. Instead, Congress put language into the 1988 trade bill restricting the sale of Toshiba products. Foley met with the Japanese Minister of Trade and

Finance to express his "very deep concern," and said he was assured that Tokyo was moving toward preventing future "illegal exports" of this kind.[56] The *Seattle Times* later said that Foley told them "the Japanese government has taken steps that should help prevent similar sales."[57]

Foley seemed to smooth over the issue, and trade between Washington and the Pacific Rim continued apace. In 1988, Japan exported $15.3 billion worth of goods to Washington, the most of any country to the state, with Canada a distant second at $3.6 billion. The state did its share to try to balance the US trade deficit with Japan, only importing $6.3 billion in Japanese goods. Washington also harvested more than 2.6 million acres of wheat, barley, and oats that year, most of it for export, and much of it from counties in Foley's Fifth District: Whitman County led the way with 565,500 acres of wheat and 183,000 barley acres.[58] Foley looked not just to maintain ongoing trade relationships, but to open new trade routes as well. He supported an additional Boeing plant for Spokane, thereby bringing to his district by far the state's biggest private sector trader abroad. The *Seattle Times* reported that the new $23 million plant in Spokane would produce fiberglass and plastic ductwork for the air systems in Boeing's commercial jets, while also housing research and development facilities for automated production of airplane floor panels. The plant would employ a total of 350 people, mostly from the Spokane area. When the plant broke ground in the spring of 1989, Foley said "the coming of Boeing to Spokane is a tribute to the outstanding work ethic of the area." By 2018, the partnership of local work ethic and Boeing had added up to a total of 4,300 aerospace industry jobs in Spokane County, paying an average of $63,000 annually.[59]

Although Foley stepped back somewhat from personal involvement on international trade issues in his district after becoming Speaker of the House, some local projects did get his attention. In 1992, he led efforts to get US government support for the Russian-American Technical and Economic Development Consortium, in which Washington State University played a key role. "This effort has the potential to help us change and reorient Russian research and education patterned after the US Land Grant University System," Russian Ambassador to the US Vladimir Lukin told Foley, adding that WSU's work contributed to Russia's move toward becoming a market economy.[60]

Foley was also involved in efforts to assist the Spokane company Gold Reserve Corporation with business dealings in Venezuela. In March 1993, Gold Reserve CEO Rockne Timm asked Foley to connect him to Venezuela's president, as well as its Ministry of Energy and Mines, to overcome business difficulties Gold Reserve was experiencing in that country. Gold Reserve wanted to obtain the rights to two properties to which it had mining titles: the Alfa Concession, for which Timm desired a ten-year extension he said would create jobs and tax payouts to the Venezuelan government; and the Brisas del Cuyuni Concession, a sulfide/hard rock deposit which Gold Reserve was trying to hang on to despite competition from other Venezuelan interests. Foley wrote Secretary of State Warren Christopher seeking assistance for Gold Reserve to compete fairly against its Venezuelan competitors.[61]

In the following months, some progress was made, but apparently not what Gold Reserve hoped for. On September 24, Raymond A. Hanson of the R. A. Hanson Company in Spokane wrote Foley that he thought "there are funny things happening there" regarding Gold Reserve, and that "considering Venezuela's desire for foreign investment, particularly American, it seems strange that we cannot get this resolved."[62] Hanson enclosed a letter from Timm, saying that Gold Reserve received a ten-year extension for the Alfa concessions, but that it applied for other concessions and received verbal assurances that these would be granted, yet with no results. When Timm filed a lawsuit to receive his concessions, he discovered that the judge was "prepared to issue certain rulings without following established Venezuelan procedures," causing him "great concern."[63] Foley followed up by writing Venezuelan Ambassador to the United States Simon Alberto Consalvi to ask for his assistance.[64] It is unclear whether this yielded positive results for Timm, but the episode demonstrated Foley's continued use of power and contacts to attempt to aid small businesses in international trade matters, even after becoming House Speaker.

In terms of farming, when Foley first became House majority whip in 1981, he convinced his agricultural constituents that by entering the leadership, he could more easily expedite wheat and grain legislation vital to them to the House floor. Foley said he would also have greater clout overseas, such as when he met with Japanese officials at an international food conference and convinced them not to resell wheat they bought from the United States to other countries at a higher price. In 1982, Foley led a congressional delegation to Japan in which he pushed Japan's agriculture minister and officials from the Japanese Flour Millers Association to buy eastern Washington farm products and to reduce import barriers on grains, fruits, beef, and forest products. His efforts generally met with approval at home. The *Spokane Chronicle* praised Foley in 1984, for example, for sponsoring a bill to establish a commission to study the expansion and improvement of agricultural export programs, in an attempt to stem a decline in the value of agricultural exports from $43 billion in 1981 to $38 billion in 1984.[65]

Midwest farmers, meanwhile, pursued protectionist trade measures because their red wheat—as opposed to the white wheat of the Northwest—was used for domestic consumption. Foley was in a tight spot when a farm bill came up for vote in 1985 that favored protectionist interests which he, as majority whip, had to conciliate in ways that brought into conflict his regional and national constituencies. The Washington Wheatgrowers Association lobbied for measures in the farm bill that would help them reclaim lost export markets. Both the House and Senate Agriculture Committees approved versions of the bill that allowed the Reagan administration to cut the guaranteed price of wheat, theoretically making it more attractive to export, but the Senate bill contained a provision that could increase wheat prices by establishing strict production quotas if desired by a referendum of farmers. The referendum question put Foley in a tough position because it was opposed by Washington wheat growers yet supported by Midwest Democrats with farm constituents. In the end, Foley reluctantly supported a referendum provision in the House's farm bill, only agreeing to include it because he would have lost the votes of many Democrats on the committee otherwise.[66] Foley biographer Baodi Zhou argues that he supported the bill because he was concerned that if he did not, he would be deposed as House Majority Whip or eliminated from future consideration for further promotion in the House. In this instance, Foley's national political ambition outweighed regional concerns. When Reagan vetoed the bill, Foley voted "present" on an override attempt that he knew would fail. By not voting for or against the legislation in its final form, Foley saved face with Congress and did not have to face the consequences of the potential negative trade repercussions that would hurt his farm constituents.[67]

Overall, Foley's attention to agricultural issues diminished as he rose in the leadership. From 1977 to 1980, while he was chair of the House Agriculture Committee, over 19 percent of the bills he introduced were related to agriculture; but from 1982 to 1985, that number decreased to just 6.2 percent.[68] When constituents with farming concerns wrote Speaker Foley in the early 1990s, moreover, his responses were rarely substantive. For example, the head of the international sales department of Arbor Crest Wine Cellars in Spokane asked Foley to help her fix a bureaucratic error that had denied Arbor Crest federal funding it needed to participate in an international trade show in Paris in April 1992. Foley forwarded the letter to Richard Crowder, the undersecretary of agriculture for international affairs and commodity programs.[69] There was no further indication in Foley's files of any action taken on behalf of Arbor Crest, however. The exchange reflected not just the growth of the region's wine industry, but also frustrations about red tape and a growing antigovernment attitude in the Fifth District that would, despite Foley's perennial support for agricultural exports, eventually doom his seat in Congress. Foley's support for trade, even when it benefited his constituents, could not save him from being felled by the Republican resurgence during the 1994 midterm elections. His work did benefit the region, even as his constituents failed to show their appreciation by returning him to office.

SENATOR MARK HATFIELD AND THE PUSH TO MOVE OREGON BEYOND A TIMBER-BASED ECONOMY

Back in Oregon, although Senator Mark Hatfield was primarily concerned with redirecting national security dollars toward domestic economic growth, he was also a strong proponent of international trade, and his work on behalf of trade interests in Oregon helped to strengthen the state's economy throughout his career. While Hatfield is most well known for his opposition to defense spending, he did not block projects when he did not have the votes to do so, and this selectiveness aided him in his ability to use his political capital in ways that would help international trade interests. Hatfield "kept close friendships on both sides of the aisle" as he followed the model of Henry Jackson and Warren Magnuson, watching their power and ability to bring home federal dollars in the

1970s. During his tenure as Senate Appropriations Committee chairman or ranking member in the 1980s to mid-1990s, Congress approved many Oregon trade-friendly projects, including the installation of new locks at Bonneville Dam to increase the shipping of wheat and other commodities, and funds for improvements to small coastal ports. Critics accused Hatfield of pork-barrel spending, but the senator retorted that "Oregon received little in the way of defense spending and this federal money was a way of evening the score."[70]

Hatfield was engaged in expanding international trade opportunities for Oregon long before his days in the Senate. During his gubernatorial inaugural speech in 1959, Hatfield mentioned the forthcoming Centennial Exposition in Portland, arguing that "we should be aware among our people of an air of enthusiasm and excitement." Dreaming big dreams for the state, Hatfield said that "such an event, properly conducted, could . . . bring Oregon to the forefront of the nation, . . . accelerate our economy, and . . . leave lasting benefits of immeasurable proportions."[71] In the coming years, Hatfield continued to boost for what he believed to be the exceptional state of Oregon. As Northwest politicians did repeatedly, Hatfield sought to strike a balance between promoting growth and protecting Oregonians. "We are developing job opportunities for native-born Oregonians," Hatfield told the *Oregonian* in 1963. In an interview with reporter Gerry Pratt, he remarked that "there are people who feel we ought to close the borders and preserve Oregon for the Oregonians." Arguing this opinion was "wrong," Hatfield said the question was "not how do we keep Oregon from growing, but how do we make certain that it is growing with orderly development, growing in a manner that is compatible with our liveability factors? Our clean air? Our schools?"[72]

One of Hatfield's biggest initiatives aiding local defense and trade interests while he was governor was the development of Silicon Forest, a high-tech hub in the Portland suburbs that would garner a significant amount of investment from both the federal government and foreign companies in the coming decades. In 1962, Hatfield helped Electro Scientific Industries, a producer of electrical measuring instruments, get a zoning permit to build a new high-tech industrial park. ESI already had a contract with the United States Air Force, and it contributed to the development of the US intercontinental ballistic missile program.

Governor Mark Hatfield examines a new kind of telephone at the Swedish exhibition during the Oregon Centennial Exposition and International Trade Fair in 1959, flanked by delegate Lars Lewendal. Hatfield promoted the exposition as an opportunity to increase Oregon's trade and cultural links with the world. Reprinted by permission from Oregon Historical Society, accession no. 8215.

By the end of the 1960s, ESI counted Boeing among its customers, and was internationally known, as it developed foreign subsidiaries to get around other countries' trade barriers, including in Japan, France, and the United Kingdom.[73]

Unlike Seattle, however, Portland did not have a major university serving it to receive federal aid from the National Defense Education Act that went toward boosting the high-tech sector through education in the late 1950s and 1960s. Hatfield instead shepherded the creation of the Oregon Graduate Center, which trained local graduate students for high-tech careers and helped the regional economy. The Oregon Legislature, however, slashed Hatfield's $1.5 million funding request for the OGC to $596,000 in 1965. After Hatfield went to the Senate, Ira Keller, a major Portland powerbroker from his position as chair of the Portland Development Commission, took over the OGC in the early 1970s and greased the wheels for additional donations from Silicon Forest companies to fund faculty for the center. But the center's lack of funding in the 1960s hurt Oregon vis-à-vis Washington in attracting tech companies to boost Oregon's jobs numbers and international trade. While the Oregon Legislature bickered over $500,000 of potential state support for high-tech interests, Washington's legislature "designated $10 million for educational programs designed to meet the needs of high technology and created a technology resource center funded at between $12 million and $14 million to pool the resources of public universities and private industries."[74] As a result, Washington's high-tech sector flourished, but it would not be until Vic Atiyeh was Oregon's governor in the 1980s that Silicon Forest took off in terms of foreign trade investment.

Even though the OGC got cut out from under Hatfield, he sought additional means to strengthen Oregon's international trade potential, most notably by undertaking a major trip to Japan in the fall of 1964. Hatfield had a strong relationship with Governor Kingo Machimura of Hokkaido province, and between 1961 and 1964, they formed the Oregon-Hokkaido Rural Cooperation Society, which brought Japanese students to the state to study American agricultural methods. Machimura visited Oregon in the spring of 1964, and in November Hatfield reciprocated, bringing with him several Oregon business giants, including Meier and Frank department store heir Gerry Frank, Tektronix cofounder Howard Vollum, and Jack Brandis, a lumber baron from the southern part of the state. "Much of our destiny in the West lies in the trade potential of the Orient and Asia," Hatfield asserted. "Japan . . . is our gateway to these markets. We in Oregon want to be sure we are their gateway to American markets."[75]

The trip featured meetings with Kingo and businessmen in Hokkaido, as well as official luncheons, a meeting with the Japanese Diet, and visits to Honda and Sony headquarters. Hatfield arranged an audience with Japanese Emperor Hirohito and received some 200 Japanese political and business leaders at the Hilton Hotel in Tokyo. Visiting Kobe, Hatfield contended that Oregon's trade with the city was increasing while Seattle was seeing a decline. He trumpeted the potential for still greater agricultural exports to Kobe in particular and attended a Japanese-language Christian church service. Upon returning home, Hatfield remarked that Oregon businessmen had "only begun to scratch the surface of the trade potential of the Far East." Noting that the state was already working to open up the full potential of the Columbia River channel for trade downstream to Japan via the Pacific Ocean, the governor said that the goal of the trade mission was "to become better acquainted with the people of the Orient" and this was accomplished. Noting that he was "embarrassed at his own inability to speak Japanese," Hatfield recommended that more Oregonians study the language.[76] A later *Oregonian* article credited Hatfield's visit with paving the way toward the opening of a Bank of Tokyo branch, a Japanese consulate, and an office of the Japanese External Trade Recovery Organization in Portland.[77]

The *Oregon Journal* also proclaimed the trade mission a success. "Kipling's 'East is East and West is West and never the twain shall meet' was proved wrong many years ago," the *Journal* noted, proclaiming that "Oregon political and business leaders are continuing to demonstrate how wrong Kipling was." The trade mission, stated the *Journal*, "has been described by those who participated as a striking success, with praise unanimously accorded Hatfield for his leadership. As one of them put it, 'The governor fractured Japan.'" The article said the trip mostly consisted of making contacts for future trade opportunities, noting that six of Portland Harbor's top seven exporters were already from East Asian nations. The *Journal* also credited the Oregon Wheat Growers League's work to expand exports, and the efforts of Portland Mayor Terry Schrunk in cementing sister-city relations with Sapporo: Schrunk had been on many trade missions to Japan and received Japanese emissaries in Portland. It finally noted that the city-run Portland Commission of Public Docks (a predecessor agency to the Port of Portland) was "actively promoting trade with the Orient" and that "its field office in Tokyo is flourishing."[78]

International trade was on Hatfield's agenda as he met with representatives from regional chambers of commerce in February 1965. The governor credited the Northwest's rapid postwar population growth to ex-servicemen who decided to settle in the region and said that while a boom followed in "the lumber industry, the metals industry, and in electro-processing," international trade was also key to this growth. He noted that the Port of Portland "has become the largest dry-cargo port on the entire Pacific Coast." At that time, the port exported $100 million to Japan annually, but was only scratching the surface of its potential, according to findings from his recent trade mission.[79] As Hatfield prepared for his Senate run, he could brag that the dollar value of Oregon imports had increased 64.5 percent and that of exports was up 73.6 percent. On his watch, the state created an Import-Export Committee to encourage overseas markets for Oregon crops, and Hatfield pledged in a 1966 campaign ad to seek acreage control programs so farmers could increase their exports.[80]

Hatfield was remembered upon his retirement for having used his power as governor to increase international trade into Oregon. Political commentator Brent Walth said that "as governor, [Hatfield] launched the first significant effort by state government effort to diversify Oregon's economy. His trade missions and industrial recruitment drew attention to the state, and his founding of the Oregon Graduate Center helped foster Washington County's high-technology industry."[81] The *Oregonian* similarly editorialized that "he paid particular attention to diversifying the state's economy from its dependence on King Timber."[82] International trade continued to be a major vehicle through which Hatfield addressed the issue of economic diversification during the remainder of his career.

HATFIELD'S TRADE EFFORTS DURING HIS SENATE YEARS, 1967–1997

Aside from the complex and emotional issue of timber, international trade was one of Hatfield's main interests, and his policies in this area helped Oregon-based companies bloom. For example, in the late 1970s, he established good relations with a young Portland-area entrepreneur named Phil Knight. After tariffs raised the rates to ship shoe parts from Europe and East Asia for his burgeoning company, Knight worked with the Oregon congressional delegation to get those tariffs reduced. In a move that does not seem coincidental, Knight also made donations to the political campaigns of many Oregon politicians: for example, he and his employees gave $3000 to Hatfield. In 1978, Hatfield wrote the US Special Trade Representative, endorsing a recommendation by the International Trade Commission to reduce the tariffs on Knight's Nike sneaker imports. Although Nike counsel Richard Werschkul said it would take years and a new GATT treaty for tariffs to be reduced, the Nike case shows significant involvement by Hatfield on behalf of a highly successful local entrepreneur doing business abroad.[83] In later years, Senator Bob Packwood was even more helpful to Nike in terms of reducing duties on shoes; in 1992, Knight memorably endorsed Packwood during the latter's reelection campaign as "the single most important man standing between Customs and the rape of our corporate body."[84]

While Packwood spent the 1980s and the early 1990s assisting Oregon international trade efforts by working, Tom Foley-like, on forestalling protectionist legislation as chair of the Senate Commerce and Finance Committees, Hatfield spent federal money to increase Oregon's trading capability. His position as head or ranking member of the energy and water subcommittee of the Senate Appropriations Committee gave him power in regional trade matters. J. Keith Kennedy, Hatfield's chief of staff on the committee, recalled that the subcommittee had jurisdiction over national security issues such as nuclear weapons manufacturing, but also, "more important to the members[,] issues like the annual dredging of a particular port in order to maintain a sufficient depth for commerce to go in and out, which might be only an annual expenditure of a quarter of a million dollars but was real significant to the local community." Indeed, Hatfield shepherded many port-related projects through this subcommittee. Kennedy recalled that Hatfield helped garner a new lock at Bonneville Dam to assist passage of barge traffic up and down the Columbia River. In addition, he noted Hatfield's efforts to help Oregon's seaport communities, which have "port entrances that have to be dredged in order for the traffic to continue." Kennedy said dredging was an annual effort, especially at the mouth of the Columbia River where it meets the Pacific Ocean, "to build jetties out of the mouth of the river into the ocean to try to maintain that channel." A large part of Hatfield's success in getting the funding needed to keep up this annual work had to do with his reciprocal relationship with Democratic Senator J. Bennett Johnston of Louisiana, who—depending upon which party controlled the Senate—alternated with Hatfield as chair of the energy and water subcommittee. "Because Mark Hatfield worried about the Columbia River he had an appreciation for Bennett Johnson worrying about the Mississippi, and vice versa," Kennedy surmised. "So, when the two of them took the Energy and Water bill to the floor . . . the bill would pass 88 to 12, year in and year out."[85]

The successful passage of these bills was paramount to the economic diversification of the region, particularly Portland, Oregon's largest city and economic hub. The city's economic revitalization during Hatfield's Senate years was largely due to the rejuvenation of its "river city" role

Terminal 6, the part of the Port of Portland which handles automobile imports and exports, in 2019. Senator Mark Hatfield and Governor Victor Atiyeh both worked in the 1980s to increase the trade in automobiles out of the port to provide more Oregonians with jobs. Photo by author.

as it modernized shipping facilities and expanded the Port of Portland to regain ground lost to Seattle earlier in the postwar period. Thanks to Honda and Toyota, Portland became the largest car importer on the West Coast. This was a boom time: whereas in 1970, foreign commerce out of West Coast ports was 17 percent of the national total, by 1983 the figure went up to 24 percent. Ships from Portland went to Asia and Latin America, importing steel, oil, cars, and general merchandise, while exporting products from lumber to McDonald's French fries. As a result, the value of trade out of Portland tripled between 1966 and 1983.[86]

Clearly the stakes were high for Portland and the region. By the early 1980s, half a dozen ships per day loaded cargo at the Port of Portland, with Japan, Taiwan, East Asia, British Columbia, South America, and the Panama Canal as top destinations. Seventy percent of jobs in Portland and 50 percent of metropolitan-area jobs were based within a mile of either the Willamette River or the Columbia River. "The focus of the industrial and commercial city has moved steadily downstream," Carl Abbott noted in 1983. "The filled lands on both banks of the Willamette as it nears the Columbia have provided space for newer and larger facilities to serve bigger ships and expanded trade."[87] The simultaneous expansion of container transport made Portland even more significant as an importer/exporter of containers full of cars, barges, and grain. The 1980s were also a turning point for Oregon and its West Coast counterparts because, for the first time, the volume of cargo in trans-Pacific trade surpassed the trans-Atlantic volume. Portland went from being a port of secondary significance in the national economy to one of primary importance to broader national and international markets.[88] These changes were not lost on Hatfield. A free market proponent who wanted Oregon to become involved in trade, Hatfield did this mainly by throwing his support behind dredging projects. In fact, it was a predominant interest of not just Hatfield, but the entire Pacific Northwest congressional delegation, to protect the Columbia River and keep it open for trade, because it was among the region's most valuable natural assets.

Hatfield worked for interests in marketing and shipping wheat through Portland as well. Portland exported twice as much grain in 1980 as in 1975 due to new investment in river grain terminals and navigation capability. Portland's wheat exports decreased in the 1980s, but not as much as other ports because of the "efficiencies" of Columbia River transportation.[89] In 1988, Hatfield obtained funding for the city to receive a wheat marketing center. The center "could stand by itself as a major addition to regional commerce," noted the *Oregonian*. But it also represented, the editorial argued, "the opportunity for Portland to be the principal export center of farm commodities to the Pacific Rim." The article contended that the center would allow procommodity groups to "unite into effective marketing forces and run their distribution and export operations out of Portland." The Port of Portland already exported one-third of the nation's wheat exports and half of its potato exports, and, the paper believed, was now "destined to become an even larger player in international agricultural trade." According to the *Oregonian*, Hatfield had "used the federal appropriations process to transform vision into reality." The wheat marketing center was established with $4.8 million in federal funds obtained by Hatfield, leading the paper to anticipate that "barriers that have divided the wheat industry are coming down," including those separating growers, processors, distributors, and exporters, as well as political boundaries dividing states and regions of the western United States, and even between soft white and hard red wheat producers. The *Oregonian* envisioned that "all are expected to come together in the center as a single force to create markets and expand uses of the product."[90] Hatfield's leadership in large part made this vision possible.

Hatfield also attempted to use his political muscle to get the Commerce Department to establish an export assistance center in Portland as mandated in the 1988 omnibus trade bill. Responding to a plea from the department that it needed more time to study the proposal, the senator said, "Hell, you can study something to death. . . . That is a delay or a tactic to block." Hatfield hoped that the center would expedite the export of high-tech goods from Silicon Forest. With other trade assistance bureaus opening in California, the senator fretted that Oregon would be left behind in the increasing pace of West Coast exports. The assistance center was eventually opened in downtown Portland.[91]

Hatfield downplayed the idea that unfair trading practices with Japan were problematic: on the contrary, he launched new efforts to extend Oregon-Japan ties. Former aide Steve Nousen recalled that Hatfield was particularly active in securing new direct flights between Oregon and Japan for Portland International Airport. The State Department and Japan had to negotiate new routes, and Hatfield's office attempted to influence the negotiators from the State Department and the Department of Transportation to include Portland on their list of routes. Nousen credited Bob Packwood and Hatfield, saying that "we had the guy who raised all the funds and the guy who spent all the funds as chairs of the two most powerful revenue committees in Congress." Thus, when Hatfield and Packwood wrote the State and Transportation Departments on behalf of Oregon, "they carried weight."[92]

In March 1987, Delta Airlines commenced a direct flight between Portland and Tokyo which operated five days per week.[93] Nousen, then working at the Port of Portland—which ran the airport—pushed Hatfield and Packwood to lobby for a route to Korea or to another Japanese destination. In 1990, the port won a nonstop route for Delta Airlines to Nagoya, Japan, and the first flights commenced in early 1991. The port invited Hatfield and his wife, Antoinette, to be emissaries on the trade mission to Japan scheduled for the first Nagoya flight in February. A major part of the mission was to aid a Northwest forest products lobby in Hiroshima as they bid on what they hoped to be an "Oregon Village" housing project outside the city. Along the way, the Hatfields called on Japanese emperor Akihito. Nousen, who by now served as Hatfield's chief of staff, recalled that Hatfield had a portrait of the emperor on his side table in his office. When visitors asked him why he had that portrait, Hatfield would remind them that World War II was long over. In fact, the Hatfields had a warm relationship with the Japanese imperial family dating back to his days as governor in 1960, when Akihito stopped in Portland during a state visit. Akihito's wife, Michiko, had just given birth and Antoinette Hatfield was pregnant, so the two bonded while shopping for baby clothes together at Portland's Lloyd Center. Michiko purchased clothing and a car seat for eight-month-old son Naruhito, and Nousen believed this early connection may have helped the Hatfields get an audience with Akihito once he became emperor many years later.[94]

Ultimately, Nousen said he felt that Hatfield's biggest trade-related legacy was in securing nonstop flights to Japan and South Korea and helping to resolve customs issues around those flights. But the senator had to contend with a reputation Portland International Airport developed: it detained foreign arrivals at the gate and in customs at a higher rate than other airports. This reputation threatened to stymie new businesses from coming to Portland from abroad, and foreign airlines questioned why they should come to Portland when they could go elsewhere and not have the same customs difficulties. Hatfield was long a champion of the rights of foreign travelers, immigrants, and refugees, however, and his office routinely helped foreign nationals traverse the federal immigration system during his career. According to local refugee aid agencies, "no other Oregon congressional office [came] close."[95]

Problems continued after Hatfield left office, however. An ugly 2000 incident in which a Chinese businesswoman was forced to strip to her underwear, searched, and briefly jailed by the Immigration and Naturalization Service—one of the precursor agencies to the US Immigration and Customs Enforcement agency, better known as ICE—after being mistaken for an illegal immigrant became an embarrassing national news headline for Portland. INS data confirmed that foreign arrivals to Portland International Airport were turned back at a higher rate (0.17 percent between May and July of 2000) compared to Seattle and Los Angeles, both of which turned back 0.06 percent of new arrivals. Portland's mayor, the director of the Port of Portland, and Senator Gordon Smith—the successor to Hatfield's seat—all condemned the incident and urged reform. Despite threats by airlines and East Asian cities to stop doing business in Portland, international flights continued.

As of 2019, Portland International Airport offered nonstop passenger flights to cities in Canada, Germany, Great Britain, Iceland, Mexico, and the Netherlands. In August 2019, furthermore, federal regulators approved a proposal by Delta Airlines to shift the Portland airport's Tokyo flight to Haneda, Tokyo's central airport, from the more-distant Narita airport.[96]

Hatfield's efforts helped Portland become a world-class city in the 1990s. During the decade, non-timber businesses as diverse as architectural firm Zimmer Gunsul Frasca (now ZGF Architects) and public relations firm Wieden+Kennedy gained international clients. Portland ranked sixteenth out of eighty-five cities in the world as a top "Internet information center" at the end of the decade. The city had 150,000 export-oriented manufacturing jobs, and that number was growing, not shrinking as it was in the rest of the country. When Hatfield retired in 1996, the Portland-Salem combined metropolitan area ranked tenth in the nation in exports at $9.2 billion.[97] The state's prosperity was not just limited to the Willamette Valley: Hatfield used the appropriations process to make sure that all cities on the Oregon coast had a jetty built by the Army Corps of Engineers. By the end of his time in office, Hatfield's Appropriations Committee had pumped $28 million into a jetty extension at the port of Siuslaw, $16 million into a similar extension at the port of Umpqua, and $7.3 million to deepen the channel of the Columbia River, to name just a handful of the coastal public works projects the senator helped fund.[98]

CONCLUSION

Despite pressure in Congress and among the public to restrict imports during the late twentieth century, Slade Gorton, Tom Foley, and Mark Hatfield kept goods flowing into Oregon and Washington, aiding a largely trade-dependent regional economy, while opening new avenues of opportunity for Pacific Northwest businesses as diverse as timber and aerospace to export their goods abroad. These businesses and the Pacific Rim nations they served were clearly the biggest beneficiaries of expanded trade in the Northwest. Regional politicians were feted and cajoled by Chinese and Japanese businesspeople and politicians in particular to stimulate Pacific Rim trade. The people of the Northwest,

Part of the grain terminal at Port of Portland's Terminal 5 in 2019. Much of the grain exported from the Port has historically gone to Japan. Photo by author.

despite some resistance—most notably in the form of protests against the World Trade Organization in Seattle in December 1999—went along with increased international trade for the most part, because through the 1990s, their economic prosperity increased. More people moved to the Northwest both from other places in the United States and from other nations. The free-trade paradigm that seemed under siege at the beginning of the Reagan administration had prevailed by 2000. Thanks largely to the patience, mediation, and personal diplomacy politicians used both with domestic constituents and international politicians and business clients, big names like Boeing, Microsoft, Nintendo, and Nike were making world-class products, creating jobs, and spreading prosperity worldwide, especially in the Pacific Northwest. As the years went on, however, they often had to do this without federal assistance: trade-assistance subsidies and federal programs to shore up local unemployment were not as plentiful as they had been during the flush midcentury postwar economy. Instead, it was up to state and local-level politicians like Oregon Governor Vic Atiyeh to follow up on federal-level efforts to deepen trans-Pacific ties through forging local connections with international people and companies.

CHAPTER 6

"We Were Way Out in Front": Vic Atiyeh and the Growth of International Trade in Oregon[1]

On July 7, 1993, former Oregon Governor Victor Atiyeh sat down for the latest in a series of interviews conducted by Clark Hansen, an oral historian for the Oregon Historical Society, and discussed trade relations between Oregon and its international business partners, especially in East Asia. Along the way, Atiyeh related Oregon's many triumphs in attracting foreign businesses to the state and in securing export growth abroad for Oregon businesses. He also rued the opportunities lost, however. Atiyeh particularly recalled a May 1985 trip to Japan when he attempted to convince the Sharp-RCA Corporation to locate a new factory in Oregon. The Sharp faction in the corporation, Atiyeh recalled, wanted to come to Oregon, but the RCA faction won out and the plant ended up just across the river in Camas, Washington. Atiyeh was particularly peeved at the reaction of the press, which pointed out that the plant was at least still sited in the Portland, Oregon, metro area. "I'm so intensely competitive and I want things for Oregon," Atiyeh said. "My reaction was baloney. I'm not the governor of Washington, I'm the governor of Oregon. . . . There was no comfort to me that it was in the area." Although he was certainly not against foreign investment in Washington, Atiyeh had a competitive streak that, perhaps, belied an inferiority complex toward his neighbor to the north. "I wanted Oregon to have something," Atiyeh recalled. "I expect to make every sale. I'd get disappointed if I didn't make every sale."[2]

Atiyeh had a point: as a review of the careers of Wayne Morse, Mark Hatfield, and other Oregon politicians has shown, Oregon was more starved than Washington for economic stimulus in the post–World War II years, in part because of a relative lack of military bases and prime defense contracts, but also because of the state's historic overreliance on the lumber industry as a manufacturer and exporter of raw and finished logs. Oregon's economy did diversify away from timber to a degree in the postwar years, but the state still depended considerably on exports at the end of the twentieth century. A 2001 report by the Oregon Economic and Community Development Department showed Oregon to be one of the top ten states in both exports per capita and dependence on sales abroad. Of the state's manufacturing jobs, one in five was related to international business and trade. Semiconductors and wheat became the state's two largest exports by 2000, totaling 29 percent of all state exports. Those trends continued through the 2010s, as Oregonians lamented seemingly disparate occurrences connected by trade, including the Substation Wildfire that wiped out much of the state's white wheat crop in 2018, as well as President Donald Trump's trade wars that threatened Oregon plywood, wheat, and cattle sales abroad. While Oregon politics fragmented in many areas, conservatives, liberals, and progressives alike agreed that trade was a necessity.[3]

Wayne Morse and Mark Hatfield were crucial to the growth and development of postwar Oregon because they obtained federal funds first to sustain the state's defense industry, then later to redirect defense dollars toward infrastructure and building up Oregon Health and Science University, and eventually to augment foreign trade. Another important figure in the diversification of Oregon's economy and the expansion of its international trade, however, was Vic Atiyeh, an Oregon legislator and Republican governor who was relatively unknown nationally. Historians and political scientists have recently attempted to rescue Atiyeh from obscurity, but the governor was generally dubbed a failure upon his departure from office in 1987. Widely criticized by the media as being hands-off and indecisive on a wide variety of affairs, from the occupation of the small town of Antelope by the Rajneeshpuram commune to Oregon's economy, the surprising defeat of his heir apparent to the governorship—the widely popular Secretary of State Norma Paulus—at the ballot box triggered a Democratic Party lock on the governorship not broken in over thirty years, as of 2020.[4]

Upon Atiyeh's death in 2014, when *Capital Press* reporter Peter Wong summarized his contributions to the state, he highlighted the nine trips to Pacific Rim nations—out of 20 trade missions overall—that earned the governor the moniker "Trader Vic." Wong noted that

Atiyeh had convinced a number of foreign businesses to build factories in Oregon, with the biggest breakthrough in 1984, when Nippon Electric Corporation of Japan committed to build an assembly plant in Hillsboro. Oregon exports, meanwhile, went from $2.4 billion in 1978, when Atiyeh was elected governor, to $4.1 billion in 1984, all the way to $18 billion by 2011, or "about 10 percent of Oregon's goods and services produced that year."[5] Greg Walden, US Representative for Oregon's Second Congressional District from 1999 to 2020 and a former Atiyeh staffer, argued that "he reset the state to become a very active participant in international trade. He helped create a whole new economy. . . . The ribbon cuttings and the building openings occurred after that. He laid out the markers. He dug the ditches and he poured the foundations for what really developed, especially in the Portland metro area and the high-tech growth that occurred there."[6]

This chapter explores the extent to which Atiyeh not only maintained preexisting trade links between Oregon and its major trading partners but expanded its presence in the Pacific Rim and beyond during the 1980s. Atiyeh's ethnic background as a second-generation Arab American, his business connections garnered from decades as head of the major exporting/importing Oriental rug company Atiyeh Bros., and his gubernatorial power played a large role in his success in generating new exports from Oregon as well as new foreign direct investment to the state. Atiyeh did have the misfortune of leading the state during one of its worst economic downturns, and he endured a considerable amount of criticism from Democrats and the media during his time in office. Arguably, however, Atiyeh was as effective—if not more—than his colleagues at doing what he believed to be his calling, namely, to sell Oregon abroad. Atiyeh's work particularly seems to have borne fruit after his time in office, when Oregon—and the Pacific Northwest as a whole—became synonymous with globalization and the region's economic transformation.

FILLING THE VOID: STATES AND INTERNATIONAL TRADE

On August 5, 1985, at the height of Vic Atiyeh's efforts to diversify Oregon's economy by increasing the state's international ties, the *New York Times* published a story discussing the push by other states to do the same. It reported that one of the major conclusions of that year's annual meeting of the National Governors' Association was that "the apparatus set up by Congress to help American exporters and increase foreign investments in this country is inadequate to meet the need." The Reagan administration, as part of an effort to decentralize federal functions, endorsed state efforts to accelerate international trade. Among the tactics states used to increase foreign trade was increasing foreign trade appropriations, sending representatives abroad to search for markets, aiding exporters and foreign plants in the domestic market, sponsoring trade missions, and establishing sister-state relationships. The piece mentioned Tennessee, Michigan, Minnesota, and New York as examples of states courting international trade through a variety of tax incentives, subsidies, and mutual exchanges of technological expertise.[7]

Vic Atiyeh was hardly unique in his drive to open his state to international trade relative to others in the United States. As early as the 1950s, state governors sought to expand their relationships outside of the United States, but the trend accelerated as the American economy trended downward in the 1960s and '70s. From Oregon, Mark Hatfield was succeeded by Tom McCall and Robert Straub in courting Japanese takers for the state's exports. Ohio Governor Jim Rhodes at one point hoped to build a bridge between Cleveland and the southern border of Canada to ease trade relations. In 1977, he negotiated an agreement with the top management at Honda to bring what was initially just a motorcycle assembly plant to the state. Rhodes memorably blundered when asked by a reporter whether the plant would build more than just motorcycles, responding, "I wouldn't be surprised. . . . You know, those Japs are pretty smart." (Rhodes tried to clarify that by "Japs," he actually referred to his "Jobs and Progress" slogan.) Nevertheless, by 1982, the motorcycle plant turned into a major auto plant in the city of Marysville. By 2000, as its Accord model became one of the most popular cars in the country, Honda employed 16,000 people in Ohio and may have been indirectly responsible for 128,000 ancillary jobs.[8] It is little wonder why Atiyeh and others were scrambling for investment by Japanese and other East Asian companies.

A biography of Governor Tom Kean of New Jersey, an Atiyeh contemporary, shows that his situation was more analogous to Atiyeh's: for one, his state was also geographically positioned on a coastline in between two much larger states. Furthermore, "because of its close proximity to New York and Pennsylvania, its good transportation network, skilled workforce, competitive tax rate, and good research universities and research laboratories, Kean maintained that New Jersey could be . . . attractive to foreign companies expanding their operations." Kean hired a special trade representative, a Chinese national named Ming Hsu who was the daughter of a member of Taiwanese leader Chiang Kai-shek's cabinet. During Kean's administration, he and Hsu entered New Jersey into foreign trade shows, where officials stressed New Jersey's suitability for foreign investment. By 1984, Korean companies Samsung, Daewoo, Hyundai, and Lucky Star all opened facilities in the state. In 1986, Kean embarked on his first trade mission to China, Hong Kong, and South Korea, and renewed a sister-state relationship his predecessor, Brendan Byrne, had signed in China's Zhejiang Province. The trip was a success, and Kean later led a trip to the United Kingdom, spearheaded the opening of a New Jersey trade office in Tokyo, and hosted "China Expo '88," bringing in former Nixon National Security Adviser Henry Kissinger to regale guests "with stories of his early experiences trying and failing to outfox Chinese diplomats." Ultimately, New Jersey ranked fourth among all states in terms of foreign investment by the end of Kean's tenure. During his foreign trips, however, Kean discovered growing competition among US states for foreign investment. He also came under scrutiny from the *Bergen Record*, a major New Jersey newspaper, which questioned whether his trips made a difference in determining whether companies opened branches in New Jersey. Kean defended himself by arguing that he'd only gone on three trade missions in six and a half years as governor, which he characterized as placing himself in the "bottom fifth" among governors.[9]

Atiyeh's record in terms of international trade was strikingly like that of Tom Kean, with a major difference—Atiyeh went on more trade missions than did Kean, in part supporting Kean's theory that he did not actually participate in that many trade missions relative to the norm for American governors. Atiyeh was also questioned contemporaneously on whether he was getting bang for his buck, though he is today much more remembered for his record on international trade than is Kean, whose exploits, for all their apparent success, garnered barely three pages of mention in his biography. For better and worse, Atiyeh was justifiably nicknamed "Trader Vic," since his international trips were a major part of his legacy.

GLOBAL CONNECTIONS AND ATIYEH'S RISE TO POWER

Vic Atiyeh's heritage as a second-generation Arab American arguably played a major role in his inclination toward and interest in expanded trade relations between Oregon and other countries. Atiyeh was born in Portland on February 20, 1923, to Syrian immigrants. His father, George Atiyeh, came to the United States close to the end of the nineteenth century; by 1900, he and his brother Aziz operated Atiyeh Bros., a regionally well-known importer, wholesaler, and retailer of Middle Eastern rugs and carpets. "Somebody apparently had come through and said that this area was a good place to sell Oriental rugs," Atiyeh recalled. When that individual proposed going into business with George, then backed out on the deal, Aziz stepped in "to protect his interest, and apparently liked what he saw . . . and came to Portland in 1900." Before Vic was born, the family business was already well-established and acculturated into the city's business mainstream. In fact, the Atiyehs won medals at the Lewis and Clark Exposition in Portland in 1905 and the Alaska-Yukon-Pacific Exposition in Seattle four years later. Years later, Atiyeh's father went back to Syria to take a bride after his first wife died. "There was this feeling that you marry someone of your own ethnic background," in the Syrian-American community at that time, Atiyeh believed, explaining why his father went to Beirut (then part of Syria) to marry his mother, Linda Asly Atiyeh. In addition to Vic, the Atiyehs had twins, Edward and Richard, who survived capture and imprisonment in Nazi Germany during World War II. Vic remained home during the war, attended the University of Oregon, and passed up an offer from the Green Bay Packers to play football, choosing instead to follow in his father's footsteps and join Atiyeh Bros.[10]

Atiyeh was a member of the Oregon House of Representatives from 1958 until 1964, and the Oregon State Senate from 1965 until his election as governor in 1978. Mark Hatfield was elected governor the same year that Atiyeh was elected to the House, and Atiyeh remembered that he and Hatfield were often referred to as the "Young Turks" of the state's

Republican Party.[11] Both men worked for economic diversification and development in Oregon beyond the timber industry. They differed, however, on a major trade-related initiative during the 1960s: the proposed development of the Boardman Space Age Park as an industrial site that would lure Boeing to eastern Oregon. Atiyeh said he voted against legislative approval for development "because there is all this desert land out there . . . Why in the world are you going to do something out there?" Atiyeh believed Hatfield "was going to get Boeing in" but argued "they were making money on it and we weren't making anything on it," because it went undeveloped for many years.[12] Indeed, Boeing never built a plant in Boardman, although the nearby Port of Morrow is today a hub in the Columbia River system of international trade.

Atiyeh was more concerned about issues on his legislative committees such as taxation, food and dairy, fish and game, and education. He also focused on economic development for his district, which encompassed much of Washington County west of Portland. That area, along with Portland's Southwest neighborhoods, was becoming known as the Silicon Forest—a stepsister to California's Silicon Valley—because many of the developments taking place in the state's high-tech sector were centered there. Low taxes and cheap, abundant land lured the growing tech companies out to the suburbs. Electro Scientific Industries, which counted Boeing and the Defense Department among its customers, was a Silicon Forest mainstay from its beginning, and eventually developed subsidiaries in Tokyo and Munich, West Germany. Tektronix, an exporter of measuring equipment which also developed subsidiaries in England, Switzerland, and Japan during the 1960s, also relocated its headquarters from Portland to Washington County during this time. Intel built a plant in the county in 1976 that would become one of its largest in the United States. In 1978, Portland Mayor Neil Goldschmidt convinced German-based Wacker Siltronic Corporation to locate a plant in Silicon Forest that eventually employed 800 people.[13] As Washington County looked beyond US shores, Atiyeh likely took notice of these developments and may have seen them as a harbinger of future economic growth to come.

After several decades at Atiyeh Bros. and in the state legislature, Atiyeh first threw his hat in the ring for governor in 1974 but lost to Democrat Robert Straub. Trying again in 1978, Atiyeh first convinced

Republicans to select him for the party nomination over liberal former governor Tom McCall and conservative Roger Martin, then won over voters in the general election, contending that the McCall-Straub years of the 1960s and 1970s had been ones in which the state had received a national and international reputation as being unfriendly to business. Oregon had pioneered in developing environmental regulations that spread across the country, but the state's economy was beginning to slump, and Atiyeh positioned himself as the man to turn it around in an era in which conservative voters nationwide sought lower taxes to stimulate the economy. He scored a surprising upset over Straub in the fall, perhaps because, as longtime Oregon journalist Floyd McKay put it, "Vic was ideal for the new climate; moderate in public and private life, seldom flummoxed by events, he fit the image of quiet competence that voters wanted."[14]

Upon becoming governor, Atiyeh worked to strengthen international contacts for the state in the Pacific Rim, visiting Japan for the first time in 1979. During his first year in office, he made international contacts by visiting several Asian nations, including Japan. The governor believed Oregon to be a natural trade partner with Asian markets, but he nonetheless faced challenges. Both Atiyeh and his chief of staff Gerry Thompson believed Japanese businesspeople perceived Oregon as having an antigrowth mentality. "Everywhere we went, when Vic would say he was from Oregon, they would say, 'that's the state that says come visit, but don't stay,'" Thompson remembered, referring to McCall's famous 1971 remark contending the need to limit population growth to preserve Oregon's ecological balance. "It used to anger [Atiyeh] every time. . . . He could recite people, who they were, and where they were when they heard that comment made."[15] Japan was Atiyeh's primary target, Thompson recalled, because the timing for Oregon-Japanese trade was better than with any other potential Asian trading partner. China, Taiwan, and South Korea "just weren't ready" for various reasons, including, for example, China's recovery from the internal purges of the Cultural Revolution, which had only recently concluded with premier Mao Zedong's death in 1976. "It's all about timing," Thompson said. "Japan was doing well economically and they were ready to grow."[16]

From his experience with Atiyeh Bros., the governor thought Oregon to be a natural trade partner with Asian countries, but he ran into some initial difficulties, journalist Jeff Mapes recalled: "On his first trip to Japan, in 1979, Atiyeh joked that the people knew what a governor was 'but they didn't know what Oregon was.'"[17] Given previous governors' trade missions and the evidence showing strong levels of Oregon-Japan trade prior to 1979, Atiyeh's quote likely reflects his attempts to broaden Oregon's trading partners in Japan beyond the usual purchasers of the state's lumber exports. The governor's visits there and attempts to establish new contacts would take years to bear fruit for the state, as he had to build relationships with Japan's business and political leadership in order to encourage new importers of Oregon goods, as well as foreign direct investment. The governor also focused on other local trade issues: along with now-Senator Hatfield, Atiyeh focused on upgrading Oregon's ports of entry to better accommodate international trade. One project he recalled was an attempt to put a car loading dock at the former Tongue Point Naval Station at Astoria. "They did some dredging right around there so the ships could come in," Atiyeh said. Considering Oregon's historic disadvantage with Washington and California because of its lack of deep sea ports, Atiyeh acknowledged that "we have to continually dredge." Washington ports, he recalled, "jumped on the container thing very early, and we were behind that power curve, so we lost out on that." Atiyeh did assert, however, that Oregon ports fared "much better" in automobile imports than Washington and continued to do so after the end of his term in office.[18]

Atiyeh faced plenty of challenges, however, in making Oregon economically prosperous. An oil embargo by Mideast countries in 1979 caused an increase in interest rates, which led to a sharp drop in housing starts, in turn causing a drastic slowdown in the wood products industry. State revenues, largely dependent on the sale of state timber, declined, along with many private-sector timber-dependent individuals and businesses. In addition, Oregon and the United States slumped into a sharp recession in the early 1980s characterized by double-digit unemployment. Atiyeh called multiple emergency special sessions of the legislature to shore up state funding, but the governor's critics charged that his efforts at economic diversification—including an international trade program—were not producing sufficient results to compensate for the state's overall economic decline. In his 1982 reelection bid, Atiyeh was challenged by Democrat Ted Kulongoski, who came out swinging on the trade issue during a debate against the governor. "Oregon today needs to expand its markets within our state with a 'Buy Oregon' program and expand our markets worldwide with an aggressive Oregon exports program," Kulongoski said. "It is time we begin to help our mills retool to compete in the worldwide markets by operating at the highest efficiency for the greatest sales, payrolls, and profits."[19]

Atiyeh waged a bruising, successful campaign, however, built in part on new plans for expanding international trade. In a speech to civic groups in the spring of 1982, Atiyeh reflected on thirteen trade missions and overseas trade exhibitions the governor's office had sponsored. He also discussed nine foreign trade delegations his office had hosted and numbered at twenty-six the Oregon firms that were introduced to exporting. Atiyeh said five Oregon firms participating in trade missions would receive $28 million in exports, adding that "we opened up direct lines to Japanese and other overseas markets for Oregon lumber firms, markets that are now helping many of them stay alive in this depressed domestic market."[20] Despite the persistence of high unemployment, Atiyeh won reelection in 1982. Early polling had shown a near-deadlock between the governor and Kulongoski, but Atiyeh opened the gap in October, as Kulongoski never made an impact on Oregon voters who had similarly sent him to defeat two years earlier in his race against Bob Packwood for the US Senate. Atiyeh successfully portrayed Kulongoski as antibusiness and took advantage of his fundraising woes, outspending Kulongoski by a nearly two-to-one margin.[21]

Atiyeh turned away Kulongoski's challenge and won a second term in office, but he had yet to produce results toward achieving his goal of diversifying Oregon's economy. The state's timber industry laid off 10,000 workers during the 1980s as it sought to be more profitable against competing Canadian firms, primarily through increased assembly line mechanization.[22] Washington, meanwhile, threatened to race ahead of Oregon in the regional competition to attract Pacific Rim trade. In 1982, Washington Governor John Spellman led a delegation of state leaders in starting a trade relationship between Washington and Sichuan Province in China, commencing a "sister-state" relationship negotiated by the Chinese in conjunction with the well-connected pro-trade lobby Washington State China Relations Council (WSCRC). In 1983, WSCRC negotiated sister-city relations between Seattle and

Chongqing, China. WSCRC was active in "receiving Chinese delegations visiting Washington, assisting American delegations going to China, briefing American embassy officials returning from Beijing, acquainting Chinese diplomats with Washington state, providing member firms with information on China, giving them advice and assistance in their contacts with China, [and] endorsing China related events."[23] If Atiyeh wanted *something* for Oregon, he had his work cut out for him.

TO *AND* FROM OREGON WITH LOVE: INCREASING JAPANESE EXPORTS AND INVESTMENT IN OREGON

Atiyeh's second term saw a number of breakthroughs in terms of garnering international trade opportunities. In 1983, Atiyeh helped inaugurate the first direct commercial flight between Portland and Tokyo, undertaking the first of many trade missions to Japan during his final four years in office. Japanese businesses accelerated into foreign markets during the 1980s, as Japan became an integral player in American industry and culture through foreign direct investment. Auto manufacturers Honda, Toyota, and Nissan exported cars and opened factories in the United States. Tech giants such as Sony and Nintendo transformed the entertainment industry by winning a dominant US market share in televisions, videocassette recorders, and the home videogame industry.[24] Some Americans feared this trend. Missouri Senator John Danforth, for example, referred to the Japanese as "leeches."[25] But in public opinion surveys taken throughout the 1980s, most Americans thought highly of Japan: one 1987 survey indicated that only 19 percent of respondents thought US-Japanese relations were "unfriendly."[26] Local leaders such as Atiyeh realized the opportunity Japan and Japanese companies presented to aid their states' flagging economies. It was in this economic climate that Atiyeh experienced his most significant achievements with Japanese businesses.

Atiyeh had to engineer a major and potentially controversial change to state law, however, to win over Japanese business leaders keen on investing in Oregon. In July 1984, the governor called the Oregon Legislature into special session and asked it to repeal the state's unitary tax, which allowed Oregon to tax international companies on both their Oregon and home-country earnings. Atiyeh had spent years

negotiating with the Japan Federation of Economic Organizations—
known in Japan as Keidanren—to persuade its member businesses to
invest in Oregon. Keidanren claimed the unitary system was unfair
because it constituted "double taxation" against both parent companies
and their foreign subsidiaries by considering them as one company.
Eliminating the unitary system meant Oregon would only tax the
subsidiary company, independent of the parent.[27] Pressure from Japanese businesses appears to have weighed heavily in Atiyeh's decision
to push for the tax repeal. Earlier in 1984, high-tech Nippon Electric
Corporation (NEC) announced plans to build a manufacturing plant in
Oregon, but the company asked Atiyeh for assurance that the unitary
tax would be repealed. Gerry Thompson recalled a negotiating session
in Portland with NEC during which their representatives "absolutely"
had to be promised that unitary repeal would occur before committing
to investing in Oregon. NEC, she said, "made it perfectly clear they
didn't like our unitary tax. Period. End of subject." A couple of days
after the Portland meeting, Atiyeh called her into his office and said
"Gerry, we're going to do it. Let's repeal the unitary tax."[28]

Atiyeh understood that repeal would be criticized by some legislators, particularly because the state stood to lose as much as $15
million in annual revenue from unitary tax collection. He reacted to
these criticisms by arguing to the Oregon Legislature that it should
favor broad economic growth, especially in an election year. "I said to
my Republican colleagues I was going to call a special session," Atiyeh recalled. Advised not to call the session because "the Democrats
will just raise all kinds of hell," the governor held firm, using electoral
politics to his advantage: "The Democrats are out campaigning, too,
all of the House and half the Senate, and they have to be for economic
development."[29]

To be certain of victory, however, Thompson met with certified
public accountants and members of the American Electronics Association, encouraging them to lobby the legislature on behalf of repeal.[30] On
the opening of the special session, Atiyeh told legislators that unitary
repeal constituted "an issue of extraordinary importance to the future
of our State and to the future of its citizens." If the legislature failed
to act, Atiyeh argued, Oregon would "languish in the grips of cyclical
economic fevers that will continue to sap our strength and diminish our

future . . . [and] the pall of economic darkness will cover our State for decades to come."[31]

Atiyeh also benefited from good publicity for the tax repeal. Portland lawyers Clifford B. Alterman and Gary P. Compa acknowledged it would cause a loss in state revenue, but contended that repealing the unitary tax "would go a long way toward changing the antibusiness attitude under which Oregon has labored for so long."[32] Whether convinced by the governor, the lobbyists, or the weight of public opinion, these tactics worked on legislators: repeal easily passed on July 30, with only nine votes in opposition from both chambers.[33]

The response from the Japanese business community was positive. After the repeal of the unitary tax, Keidanren issued a press release stating that "this shift in policy clearly guarantees fair treatment to present and future investors in Oregon, making the state highly attractive for foreign investment."[34] The *Japan Economic Journal* also favorably noted the pending end of the unitary system and extolled Oregon's geographic and economic climate. "Geographically speaking, Oregon is a good place to do business in the age of the 'Pacific Rim,'" said writer Juniciii Umeda, arguing that Oregon was favorable because of excellent ports, cheap electricity, and a workforce the author believed to be more loyal and productive than that in California.[35]

The unitary tax was not the sole hurdle in the way of NEC's arrival in Oregon. In a memo to Atiyeh, Thompson said she had heard the *Oregonian* was preparing a story on NEC's arrival in Oregon, but that the Hillsboro school board had not yet signed off on giving NEC land for its factory. Thompson negotiated with reporter Steve Jenning to get him to hold the story in exchange for "private interviews" with NEC officials when they arrived in Portland. Jenning was overruled by the *Oregonian*'s Dick Thomas, who, Thompson wrote, informed her that her request was "irrational, unreasonable and could not be granted."[36] Thompson also worked to broker a deal to improve Shute Road in Hillsboro by increasing a nearly mile-long stretch by two lanes to meet NEC's desire for a bigger roadway near its planned manufacturing centers. Thompson worked on the plan with the Oregon Department of Transportation and the Washington County Board of Commissioners. She had to do damage control because NEC "was misled that this section of Shute Road was scheduled for improvement." Thompson warned Atiyeh that NEC "must have assurance of the improvement" to proceed with construction.[37] In the end, the school board approved the land transfer, and the Shute Road expansion plan went through. NEC built its Hillsboro plant to rave reviews and succeeded at increasing local employment. "I call them our pioneers," Atiyeh remembered. "They're the ones who really did it." Soon after unitary repeal, other Japanese tech companies, most notably Fujitsu and Epson, announced they would build in Oregon.[38] By the end of the decade, Fujitsu opened plants in Hillsboro and Gresham, and Epson opened a plant in Hillsboro.

With the unitary tax repealed and Keidanren impressed, Atiyeh believed that Oregon had the "inside track" on trade with Japan. "We are better positioned than any other state," Atiyeh said in September 1984, shortly after he went to Japan to attract more business for Oregon.[39] His trips typically included meetings and speeches wherein he or other representatives from Oregon state government agencies or businesses would tout the state's livability and business climate. Such was the tenor of a bullish speech Atiyeh gave to the Keidanren on September 14, 1984. The governor played up the history between Oregon and Japan, glowingly professing that the trade and appreciation between Japan and Oregon "has grown steadily as we have cemented our friendship." Vowing that Oregon was "steadfastly" committed to trade, Atiyeh touted Japanese companies' announcements that they would build new plants in Oregon as indicative of the growth of the Japanese business presence in Oregon and the hospitality of the state's business climate. "We can offer you close proximity to California markets without asking you to pay the high price of crime, congestion, and pollution," he argued. Atiyeh also pointed out that 8,000 Japanese-Americans lived in Oregon, that Portland had a Bank of Tokyo branch, and that Oregon had Japanese churches, study groups, service organizations, and schools. Above all, he concluded, Oregon was a progressive place to do business in what he envisioned as a Pacific-oriented future. "We see our future as a state . . . and our destiny as a people . . . as we look out over the Pacific," Atiyeh said.[40]

An internal staff memorandum written after Atiyeh's visit concluded that "the mission to Japan was very successful." During the mission, Fujitsu announced it would build two plants in Oregon. Fifty delegation members, meanwhile, constituting "the largest Oregon trade mission

Oregon Governor Victor
Atiyeh (seated, left) meets
with Japanese Crown Prince
Akihito and Crown Princess
Michiko during one of the
governor's eight trade trips
to Japan while in office.
Reprinted by permission
from Pacific University
Special Collections, Victor
Atiyeh Collection, identifier
PUA_MS96_2014.

ever assembled" made Japanese contacts in the realms of trade, tourism, and investment. The memo said that "at least" fifteen newspaper articles appeared in the Japanese press about the visit, and that Japanese banks and securities agencies—including Fuji Bank, the Osaka Chamber of Commerce, Nomura Research, and Long Term Credit Bank—announced their intentions to study Oregon's economic climate. The outreach mission sold tourist packages for Timberline Lodge on Mount Hood, and got the United States Travel and Tourism Administration to arrange for tour operators to travel to Oregon for "familiarization" tours. The memo also apparently took a dig at one of Oregon's rivals: a meeting with Oklahoma Governor George Nigh was said to have seen him urge the Oregon trade mission to "Leave Us Something."[41]

Another highlight of the mission was that Japan's Fuji TV announced production of the miniseries *From Oregon With Love*, which promised to promote harmonious relations between Oregon and Japan. *From Oregon With Love* (known as *Oregon Kara Ai* in Japan) aired in 1984 and spawned numerous sequels in the 1980s and 1990s, further cementing Oregon-Japan cultural ties and strengthening the economic benefits of the Oregon-Japan relationship. Atiyeh recalled that the series "spread the word of Oregon throughout all of Japan" and that it was "exceedingly popular." The series featured a young boy who, after his parents' death, came to live with his aunt and uncle in Oregon. Atiyeh praised the series' "beautiful photography" and its central Oregon setting.[42]

From Oregon With Love filmed follow-up programs in Oregon through 1996, when Atiyeh recognized Fuji TV at a tribute speech at the Governor Hotel in Portland for its cultural contributions to Oregon. Among his fondest memories as governor, Atiyeh claimed, "right up there in my memory bank is Fuji TV." Noting that the Fuji TV crew laid a plaque at Lake Billy Chinook to memorialize filming nearby and the company contributed funds to help build the Museum at Warm Springs, Atiyeh believed that the series' accomplishments were sometimes overlooked compared to the manufacturing plants he had helped secure in Silicon Forest.[43] The series clearly made the state friends in Japan. In a letter to Atiyeh, Fuji TV CEO Hisashi Hieda wrote that as late as 1983, no Japanese TV network had ever tried to film abroad. "It was just then that I received a letter from you, which encouraged me strongly and made me feel so confident that we could make this project come true," Hieda recalled. "I have never forgotten the day I met with you at the location set in the State of Oregon and how I was impressed with your heartfelt warmth and thoughtfulness," Hieda continued, and then thanked Atiyeh for his "years of close support and encouragement."[44]

In addition to luring economic and cultural investments from Japan, Atiyeh built upon his predecessors' work to get Japan to buy more Oregon goods. He took a dramatic step by joining with Portland Mayor Frank Ivancie to found Oregon's first official foreign trade office in Tokyo. "If you're trying to get people in Japan to do business . . . you can't do it on a hit-and-run deal, go there for two or three days and come home and expect anything to happen," Atiyeh recalled. "I said, 'Okay, we've got to have some kind of a continuing presence.'"[45] To cover startup costs, the Oregon Legislature Emergency Board provided $250,000.[46] That funding allowed the office to serve as an intermediary for Oregon exporters and potential Japanese clients as well as Japanese companies investing in the state. "It was a gesture of good will; that we're serious," Thompson recalled. "It became the hub of the wheel for whatever activity we had going from Japan or to Japan."[47]

Atiyeh's work in Japan received positive press at home as well as abroad. The *Capital Press* praised his hard work, good humor, and openness to press coverage during the September 1984 trade mission.[48] The *Seattle Weekly* proclaimed that "this is the year that Oregon moved out of the shadows and into the sun in the growing West Coast competition for investment, tourism, and other business favors from the Pacific Rim." The paper noted that Oregon went from zero to four Japanese manufacturing plants in 1984, adding five thousand new jobs. The *Weekly* judged Atiyeh's September 1984 visit as "probably the most successful such Pacific Rim trip by a Western governor in years."[49] Thanks to Atiyeh, Oregon and Japan cemented a strong relationship that set a high bar for the state's future international trade missions.

ATIYEH IN THE MIDDLE EAST

Atiyeh was also active in trying to grow trade links between Oregon companies and Middle Eastern countries in March of 1984. Atiyeh believed that no Oregon governor had ever taken a trade delegation to the Middle East. Some small Oregon companies already were doing business there, however, including Niedermeyer Martin (lumber sales), and Western Power Products of Hood River, which was operating in Saudi Arabia, the country where the trade mission began.[50] Portland's KATU TV station reported in 1984 that 500,000 US jobs were dependent upon trade with Saudi Arabia, as the kingdom was the sixth largest trading partner of the United States and the nation's largest Middle East trading partner. The station characterized Atiyeh as "attempting to cash in" on this relationship for Oregon, which already exported $34 million of goods to Saudi Arabia. Overall Atiyeh and six Oregon businessmen spent a week in the kingdom. The Saudi Minister of Commerce told KATU reporter Lisa Stark that "there remains plenty of opportunities for Oregon companies," though a worldwide decrease in oil prices meant that the kingdom would not be importing as much as in the past. Niedermeyer-Martin officials said they had been selling to Saudi Arabia since the 1940s and were continuing to do so, particularly playground equipment for new schools in the country. Saudi businessman Amar Kassoghi said he hoped to open up a company in Lake Oswego, Oregon. Stark closed her report on a down note, however, noting that the Saudis were not interested in buying Northwest wheat.[51] Fellow journalist Mike Donahue from KOIN TV reported that Saudi Arabia had reached self-sufficiency in grain growing and that Oregon could not convince Saudi officials to use the state's soft white wheat in its blend of flours.[52]

Atiyeh still felt as though the Saudi Arabia visit was worthwhile. When he made his first step out of the plane at Jeddah—a major port destination for Oregon goods heading to Saudi Arabia—the governor remembered getting "this huge emotional feeling. . . . I just couldn't hardly wait to get down on the ground. And I'm in Saudi Arabia, I'm not in Syria yet." Atiyeh recalled that the trip overall was more about laying the groundwork for future deals, rather than making any deals at that time. In that sense, he thought that his mission in the Middle East was much more ceremonial and less hands-on than in the Pacific Rim. "When a governor takes a trade delegation, it's kind of to open doors," Atiyeh said. "And I said to them, because of my business background, you know, 'If you want me to make calls with you, I'll be glad to do that,' when they have their own business appointments." To Atiyeh, it was commonplace to have ceremonial visits with foreign dignitaries and play tourist in the name of improving relations between the leaders of his state and foreign leaders, but his visits had an important business component as well. "I was willing to go talk to their prospects," Atiyeh said. "I was always for them and their business, and so I was lending the prestige of the governor's office."[53] The trip was also apparently success-ful from the official Saudi perspective: King Fahd bin Abdul Aziz later wrote to US Ambassador to Saudi Arabia Walter Cutler that "we were pleased with his visit made to the Kingdom, and extend to him our best regards."[54] Even the more critical Donahue acknowledged Atiyeh's suc-cess in opening doors for Oregon businessmen, noting: "It's not unusual to wait weeks to get an appointment with a Saudi cabinet minister but with Governor Atiyeh leading the way Oregon's trade delegation got in to see three ministers the first day," including the ministries of com-merce and industry and electricity.[55]

The trade mission next proceeded to Egypt, where delegates met with representatives from the Egyptian wheat industry, the US Cham-ber of Commerce in Egypt, and a variety of other small firms in the country.[56] According to KATU TV, Egypt was already one of Oregon's largest trade partners, accounting for $100 million in business with the state, largely in the sale of wheat provided as part of US food aid to the country. The Oregon business delegation learned that Egypt was trying to attract more foreign investment, including American companies that could manufacture toothpaste and other toiletries. Electrical supplies,

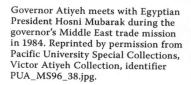

Governor Atiyeh meets with Egyptian
President Hosni Mubarak during the
governor's Middle East trade mission
in 1984. Reprinted by permission from
Pacific University Special Collections,
Victor Atiyeh Collection, identifier
PUA_MS96_38.jpg.

medical equipment, construction equipment, and agricultural machinery were seen as the best export trade possibilities to Egypt. Atiyeh
vowed to try and add Northwest companies to the Cairo Trade Fair, a
major exhibition of foreign business firms in Egypt that did not feature
a single Oregon company.[57] Atiyeh recalled in an interview conducted
almost two decades before the Arab Spring of 2011 ousted President
Hosni Mubarak's Egyptian regime that "they're going in the right direction. . . . Again, we were interested in wheat, and incidentally, even
today, one of the big importers of Oregon wheat is Egypt." Atiyeh said
his meeting with Mubarak was very successful: "Several times they
knocked on the door and there was a delegation from Sudan that he
had an appointment with, and he'd tell them to wait," Atiyeh recalled.
"We spent more time than I think he'd planned on, and certainly more
time than I planned on."[58]

As the trip progressed to Atiyeh's ancestral homeland of Syria, he
recalled that "we met with a lot of dignitaries and cabinet officials"
and that "the business people that were with us, they were impressed
with the entree that we were able to provide for them."[59] Mike Donahue reported that some Oregon businessmen had to cancel appointments with customers in Egypt to come to Syria with the governor's
entourage, but others hoped that new contacts in Syria would help to
compensate.[60] The governor met with a number of high-ranking Syrian officials, including President Hafez al-Assad, and the governor of
Damascus, the capital of Syria. With tensions high over Syria's hostility
toward staunch US ally Israel, Atiyeh's visit was nearly canceled; and
while he was there, he was shown carefully orchestrated tours of Syrian
battle sites, such as at the Golan Heights near Israel. Much more was
made in the press of Atiyeh's visit to his ancestral hometown of Amar

Governor Atiyeh poses by the road sign for Amar, Syria, during his Middle East trade mission in 1984. Atiyeh's father was born in Amar and the governor spent time there touring and visiting with friends and family. Reprinted by permission from Pacific University Special Collections, Victor Atiyeh Collection, identifier PUA_ MS96_2346.

than of any progress on investment in Oregon or by Oregon business-men. Bob Buchanan, a wheat rancher from Milton-Freewater and vice president of the Oregon Wheat Growers League who accompanied Atiyeh on the trip, said Syria had "real market potential" to import eastern Oregon's white wheat. Nonetheless, Buchanan returned home disappointed that conflict between the United States and Syria over American support for Israel, as well as the weak value of Syrian currency relative to the US dollar, prevented the Syrians from being able to buy more Oregon wheat.[61]

When asked what he hoped to accomplish by going to Israel at the end of the trade mission, Atiyeh indicated he was mainly going there on behest of Jewish constituents back home who wanted Israel to be included on Atiyeh's Middle East itinerary. "I have a lot of good [Jewish] friends in Portland . . . and I mean real good friends," Atiyeh recalled. "And they wanted me to go to Israel."[62] Meanwhile, the business delegation that accompanied Atiyeh to the Arab countries of the Middle East did not join him in Israel. For some, this was out of fear that if they did business with the Jewish state, they would lose business from Muslim-majority Arab nations that refused to cooperate with foreign companies dealing with Israel. For his part, Nofal Kasrawi, the Syrian-born vice president of CH2M Hill International, said "I will never set foot in Israel" because of what he perceived as Israeli aggression against Arab nations.[63] Atiyeh nevertheless spent nearly two weeks in Israel, more than in any other Middle East nation.

Overall, the trip seemed like a mixed bag. Upon Atiyeh's return home, KOIN TV noted that "Oregon's first trade mission to the Middle East did not return with [a] pad full of orders for Northwest white wheat," since Saudi Arabia claimed self-sufficiency and Syria would only be able to buy on credit. The report warned, furthermore, that Egypt was moving toward self-sufficiency and would eventually not have to buy as much Northwest wheat.[64] The governor, however, declared the trade mission a success. "The trade mission would have been success-ful if we had just had impact," Atiyeh told the *Eugene Register-Guard*, "but we had both impact and sales." The paper reported that the mis-sion helped David Grinwood, a doctor and business consultant from Portland suburb Lake Oswego, aid client Riedel International Inc. in building a $100 million pipeline in Saudi Arabia. In Egypt, CH2M Hill International stationed eight Oregon engineers on a $10 million per year sewer system planning project.[65] When later asked what the Mid-dle East trip accomplished, Atiyeh said he thought "we bolstered the amount of work that Oregonians were doing over there." He empha-sized that the trip gave leads to the delegation members, but that it was up to them to pursue their new contacts further. "They did get a better feel—mainly in Saudi Arabia, but to a lesser degree Egypt, and even lesser in Syria—as to the potential for business, so that they could, you know, have their antennas out and see if they could do business," Atiyeh recalled. "The trade mission was the basic fundamental reason that we put this group together and went to that part of the world."[66]

Atiyeh oral historian Clark Hansen recalled that critics believed "that there were no real important business reasons to be going to the Middle East for Oregon, but that it was basically a vacation." Indeed, an extensive photographic collection exists in Atiyeh's personal papers at Pacific University along with video footage of the trip showing the governor touring historic sites.[67] Atiyeh openly acknowledged experi-encing nostalgia in returning to his parents' homeland for the first time in over half a century and spent a great deal of time on the trip visit-ing family. More troubling was his apparently cozy relationship with dictators Hosni Mubarak and Hafez al-Assad, which was likely already uncomfortable upon reflection when Hansen interviewed Atiyeh in 1993 because those leaders had been repressing dissent in Egypt and Syria respectively for decades, sometimes brutally so. Nevertheless,

Atiyeh reasserted his positive feelings about the trade mission. "All you'd really have to do is ask those that went on the trade mission, and they were all perfectly happy," he said. "Matter of fact, they were ecstatic. We met more cabinet heads in one day that they would probably receive in two years. . . . That's what a Governor does, open those kind of doors. And the fact that they were with the Governor raised their prestige among the people they were trying to do business with." Though he acknowledged that Saudi Arabia, for example, never developed into a major Northwest trading partner, he still asserted that "if you take a company or two, they're real important to them."[68]

A DELICATE BALANCE: ATIYEH AND THE TWO CHINAS

Following particularly on the heels of politicians in Washington state, Atiyeh saw Taiwan and China as a major international trade priority. The governor said that his active involvement with Taiwan trade relations began when Oregon State Senator Ken Jernstedt put forth a resolution in the legislature calling for Oregon and Taiwan to have a sister-state-province relationship. After determining how to sort out the situation vis-à-vis Oregon's burgeoning trade relationship with China, which adamantly opposed most US relations with Taiwan, the legislature passed the resolution and Atiyeh signed it. "Taiwan was a great trading partner with Oregon," Atiyeh recalled. "Had been for a long time. I even met with the consul-general of Taiwan in my office on the afternoon and that evening" of the signing.[69]

For Atiyeh, Oregon's relationship with Taiwan was personally important, and he had mixed feelings after the Carter administration formally recognized China in 1979 and ended official US relations with Taiwan. As he recalled,

> I felt very offended by all of that, because Taiwan was such a great trading partner with Oregon, and they'd send delegations and they would buy. . . . They bought a lot of wheat from us. . . . To me it's a matter of loyalty. And I'd visited Taiwan and had good friends there. . . . I just wanted to make sure that the people in China understood where I stood. And basically [my position] was, "I have no problem signing this relationship with

China. I think it's a good move, and a wise move. . . . But you do understand that I personally have a loyalty to Taiwan, and that I intend to do everything that I can to continue our good relationship because they are our good trading partners. You, China, might be. Taiwan is." And I had that discussion when I met with [then-PRC premier] Zhao Ziyang. . . . We had a very frank and friendly, very friendly discussion. The only understanding that we had was that if—we never quite said I was going to work for a province-state relationship with Taiwan, but it was kind of understood that if we did that, we would not refer to the Republic of China—ROC—because we were talking with, dealing with the People's Republic of China. And that was kind of an agreement.

For Atiyeh to deal with both Taiwan and the PRC was obviously going to be diplomatically tricky. The governor recalled that he made it work largely on the strength of his friendship with Taiwanese Deputy Minister of Affairs John Chang. He also had precedent to go on, as Montana had signed a "province-state relation" with Taiwan. In December 1986, shortly before Atiyeh left office, Oregon and Taiwan formally concluded the sister-state relationship begun with the Oregon State Legislature's 1984 resolution, and Atiyeh noted that the so-called "Atiyeh formula" was later emulated by other US states.[70]

Atiyeh also jump-started relations between Oregon and mainland China, on its way to becoming the state's biggest trade partner. In the spring of 1984, Atiyeh flew to China to meet with Premier Zhao Ziyang and sign a sister-state agreement with Fujian province. In the process, Atiyeh and his delegation undertook the sort of on-the-ground, meet-and-greet diplomacy he believed was key to winning over foreign business constituents. During his meeting with Zhao, Atiyeh was filmed small-talking, drinking, eating dinner, giving the premier a book of Oregon pictures, and inviting him to visit Oregon. Atiyeh later toured a museum displaying antiquities from the Han dynasty, as well as an electronics plant. Upon the signing of the Oregon-Fujian agreement, Atiyeh told a press briefing that committees from the Oregon and Fujian delegations signed agreements "in the areas of forestry, agriculture, fisheries, electronics and the light industry, education, trade, and culture." He declared that "we are not only signing a document

Governor Atiyeh shakes hands with Zhao Ziyang, premier of the People's Republic of China, during a trade mission to China in the mid-1980s. Oregon's trade with China, negligible before Atiyeh's tenure in office, eventually surpassed the state's trade with all other countries. Reprinted by permission from Pacific University Special Collections, Victor Atiyeh Collection, identifier PUA_MS96_1948.

but we are making initial agreements for immediate exchange," touting the relationship to come as "the envy of all of the states in the United States." When pressed to discuss the substance of the agreement, Atiyeh said it included "efforts in regard to freeze-dried food, some efforts in regard to paper craft sawmills, exchange of students between Fujian and Oregon in terms of education, exchange of cultural visits" and artistic exchanges.[71]

The success of the Fujian trade mission led a Chinese delegation to come to Oregon. Fujian government officials, an economic study group, Chinese media, and the provincial consul general were in attendance. Fujian governor Hu Ping's delegation visited Portland and San Francisco between November 27 and December 9, 1984. The mission began by touring Portland State University, the Port of Portland, and Oregon Health & Science University. On December 1, the delegation saw Bonneville Dam before having dinner with the Chinese-American community in Portland's Chinatown. On December 2, the mission visited Hatfield Marine Science Center in Newport and the fish-processing plant at Depoe Bay Fish Company. On December 3, the group toured the University of Oregon, Normarc Inc. in Tangent, the National Fruit Canning Company and the Plywood Components plant in Albany, and Oregon State University and the Hewlett-Packard plant in Corvallis. On December 4, the group toured Cuddeback Lumber in Eugene, a "sawmill with equipment and technology appropriate to Chinese needs," apparently trying to see if it could export finished lumber to China or jump-start Chinese investment in the sawmills. The group also looked at Pierce Corporation, a "manufacturer of irrigation equipment that is very involved in the export market and utilizes off-shore manufacturing." They headed to Salem on December 5 to present their "specific projects"—presumably to Atiyeh—before lunching at Willamette University and touring the Siltec and Salem Equipment companies. On December 6, the Chinese visited Tektronix, Nike, and Washington Square Mall in Atiyeh's home Washington County, before finishing the day with a Chamber of Commerce reception and a Portland Trail Blazers basketball game. On December 7, the Fujian group concluded their stay with a breakfast meeting with the Northwest China Council, an economic study group meeting in Portland.[72] The trip was a success, according to Atiyeh, as Hu Ping's "seventeen-man party" completed "ten tentative deals," capping off a strong 1984 for Oregon and international trade.[73]

PUSHING TRADE FRONTIERS IN ATIYEH'S FINAL YEARS IN OFFICE

Atiyeh's final years in office saw a push for more international trade during a time when the climate seemed particularly ripe for new Japanese investment in Oregon. The *Nomura Newsflash*, a publication that circulated to 100,000 Japanese businessmen, reported in March 1985 that "Oregon . . . is now in the foremost limelight in America" as a production base for high-tech semiconductor, computer, and telecommunications industries. The article contended that Oregon had become increasingly advantageous over California because of its higher quality of life as well as the abolition of the unitary tax. "Japanese leading enterprises' advance to Oregon has worked to raise more 'Oregon fever' among Japanese industries," the *Newsflash* argued.[74]

Atiyeh returned to Japan for another trade mission in May 1985, but this visit ended in disappointment, especially with the loss to Camas, Washington, of the hoped-for Sharp-RCA Corporation factory. According to Atiyeh oral historian Clark Hansen, Washington Governor Booth Gardner "was taking the same representatives from the companies on tours at the same time," demonstrating an interregional competitiveness with Oregon.[75] Atiyeh took flak for the Sharp-RCA loss amid a public assessment that he was not turning the state's economy around. At year's end, Charles Humble of the *Oregonian* editorialized that "where 1984 brought a sense of euphoria from the announcements of several Japanese electronics firms that they would invest in the state, 1985 brought layoffs by the existing stable of high-tech mainstays," particularly Tektronix in Atiyeh's Washington County, which laid off 1,200 workers. "Atiyeh was unable to repeat the kind of success" he enjoyed in 1984, largely, Humble argued, because Oregon Economic Development Department director John Anderson was lured away to Washington for a higher salary and a similar post, taking all hope of landing Sharp-RCA with him. "As much as Oregonians tried to shroud their hurt, it was another case of Oregon's failing to land a big one after reeling it boatside," Humble concluded.[76] Years later, Atiyeh recalled that Booth Gardner "stole [Anderson] from me," but also claimed he was "very unhappy" with Anderson because he "wouldn't return phone calls [and] took credit for everything that happened" during his department's period of success in increasing Oregon-Japan relations. Fed up with Anderson, Atiyeh said he was "delighted when he got stolen from me" and was "quietly smiling" at the negative press coverage from the *Oregonian*. Atiyeh said he was much happier with Tom Kennedy, Anderson's replacement at the OEDD, saying, "I'd wished I'd started with him years earlier because Tom was a good, good director of economic development."[77]

As 1985 ended, Atiyeh was increasingly fighting criticism from constituents for being away from home too much. Syndicated columnist Richard Reeves reported that Atiyeh had spent over a month out of Oregon in 1985, earning himself the derisive nickname "Trader Vic." He noted that Atiyeh's last trip cost more than $15,000, but defended the governor, arguing "that money seems to be earning more money." His report indicated that in 1984, Oregon imported $2.2 billion and exported $2.5 billion in goods and services to Japan, compared with 1983 imports of $1.7 billion and exports of $1.6 billion. Noting that nearly three-quarters of US governors went on trade missions in 1985, Reeves advocated for more such missions, contending that "anybody who doesn't like his junketing doesn't understand what government has to do at the end of the 20th century." Because national leaders, including within the Reagan administration, were "grumbl[ing] about 'government interference in business'" and failing to come up with a coherent policy to help US businesses make international connections, Reeves said, states like Oregon were rightly taking up the cause themselves.[78]

The junketeer charge stuck to Atiyeh, however, and he had to appeal directly to Oregonians to repel charges that his trade missions were wasteful uses of taxpayer money. His April 4, 1985, "State of the State" address touted the international efforts of the State Agriculture Department, including its work "promoting Oregon-grown foods in Japanese supermarkets." In his July 24, 1986, "State of the State," Atiyeh said Oregon's Tokyo trade office had met with representatives from Japan's fourth-largest "home-center chain," bringing the company to Oregon to meet wood manufacturers who assisted them in purchases of finished wood products. Because the chain store was ready to buy these products, Atiyeh contended the sale would produce jobs for Oregonians. Overall, he claimed, the trade office regularly worked with Oregon suppliers to find prospective Japanese buyers. He told numerous success stories, such as when a Tokyo buyer purchased cod from an Oregon supplier.[79]

Japanese opinion of Oregon remained favorable as Atiyeh's administration wound down. Keidanren members were again impressed with Oregon on a return visit in the spring of 1986. Kazuo Nukazawa, coordinator of Keidanren's mission to Oregon, wrote Atiyeh that the state's "industrial workers share such qualities as diligence and frugality with their Japanese counterparts." Keidanren again praised the end of the unitary system and the success of *From Oregon With Love*. It also noted that "the state is heavily committed to an economic principle of free trade and competition with foreign corporations. This is a posture very encouraging to us."[80] Atiyeh kept up that posture during his waning months in office. In the spring of 1986, the governor, through the state Agriculture Department, landed a deal for Superior Packing, an Oregon lamb wholesaler, to sell 250,000 pounds of lamb and up to twenty containers of lamb skins annually to Japan.[81] A chemical factory named American Tokyo Kasei, meanwhile, broke ground at the Port of Portland on a world distribution center, including a warehouse and research laboratory that would house up to fifty chemists to distribute chemical and pharmaceutical products across the world. Port commissioners also concluded a lease agreement with Toyota to become the port's largest automobile import customer.[82]

At the end of Atiyeh's administration, fellow politicians and businesspeople heaped praise upon the governor for his efforts to stimulate
the Oregon-Japan relationship. On December 28, 1986, Senator Mark
Hatfield wrote Atiyeh that Oregon got high marks from US Ambassador to Japan Mike Mansfield during a recent meeting. "Oregon is
the exception to a pattern of neglect of the growing trade imbalance
between our two countries," Hatfield wrote. "Ambassador Mansfield
made specific reference to your work which is well deserving of such
praise."[83] D. James Manning, director of the International Trade and
Commerce Institute at Portland State University, congratulated Atiyeh, meanwhile, for "foresight and leadership in the development of
the international dimensions of Oregon's economy," arguing that his
"efforts in this area are reflected through the significant growth and
development in recent years of Oregon's international business community." Manning noted, "The record clearly indicates your success in
the promotion of investment in Oregon, exporting from Oregon and
Oregon as a state 'Open For Business.'"[84]

The Japanese businesspeople Atiyeh worked with during his administration also showered him with praise on his departure from office.
Toyoo Nariai, manager of the international division of the Japan/Tokyo
Chambers of Commerce and Industry, wrote Atiyeh that his "role in
the growth and development of industry in Oregon has been great
indeed . . . thank you for all you have done to deepen our relationship
between Oregon and Japan." Hiroo Kobayashi, president of Epson Portland Inc. in Hillsboro, wrote that "we are impressed by your initiative
and efforts to welcome Japanese investments into Oregon."[85] Portland
consul-general Shosaku Tanaka said in farewell remarks to Atiyeh at
the Alexis Hotel in Portland on November 24, 1986, that "everyone in
the Japanese community has been deeply impressed with Governor
Atiyeh's warm personality and respects him as a man of sincere, moderate and broad-minded views." Tanaka argued that "there is not one
Japanese business executive who doesn't know the state of Oregon as
one of the most promising sites for their new investments."[86]

Press and public opinion on the Atiyeh administration's trade
efforts were more mixed. The *Oregonian* contended that "it is easy to
disparage a politician's overseas travel, but it is also easy to overlook the
benefits that high-level contacts produce"—such as convincing Atiyeh

that Oregon's unitary system was a barrier to Japanese investment. "At least some of the additions to Oregon's so-called Silicon Forest were dividends from that policy change," the paper concluded.[87] The *Klamath Falls Herald and News* noted that Atiyeh predicted that "visits he made to Pacific Rim countries will continue to pay off in the future. . . . We hope so," the paper opined, warning that recent layoffs at Tektronix, in particular, threatened to dampen the gains he had made.[88] The *Eugene Register-Guard* pointed out that a recent poll gave Atiyeh ratings of just 45 percent "excellent" or "good" and 44 percent "not very good" or "poor" over his governorship. Of his trade missions, the paper editorialized that "it's impossible to say how much good these have done, but Atiyeh's missionary work could pay off in expanding Pacific Rim trade and investments in Oregon long after he is out of office." The editorial contended that Atiyeh "deserves credit for trying, and for realizing that this selling job could only be done by the governor."[89]

Atiyeh's efforts at increasing Oregon-Japan trade continued to bear fruit after his retirement as governor in 1987. In August Atiyeh was present as Fujitsu unveiled plans for its Gresham plant. The *Oregonian* reported that Atiyeh and former Gresham mayor Margaret Weil, a like-minded international trade advocate, were probably the officials most responsible for getting the plant sited in Gresham, with Atiyeh visiting Japan and Fujitsu corporate offices nine times. Personal diplomacy played a role as well in securing the plant, as Vic and Dolores Atiyeh became friends with Fujitsu's top executive, Rinzo Iwai, and his wife. The couples got to know each other so well that Vic credited Dolores with helping to bring Fujitsu to both Gresham as well as its earlier Hillsboro plant.[90]

Atiyeh believed he had stood up well against competition for foreign investment. He praised his staff as "a good team of people, well-organized, well-equipped . . . continually pushing, moving forward, to diversify the economy of the state." When his governorship began, Atiyeh noted, Oregon's economic base was agriculture, wood products, timber, and some tourism. When he left office, tourism, high-tech, and international trade had been added to that base.[91] Gerry Thompson acknowledged that while Washington "was really competing against us . . . we were way out in front" of other states in international trade.[92] Some business leaders certainly seemed to agree. When in 1986, Atiyeh addressed an annual meeting of Japanese and business executives from western states, he met with a group formerly known only as the Japan-California Association at Salishan Beach near Lincoln City in Oregon. The California-based event moderator noted that this was the first time the meeting had been held outside California and said that Atiyeh was "a leader, and we're a follower."[93]

Sales of grain and wood products abroad, still Oregon's leading export items despite the high-tech surge, increased late in Atiyeh's term and continued into that of his successor, Neil Goldschmidt. Steve Newman, president of Newman, Wilson & Co., a Portland freight forwarder, told the *Oregonian* in October 1987 that his export business was "substantially better than any of the last three years." As the national economy continued its recovery from the recession of the early 1980s, grain exports increased 2 percent in the first half of 1987, and softwood lumber exports from the Northwest states in general were up 20 percent in 1987 over 1986 numbers, which had shown a 24 percent gain from 1985.[94]

As Goldschmidt prepared for his own Asian trade mission in October 1987, Bob Buchanan, by now the director of the Oregon Department of Agriculture, contended that Oregon needed to modify its approach from the Atiyeh years to be competitive. In putting together trade shows in Taiwan and Japan, multiple state agencies and industries jointly staged trade exhibits for the first time. The *Oregonian* reported that in the past Oregon companies and agencies exhibited "at specialized overseas shows, such as agriculture shows." Noting that a single-industry focus was common to most state trade delegations, Buchanan said that Oregon, by contrast, "needed a statement" to position it better vis-à-vis other states. Perhaps this was true: as the article noted, nearly every state was now lobbying hard for business in East Asia.[95] On his return, Goldschmidt acknowledged that more work would be necessary to boost Oregon's international trade portfolio. "The message we got was presence and perseverance," Goldschmidt said. "If you're not back within 12 months, it won't pay off." The governor and Port of Portland Commission president Cecil Drinkward met with officials of shipping lines to try and make Portland a port of first call. Even during the Atiyeh years, no shipping line stopped at Portland first, and half of Oregon's cargo went through Puget Sound ports.[96] This point contrasts to some degree with Atiyeh's rosy picture of Oregon in the lead in terms of international trade among other states.

The state as a whole certainly became more dependent on international trade during Atiyeh's tenure. One in six jobs were tied to trade in 1987 versus one in nine before he entered office. This sort of expansion had been Atiyeh's goal, and he believed he had done the right thing by pushing so hard in this arena. Trade, he contended, was a more stable source of economic prosperity than the federal or military investment sought by Henry Jackson, Wayne Morse, and even Mark Hatfield. "The military budget's constant in being attacked by a lot of people," he said. "To me it was kind of transitory . . . too thin a reed for us to hang our hat on." Atiyeh contended that in contrast to Oregon, California struggled because it had been "heavily dependent" on the military and endured cutbacks costing thousands of employees their jobs when the Cold War ended. A 1998 analysis by the Legislative Analyst's Office of California backs up Atiyeh's claims somewhat: it indicated that while economic growth was strong in some parts of the state, "defense cutbacks have taken a major toll on California," with over 200,000 job cuts in the state's aerospace industry between 1988 and 1996 and the closure of twenty-five military bases in the state during the 1990s.[97] Oregon avoided being directly affected by Pentagon cuts, although there was little in Oregon to cut because nearly all of the state's military outposts were shuttered or turned over to control of the Oregon National Guard during the Cold War. Oregon's trade relationships, meanwhile, continued to grow with Japan and other East Asian countries Atiyeh had cultivated relationships with during his tenure as governor.

Documents relating to America Japan Week 1992, which Atiyeh helped organize in Portland, show that Oregon-Japan links continued to grow and benefit the state in the years after he left public office. America Japan Week organizers claimed that Oregon's total bilateral trade with Japan had increased to $7 billion, that the majority of the 1,400 Oregon companies that traded in the Pacific Rim did so with Japan, and that Delta Airlines' direct link to Tokyo, a successor to the United Airlines flight Atiyeh had helped inaugurate nearly a decade earlier, had created 1,000 jobs. Japanese foreign direct investment to Oregon totaled $375 million during the 1980s and had created 4,300 jobs.[98] In 2007, the Port of Portland unveiled a sculpture of Atiyeh to greet overseas arrivals at the Victor G. Atiyeh International Concourse at Portland International Airport. The *Oregonian* editorialized that while "others have built on Atiyeh's work, both in trade and economic development... Atiyeh's efforts to lead Oregon... laid the foundation."[99] Working in concert with local business leaders, Japanese business and government officials, and other Oregon state agencies, Atiyeh attracted Japanese foreign direct investment and increased Oregon exports to Japan and other East Asian nations, diversifying Oregon's economy in the face of the collapse of much of the state's timber industry.

Atiyeh's work did not, however, broadly transform Oregon into a high-tech manufacturing hub that rivaled its neighbors, nor was the governor able to stabilize Oregon's economy during his time in office. As early as 1985, when Tektronix announced layoffs despite a broader economic recovery in Oregon and the nation as a whole, it was clear that high-tech could not replace timber as an economically stable industry on which the state could lean. His own administration acknowledged near the end of his tenure that, despite the influx of Japanese investment, the state's old staples of timber, agriculture, and tourism remained Oregon's three largest industries.[100] Meanwhile, the big three tech companies Atiyeh lured to Oregon—NEC, Fujitsu, and Epson—expanded and thrived. In 1993, outgoing Epson Portland executive adviser Mas Tomita predicted a bright future for the company, noting Atiyeh's work to convince him to build in Oregon.[101] The bottom nonetheless dropped out on the big Japanese manufacturers Atiyeh lured to Oregon by the beginning of the new millennium, due in part to external factors. The economic "miracle" fueling Japan's foreign investment slowed during the early 1990s, and the Japanese economy went into recession during the Asian economic crisis of the late 1990s. To make up for its losses, Japan turned to its East Asian neighbors for cheaper labor costs, removing jobs from Oregon as well as elsewhere in the United States. NEC America was the first to leave Oregon altogether in 1999, with Fujitsu Microelectronics' Gresham plant following in 2001.[102]

Historian Andrew McKevitt contextualizes this shift in fortunes for Japanese subsidiaries in the United States by contending that "American companies like IBM, Microsoft, and Apple benefited most" from the personal computer boom following Atiyeh's administration, not merely as a result of Japan's economic decline but also because "Japanese corporations structured to maximize productivity, efficiency, and distribution in a global marketplace were too hierarchical and inflexible to keep pace with the rapidly innovating, smaller American firms."[103] In essence, if Atiyeh had bet that Japan represented a stable source of future economic growth in the manufacturing sector, that gamble did not pay off.

Of the major companies Atiyeh lured to Silicon Forest, only Epson's Hillsboro plant clung to life. In May 2000, the ex-governor predicted that Epson was in Oregon to stay, contending that "the EPI [Epson] story is a good one that demonstrates the enormous concern of our Oregon business employees and leadership that quietly gives to our community."[104] Amid a global economic slowdown, Epson laid off Oregon employees and discharged Atiyeh as a paid consultant in August 2000.[105] Despite its downsizing, Atiyeh's prognostication about Epson's future in Oregon, at least, held true. In addition, smaller Japanese companies—for example, Yamasa Soy Sauce, which built its American factory in Salem in 1994—invested in Oregon during and after the Atiyeh years, following the path laid out by the manufacturers Atiyeh lured to the state during the mid-1980s.[106]

As the hemorrhaging of the timber industry has proven, Atiyeh, like Mark Hatfield, was right to assert that Oregon could not remain dependent on the forests alone for its economic health. Atiyeh should be credited for recognizing that Oregon needed to diversify its economic portfolio, even if such diversification yielded variable benefits. Atiyeh should also be credited for creative, unconventional thinking in terms of expanding Oregon's economy, as shown in the evolution of Oregon's relationship with East Asian and Middle Eastern nations during the 1980s and beyond. Through his travels abroad, hosting delegations from overseas, securing foreign direct investment to Oregon, and maintaining his connections abroad after leaving office, Atiyeh opened doors to the state throughout the world, helping make Oregon less insular and parochial than in past decades and more fully integrating the state into the global economy. While hardly the economic savior contemporary accounts make him out to be, Atiyeh did make a leap forward in contrast to his gubernatorial predecessors by recognizing that Oregon's economic future relied on foreign trade and investment into the state. With respect to those who cemented Tom McCall and Robert Straub in popular discourse as Oregon's most important post–World War II governors, recognition on Atiyeh's part of the value of foreign markets earns him a chapter in the "Oregon Story" of the last half of the twentieth century.

Conclusion

Since 1945, US senators and representatives, and governors from the Pacific Northwest have exercised political power to turn a region once considered a hinterland by the rest of the United States into an economic powerhouse. They fought for national security state-building dollars from the federal government, as well as for trade deals with government and business officials from the United States as well as abroad. Decades of policy shifts and lobbying by governmental officials ultimately brought about increased economic prosperity for Washington and Oregon, although that prosperity was divided somewhat unevenly. Ultimately this process provides insights into the regional impact of post–World War II economic growth and transformation.

In the realm of national security, Henry Jackson and Warren Magnuson recognized that with Hanford as a producer of plutonium and Boeing producing vital military aircraft, they had chips to play that would, if they gained power, keep the region from losing defense dollars and military personnel in a postwar era in which seemingly the entire nation was scrambling for the material benefits of the national security state. Indeed, during the 1960s, their committee and subcommittee chairmanships enabled them to maintain and strengthen the defense establishment in Washington. In the 1980s, Tom Foley used his burgeoning power to maintain Fairchild Air Force Base. Although he could not maintain Hanford's nuclear mission, Foley and Oregon's Mark Hatfield redirected federal dollars to clean up one of the United States' great environmental catastrophes. The "Scoop and Maggie" legacy has helped federal- and state-level officials keep Washington intricately linked with national security interests. Boeing remains a major jobs producer for the Seattle area, and the naval bases of the

Puget Sound as well as Joint Base Lewis-McChord near Tacoma are lasting legacies of the Jackson/Magnuson years.

The relationship of the national security state to Oregon was weaker. The industrialist Henry Kaiser's shipyards, which were for a time Oregon's equivalent to Boeing, shut down after World War II as the nation leaned on air power and nuclear weapons to fight the Cold War. The Pentagon gradually eliminated Oregon's military installations or transferred them to National Guard control in the decades following the war. A lack of political power by Oregonians played a role in the state's fate relative to the growth of military industries. Before 1981, Second District Representative Al Ullman was the only Oregonian to chair a full committee—Ways and Means—which had limited authority over national security affairs. Though Wayne Morse fought for national security interests, he ultimately was no Jackson or Magnuson in his efforts, nor was long-serving Representative Edith Green. It was thus easy for both Morse and Green, as well as Governor-turned-Senator Mark Hatfield, to break ranks and oppose the Vietnam War, because the national security state's presence in Oregon was relatively small by the late 1960s. Mark Hatfield was at the congressional vanguard in terms of redefining national security once he became Senate Appropriations Committee chair in the 1980s. His moral and ethical opposition to war and desire for reduced military spending, combined with the lack of a national security apparatus in Oregon, led him to redirect funds toward efforts that he believed more vital in the maintenance of national security. Hatfield turned defense dollars toward the education and health of the region's citizenry, particularly through his fostering of the growth of Oregon Health and Science University.

Regarding international trade, meanwhile, it is ironic that prior to the New Deal, arguably the region's biggest contribution to the national debate on tariffs came from Willis Hawley. The Republican Congressman from Oregon cosponsored the Smoot-Hawley Tariff and pushed it through his Ways and Means Committee, where it was later approved by the Senate and President Herbert Hoover in the early 1930s. This legislation dramatically raised import tariffs and is considered by some historians to have exacerbated the Great Depression.[1] In the decades thereafter, Northwest politicians progressed steadily farther from Smoot-Hawley-style protectionism. They have not been alone among their colleagues from other regions in embracing international trade, but given the proximity of their region to the growing economies of the Pacific Rim, as well as the Northwest's economic dependency prior to the Cold War (particularly in Oregon), they reaped clearer benefits from such openness.

The efforts of politicians in the post–World War II era accelerated the already robust movement of extractive agricultural commodities from the Pacific Northwest. Timber, wheat, and apples were exported to Pacific Rim countries in increasing quantities, particularly as Japan recovered from the devastation of World War II and as Communist China reopened to western trade after President Richard Nixon's visit there in 1972. Politicians worked to expedite this trade and to introduce new Northwest commodities and businesses to foreign markets. At the same time, they encountered occasional protectionist impulses from elements in their constituencies, as well as at the national level. Tom Foley discovered during the 1980s that his power to shape national trade policy could be a double-edged sword, as he had to balance the needs of free-trade-oriented eastern Washington farmers with Midwest farmers who wanted to keep wheat prices low so that they could sell more of their domestically bound wares to consumers. The fact that he did so successfully speaks to a high level of political skill that benefited the pro-foreign trade constituency in his home district and enriched the Pacific Northwest.

During the 1980s and 1990s, the increasing ubiquity of jet travel and high-tech goods and services further globalized the Pacific Northwest. Oregon stood to gain in these years after decades of slipping behind its northern neighbor in economic and political power. Democrats Henry Jackson and Warren Magnuson died and passed from the political scene. After Republicans swept to power in the Senate in the 1980 elections, Mark Hatfield became Senate Appropriations Chair, while Bob Packwood chaired the Senate Commerce Committee and later the Finance Committee. At the same time, the state had a staunchly pro-trade Republican governor in Vic Atiyeh, a former rug exporter used to hustling for international trade partners. These men all worked to increase trade of traditional agricultural goods to Japan while encouraging foreign direct investment, but also boosted trade with China, Saudi Arabia, Syria, Egypt, Taiwan, and others.

Sometimes they endured criticism for what opponents considered to be extravagant and excessive overseas trips. It is clear, however, that they achieved positive results for Oregon businesses and improved the state's reputation abroad as a business partner and as a destination for foreign investment, particularly through Atiyeh's repeal of the state's unitary tax in 1984.

Ultimately, an examination of trade and security issues facing Oregon and Washington shows the real effects of political power and the politicians that wielded it. These individuals were effective at their jobs, they were well-liked by voters, and they held a strong interest in US foreign relations. In some cases, as with Wayne Morse and Mark Hatfield, the interest was innate in their character: they felt it was their moral and ethical duty as senators to be citizens of the world beyond their narrow constituencies, although they certainly did their best to represent their voters. The Washingtonians, meanwhile, looked to the Pacific and saw that the shores beyond them represented danger which threatened their state (particularly in the case of anti-Communists Henry Jackson and Warren Magnuson) but also opportunity for their state (particularly in the case of Tom Foley and Slade Gorton). Once these senators and congressmen finally obtained positions of power via committee chairmanships, they brought federal dollars to their states for economic development, and they paved the way for governors like Vic Atiyeh to use political power to help local businesses reap benefits from international connections as well.

In obtaining and harnessing political power, Pacific Northwest politicians shed national perceptions that the region was just a colonial hinterland. Just like congressional giants Lyndon Johnson and John Stennis in the South, Ted Kennedy in the Northeast, or Stuart Symington in the Midwest, the delegation from Washington and Oregon used their chairmanships and authority to economically strengthen their region during the Cold War and beyond. Such political power, whether used wisely or for pork-barreling purposes, offers a lens illuminating the place of the Pacific Northwest in the United States vis-à-vis the world. The debates in Oregon in 1966 and 1968 over the Vietnam War, and in 1984 over the unitary tax; as well as Washingtonians' continued dependence on defense contracts and spending for military bases show a region changed and challenged by international events during the

Snow sculpture of Portland, Oregon, City Hall constructed in Portland's sister city of Sapporo, Japan, in 1987. The inscription indicates the photo was sent to Portland Mayor Bud Clark by an acquaintance who was an admiral in the US Pacific Fleet. US and Japanese flags flank the sculpture. Reprinted by permission from City of Portland (OR) Archives, A2010-011, 1987c.

Cold War. Successful politicians alternately rode the waves of change or influenced the shape of those waves. As important as it was for Nixon to go to China in 1972, for example, it was also crucial that Northwest senators like Henry Jackson and Warren Magnuson followed up later in the decade, forming connections that would increase trade to the region and ultimately to the nation. Northwest politicians were not the only Americans influencing the increase of national security and trade flows, but it is important to understand the role that people from this region played in the expansion of trade in the Pacific Rim and in the growth of—and debates about—the national security state.

National security state dollars and increased global trade alone could not solve all the economic dilemmas of the Pacific Northwest or the United States as a whole in the postwar years. After decades of electing presidents who pumped immense resources into defense and trade, American voters went to the polls on November 8, 2016, and elected Donald

J. Trump, a Republican presidential candidate who vowed to rebuild the nation's military while reducing American commitments worldwide, and who also did not look kindly on American trade deals of the past. In his inaugural address, Trump emphasized his belief that "a small group" in Washington, DC, benefited while "the jobs left, and the factories closed." The triumphs of the few, said Trump, had not been celebrated by most Americans. Saying that the United States had decayed while enriching others abroad, Trump put forth an "America first" policy, saying that "we must protect our borders from the ravages of other countries making our products, stealing our companies, and destroying our jobs."[2]

Although most of the national attention with regard to Trump's work to "protect our borders" has been focused on his administration's controversial immigration policy, his trade policy seems to stand in stark contrast to the worldview of most in the Pacific Northwest, arguably signaling a fundamental threat to the relationship the region had built with the world. Indeed, Oregon and Washington voters resoundingly rejected Trump at the ballot box. Yet the president's message clearly struck a chord with those who felt left behind by the economic transformations discussed in this book, and the residents, businesses, and politicians of the Pacific Northwest are already reckoning with the voices awoken by his stridently nationalist campaign. By September 2019, sales of Pacific Northwest beef and wheat to China had come to a halt because of Trump's "trade war" against Beijing. Retaliatory tariffs imposed by China on Oregon exports of hazelnuts and cherries hit 65 percent and 60 percent, respectively. Oregon was particularly hit hard because 40 percent of its agricultural exports went outside the United States, compared to 20 percent for the rest of the United States. Directors of the main ports of the West Coast warned Trump of "irredeemable economic harm" if the trade war continued.[3] Oregon Democrats railed against the Trump administration's actions, while Republican Representative Greg Walden stood by the president. Oregon's divided congressional delegation seemed to have little clout in influencing Trump's trade policy.

Even before Trump came to power, in recent decades political gridlock at the state and federal levels rendered Northwest politicians relatively impotent in terms of attracting national security dollars and trade routes in comparison to their famous predecessors. Oregon

Democratic Senator Ron Wyden briefly served as chair of the Finance Committee in 2014 and did not pass any meaningful legislation before the Republicans regained the majority in that chamber in that year's midterm election. Wyden had long been a strong advocate of the Trans-Pacific Partnership (TPP), a trade deal he argued would benefit the Pacific Northwest by expediting foreign trade with many of the region's major international partners, including Japan. Many in the Northwest agreed with Wyden. But during the 2016 presidential campaign, both Trump and Democratic presidential candidate Bernie Sanders fired up crowds and attracted voters in part through vociferous opposition to the TPP, which they believed would take American jobs and investment overseas. Hillary Clinton, Sanders's Democratic opponent, was forced to oppose the TPP in the general election, and one of Trump's first acts upon taking office was to withdraw the United States from TPP negotiations.[4] While Trump left the door open to future bilateral trade deals with Pacific Rim nations that could benefit Northwest workers and businesses dealing abroad, the US withdrawal was still a major blow in the short term to pro-trade interests in the region.

Power and globalization in the Pacific Northwest clearly benefited the region, but Trump's election and the devotion of his base of supporters—even in Oregon and Washington—demonstrate that it is important to point out the unevenness of the benefits of defense spending and trade across the region. Federal government intervention into the lives of Pacific Northwesterners has presented drawbacks as well as benefits. While most Americans have positively viewed the economic benefits that have come with the national security state, for example, the needs of the Pentagon have nonetheless "clashed with long-cherished ideas about property, land ownership, and citizenship."[5] Indeed, it cannot be forgotten that property owners from Hanford to Bremerton clashed with the federal government over the loss of their land, even in the name of national security. Tom Foley's electoral defeat in 1994 was clearly linked to growing antigovernment sentiment, even in the face of his support for federal agencies that were giving his constituents jobs, like Fairchild Air Force Base near Spokane or the Veterans' Administration Hospital in Walla Walla.

On issues of international trade as well, some Northwesterners had very real concerns that the globalization of the region was not working out in their favor. At the turn of the millennium, Oregon's economy was no longer dependent solely upon natural resources. Housing and industrial subdivisions ate up an increasing share of farmland, especially on the state's growing west side, leading to sprawl and, some believed, an erosion of the livability that state boosters like Mark Hatfield and Vic Atiyeh had touted for decades.[6] The question of whether the benefits of globalization were being evenly spread was also subject to intense debate. Japanese and Koreans who came to Oregon to work in Silicon Forest–related industries because of Atiyeh's push for foreign direct investment increased the Asian population of Washington County from 5,000 to 14,000 during the 1980s, giving the Portland suburb of Beaverton a distinctly multicultural feel. Yet these migrants were mostly well-heeled technicians, engineers, and managers. Foreign trade to and from the Northwest did not clearly benefit large numbers of people in the working or lower classes in the region.[7]

In general, Silicon Forest has not proven to be the cure for Oregon's ailing economy. While its boom created new jobs, its factories also outsourced labor to manufacturers in developing countries, leaving laid-off employees to retrain or look to the service sector to find work. Ancillary job creation also occurred alongside the main Silicon Forest plants, but this was mostly in the consultation industry, with venture capital firms being the biggest winners. Women were well represented in blue-collar work on the Silicon Forest assembly lines, but not in management. At the same time, there was growing concern that the supposedly clean high-tech sector was damaging the natural landscape, mostly by leaking potentially deadly chemicals into the soil and water. But while new businesses had to endure high property taxes in Portland, the cost of land was half as much as in Seattle and a quarter of that in Los Angeles. The high-tech sector was generous in terms of philanthropy and thus worked to strengthen the region's arts, culture, and educational landscape.[8]

Indeed, when it came to foreign trade, Pacific Northwesterners exuded a mixed spirit of optimism, anxiety, and even nostalgia as the region passed into the new millennium. Historian and *Oregonian* columnist David Sarasohn, for example, positively reflected on the one-hundred-year history of Jake's, a historic seafood restaurant in downtown Portland. At the same time, however, he noted the effect globalization had on the restaurant. Its legendarily fresh fish, he reported, was less likely to come from the Columbia River, and more likely to come from the Atlantic Ocean, or from Pacific Rim destinations like Alaska, British Columbia, or Hawaii, thus causing loss of an intrinsic regionalism that characterized the restaurant. Pointing out the growth of the regional wine industry—which in and of itself was a manifestation of a global economic force traditionally felt far from the Pacific Northwest—Sarasohn noted that "in Oregon restaurants at the start of the century, the fish was local and the wine came from far away. At the end of the century, it's been reversed." In 2018, only about half the fish on the menu at Jake's came from Oregon or Washington waters.[9]

Another turn-of-the-millennium report indicated that, from a macroeconomic point of view, globalization seemed to benefit Oregon, which by the end of the 1990s sent $4.59 billion in exports to the developing world and $5.23 billion to industrialized countries, numbers that had dramatically increased from the 1980s. Columnist Jennifer Bjorhus argued that the success of small businesses like Weitech, a pest-repellant-assembly company that filled orders from around the world, reflected the successes of globalization. On the other hand, Bjorhus pointed out that Pendleton Woolen Mills, a maker of blankets and clothing based in eastern Oregon, had lost over half its jobs—employing only 350 workers, down from a peak of 800—to Mexican textile plants offering cheaper wages because of the North American Free Trade Agreement. Silicon Forest mainstay Tektronix, meanwhile, suffered after US sanctions against India and Pakistan for testing nuclear weapons in 1998 meant the loss of the oscilloscope trade to those countries, on which the company relied heavily. Bjorhus noted that Oregon had also suffered "thousands" of job losses during a major Asian financial crisis in 1997 that barely dented the US economy.[10] Columnist James Mayer, meanwhile, contended that globalization was largely to blame for Oregon experiencing the second-highest growth in the nation in economic inequality in the 1990s. Increased international connections, he argued, led to the creation of mainly low-wage, service-sector jobs, while high-paying jobs in lumber and industry went overseas or were eliminated.[11] Globalization, therefore, entailed a loss of control by the state of Oregon and the nation as a whole over what economic sectors grew, where they grew, and who benefited.

The Northwest was also shocked by the disruption and destruction caused by violent protests against the World Trade Organization (WTO) meeting in Seattle in early December 1999. Even the nonviolent protests by a broad coalition of environmentalists, trade unionists, and their allies showed that globalization did not have consensus backing in the region. Columnist Richard Read argued that the conference was an embarrassment and failure for Seattle. Its image as a global city, Read believed, was sullied by riot damage, allegations of police brutality, and calls for the resignations of public officials by antiglobalization protesters. The highest hope of WTO organizers was that the meeting would trigger a successful Seattle round of global trade talks, but instead, Read contended, Seattle was synonymous with the chaos which could happen "when globalization turns sour."[12] The WTO protest lingered in the minds of Pacific Northwesterners on both sides of the debate, particularly when a similar protest wrecked parts of downtown Portland on May 1 of the following year.

The Al-Qaeda attacks on New York City and Washington, DC, on Sept. 11, 2001, further threatened to expand the gap between those who advocated for global ties and others who wanted to turn more inward. A series of letters to the editor of the *Oregonian* highlighted a wide variety of positions on the place of the United States in the post-9/11 world. Marjorie Sandoz of Portland called for the world to share global wealth more equitably. Eric Rhodes of Aurora argued that the United States needed to remain engaged in the world because backing off, he believed, meant the terrorists would win. Stephen Bachhuber said globalization was the reason the 9/11 attacks happened, arguing that redistribution of wealth and the subsequent end to economic inequity would stop terrorism more effectively than war.[13] A subsequent letter to the editor also assailed globalization as the cause of 9/11. Author Susan Banyas feared World War III was soon at hand, and blamed Congress for not doing enough to build bridges toward the developing world.[14]

It is noteworthy, however, that none of the voices in the post-9/11 debate illuminated in the pages of the *Oregonian* called for the Pacific Northwest to shut its borders and become aloof to the world, a sign, perhaps, of how much the region had evolved since World War II thanks in part to the actions of politicians engaged in foreign affairs and trade. Subsequent columns highlighted the urgency of the region's remaining

CONCLUSION259

open in its dealings with the outside world, and the consequences of the threat of global terrorism to Oregon's foreign ties. Richard Read reported, for example, that each container ship going out of the Port of Portland to the Middle East would be tagged with a $125 war insurance surcharge. In the wake of 9/11, Governor John Kitzhaber canceled a trip to Mexico meant to boost the state's sagging export portfolio there, after reports that exports were already off 49 percent from 2000 even before the attacks. Oregon's trade with the European Union was down 6 percent, and trade with Asia was off 30 percent due to uncertainty in the global economy.[15] Read argued that more trade, not less, was the answer.

Willamette University President M. Lee Pelton also advocated for continued Northwest engagement in the world. Although clearly speaking from the standpoint of his university's economic interest in maintaining high numbers of enrollees from outside the United States, Pelton eloquently argued against calls for curtailing study abroad programs both to and from the United States, saying those arguments were contrary to the goals of education. He argued instead for strengthening ties of "human capital" and development at home and abroad through study abroad, contending that increased international research opportunities were also needed. He argued that Willamette and the nation's schools had to "uphold the values of a liberal education" and said he believed that embracing the world at home through programs such as Willamette's Tokyo International University of America would aid that cause.[16]

In the end, the Pacific Northwest did not turn its back on the world after the antiglobalization protests or 9/11—far from it. By 2006, Seattle had become the top exporting city in the United States, with Portland continuing to make strong gains, even though it was secure in its position as the region's second city. Historian Bruce Cumings contended that by and large, things ended up working out for Americans living in the Pacific Rim—including in Oregon and Washington—better than anywhere else in the United States.[17]

After Trump's inauguration, however, the deterioration of relations between the United States and many parts of the world threatened the dreams of post–World War II politicians to enrich the region through global contact. The president's call to rebuild the nation's military did not immediately result in any new major defense contracts, military bases, or armed forces deployments for Oregon or Washington. His rhetoric, however, had a chilling effect on future prospects for trade to and from the region, even as many of its politicians remained free-traders. In Oregon, Schnitzer Steel stood to benefit from Trump's imposition of tariffs on steel and aluminum, but the Evraz North America mill in Portland prepared to suffer because it imported Canadian metal for its mills. Cherry producers in rural areas of the state, meanwhile, fretted losing out on the China market due to Trump's tit-for-tat tariffs with Beijing, and state analysts feared a broader trade war would dampen the state's broadly export-dependent economy.[18]

The work of people at the local level—in businesses, through immigration, and via multiple and complex levels of private and public civic engagement—clearly resulted in a great deal of the economic development and globalization of Washington and Oregon. In the years ahead, it might appear that if regional politicians and their constituents join together, they could achieve the dream of livability, a balance between growth and environmental preservation, that the post–World War II generation wished upon the Pacific Northwest. But the region is currently void of powerful leaders like Henry Jackson, Mark Hatfield, and Vic Atiyeh that used their power to make economic growth—if not environmental preservation—a reality. Worse, even if those leaders were alive today, increased partisanship, trade wars, a heightened sensitivity to damaging the natural environment because of the imminent danger posed by climate change, and legitimate concerns about economic inequality created by unfettered trade would dilute their power. Speaker of the House Tip O'Neill once famously said that all politics are local. An era in the politics of this region, and perhaps in all regions of the United States, where locals had political power to sway national policy, seems to have passed.

Appendixes

Appendixes

APPENDIX A
Selected Senators, Representatives, and Governors from Oregon and Washington Since 1945

OREGON, CLASS 2 SENATORS

GUY CORDON
Party: Republican
Years in office: 1944–1955
Committees: Interior and Insular Affairs (*chair 1954*),
Appropriations, Atomic Energy

RICHARD NEUBERGER
Party: Democratic
Years in office: 1955–1960 (*died in office*)
Committees: Interior and Insular Affairs, Post Office,
Public Works

HALL LUSK
Party: Democratic
Years in office: 1960–1961 (*appointed to serve remainder of Richard
Neuberger's term*)
Committees: Interior and Insular Affairs, Public Works

MAURINE NEUBERGER
Party: Democratic
Years in office: 1961–1967
Committees: Banking and Currency, Agriculture and Forestry,
Commerce

MARK HATFIELD
Party: Republican
Years in office: 1967–1997
Committees: Appropriations (*chair 1981–86, 1995–96*), Interior and Insular Affairs/Energy and Natural Resources, Agriculture and Forestry, Aeronautical and Space Sciences, Commerce, Rules and Administration, Small Business, Nutrition and Human Needs, Equal Educational Opportunity, Secret and Confidential Documents, Intelligence, Indian Affairs, Ethics, Library, Printing

OREGON, CLASS 3 SENATORS

WAYNE MORSE
Party: Republican (1945–52), Independent (1953–54), Democratic (1955–1969)
Years in office: 1945–1969
Committees: Labor and Public Welfare, Armed Services, District of Columbia, Foreign Relations, Small Business, Public Works, Banking and Currency, Foreign Aid Program, Aging, Railroad Retirement Legislation, Washington Metropolitan Problems

ROBERT "BOB" PACKWOOD
Party: Republican
Years in office: 1969–1995 (*resigned from office*)
Committees: Finance (*chair 1985–86, 1995*) Commerce, Science, and Transportation (*chair 1981–85*); Banking and Currency, Public Works, Labor and Public Welfare, Budget, Small Business, Committee on Committees, Official Conduct, Taxation

SELECTED OREGON REPRESENTATIVES

LES AUCOIN
District: First
Constituencies: West Portland and suburbs, North Coast, and Coast Range
Party: Democratic
Years in office: 1975–1993
Committees: Merchant Marine and Fisheries, Banking, Currency, and Housing (later renamed Banking, Finance, and Urban Affairs), Appropriations, Outer Continental Shelf, Hunger

AL ULLMAN
District: Second
Constituencies: Salem, Central/Eastern Oregon
Party: Democratic
Years in office: 1957–1981
Committees: Ways and Means (*chair 1975–81*), Budget (*chair 1974–75*), Interior and Insular Affairs, Energy, Taxation, Reduction of Federal Expenses, Study Budget Control

EDITH GREEN
District: Third
Constituencies: Portland, unincorporated Multnomah County, Gresham, northern Clackamas County
Party: Democratic
Years in office: 1955–1974 (*resigned in office*)
Committees: Education and Labor, Interior and Insular Affairs, Merchant Marine and Fisheries, House Administration, District of Columbia, Appropriations, Congressional Pages, House Beauty Shop, Disposition of Executive Papers

ROBERT "BOB" DUNCAN

Districts: Fourth (1963–1967), Third (1975–1981)
Constituencies: Fourth: Eugene, Roseburg, rural timberlands.
Third: Portland, unincorporated Multnomah
County, Gresham, northern Clackamas
County
Party: Democratic
Years in office: 1963–1967, 1975–1981
Committees: Appropriations (*chair of transportation subcommittee 1979–1981*), Agriculture, Interior and Insular Affairs

SELECTED OREGON GOVERNORS

YEARS	GOVERNOR	POLITICAL PARTY
1959–1967	Mark Hatfield	Republican
1967–1975	Tom McCall	Republican
1975–1979	Bob Straub	Democratic
1979–1987	Vic Atiyeh	Republican
1987–1991	Neil Goldschmidt	Democratic

WASHINGTON, CLASS 1 SENATORS

HENRY "SCOOP" JACKSON

Party: Democratic
Years in office: 1953–1983 (*died in office*)
Committees: Interior and Insular Affairs (later Energy and Natural
Resources) (*chair 1963–1981*), Armed Services,
Government Operations (later Government Affairs),
Atomic Energy, National Water Resources, National
Fuels Study, Intelligence

DAN EVANS

Party: Republican

Years in office: 1983–1988 (*selected by Governor John Spellman to temporarily replace Jackson after his death; subsequently won a special election to serve remainder of the term*)

Committees: Foreign Relations, Energy and Natural Resources, Indian Affairs

SLADE GORTON

Party: Republican

Years in office: 1989–2001

Committees: Commerce, Science, and Transportation; Agriculture, Nutrition and Forestry; Appropriations, Armed Services, Indian Affairs, Intelligence, Ethics

WASHINGTON, CLASS 3 SENATORS

WARREN MAGNUSON

Party: Democratic

Years in office: 1945–1981

Committees: Interstate and Foreign Commerce (later Commerce, Science and Transportation; *chair 1955–77*), Appropriations (*chair 1977–1981*), Judiciary, Aeronautical and Space Sciences, Budget, Space and Aeronautics, National Water Resources, Equal Educational Opportunity

Leadership: President pro tempore 1979–1981

SLADE GORTON

Party: Republican

Years in office: 1981–1987

Committees: Commerce, Science, and Transportation; Environment and Public Works, Budget, Small Business, Banking, Housing, and Urban Affairs

BROCK ADAMS

Party: Democratic

Years in office: 1987–1993

Committees: Labor and Human Resources, Appropriations, Foreign Relations, Commerce, Science and Transportation; Rules and Administration

SELECTED WASHINGTON REPRESENTATIVES

JULIA BUTLER HANSEN

District: Third

Constituencies: Vancouver, Longview, Kelso

Party: Democratic

Years in office: 1961–1975

Committees: Appropriations, Interior and Insular Affairs, Veterans Affairs, Education and Labor

DON BONKER

District: Third

Constituencies: Vancouver, Longview, Kelso

Party: Democratic

Years in office: 1975–1989

Major committee: International Relations (later Foreign Affairs), Merchant Marine and Fisheries, Aging

SID MORRISON

District: Fourth

Constituencies: Tri-Cities, Yakima, Wenatchee

Party: Republican

Years in office: 1981–1993

Committees: Agriculture, Science and Technology (later Science, Space, and Technology), Hunger

WALTER HORAN
District: Fifth
Constituencies: Spokane, Pullman
Party: Republican
Years in office: 1945–1965
Committees: Appropriations, Chemicals in Food

THOMAS "TOM" FOLEY
District: Fifth
Constituencies: Spokane, Walla Walla, Pullman
Party: Democratic
Years in office: 1965–1995
Committees: Agriculture (*chair 1975–81*), Interior & Insular Affairs, Standards of Official Conduct, House Administration, Post Office & Civil Service, Energy, Iran-Contra
House leadership: Majority whip 1981–1987, majority leader 1987–1989, speaker 1989–1995

SELECTED WASHINGTON GOVERNORS

YEARS	GOVERNOR	POLITICAL PARTY
1965–1977	Dan Evans	Republican
1977–1981	Dixy Lee Ray	Democratic
1981–1985	John Spellman	Republican
1985–1993	Booth Gardner	Democratic

Source: Nelson, Garrison. *Committees in the Congress Volume 2:1947–1992 Committee Histories and Member Assignments.* Washington, DC:Congressional Quarterly, 1994.

APPENDIX B

List of Federal Spending Earmarked by Senator Mark Hatfield (R-OR), 1979–1997

WILLAMETTE VALLEY

— Construction of Marion Street and 12th Street bridges, Salem, 1984–90, $56.8 million
— Sheridan federal minimum-security prison, 1984–87, $52 million
— University of Oregon Sciences Center Building, Eugene, 1985–88, $35 million
— High-speed rail construction costs, 1997, $11 million
— Steamboat Creek and North Umpqua highway upgrades, 1994, $10.4 million
— Eugene transit center, 1993, $10.2 million
— Oregon State University Forest Ecosystem Research Laboratory, 1995, 1996, $10 million
— Electronic weigh station pilot project, 1997, $9.7 million
— Eugene bus facility projects, 1997, $5.1 million
— West Eugene wetlands acquisition, 1994–96, $4 million
— Salem Courthouse Square transit center, 1997, $3.7 million
— Oregon State University Forage Research Center, 1984, $3.2 million

SOUTHERN OREGON

— Lost Creek Dam construction, 1977, $135 million
— Applegate Dam, 1984, $90 million
— Crater Lake Lodge restoration, 1989–94, $29.5 million
— Lake County uranium mill tailings cleanup, 1984–91, $23 million
— Upper Klamath Basin wetlands restoration, 1996–97, $9 million
— Kingsley Field runway repair, Klamath Falls, 1994, $8.5 million
— Ashland Fish and Wildlife Forensics Lab, 1987–93, $6.8 million
— Klamath Falls air traffic control tower, 1997, $3.9 million

PORTLAND AREA

— Westside light rail, 1991–1998, $532 million
— Banfield Freeway light-rail and highway, 1981–87, $320 million
— Mark O. Hatfield Courthouse, 1989–93, $132 million
— Portland Veterans Affairs Medical Center hospital construction, Portland, 1983, $131 million
— Federal jail and law enforcement center, 1997, $86 million

- Biomedical Information Communication Center, Oregon Health & Science University, 1983–96, $37.4 million
- Burlington Northern railroad bridge replacement, 1985–87, $34 million
- OHSU Neurosensory Research Center, 1990–91, $22 million
- OHSU Ambulatory Research Center, 1992–93, $20 million
- Vollum Institute for Biomedical Research, Oregon Health & Science University, 1981, $20 million
- Oregon Graduate Center developmental grants, Beaverton, 1986–90, $17 million
- Portland Veterans Affairs Medical Center expansion, 1997, $16 million
- Portland International Airport air traffic control tower, 1997, $14.9 million
- Portland South Transit Mall extension and Portland State University Transportation Plaza, 1997, $12.8 million
- OHSU School of Nursing building, 1989, $12 million
- Columbia Slough project, 1995, $10 million
- Tanner Creek environmental work, 1996–97, $9 million
- OHSU skybridge, 1988–89, $6.7 million
- South-North light-rail project, 1997, $6 million
- Tualatin National Wildlife Refuge, 1996–97, $3 million

OREGON COAST

- Port of Siuslaw jetty extension, 1983, 1984, $28 million
- Alsea Bay Bridge replacement, 1986, $20 million
- Port of Umpqua jetty extension, 1978–80, $16 million
- Yaquina Head Visitors Center, land acquisition, planning, construction, 1982–97, $11.5 million
- Yaquina Bay jetty rehabilitation and extension, 1986, 1987, $8.5 million
- Columbia River channel deepening project, 1984, 1985, $7.3 million
- Hatfield Marine Science Center, Newport, 1979–97, $6 million
- Coos Bay channel deepening, 1997, $4.3 million
- Oregon State University Seafood Research Laboratory construction, Astoria, 1991–93, $3.8 million

CENTRAL/EASTERN OREGON, COLUMBIA RIVER GORGE

- Powerhouse II at Bonneville Dam, 1975–85, $681 million
- Bonneville Dam lock replacement, 1985–94, $346 million
- Umatilla Basin Project, 1988–93, $33.4 million
- Baker City Oregon Trail Interpretive Center, 1989–92, $11.5 million
- Columbia River Gorge Discovery Center, The Dalles, 1995–97, $7 million
- Umatilla Basin irrigation project, 1997, $6.3 million
- Hells Canyon land acquisition, 1991–92, $4 million
- Historic Columbia River Highway restoration, 1997, $3.7 million

All years are fiscal.

Source: "Hatfield Projects," *The Oregonian*, Sept. 29, 1996.

APPENDIX C
International Trade to/from Oregon and Washington Since World War II

Table 1: Waterborne Exports—Cargo Tonnage, by Coastal District: 1945–1969

District	Cargo Tonnage (in thousands of short tons)								
	1945	1950	1955	1960	1965	1966	1967	1968	1969
Atlantic	39,609	15,228	54,906	44,902	54,943	56,756	57,365	58,255	62,987
Pacific	7,258	7,270	13,394	19,351	26,445	30,395	36,486	39,146	41,018

Source: US Census Bureau, *Statistical Abstracts of the United States*, 1971.

Table 2: Commerce of Selected United States Ports (in short tons), 1969

Port	Imports	Exports
Coos Bay, OR	< 500	2,909
Portland, OR	1,202	3,588
Longview, WA	313	3,276
Tacoma Harbor, WA	1,906	2,112
Seattle Harbor, WA	2,483	1,437

Source: US Census Bureau, *Statistical Abstracts of the United States*, 1971.

Table 3: Waterborne Exports—Cargo Tonnage and Value, By Coastal District: 1970–1984

District	Cargo Tonnage (in millions)					
	1970	1975	1980	1982	1983	1984
Atlantic	79	80	117	119	87	82
Pacific	48	49	78	74	78	86
Value (in billions of dollars)						
	1970	1975	1980	1982	1983	1984
Atlantic	11.9	28.7	51.0	50.2	41.2	37.5
Pacific	4.1	10.0	25.2	25.5	25.1	27.2

Source: US Census Bureau, *Statistical Abstracts of the United States*, 1986.

Table 4: Exports from Portland and Seattle Customs Regions, 1970–1984
Figures in billions of $

	1970	1975	1980	1981	1982	1983	1984	1984 % of total
US total	43.2	107.6	220.8	233.7	212.3	200.5	217.9	
Portland	.8	2.0	3.8	3.9	3.3	3.7	4.1	1.8%
Seattle	1.9	4.2	12.0	12.3	8.9	10.0	10.1	4.6%

Source: US Census Bureau, *Statistical Abstracts of the United States*, 1986.

Table 5: Jobs Attributed to Foreign Direct Investment, 1981 to 1989

	Employment (1981)	Employment (1989)	% Change
United States	2,402,000	4,406,000	+101%
Oregon	13,100	28,500	+217%
Washington	26,000	67,200	+258%

Source: US Bureau of the Census, *Statistical Abstracts of the United States*, 1992.

Table 6: US Exports and Imports, 1970 to 1991

Year	Total Exports (in billions)	Total Imports (in billions)	% Change (exports)	% Change (imports)
1970	42.7	40	14.1	10.8
1971	43.5	45.6	1.9	14.0
1972	49.2	55.6	13.1	21.9
1973	70.8	69.5	43.9	25.0
1974	98.1	102.6	38.6	47.6
1975	107.7	98.5	9.8	-4.0
1976	115.2	123.5	7.0	25.4
1977	121.2	150.4	5.2	21.8
1978	143.7	174.8	18.6	16.2
1979	181.9	209.5	26.6	19.9
1980	220.6	244.9	21.3	16.9
1981	233.7	261	5.9	6.6
1982	212.3	244	-9.2	-6.5
1983	200.5	258	5.6	5.7
1984	217.9	325.7	8.7	26.2
1985	213.1	343.3	-2.2	6.0

Table 6: US Exports and Imports, 1970 to 1991 (continued)

Year	Total Exports (in billions)	Total Imports (in billions)	% Change (exports)	% Change (imports)
1986	217.3	370	2.0	7.2
1987	254.1	406.2	16.9	9.8
1988	322.4	441	26.9	8.6
1989	363.8	473.4	12.8	7.3
1990	393.6	495.3	8.2	4.6
1991	421.9	488.1	7.2	-1.5

Source: US Bureau of the Census, *Statistical Abstracts of the United States*, 1992.

Table 7: Exports and Imports for Portland and Seattle, 1980 to 1991

PORTLAND CUSTOMS DISTRICT		
Year	Exports (in billions of $)	Imports (in billions of $)
1980	3.8	2.6
1985	3.5	3.8
1987	3.7	4.6
1988	5.6	5.8
1989	6.2	5.7
1990	5.8	5.6
1991	6.0	5.3
SEATTLE CUSTOMS DISTRICT		
Year	Exports (in billions of $)	Imports (in billions of $)
1980	12.0	9.2
1985	12.1	13.4
1987	15.7	17.2
1988	20.9	17.8
1989	26.6	20.2
1990	32.6	20.9
1991	35.0	18.9

Source: US Bureau of the Census, *Statistical Abstracts of the United States*, 1992.

Table 8: Oregon Exports and Imports, 2017

Top 10 Export Destinations from Oregon Based on 2017 Dollar Value			
Position	Country	Value	% Share
1	China	$3,933,000,000	18%
2	Canada	$2,332,000,000	10.6%
3	Malaysia	$2,302,000,000	10.5%
4	South Korea	$2,031,000,000	9.3%
5	Japan	$1,805,000,000	8.2%
6	Vietnam	$1,598,000,000	7.3%
7	Taiwan	$852,000,000	3.9%
8	Germany	$498,000,000	2.3%
9	Singapore	$465,000,000	2.1%
10	United Kingdom	$451,000,000	2.1%
Top 10 Countries Exporting to Oregon Based on 2017 Dollar Value			
Position	Country	Value	% Share
1	Canada	$2,761,000,000	15.1%
2	China	$2,571,000,000	14%
3	Ireland	$2,480,000,000	13.5%
4	Japan	$2,085,000,000	11.4%
5	South Korea	$1,866,000,000	10.2%
6	Israel	$909,000,000	5%
7	Mexico	$876,000,000	4.8%
8	Netherlands	$751,000,000	4.1%
9	Taiwan	$539,000,000	2.9%
10	Germany	$486,000,000	2.7%
Total value of exports, 2017:		$21,895,000,000	
Total value of imports, 2017:		$18,308,000,000	

Source: US Census Bureau, "States by Top 25 Commodities and Countries,"
https://www.census.gov/foreign-trade/statistics/state/data/index.html.

Table 9: Washington Exports and Imports, 2017

Top 10 Export Destinations from Washington Based on 2017 Dollar Value			
Position	Country	Value	% Share
1	China	$17,967,000,000	23.5%
2	Canada	$7,712,000,000	10.1%
3	Japan	$5,415,000,000	7.1%
4	United Arab Emirates	$4,105,000,000	5.4%
5	South Korea	$3,286,000,000	4.3%
6	Taiwan	$2,580,000,000	3.4%
7	Norway	$2,154,000,000	2.8%
8	Mexico	$2,034,000,000	2.7%
9	Saudi Arabia	$1,980,000,000	2.6%
10	Russia	$1,846,000,000	2.4%
Top 10 Countries Exporting to Washington Based on 2017 Dollar Value			
Position	Country	Value	% Share
1	China	$14,575,000,000	29.2%
2	Canada	$13,339,000,000	26.8%
3	Japan	$5,262,000,000	10.6%
4	South Korea	$2,111,000,000	4.2%
5	Taiwan	$1,549,000,000	3.1%
6	Mexico	$1,280,000,000	2.6%
7	Vietnam	$1,141,000,000	2.3%
8	Russia	$882,000,000	1.8%
9	Germany	$735,000,000	1.5%
10	Brazil	$731,000,000	1.5%
Total value of exports:		$76,414,000,000	
Total value of imports:		$49,847,000,000	

Source: US Census Bureau, "States by Top 25 Commodities and Countries,"
https://www.census.gov/foreign-trade/statistics/state/data/index.html.

Table 10: Oregon and Washington Exports, 1995–2015

Year	State	Total Exports	Rate of 5-Yr Increase
1995	Oregon	$7,666,000,000	
	Washington	$21,879,000,000	
2000	Oregon	$11,441,300,000	33%
	Washington	$32,214,700,000	32.9%
2005	Oregon	$12,380,700,000	7.5%
	Washington	$37,948,400,000	15.1%
2010	Oregon	$17,682,700,000	29.9%
	Washington	$53,243,800,000	28.7%
2015	Oregon	$20,084,000,000	12%
	Washington	$86,353,000,000	38.3%

Source: US Census Bureau, US Exports of Goods by State,
https://www.census.gov/foreign-trade/statistics/state/origin_movement/index.html.

APPENDIX D

National Security and Defense in Oregon and Washington Since World War II

Table 1: Defense-Generated Employment in Oregon and Washington during the Escalation of the Vietnam War*

	Employment			
	1965	1966	1967	1968
Oregon	5,500	6,400	8,000	8,700
Washington	45,700	50,200	56,200	54,500
	Civilian Workforce 1968		Defense Employment as % of Workforce 1968	
Oregon	857,500		1.0	
Washington	1,356,700		4.0	

*Defined as "employment in private plants which are working on Dept. of Defense military prime contracts."

Source: US Census Bureau, *Statistical Abstract of the United States*, 1969.

Table 2: Defense Contract Awards and Payroll for Oregon and Washington, 1978–1980

	Contract Awards		
	1978	1979	1980
Oregon	$92,000,000	$147,000,000	$131,000,000
Washington	$1,808,000,000	$1,540,000,000	$2,110,000,000
	Payroll		
	1978	1979	1980
Oregon	$69,000,000	$71,000,000	$84,000,000
Washington	$869,000,000	$886,000,000	$1,121,000,000

Source: US Census Bureau, *Statistical Abstract of the United States*, 1981.

Table 3: Defense-Oriented Industries' Employments and Shipments to Defense Department by State, 1980 and 1983

State	Employees		Shipments to DoD	
	1980	1983	1980	1983
Oregon	2,000	4,000	$153,000,000	$268,000,000
Washington	22,000	10,000	$1,502,000,000	$944,000,000

Source: US Census Bureau, *Statistical Abstract of the United States*, 1986.

Table 4: Department of Defense Contract Awards, Payroll, Civilian and Military Personnel in Oregon and Washington, 1982–1984

State	Contract Awards		
	1982	1983	1984
Oregon	$208,000,000	$181,000,000	$230,000,000
Washington	$2,828,000,000	$3,986,000,000	$2,884,000,000
	Payroll		
	1982	1983	1984
Oregon	$103,000,000	$97,000,000	$104,000,000
Washington	$1,488,000,000	$1,573,000,000	$1,689,000,000
	Civilian Employees		
	1982	1983	1984
Oregon	2,990	3,042	2,998
Washington	26,601	29,246	29,334
	Military Personnel		
	1982	1983	1984
Oregon	823	770	772
Washington	41,336	42,570	42,958

Source: US Census Bureau, *Statistical Abstract of the United States*, 1986.

Table 5: Department of Defense Data for Oregon and Washington, Fiscal Year 1989

State	Active Duty Personnel	Army	Navy/Marines	Air Force
Oregon	665	195	407	63
Washington	40,533	22,370	8,790	9,373
Prime Contracts Over $25,000:				
	1986	1987	1988	1989
Oregon	$340,069,000	$286,582,000	$452,853,000	$178,526,000
Washington	$2,525,250,000	$3,112,025,000	$2,525,078,000	$2,951,055,000
Top Five Defense Contractors in Fiscal Year 1989				
Oregon	Contractor		Contract Total	
1	Tektronix Inc		$42,248,000	
2	Daimler Benz North American Holding Co.		$26,070,000	
3	Precision Castparts Corp		$10,330,000	
4	General Instrument Corp		$6,073,000	
5	US Inc		$5,696,000	
Washington	Contractor		Contract Total	
1	The Boeing Company		$1,804,753,000	
2	Atlantic Richfield Company		$336,894,000	
3	Litton Industries Inc.		$47,417,000	
4	General Construction Manson JV		$43,953,000	
5	Todd Shipyards Corp		$42,439,000	

Source: *Department of Defense Atlas/Data Abstract for the United States and Selected Areas, Fiscal Year 1989,* Washington, DC: US Government Printing Office, 1989.

Table 6: Department of Defense Data for Oregon and Washington, Fiscal Year 2009

State	Active Duty Personnel	Army	Navy/Marines	Air Force
Oregon	1,615	815	336	464
Washington	46,161	34,557	4,907	6,697
Prime Contracts, 2009				
Oregon	$1,546,000,000		(99 grants)	
Washington:	$5,174,000,000		(127 grants)	

Source: US Census Bureau, *Statistical Abstract of the United States,* 2012.

Notes

INTRODUCTION

1 US Census Bureau, *Statistical Abstracts of the United States 1940*, 3–4; US Census Bureau, *Statistical Abstracts of the United States 1942*, 7, 568; Craig Wollner, "Silicon Forest," *Oregon Encyclopedia*, https://oregonencyclopedia.org/articles/silicon_forest/#.Wqm8Vuch1PY.

2 "Seattle-Tacoma-Bellevue, WA Metro Area," *Census Reporter*, 2017, https://censusreporter.org/profiles/31000US42660-seattle-tacoma-bellevue-wa-metro-area; "Portland-Vancouver-Hillsboro, OR-WA Metro Area," *Census Reporter*, 2017, https://censusreporter.org/profiles/31000US38900-portland-vancouver-hillsboro-or-wa-metro-area.

3 "The 25 Best Cities to Live In," *CBS News*, n.d., https://www.cbsnews.com/pictures/the-25-best-cities-to-live-in; Samuel Stebbins, Evan Comen and Michael B. Sauter, "Most Livable: America's 50 Best Cities to Live In," *USA Today*, Oct. 13, 2017,https://www.usatoday.com/story/money/nation-now/2017/10/13/most-liveable-americas-50-best-cities-live/761013001.

4 Chet Orloff, "Mark Hatfield Interview, April 15, 1993," Folder "Mark Hatfield," Oregon Historical Society, Call No. SR 1345.

5 On the growth of American consumption of Japanese goods and direct investment in the United States, see Andrew McKevitt, *Consuming Japan: Popular Culture and the Globalizing of 1980s America* (Chapel Hill: University of North Carolina Press, 2017).

6 Carlos Schwantes, *The Pacific Northwest: An Interpretive History*, 2nd ed. (Lincoln: University of Nebraska Press, 1996), 4.

7 For more on the utopian ideal, see Schwantes, 92–98; James J. Kropp, *Eden Within Eden: Oregon's Utopian Heritage* (Corvallis: Oregon State University Press, 2009). There is also an emerging literature on the racist, nativist tone central to much of this Edenic discourse: see Schwantes, 121–122; Matt Novak, "Oregon Was Founded as a Racist Utopia," *Gizmodo.com*, Jan. 21, 2015, http://gizmodo.com/oregon-was-founded-as-a-racist-utopia-1539567040; Gray Whaley, *Oregon and the Collapse of Illahee: U.S. Empire and the Transformation of an Indigenous World, 1792–1859* (Chapel Hill: University of North Carolina Press, 2010); R. Gregory Nokes, *Breaking Chains: Slavery on Trial in the Oregon Territory* (Corvallis: Oregon State University Press, 2013).

8 Richard White, *"It's Your Misfortune and None of My Own": A History of the American West* (Norman: University of Oklahoma Press, 1991), 57.

9 For political scientists who have also made this argument, see Theodore H. Cohn and Patrick J. Smith, "Developing Global Cities in the Pacific Northwest: The Cases of Vancouver and Seattle," in Peter Karl Kresl and Gary Gappert, eds., *North American Cities and the Global Economy: Challenges and Opportunities* (Thousand Oaks, CA: SAGE Publications, 1995), 251–285.

10 Richard White, *The Organic Machine* (New York: Hill and Wang, 1995); John M. Findlay and Bruce Hevly, *Atomic Frontier Days: Hanford and the American West* (Seattle: University of Washington Press, 2011); Paul W. Hirt, *The Wired Northwest: The History of Electric Power, 1870s–1970s* (Lawrence: University of Kansas Press, 2012).

11 William G. Robbins, *A Man for All Seasons: Monroe Sweetland and the Liberal Paradox* (Corvallis: Oregon State University Press, 2015); Jeff LaLande, "Oregon's Last Conservative US Senator: Some Light upon the Little-Known Career of Guy Cordon," *Oregon Historical Quarterly* 110:2 (Summer 2009), 228–261.

12 For the linkages between domestic politics and home-front militarization, see Roger Lotchin, *Fortress California, 1910–1961: From Warfare to Welfare* (New York: Oxford University Press, 1992); Michael Sherry, *In the Shadow of War: The United States Since the 1930s* (New Haven, CT: Yale University Press, 1997); Julian E. Zelizer, *Arsenal of Democracy: The Politics of National Security—From World War II to the War on Terrorism* (New York: Basic Books, 2010). Major narratives of US history illustrating the growth—and durability—of federal spending after World War II include James Patterson, *Grand Expectations: The United States, 1945–1974* (New York: Oxford University Press, 1996); James Patterson, *Restless Giant: The United States from Watergate to Bush V. Gore* (New York: Oxford University Press, 2005); Sean Wilentz, *The Age of Reagan: A History, 1974–2008* (New York: Harper, 2008).

13 See, for example, Lotchin, *Fortress California*; Elizabeth Tandy Shermer, *Sunbelt Capitalism: Phoenix and the Transformation of American Politics* (Philadelphia: University of Pennsylvania Press, 2013); Michael Brenes, "For Right and Might: The Militarization of the Cold War and the Remaking of American Democracy," PhD diss., City University of New York, Feb. 2014.

14 For more on Morse, see Mason Drukman, *Wayne Morse: A Political Biography* (Portland: Oregon Historical Society Press, 1997), and Larry Ceplair, "The Foreign Policy of Senator Wayne Morse," *Oregon Historical Quarterly* 113:1 (Spring 2012), 6–35. For more on Oregon's disadvantages in securing military facilities, see Brian G. Casserly, "Securing the Sound: The Evolution of Civilian-Military Relations in the Puget Sound Area, 1891–1984," PhD diss., University of Washington, 2007, 48–49.

15 On McCall, see Brent Walth, *Fire at Eden's Gate: Tom McCall & the Oregon Story* (Portland: Oregon Historical Society Press, 1994); "Tom McCall," *Oregon Experience* (2013), https://www.opb.org/television/programs/oregonexperience/episodes/703. "Californication" appeared in media as early as 1966: see "Books: Nosepicking Contests," *Time*, May 8, 1966; Sandra Burton, "The Great Californicated West," *Time*, Aug. 21, 1972.

16 Helen Mershon, "Rugs to Riches," *The Oregonian* (hereafter *TO*), Oct. 20, 1990; "Appropriately Honoring a Trade Leader," *TO*, July 19, 2007; Jeff Mapes, "Former governor led Oregon through trying times," *TO*, July 21, 2014.

17 For example, see Dana Frank, *Purchasing Power: Consumer Organizing, Gender, and the Seattle Labor Movement, 1919–1929* (Cambridge: Cambridge University Press, 1994); Dwayne A. Mack, *Black Spokane: The Civil Rights Struggle in the Inland Northwest* (Norman: University of Oklahoma Press, 2014); Luke Sprunger, "'This Is Where We Want to Stay': Tejanos and Latino Community Building in Washington County," *Oregon Historical Quarterly* 116:3 (Fall 2015), 278–309.

CHAPTER 1

1   A portion of this chapter appears in a slightly altered form in Christopher Foss, "Bringing Home the (Irradiated) Bacon: The Politics of Senator Henry Jackson's Support for Nuclear Weapons and Energy during the Cold War," *Pacific Northwest Quarterly* 109:1 (Winter 2017/2018), 3–18. Special thanks to Bruce Hevly for permitting me to reprint it here.

2   Joshua B. Freeman, *American Empire: The Rise of a Global Power, the Democratic Revolution at Home, 1945–2000* (New York: Viking, 2012), 90.

3   Schwantes, 411.

4   Works on Washington's early military history include William Woodward, "Prelude to a Pacific Century: The Washington National Guard in the Philippines, 1899," *Columbia* 13 (Winter 1999–2000), 6–13; Kurt R. Nelson, *Fighting for Paradise: A Military History of the Pacific Northwest* (Yardley, PA: Westholme Publishing, 2007); Casserly, "Securing the Sound."

5   For the official account of Boeing's history, see *Year by Year: 75 Years of Boeing History, 1916–1991* (Seattle: Boeing Historical Archives, 1991); for a brief primer, see Stanley I. Weiss and Amir R. Amir, "Boeing Company," *Encyclopedia Britannica*, https://www.britannica.com/topic/Boeing-Company; "Boeing: General Information," http://www.boeing.com/company/general-info/#/employment-data. For Washington's official assessment of its top private employer in the late 1980s, see Richard Yates and Charity Yates, *Washington State Atlas & Databook, 1990 Edition* (Eugene: Information Press, 1990), 35, 39.

6   Yates and Yates, 19, 35, 54; after 1990, Washington maintained most of these military facilities, but Fort Lewis and McChord AFB merged to become Joint Base Lewis-McChord (JBLM) in 2010.

7   Shelby Scates, *Warren G. Magnuson and the Shaping of Twentieth-Century America* (Seattle: University of Washington Press, 1997); Kit Oldham, "Magnuson, Warren G. (1905–1989)," http://www.historylink.org/index.cfm?DisplayPage=output.cfm&file_id=5569.

8   Scates, 70.

9   Ibid., 126.

10 July 15, 1955, "Joint Statement in Support of $2,000,000 Appropriation to Finance Architectural and Engineering Work on a New Dry Dock for Puget Sound Naval Shipyard in Bremerton, Washington," Warren G. Magnuson Papers, University of Washington Special Collections (hereafter WGM Papers), Accession 3181-003, Box 147, Folder 248; "For Release to P.M.'s of Monday, February 13, 1956," WGM Papers, 3181-003, 148, 42.

11 WGM to constituent, July 29, 1957, WGM Papers, 3181-004, 93, 10 (per access rules of the WGM Papers, the identities of private constituents must be kept anonymous).

12 "Purchase O.K.'d For Reserve Flight Center," *Seattle Times* (hereafter *ST*), Aug. 25, 1954; "Navy Air Station at Whidbey Isle Gets More Land," *Bremerton Sun* (hereafter *BS*), May 29, 1956; "McChord Gets Housing Units," *Tacoma News Tribune* (hereafter *TNT*), Oct. 14, 1956.

13 Marquis Childs, "Defense Cuts May Impair Security," *ST*, Apr. 6, 1953.

14 Constituent to Henry Jackson (hereafter HMJ), June 27, 1956, Henry M. Jackson Papers, University of Washington Special Collections (hereafter HMJ Papers), Accession 3560-003, Box 120, Folder 5 (per access rules for the Jackson papers, private constituents' names must be kept confidential).

15 "Jackson Calls for New Civil Defense Program," *Wenatchee Daily World* (hereafter *WDW*), Feb. 23, 1955.

16 Robert G. Kaufman, *Henry M. Jackson: A Life in Politics* (Seattle: University of Washington Press, 2000), 53.

17 Richard S. Kirkendall, "The Boeing Company and the Military-Metropolitan-Industrial Complex, 1945–1953," *Pacific Northwest Quarterly* 85 (Oct. 1994), 137–149.

18 Peter J. Ognibene, *Scoop: The Life and Politics of Henry M. Jackson* (New York: Stein and Day Publishers, 1975), 74.

19 William G. Robbins and Katrine Barber, *Nature's Northwest: The North Pacific Slope in the Twentieth Century* (Tucson: University of Arizona Press, 2011), 136.

20 William W. Prochnau, "Boeing TFX Pricing Wins Probers' Support," *ST*, Mar. 6, 1963.

21 HMJ to constituent, May 8, 1963, HMJ Papers, Accession 3560-3, Box 90, Folder 7.

22 Kaufman, 144.

23 William M. Allen, "Criticism of Senator Jackson over TFX Is Improper," *ST*, Sept. 20, 1964.

24 Robbins and Barber, 136.

25 Recording of telephone conversation between Lyndon B. Johnson and Henry M. Jackson, Apr. 4, 1967, Citation No. 11703, Tape WH6704.01, Program No. 3.

26 Constituent to HMJ, Aug. 1, 1969, HMJ Papers, Accession 3560-4, Box 87, Folder 19.

27 "SST in Trouble," *TO*, Nov. 10, 1969.

28 John C. Hughes, *John Spellman: Politics Never Broke His Heart* (Washington State Legacy Project, 2013), 129.

29 Scates, 280–281.

30 "Boeing Purchases Surplus Property," *Ellensburg Herald* (hereafter *EH*), Jan. 23, 1968; "Boeing Does Well in Budget," *BS*, Jan. 30, 1968; John C. Hughes, *Slade Gorton: A Half-Century in Politics* (Washington State Legacy Project, 2011), 175–176; Ann Markusen et al., *The Rise of the Gunbelt: The Military Remapping of Industrial America* (New York: Oxford University Press, 1991), 34, 159.

31 Gretchen Heefner, *The Missile Next Door: The Minuteman in the American Heartland* (Cambridge, MA: Harvard University Press, 2012), 65.

32 Richard Colby, "Business Takes Off at Boeing Plant," *TO*, May 7, 1989.

33 Ognibene, 102; Kaufman, 112.

34 C. Mark Smith, *Community Godfather: How Sam Volpentest Helped Shape the History of Hanford and the Tri-Cities* (Richland, WA: Etcetera Press, 2013), 148; William W. Prochnau and Richard W. Larsen, *A Certain Democrat: Senator Henry M. Jackson: A Political Biography* (Englewood Cliffs, NJ: Prentice-Hall., 1972), 160; Ognibene, 51.

35 Findlay and Hevly, 143.

36 "AEC to Spend Millions in Hanford Expansion," *TO*, Oct. 19, 1949; Kaufman, 53.

37 Prochnau and Larsen, 160.

38 Findlay and Hevly, 154.

39 "Atomic Plant Waste Seen," *TO*, June 19, 1951.

40 "Atom Power Breakthrough," *TO*, June 26, 1958.

41 Findlay and Hevly, 156.

42 Findlay and Hevly, 162–165.

43 John W. Finney, "Atom Power Plan Rejected in House," *New York Times* (hereafter *NYT*), July 14, 1961.

44 *Congressional Record,* July 18, 1961, 87th Congress, 1st Session, pp. 12845, 12854.

45 Findlay and Hevly, 166.

46 Findlay and Hevly, 168.

47 Smith, 103–104.

48 Smith, 109.

49 Ibid., 169–170, 175; "Pact Signed for Hanford," *TO,* Jan. 1, 1965.

50 "Address by Senator Henry M. Jackson: Battelle Pacific Northwest Laboratories Dedication—Oct. 27, 1967," HMJ Papers, Accession 3560-004, Box 231, Folder 54.

51 "Hanford House Dedication, Richland, WA, 10-6-69," HMJ Papers, Accession 3560-004, Box 233, Folder 32.

52 Smith, 181.

53 "Remarks by Senator Henry M. Jackson at Groundbreaking for High Temperature Sodium Facility, Richland, Washington, September 24, 1970," HMJ Papers, Accession 3560-004, Box 234, Folder 59.

54 Findlay and Hevly, 185.

55 Jackson quoted in Leverett Richards, "Closure of Hanford N-Reactor Held Threat to U.S. Security," *TO,* Feb. 4, 1971.

56 Leverett Richards, "Forces Rally against Reactor Close," *TO,* Feb. 2, 1971; Elsie Carper, "Dismantling Is Stopped at Hanford," *Washington Post,* Feb. 5, 1971; anonymous Nixon official quoted in Philip Shabecoff, "Reactor on Coast Called a Hazard," *NYT,* Feb. 7, 1971.

57 Findlay and Hevly, 189.

58 For more on the embargo, see Meg Jacobs, *Panic at the Pump: The Energy Crisis and the Transformation of American Politics in the 1970s* (New York: Hill and Wang, 2016); for the Pacific Northwest impact and response to the crisis, see Walth, *Fire at Eden's Gate,* 373–381, 389.

59 "Address by Senator Henry M. Jackson at Tri-City Nuclear Council Luncheon," Richland, WA, Aug. 19, 1976, 12:00 noon," HMJ Papers, Accession 3560-005, Box 262, Folder 168.

60 "Remarks before the Tri-City Nuclear Industrial Council, Richland, Washington, December 18, 1978, by Senator Henry M. Jackson, Why Not the Best—Nuclear Energy," HMJ Papers, Accession 3560-005, Box 246, Folder 13.

61 "Fusion at Hanford," *Tri-City Herald* (hereafter *TCH*), June 15, 1981; "Plutonium Refinement Plan Revealed for Hanford Site," *TO,* Aug. 5, 1983.

62 "Remarks by Senator Henry M. Jackson to the Pasco Chamber of Commerce, September 25, 1982," HMJ Papers, Accession 3560-005, Box 247, Folder 73.

63 Robert Lindsey, "Reactor Shutdown in Northwest Threatens Fragile Prosperity," *NYT,* Dec. 15, 1986; Findlay and Hevly, 190, 194.

64 "Senator Henry M. Jackson Centennial Celebration," YouTube video posted by "The City of Everett," Aug. 6, 2012, https://www.youtube.com/watch?v=lusZLHl-UUI.

65 Casserly, 2, 29–30.

66 Ognibene, 74; "Russia Declared Leading the U.S. in Missile Race," *Spokane Daily Chronicle* (hereafter *SC*), Jan. 23, 1958; Kaufman, 93.

67 HMJ to constituent, Jan. 26, 1962, HMJ Papers, Accession 3560-3, Box 85, Folder 2.

68 "The Bangor Expansion Is a Tribute to Senator Jackson," *BS,* Jan. 15, 1962; "Cuba Is Serious but Just a 'Speck,' Jackson Says," *BS,* Nov. 3, 1962; William W. Prochnau, "$50.5 Million Navy Job Awarded to Seattle Yard," *ST,* May 22, 1963.

69 "Bremerton Yard Escapes Navy Cutbacks," *ST*, Mar. 20, 1964.

70 "Senator Says A-Subs to Dock at Bangor Soon," *TNT*, Feb. 10, 1964.

71 "Navy Opens Bangor Plant," *Kitsap County Herald*, Sept. 16, 1964.

72 Kaufman, 184–185; "Address by Senator Henry M. Jackson: Battelle Pacific Northwest Laboratories Dedication," Oct. 27, 1967, HMJ Papers, Accession 3560-004, Box 231, Folder 54; for more on antinuclear protests see April Carter, *Peace Movements: International Protest and World Politics since 1945* (London: Routledge, 1992); Lawrence S. Wittner, *Resisting the Bomb: A History of the World Nuclear Disarmament Movement, 1954–1970* (Stanford, CA: Stanford University Press, 1997).

73 Prochnau and Larsen, 296–299.

74 Casserly, 28.

75 Ognibene, 162–165; Casserly, 469; Kaufman, 242.

76 Casserly, 472–473.

77 Casserly, 475, 491–492; "Construction Funds Sought," *TO*, Mar. 30, 1974.

78 Casserly, 474–475.

79 Casserly, 43.

80 "Navy to Spend a Lot on Roads," *TO*, June 2, 1975.

81 "Remarks by Senator Henry M. Jackson, Armed Forces Day, Puget Sound Naval Base Association," May 15, 1976; HMJ Papers, Accession 3560-5, Box 245, Folder 28; HMJ address to the Washington State AFL-CIO Labor Council Convention, Seattle, WA, Aug. 17, 1976; HMJ Papers, Accession 3560-5, Box 262, Folder 168.

82 Constituent to HMJ, Aug. 25, 1977, Accession 3560-5, Box 72, Folder 35.

83 Janet Staihar, "Congressional Gift Grab Generous to Northwest," *TO*, Dec. 14, 1980; "Launching Ceremony of the Guided Missile 'Crommelin,' Todd Pacific Shipyards Corp, Seattle, WA, July 2, 1981," HMJ Papers, Accession 3560-5, Box 247, Folder 44; Martin Heerwald, "Navy Plans New Home for Ships," *TO*, Oct. 14, 1982.

84 Alan K. Ota, "Campaign against Sub 'Just Begun,'" *TO*, Aug. 15, 1982.

85 For more on the nuclear freeze, see David S. Meyer, *A Winter of Discontent: The Nuclear Freeze and American Politics* (New York: Praeger, 1990); William M. Knoblauch, *Nuclear Freeze in a Cold War: The Reagan Administration, Cultural Activism, and the End of the Arms Race* (Amherst: University of Massachusetts Press, 2017).

86 Constituent to HMJ, Aug. 31, 1982; HMJ Papers, Accession 3560-5, Box 210, Folder 36; constituent to HMJ, Feb. 5, 1983; accession ibid.; Kaufman, 413–414.

87 Dan Mintie, "Military Spending in the Northwest," *Northwest Magazine*, May 20, 1984.

88 Findlay and Hevly, 138.

89 Jeff Mapes, "Primary Turns into Crucial Straw Poll between Gorton, Adams," *TO*, Sept. 15, 1986; Roberta Ulrich, "Triumphant Gorton Hints at Cabinet Post for Evans," *TO*, Nov. 10, 1988; Findlay and Hevly, 240.

90 President Donald Trump's proposed fiscal year 2019 budget featured $230 million in spending cuts on the Hanford nuclear reservation; see Annette Cary, "Trump Administration Proposes Smaller Hanford Budget," *TCH*, Feb. 12, 2018, http://www.tri-cityherald.com/news/local/hanford/article199668254.html.

91 Casserly, 30–31.

92 For a more comprehensive biography of Foley, see Jeffrey R. Biggs and Thomas S. Foley, *Honor in the House: Speaker Tom Foley* (Pullman: Washington State University Press, 1999).

93 Yates and Yates, 9, 48, 59–60.

94 Foley beat Republican challenger Marlyn Derby in 1988 with 160,654 votes to 49,657—fewer votes than Bush garnered in Spokane County alone; see *Statistics of the Presidential and Congressional Election of November 8, 1988* (Washington, DC: United States Government Printing Office, 1989), 51.

95 "My Congressional District, Washington, Congressional District 5," *United States Census Bureau,* http://www.census.gov/mycd (these figures are 2014 estimates).

96 Yates and Yates, 26–27; Walla Walla College is today known as Walla Walla University.

97 Nicholas K. Geranios, "Census Shows That the Fifth District is the Poorest in State," *Moscow-Pullman Daily News,* Mar. 24, 1993.

98 David H. Stratton, "The Inland Empire," in Stratton, ed., *Spokane and the Inland Empire: An Interior Pacific Northwest Anthology* (Pullman: Washington State University Press, 2005), 3.

99 Robert Kenton Bird, "The Speaker from Spokane: The Rise and Fall of Tom Foley as a Congressional Leader," PhD diss., Washington State University, Aug. 1999, 30–31; Margo S. Horn, *Thomas S. Foley, Democratic Representative from Washington* (Washington, DC: Grossman Publishers, 1972), 6.

100 "Spokesman-Review Questionnaire to U.S. House and Senate Candidates—Foley 1982," Thomas S. Foley Papers, Manuscripts, Archives and Special Collections, Washington State University (hereafter TSF Papers), Box 416, Folder "Press Files/1989/District Questionnaires."

101 Sherry Devlin, "Foley: Voice of Eastern Washington, or Inland-Empire Builder?" *ST,* Oct. 19, 1982.

102 Frank Bartel, "Chamber of Commerce Fights False Impressions to Earn Support," *Spokane Spokesman Review* (hereafter *SSR*), Mar. 25, 1991.

103 "From the Office of Senator Henry M. Jackson, for Sunday release, June 13, 1965," TSF Papers, Box 412, Folder "Press Files/Press Releases, 1965"; "June 29, 1967 Notification Calls," Lyndon B. Johnson Archives, Congressional Favors File, Box 10; Lyndon Baines Johnson Library, Austin, TX; "Construction Plans Made at Fairchild," *SC,* Jan. 31, 1976; Neil Felgenbauer, "Fairchild to Add Pair of B52s," *SC,* Mar. 11, 1976.

104 "Foley Opposes Plan to Move Survival School," *ST,* Apr. 21, 1985; Jim Camden, "Fairchild Will Open Dorm, Dining Hall," *SSR,* Mar. 16, 1991.

105 TSF to Representative W. G. Hefner, Mar. 20, 1986, TSF Papers, Box 133, Folder 3851; TSF to Hefner, May 19, 1987, TSF Papers, Box 135, Folder 3891; Representative Ronald V. Dellums to TSF, Apr. 27, 1987, TSF Papers, ibid.

106 TSF to Edwin Frost, Oct. 24, 1989, TSF Papers, Box 48, Folder "Foley Papers 1987–1989: Legislative-Armed Services/Foreign Affairs"; Keith Aubrey to TSF, Aug. 17, 1989, TSF Papers, ibid.; Mason D. Moos to TSF, Apr. 11, 1990, TSF Papers, Box 48, Folder "Foley Papers 1240 1990–1992: Legislative-Armed Services/Foreign Aid."

107 TSF to Patricia Schroeder, Apr. 24, 1991, TSF Papers, Box 138, Folder 3975; TSF to Dave McCurdy, May 25, 1993, TSF Papers, ibid.; TSF office press release, May 27, 1993, TSF Papers, Box 138, Folder 3974.

108 "Testimony of the Honorable Thomas S. Foley Before the Defense Base Closure and Realignment Commission," June 4, 1993, TSF Papers, ibid.

109 "Testimony of the Honorable Thomas S. Foley Before the Defense Base Closure and Realignment Commission," June 16, 1993, TSF Papers, ibid.

110 "Fairchild Measures Up to Toughest Standards," *SSR*, June 4, 1993; Jim Camden, "Panel Hints Fairchild Too Costly to Close," *SSR*, June 24, 1993; Jim Camden, "Fairchild Survives Cuts," *SSR*, June 25, 1993.

111 Kevin Taylor, "Fairchild Planes Headed for Bosnia," *SSR*, July 18, 1993; TSF office press release, Feb. 28, 1994, TSF Papers, Box 424, Folder "Press files/1994/ Fairchild."

112 Bird, "The Speaker from Spokane," 95–97.

113 "Foley," *TNT*, Mar. 31, 1991.

114 Bird, "The Speaker from Spokane," 145–146.

115 Kenton Bird, "Tom Foley's Last Campaign: Why Eastern Washington Voters Ousted the Speaker of the House," *Pacific Northwest Quarterly* 95:1 (Winter 2003/2004), 6.

116 For more on the 1994 midterm swing and its implications, see Donald T. Critchlow, "When Republicans Became Revolutionaries: Conservatives in Congress," in Julian Zelizer, ed., *The American Congress: The Building of Democracy* (Boston: Houghton Mifflin Company, 2004), 703–728; Wilentz, 323–354.

117 Daryl C. McClary, "Dean A. Mellberg Shoots and Kills Four People and Wounds 22 at Fairchild Air Force Base Hospital on June 20, 1994," Historylink.org, http://www.historylink.org/File/8767; for Foley's response, see Biggs and Foley, *Honor in the House*, 248; Bird, "The Speaker from Spokane," 185–186.

118 Jim Camden, "Timing of Fairchild Announcement Blasted," *SSR*, Oct. 14, 1994.

119 "Voters Are Fed Up," *SSR*, Oct. 16, 1994; "Washington Congressional Debate," *C-SPAN* video, Oct. 17, 1994, http://www.c-span.org/video/?60916-1/washington-congressional-debate; Bird, "The Speaker from Spokane," 217.

120 Jim Camden, "Foley Misread Mood of the Electorate," *SSR*, Nov. 12, 1994.

121 Jim Camden, "It's Final," *SSR*, Nov. 29, 1994.

122 Jess Walter, "Tom Foley Wraps Up 30 Years in the House," *SSR*, Dec. 12, 1994.

123 Bird, "The Speaker from Spokane," 2, 4.

124 Markusen et al., *The Rise of the Gunbelt*; Heefner, *The Missile Next Door*; Sherry, *In the Shadow of War*; Lotchin, *Fortress California*; "State and County QuickFacts: Washington," United States Census Bureau, http://quickfacts.census.gov/qfd/states/53000.html.

CHAPTER 2

1 When Mason Drukman conducted interviews for his book on Morse, "it was foreign policy above all, and Vietnam in particular, that most people recalled when they thought about Morse"; see Drukman, *Wayne Morse*, 462. Even the most recent scholarship on Morse focuses on his foreign policy and dwells little on the senator's work for Oregon: see Larry Ceplair, "The Foreign Policy of Senator Wayne Morse," ; "US Sen. Wayne Morse," *Oregon Experience* (2012), https://www.opb.org/television/programs/oregonexperience.

2 "Department of Defense Programs in Fiscal Years 1966 and 1967: Oregon," Frederick Panzer Papers, Box 140, Folder "Federal Programs 66–67 by State O-U 1st of 3 Folders," Lyndon B. Johnson Library, Austin, TX (hereafter LBJL); "Department of Defense Programs in Fiscal Years 1966 and 1967: Washington," Panzer Papers, Box 140, Folder "Federal Programs 66–67 V-Z 1st of 3 Folders By State," LBJL.

3 Schwantes, 427.

4 Bruce Cumings, *Dominion from Sea to Sea: Pacific Ascendancy and American Power* (New Haven, CT: Yale University Press, 2009), 371.

5 Gordon Dodds, *Oregon: A Bicentennial History* (New York: W. W. Norton, 1977), 216.

6 Maurine Neuberger oral history interview by Clark Hansen for the Oregon Historical Society, conducted Aug. 26–Dec. 12, 1991; ed. Sara Stroman, 2018; 81, 197, 201–202, 250.

7 Eckard V. Toy, "Oregon at War," *Oregon Historical Quarterly* 102:4 (Winter 2001), 431.

8 Randall B. Woods, "The Cold War," in Julian E. Zelizer, ed., *The American Congress: The Building of Democracy* (Boston: Houghton Mifflin Company, 2004), 506.

9 Wayne Morse (hereafter WLM) to Arthur T. Blackley, May 8, 1948, WLM to Leon French, Mar. 4, 1949, Wayne L. Morse Papers, Special Collections and University Archives, University of Oregon, Eugene, OR (hereafter WLM Papers), Series A, Box 1, "Air Defense"; Dorothy Lee to WLM, Nov. 20, 1950, WLM to Henry Hansen, Mar. 13, 1951; WLM Papers, Series A, Box 1, "Air Academy Location on the West Coast, 1950–1951"; WLM to Thomas Larkin, Feb. 28, 1952; WLM Papers, Series A, Box 110, "Portland—1952"; "A.F. Action Explained," *TO*, Oct. 6, 1957.

10 "Radio Broadcast Sen. Morse August 6, 1958," WLM Papers, Series H, Box 28, "S. 3187."

11 Had Hadgren to Edith Green (hereafter ESG), Feb. 28, 1957, Edith S. Green Papers, Oregon Historical Society, Portland, OR (hereafter ESG Papers), Series A, Box 22, Folder 12; Maj. Gen. Joe Kelley to ESG, Mar. 4, 1957, ESG Papers, ibid. series/box/folder; Robert Holmes and Terry Schrunk to ESG, July 23, 1957, ESG Papers, ibid.; Carl Vinson to ESG, July 25, 1957, ESG Papers, ibid.; ESG to Jim Harding and Jim Goodsell, July 29, 1957, ESG Papers, ibid.; Maj. Gen. Joe Kelley to ESG, Oct. 2, 1957, ESG Papers, ibid.

12 "U.S. Orders Cutback in Bases," *TO*, Mar. 31, 1961; for population figures, see Riley Moffat, *Population History of Western U.S. Cities & Towns, 1850–1990* (Lanham, MD: Scarecrow Press, 1996), 206.

13 "Morse Plugs Tongue Point," *TO*, Mar. 23, 1961.

14 "Norblad, Morse Oppose Closure of Tongue Point," *TO*, Mar. 31, 1961.

15 "Navy Station Use Studied," *TO*, July 17, 1961.

16 Lawrence Barber, "Portland Firm Wins Bid for Space Project Work," *TO*, Aug. 18, 1961.

17 "The Others Must Join In," *Daily Astorian*, Mar. 22, 1962.

18 Mervin Shoemaker, "Union Man Promises He'll Oppose Morse," *TO*, Mar. 9, 1962.

19 "Morse in Trouble?" *TO*, Apr. 28, 1962.

20 Wayne Morse, "Is Present United States Cuba Policy Adequate: Pro," *Congressional Digest* 41:11 (Nov. 1962), 268–274.

21 "Morse Declines Reply to 'Guttersniping' Book," *TO*, Oct. 18, 1962; "Unander: A Reasonable Senator," *TO*, Oct. 28, 1962.

22 Yet by the early 1950s, Morse "had become an avid supporter of a bigger, more powerful military machine to meet the ominous threat from the East"; see Drukman, 174–175.

23 "Unander Raps Morse In Chamber Address as Appeaser, Opponent to Cuba Blockade," *TO*, Oct. 30, 1962.

24 Donald G. Balmer, "The 1962 Election in Oregon," *Western Political Quarterly* 16:2 (June 1963), 454, 456.

25 John F. Kennedy, "Remarks at Tongue Point, Oregon," Sept. 27, 1963; Gerhard Peters and John T. Woolley, *The American Presidency Project*, http://www.presidency.ucsb.edu/ws/?pid=9440.

26 Some historians argue white Pacific Northwesterners have had historically poor relationships with Native American tribes even relative to other western states; see Gray Whaley, *Oregon and the Collapse of Illahee*; Schwantes, *The Pacific Northwest*.

27 "TP School Ruled Out at Astoria," *TO*, Mar. 14, 1964.

28 "TP Defeat Stirs Morse," *TO*, Mar. 15, 1964.

29 Bill Moyers to Larry O'Brien, Mar. 12, 1964, Office Files of Lawrence F. O'Brien, Box 28, Folder: Morse, Sen. Wayne (D) Oregon, LBJL.

30 WLM to Moyers, Mar. 12, 1964, O'Brien Files, ibid.

31 "Extracts from Statement of Senator Wayne Morse before Subcommittee on Department of Interior and Related Agencies of Senate Committee on Appropriations, March 5, 1964," O'Brien Files, Box 28.

32 A. Robert Smith, "Washington Observers See Tongue Point Training Base Victory for Wayne Morse," *TO*, Dec. 20, 1964.

33 Dan Dimick, *Wayne Morse: The Record of a Working Senator ... in Detail: A 1968 Handbook for Morse Workers* (1968 Re-Elect Wayne Morse Committee), 73.

34 Dimick, 68.

35 Judy Chapman, "Beaver Army Terminal Dock," *Oregon Encyclopedia*, https://oregonencyclopedia.org/articles/beaver_army_terminal_dock/#.WuuTqpch1PZ; "Department of Defense Actions to Effect Consolidations, Reductions and Closures of Field Activities," Apr. 24, 1964, WLM Papers, Series B, Box 106, Folder "Military-4 (Beaver Army Terminal, 1965)."

36 WLM and Senator Maurine Neuberger (D-OR) to Secretary of the Army Stephen Allen, Apr. 28, 1964, WLM Papers, Series B, Box 106, Folder "Military-4 (Beaver Army Terminal, 1965)."

37 WLM to Lyndon Johnson, Dec. 30, 1965, WLM Papers, Series B, Box 108, Folder "Military-4 (Portland Air Force Base, 1966)."

38 WLM to G. Linfield, Feb. 8, 1966, WLM Papers, ibid.

39 WLM to Richard T. Deaver, Feb. 18, 1965, WLM Papers, Series B, Box 106, Folder "Military 2 1965."

40 WLM to Mrs. Martin Norris, Mar. 30, 1967, WLM Papers, Series B, Box 109, Folder "Military-9 (Weapons-Arms-Ammunition) 1968."

41 J. L. Blackwell to WLM, May 12, 1967, WLM Papers, ibid.

42 WLM to Mrs. Martin Norris, May 18, 1967, WLM Papers, ibid.

43 Dimick, 131–133.

44 Drukman, 437.

45 "For Release Saturday, May 7, 1966," WLM Papers, Series B, Box Box 54, Folder "Foreign Relations 2: Viet-Nam Speeches of Senator Morse, July 11–March 25 1966."

46 "Remarks of Senator Wayne Morse, Portland Rotary Club, Portland, Oregon, May 31, 1966," WLM Papers, ibid.

47 Robbins, *A Man for All Seasons*, 221.

48 Balmer, "The 1966 Election in Oregon," 594.

49 Ibid., 595–596.

50 Lillian Claire Wilkins, "Wayne Morse: An Exploratory Biography," PhD diss., University of Oregon, March 1982, 11, 15, 18.

51 Kenneth E. Stullerly, "Quite Plain," *TO*, Jan. 10, 1968.

52 Richard K. Washburn, "Retirement Plan," *TO*, Jan. 14, 1968.

53 Mark Jacobs, "Nothing False," *TO*, Jan. 20, 1968.

54 "Morse Backs Callup Decision, Praises President's Coolness," *TO*, Jan. 26, 1968; for more on the *Pueblo*, see Mitchell Lerner, *The* Pueblo *Incident: A Spy Ship and the Failure of American Foreign Policy* (Lawrence: University Press of Kansas, 2002).

55 "Support Told for Duncan," *TO*, Jan. 27, 1968.

56 Warren Weaver Jr., "Morse Seen Leading Duncan in Oregon Contest," *NYT*, Jan. 28, 1968.

57 For more on Packwood, see Mark Kirchmeier, *Packwood: The Public and Private Life from Acclaim to Outrage* (New York: HarperCollins Publishers, 1995) and the Packwood papers collection at Willamette University Archives, Salem, OR, that opened in 2017.

58 "Packwood Enters Senate Race with Blast at Morse's Record," *TO*, Feb. 7, 1968.

59 Kirchmeier, 101–102.

60 Dale M. Harlan, "Trying for Record?" *TO*, Mar. 3, 1968.

61 "Dangerous Division," *TO*, Mar. 13, 1968.

62 Lawrence E. Davis, "Oregon Democrats Urge Vietnam Peace," *NYT*, Mar. 18, 1968.

63 "Duncan Preferred," *TO*, Apr. 8, 1968.

64 "Who Was Right?" *TO*, May 19, 1968.

65 Wilkins, 258.

66 Ibid., 251–252.

67 Mary Courtney, "The Significance of the 1968 Packwood-Morse Debate, with Special Emphasis upon Robert Packwood," B.A. thesis, Linfield College, March 1970, 25.

68 Ibid., 32.

69 Ibid., 44.

70 Ibid., 30–31.

71 Ibid., 40–41.

72 Ibid., 41.

73 Ibid., 42.

74 Ibid., 44.

75 Ibid., 46.

76 *The Last Angry Man: Senator Wayne Morse*, DVD (Portland, OR: Square Deal Productions, 1999).

77 "Wayne Morse," *Oregon Experience*.

78 Harry Bodine, "Packwood Sees Victory in Down-to-Wire Finish," *TO*, Nov. 9, 1968; Harold Hughes, "Morse Overlooks Chance at Victory," *TO*, Nov. 10, 1968.

79 "Behind Morse Loss," *TO*, Nov. 12, 1968.

80 Joann E. Burton, "Way Off Base," *TO*, Nov. 15, 1968.

81 Gerald L. Cogan, "Massive Debt," *TO*, Nov. 18, 1968.

82 Joseph M. Allman, "The 1968 Election in Oregon," *Western Political Quarterly* 22:3 (Sept. 1969), 519, 522; Tom Marsh, *To the Promised Land: A History of Government and Politics in Oregon* (Corvallis: Oregon State University Press, 2012), 293.

83 Wilkins, 257, 262–264.

84 Ibid., 303.

85 Ernest Gruening, *Many Battles: The Autobiography of Ernest Gruening* (New York: Liveright, 1973), 484.

86 Drukman, 455.

87 Ron Abell, "Ron Abell Memoir 17: Some Personal Observations on the Wayne Morse Re-Election Campaign of 1968," http://www.ronabell.com/uploads/Ron_Abell_Memoir__14--Personal_Observations_of_the_Wayne_Morse_Re-Election_Campaign_of_1968.pdf, 2.
88 Abell, 4–5, 8.
89 Ibid., 6.
90 Ibid., 7.
91 Ibid., 10–11.
92 Ibid., 12.
93 Phil Cogswell, "Morse Renowned for Sharp Tongue, Viet War Opposition," *TO*, July 23, 1974.
94 Abell, 5–6, 14.

CHAPTER 3

1 "The Peace Politics of Mark Hatfield," *Arms Control Today*, 17:3 (Apr. 1987).
2 Roberta Ulrich and Alan K. Ota, "Bush Wants BPA to Speed Up Debt Repayment," *TO*, Feb. 5, 1991.
3 Jim Lynch, "Military's Big Bucks Don't Land in Oregon," *TO*, Apr. 15, 2003.
4 Adam Bernstein, "William Proxmire, Ex-Senator, Dies," *Washington Post* (hereafter *WP*), Dec. 16, 2005.
5 Robert Eells and Bartell Nyberg, *Lonely Walk: The Life of Senator Mark Hatfield* (Chappaqua, NY: Christian Herald Books, 1979), 29, 56. A more recent work along similar lines is Lon Fendall, *Stand Alone or Come Home: Mark Hatfield as an Evangelical and a Progressive* (Newberg, OR: Barclay Press, 2008).
6 David E. Settje, *Faith and War: How Christians Debated the Cold and Vietnam Wars* (New York: New York University Press, 2011), 61–94; Brantley W. Gasaway, *Progressive Evangelicals and the Pursuit of Social Justice* (Chapel Hill: University of North Carolina Press, 2014), 235–269.
7 David R. Swartz, *Moral Minority: The Evangelical Left in an Age of Conservatism* (Philadelphia: University of Pennsylvania Press, 2012), 4, 71–72.
8 "Hatfield Eyes New Plant," *TO*, Dec. 13, 1963.
9 Joel Havemann, "Poll Says 75% Favor Buildup," *TO*, Nov. 21, 1965.
10 *Gentleman of the Senate*, DVD, dir. Rick Dancer (Lake Oswego, OR: Hatfield Film Project, 2014).
11 Joel Havemann, "Poll Says 75% Favor Buildup," *TO*, Nov. 21, 1965.
12 Mark O. Hatfield, untitled editorial, *TO*, Feb. 6, 1966.
13 *Gentleman of the Senate*.
14 Mary McGrory, "Rival Beats GOP to Punch," *Washington Star* (hereafter *WS*), Mar. 7, 1966.
15 Palmer Hoyt to Lyndon Johnson, Mar. 12, 1966, Executive Files, Political Affairs/State 37, White House Central Files, Box 65, LBJL).
16 William Connell to Marvin Watson, Apr. 19, 1966, Confidential Files, Political Affairs/State 33–50, WHCF, Box 77, LBJL.
17 "Remarks of Senator Wayne Morse Portland Rotary Club, Portland, Oregon, May 31, 1966," WLM Papers, Series B, Box 54, Folder: "Foreign Relations 2: Viet-Nam Speeches of Senator Morse, July 11–March 25 1966."
18 Dan E. Clark II and Associates to unknown (likely Travis Cross, a top aide to Mark O. Hatfield (hereafter MOH) during his gubernatorial years), Travis Cross Papers,

Willamette University Archives, Salem, OR (hereafter TC Papers), Box 5, Folder "Hatfield campaign materials, 1957–1966 (2 of 3)."

19 Rolla J. Crick, "Much Apathy Found: State Poll Favors Escalation of War," *Oregon Journal* (hereafter *OJ*), Oct. 11, 1966.

20 "Oregon: The Viet Nam Race," *Time*, Oct. 14, 1966.

21 "Prelude to Manila," Thursday, Oct. 13, 1966, KGW TV," TC Papers, Box 5, Folder "Hatfield Speeches 1959–1966 (2 of 3)."

22 "Hatfield Supported," *OJ*, Oct. 31, 1966.

23 William Sanderson, "Hatfield Sets Course, Never Wavers—Wins Votes," *TO*, Nov. 13, 1966.

24 Mark O. Hatfield, *Not Quite So Simple* (New York: Harper & Row, 1968), 162–164.

25 "Judge What He Will Do . . . by What He's Done for Oregon," *TO*, Nov. 7, 1966.

26 Andrew L. Johns, *Vietnam's Second Front: Domestic Politics, The Republican Party, and the War* (Lexington: University Press of Kentucky, 2010), 123.

27 *Gentleman of the Senate.*

28 Johns, 170.

29 Hatfield, *Not Quite So Simple*, 115.

30 Mark Hatfield, May 8, 2001, "Book Discussion on *Against the Grain: Reflections of a Rebel Republican*," C-Span video, http://www.c-span.org/video/?164328-1/book-discussion-grain-reflections-rebel-republican.

31 Bernice Henderson, "Hatfield 'All Wet,'" *OJ*, May 20, 1967.

32 "Hatfield Future Held Dim," *OJ*, Apr. 27, 1967.

33 "Hatfield Urges All-Volunteer Army; Russell Is Sure It Won't Work," *WP*, Apr. 19, 1967; Bruce Chasan, "Volunteer Army," *Oregon Daily Emerald* (hereafter *ODE*), Jan. 7, 1969.

34 "No Danger in Hatfield Army Bill," *ODE*, Feb. 21, 1969.

35 "Get Rid of the Draft," *TO*, Jan. 2, 1971.

36 Robert "Bob" Packwood (hereafter RWP) to Curt Harrison, Oct. 8, 1971; RWP to John C. Schutte, Nov. 16, 1971; Robert W. Packwood Papers, Willamette University Archives and Special Collections (hereafter RWP Papers), Box 16, Folder 33.

37 Swartz, 76.

38 RWP to W. R. Lake Jr., Aug. 7, 1970; RWP to James R. Schwartz, Oct. 23, 1970; RWP Papers, Box 8, Folder 8.

39 Johns, *Vietnam's Second Front*, 283–284.

40 Johns, *Vietnam's Second Front*, 289.

41 Henry E. Baldridge to MOH, Aug. 19, 1970; RWP Papers, Box 8, Folder 8.

42 Edith Green to Francis J. Stohosky III, June 19, 1970; ESG Papers, Box 188, Folder "Foreign Affairs Cambodia."

43 "End War Amendment Right Down Red Alley," *TO*, Aug. 20, 1970; "What 'Moral' Victory?" *TO*, Aug. 31, 1970.

44 "Let Harassment Stop," *TO*, Sept. 2, 1970.

45 Johns, *Vietnam's Second Front*, 337.

46 RWP to Glenn M. Gordon, June 17, 1971; RWP Papers, Box 17, Folder 42; Olin Harrison, "'Shabby' Display," *TO*, Apr. 21, 1971.

47 Fendall, 38.

48 Harry Bodine, "Survey Shows Green Leads Demo Prospects for Senate," *TO*, Nov. 14, 1971.

49 Jeff Mapes, "Oregon's First Statesman," *TO*, Aug. 8, 2011.

50 Mark O. Hatfield. *Against the Grain: Reflections of a Rebel Republican* (Ashland, OR: White Cloud Press, 2001), 137.

51 Walter Evans interview by author, Portland, OR; Sept. 22, 2015.

52 Evans interview.

53 Adding an additional layer of intrigue to the Hatfield-McGovern-Morse political dance, David R. Swartz asserts Hatfield "was courted" to be McGovern's running mate; see Swartz, 76.

54 "How Oregon Cast Its Ballot," *TO*, Nov. 9, 1972.

55 Aug. 9, 1974, telegram to Gerald R. Ford (hereafter GRF) from Darius Marpaung; Aug. 9, 1974, letter to GRF from Ron MacPherson; White House Central Files, Name File, Box 1374, Folder "Hatfield, Mark (Senator) (1), Gerald R. Ford Presidential Papers, Gerald R. Ford Presidential Library, Ann Arbor, MI (hereafter GRFPL).

56 MOH to GRF, Oct. 10, 1974, WHCF, Congressional Mail File, Box 17, Folder "Hatfield, Mark O. (1)," GRFPL.

57 Swartz, 132; Clyde H. Farnsworth, "Reduced Diets in Affluent Lands Argued at Food Parley in Rome," *NYT*, Nov. 7, 1974; William Robbins, "An Administrator on Hunger Urged," *NYT*, Dec. 19, 1974.

58 William T. Kendall to MOH, WHCF Name File, Box 1374, Folder "Hatfield, Mark (Senator) (2)," GRFPL.

59 GRF to MOH, Jan. 18, 1975; MOH to GRF, Jan. 31, 1975; GRF to MOH, Feb. 14, 1975, ibid.; Michaelson interview; Bill Keller, "Hatfield, Kissinger Come Out Even in Fight to Depoliticize Food Program," *TO*, Feb. 6, 1975.

60 Michael T. Kaufman, "Idi Amin, Murderous and Erratic Ruler of Uganda in the 70's, Dies in Exile," *NYT*, Aug. 17, 2003.

61 Hatfield, *Against the Grain*, 195–196; Steve Duin, "Rolf Rails Against Politics of Avoidance," *TO*, Nov. 17. 1991.

62 MOH, Don C. Frisbee, and Louis B. Perry to Hillman Lueddemann, Feb. 15, 1980, Oregon Historical Society, Hillman Lueddemann Papers, Box 2, Folder "Correspondence—Hatfield, Mark O. (1958–80) With/About."

63 Kathie Durbin, "Hatfield Backs Massive Food Campaign," *TO*, Feb. 17, 1980.

64 "Portland With a Heart for the World," *TO*, Apr. 15, 1980.

65 "There's a Hungry World at Your Door . . . ," *TO*, Apr. 6, 1980.

66 Bill Keller, "Hatfield Brings Home Bacon from Washington Pork Barrel," *TO*, Oct. 29, 1978.

67 A. Robert Smith, "Dioxin Incident Left Many Unanswered Questions about National Waste Policy," *Willamette Week* (hereafter *WW*), Dec. 29, 1976.

68 "Hatfield Fights Gas Shipment," *WW*, Aug. 2, 1978.

69 Kathie Durbin, "Air Base Closure Protested," *WW*, May 3, 1978.

70 On Panama Canal politics, see Adam Clymer, *Drawing the Line at the Big Ditch: The Panama Canal Treaties and the Rise of the Right* (Lawrence: University of Kansas Press, 2008); Ira Shapiro, *The Last Great Senate: Courage and Statesmanship in Times of Crisis* (New York: Perseus, 2012), 135–156.

71 Bill Keller, "Panama Canal Digs in as State Issue," *TO*, Aug. 28, 1977.

72 Eells and Nyberg, 160.

73 "There Is a Choice!" *TO*, Nov. 5, 1978.

74 "Treaties No Giveaway," *TO*, Mar. 12, 1978.

75 "Principal Accomplishments of Senator Hatfield in His Current Term in the U.S. Senate," Trullinger and Chamberlin Papers, Box 1, Folder "Chamberlin, Mark Correspondence with Senator Mark Hatfield 1972–1988."

76 "Senate Results," *TO*, Nov. 9, 1978.

77 Jonathan Nicholas, "If Not Now, When?" *TO*, Mar. 8, 1984; Ronald Reagan, *The Reagan Diaries* (New York: HarperCollins, 2007), 224–225.

78 "Senator Mark O. Hatfield, Silverton Speech, October 28, 1983," TC Papers, Box 5, Folder "Hatfield Campaign Materials, 1957–1966 (2 of 3)."

79 "Senator Margie Hendriksen Speaks Out on Peace and National Security," Margie Hendriksen Papers, University of Oregon Special Collections and University Archives, Eugene, OR; Box 5, Folder "Senator Margie Hendriksen."

80 Robert O'Brien, "Delving into Record," *TO*, Oct. 6, 1984.

81 "Key Concerns of Oregonians: 1984," Hatfield Backgrounder Collection, Oregon Historical Society (hereafter HBC), Box 1.

82 "Mark Hatfield of Oregon, Republican, Endorsed for the U.S. Senate by Council for a Livable World," TC Papers, Box 5, Folder "Hatfield Campaign Materials, 1957–1966."

83 David Whitney and Robert Gettlin, "Two Say Payments Made 'to Buy Help,'" *TO*, Aug. 14, 1984; Holly Danks, "Hatfield Supporters Celebrate," *TO*, Nov. 7, 1984.

84 Jeff Mapes, "Poll Says Hatfield Far Ahead," *TO*, Sept. 9, 1984.

85 "The Defense Budget: Does Increased Spending Equal Increased Security?" Oct. 1985, No. 276, HBC, Box 1.

86 David Whitney, "Daddy Taxbucks," *TO*, May 25, 1986.

87 Judy Rooks, "Tour Pursues Navy Repair Trade," *TO*, Sept. 25, 1987.

88 Richard Colby, "More Work Remains on Computer Process," *TO*, Jan. 9, 1988.

89 Foster Church, "Hatfield Says Scrapping of N Reactor Would Not Hurt U.S. Defense Capacity," *TO*, Oct. 24, 1987.

90 Foster Church, "Bill Provides for N Reactor Shutdown," *TO*, Nov. 19, 1987.

91 Linda Roache Monroe, "N Reactor's Closure: Good News . . . Bad News," *TO*, Jan. 30, 1988.

92 "Every Little Bit Helps Hanford," *TO*, Feb. 14, 1988.

93 "Extortion is Challenged," *Salem Statesman Journal* (hereafter *SSJ*), Mar. 22, 1988.

94 Steve Duin, "St. Mark Keeps Power under Wraps," *TO*, July 31, 1988.

95 "Senator Mark O. Hatfield, Portland State University Commencement, June 9, 1989," provided to author by Carrie Klein.

96 Don Hamilton, "Lonsdale Ads Charge Hatfield's Out of Touch," *TO*, Sept. 29, 1990.

97 Harry Londsale, *Running: Politics, Power, and the Press* (Bloomington, IN: 1stBooks Library, 2002), 183–184: the list included $3,000 from Boeing, $3,000 from General Atomics, $1,000 from General Dynamics, $4,000 from GE, $2,000 from Hughes Aircraft, $1,000 from ITT, $1,000 from Lockheed, $3,000 from Martin Marietta Inc., $2,000 from McDonnell Douglas, and $1,000 from Tektronix, among others.

98 Mark Hatfield, "Campaign Appearance," C-SPAN.com video, Oct. 21, 1990, http://www.c-span.org/video/?14867-1/campaign-appearance.

99 On Rajneeshpuram, see Frances FitzGerald, *Cities on a Hill: A Brilliant Exploration of Visionary Communities Remaking the American Dream* (New York: Simon & Schuster, 1986), 247–382; Carl Abbott, "Revisiting Rajneeshpuram: Oregon's Largest Utopian Community as Western History," *Oregon Historical Quarterly*

116:4 (Winter 2015), 414–447; Maclain Way and Chapman Way, dirs., *Wild Wild Country* (Duplass Brothers Productions, 2018).

100 Gail Kinsey Hill, "Political Sparks Fly in Hatfield-Lonsdale Race," *TO*, Oct. 27, 1990.

101 Carolyn Lamberson, "Hatfield Hits Back Hard at Lonsdale on Rajneesh, Labor," *TO*, Oct. 29, 1990.

102 Joan Laatz, "Hatfield, Lonsdale Fire Shots," *TO*, Nov. 1, 1990.

103 Joan Laatz and Don Hamilton, "Lonsdale Crashes Hatfield News Meeting," *TO*, Nov. 3, 1990.

104 Don Hamilton, "Senator Bests Hatfield's Challenge," *TO*, Nov. 7, 1990.

105 Mark Hatfield, "War Isn't Quick and Easy," *TO*, Jan. 13, 1991.

106 David Reinhard, "Leaving a Mark: Hatfield as Deficit Hawk," *TO*, Apr. 20, 1996.

107 *Gentleman of the Senate.*

108 Mark Hatfield, "Sen. Mark Hatfield (R-OR) on Ebola Research and NIH Funding: 1995 Senate Floor Debate on Budget Resolution," C-SPAN.com video, May 24, 1995, http://www.c-span.org/video/?c4510407/ sen-mark-hatfield-ebola-research-nih-funding.

109 Bill Graves, "Federal Largesse Benefits OHSU," *TO*, Aug. 5, 1990.

110 Mark O. Hatfield interview with Joan S. Ash, Oct. 22, 1998, *OHSU Oral History Collection*, 3, https://digitalcommons.ohsu.edu/hca-oralhist/3.

111 Hatfield interview, 8–9; William Graves, *Transformed: How Oregon's Public Health University Won Independence and Healed Itself* (Forest Grove, OR: Pacific University Press, 2017), 14.

112 Hatfield interview, 14.

113 Hatfield interview, 15; Graves, 13.

114 A. Robert Smith and Steve Forrester, "VA Hospital Appropriation: Now Hatfield Sees Double," *WW*, June 28, 1978.

115 Leonard Laster and Ruth Ann Laster interview with Joan S. Ash, Mar. 5, 1999, *OHSU Oral History Collection*, 18, http://digitalcommons.ohsu.edu/ hca-oralhist/65.

116 John W. Kendall Jr. interview with Joan S. Ash, June 23, 1999, *OHSU Oral History Collection*, 10, http://digitalcommons.ohsu.edu/hca-oralhist/63.

117 Graves, 37; fn. 15.

118 Stanley W. Jacob interview with Linda A. Weimer, Sept. 24, 1998, *OHSU Oral History Collection*, 16.

119 Jacob interview, 17.

120 Alan K. Ota and James Long, "Special Policy Got Hatfield Daughter into OHSU," *TO*, Mar. 17, 1991; Steve Duin, "Maybe We're Just Talking Half a Foot," *TO*, Aug. 27, 1991; Roberta Ulrich, "Ethics Panel Rebukes Hatfield," *TO*, Aug. 13, 1992.

121 Bill MacKenzie, "Congressional 'Pork' Is Bacon for Oregon," *TO*, Mar. 13, 1994.

122 Nancy McCarthy, "Laster to Leave OHSU for Massachusetts Post," *TO*, Aug. 13, 1987.

123 Foster Church, "Hatfield Scores Legislative Victories for Region—Despite Obstacles," *TO*, July 17, 1988.

124 Jim Hill, "OHSU Shows Off New $1.4 Million Critical Care Unit," *TO*, May 19, 1989; Patrick O'Neill, "Construction of Medical Data Center at OHSU Begins," *TO*, Aug. 11, 1989.

125 Foster Church, "Funds Set for Center at OHSU," *TO*, Sept. 15, 1989; "Hatfield Projects," *TO*, Sept. 29, 1996.

126 Oz Hopkins Koglin, "OHSU Will Renew Spirit of Research," *TO*, Feb. 15, 1998.
127 Mark Hatfield, "Book Discussion on *Against the Grain: Reflections of a Rebel Republican*."
128 Casserly, "Securing the Sound," 3–5.

CHAPTER 4

1 Biggs and Foley, *Honor in the House*, 112–114.
2 Letter, Lyndon Johnson to Warren Magnuson, May 7, 1965, Name File, WHCF, Box 9, Folder "Jackson, Henry M. (Sen) 1963–64," LBJL.
3 Wanda Rushing, *Memphis and the Paradox of Place: Globalization in the American South* (Chapel Hill: University of North Carolina Press, 2009), 1, 4.
4 Ibid, 86–87.
5 Ibid., 3.
6 Ibid., 7.
7 For more on the South as a hub of globalization, see especially James C. Cobb, ed., *Globalization and the American South* (Athens: University of Georgia Press, 2005).
8 Douglas A. Irwin, *Clashing Over Commerce: A History of U.S. Trade Policy* (Chicago: University of Chicago Press, 2017), 2.
9 Ibid., 6.
10 Kaufman, 59.
11 Michael A. Barnhart, "From Hershey Bars to Motor Cars: America's Economic Policy Toward Japan, 1945–76," in Akira Iriye and Robert A. Wampler, eds., *Partnership: The United States and Japan, 1951–2001* (Tokyo: Kodansha International, 2001), 202.
12 Guangqiu Xu, *Congress and the U.S.-China Relationship, 1949–1979* (Akron: University of Akron Press, 2007), 37; Scates, *Warren G. Magnuson*, 181–182.
13 Xu, 159.
14 WGM to constituent, June 11, 1959, WGM Papers, Accession 3181-004, Box 75, Folder 23.
15 WGM to constituent, June 18, 1959, WGM Papers, ibid.
16 Xu, 155–156.
17 Thomas Kerr to Wayne Morse, cc to HMJ, June 7, 1957; HMJ Papers, Accession 3560-3, Box 131, Folder 8; Thomas Kerr to HMJ, June 20, 1957; HMJ Papers, ibid.
18 Constituent to HMJ, June 8, 1957; HMJ Papers, ibid.
19 China Club of Seattle to HMJ, June 20, 1957; HMJ Papers, Accession 3560-3, Box 131, Folder 9.
20 "From the Office of Senator Henry M. Jackson for Release in A.M. Newspapers of July 10, 1963," HMJ Papers, Accession 3560-3, Box 232, Folder 59.
21 Ognibene, 105.
22 "Jackson Asks Less Rigid Policy Toward Red China," *Wenatchee World*, Nov. 5, 1969.
23 "Jackson Report on China and American Policy," Aug. 12, 1974, HMJ Papers, Accession 3560-4, Box 260, Folder 141.
24 Kaufman, 283–284.
25 Henry Jackson, "The Geopolitics of Oil," *NYT*, Mar. 25, 1978.
26 For Deng's 1979 visit to Seattle, see Christopher P. Foss, "Senator Henry 'Scoop' Jackson and the Intersection Between Domestic Politics and Foreign Relations in

the Postwar Era," in Andrew L. Johns and Mitchell B. Lerner, eds., *The Cold War at Home and Abroad: Domestic Politics and U.S. Foreign Policy Since 1945* (Lexington: University Press of Kentucky, 2018.)

27   "Jackson, on China Visit, Supports Trade Accord," *NYT*, Aug. 8, 1979.

28   "Taiwan Arms Sales Criticized," *NYT*, July 19, 1982.

29   "Senator Jackson, In Peking, Says Better Ties Are Ahead," *NYT*, Aug. 28, 1983.

30   H. George Frederickson to Tom Foley, Mar. 23, 1979, TSF Papers, Box 70, Folder 1989; Phil Smart to TSF, Apr. 17, 1979, TSF Papers, ibid.

31   Press release, "Foley Named to Council To Boost Exports," May 10, 1979, TSF Papers, Box 70, Folder 1987.

32   Wendy Liu, *Connecting Washington and China: The Story of the Washington State China Relations Council* (New York: iUniverse, 2005), 218; John Caldbick, "1980 Census," *HistoryLink.org*, http://www.historylink.org/index.cfm?displaypage= output.cfm&file_id=9431; Douglas Lee, "Chinese Americans in Oregon," *Oregon Encyclopedia*, http://oregonencyclopedia.org/articles/chinese_americans_in_ oregon/#.Vs33r9BCLf0.

33   Michael Bess, "Chinese Envoy Arrives," *TO*, July 30, 1980.

34   Albert Naito to WLM, Oct. 4, 1960; WLM to Koichiro Asaki, undated; Naito to WLM, Oct. 6, 1960; WLM Papers, Series A, Box 111, "Portland General 1959–60."

35   Terry Schrunk to WLM, Apr. 6, 1961, WLM Papers, Series B, Box 44, Folder "Foreign Relations 1961 Japan"; Schrunk to WLM, Aug. 31, 1961, WLM Papers, ibid.

36   "Remarks by United States Senator Wayne Morse Before a Joint Luncheon of the Japan-America Society and the American Chamber of Commerce in Japan," Nov. 20, 1965, WLM Papers, Series B, Box 142, Folder "Foreign Relations (SM's Trip—Speeches)."

37   "US-Japan Parliamentary Exchange Program," *Japan Center for International Exchange*, http://www.jcie.or.jp/pep/exchange.

38   "'The United States and Japan': Remarks of Wayne Morse, Pacific Northwest Assembly, University of Oregon, Eugene, Oregon," Feb. 12, 1966, WLM Papers, Series B, Box 42, Folder "Foreign Relations (SM's Trip—Speeches)."

39   R. J. Darling to HMJ, Apr. 7, 1953, HMJ Papers, Accession 3560-003, Box 14, Folder 24; HMJ to Walter Wilkes, Mar. 17, 1955, HMJ Papers, Accession 3560-003, Box 19, Folder 30; HMJ to Pat J. Bynum, Jan. 13, 1958, HMJ Papers, Accession 3560-003, Box 139, Folder 1; "Statement by Senator Jackson to the Committee on Ways and Means, House of Representatives Hearings on Extension of the President's Authority to Enter into Trade Agreements, March, 1958," HMJ Papers, ibid.

40   Constituent to HMJ, Apr. 23, 1958; HMJ Papers, Accession 3560-003, Box 139, Folder 1.

41   Thomas W. Zeiler, *American Trade and Power in the 1960s* (New York: Columbia University Press, 1992), 73, 83, 89.

42   "Morse Asks Wood Probe," *TO*, Jan. 7, 1961.

43   A. Robert Smith, "Japanese Trade Brings Grumbles," *TO*, July 12, 1961; A. Robert Smith, "Government Report Denies Log Exports to Japan," *TO*, July 13, 1961; "Group Requests Export Hearing," *TO*, July 23, 1963; "Labor Group Plans Meet," *TO*, Aug. 13, 1961.

44   WLM to W. J. Runckel, Oct. 10, 1961, WLM Papers, Series B, Box 151, Folder "Trade 1 Japanese Logging Materials 1962."

45 "Remarks of Senator Wayne Morse, Central Oregon District Council, Lumber and Sawmill Workers, Bend, Oregon, November 19, 1961," WLM Papers, Series B, Box 151, Folder "Trade 1 Japanese Logging Materials 1962."

46 WLM Papers, Series H, Box 43, Folder "S. 2663."

47 Zeiler, 94–97.

48 Drukman, 376–378; the WFIA apparently no longer exists, but it remained a lobby for lower-priced timber into the 1990s.

49 "Commerce Aide Backing Trade Expansion Moves," *TO*, May 23, 1962.

50 Morse robo letter to constituents, Aug. 18, 1962, WLM Papers, Series H, Box 47, Folder "H.R. 11970."

51 Zeiler, 99.

52 A. Robert Smith, "Trade Measure Offers Possible Tariff Protection," *TO*, Oct. 11, 1962.

53 Hatfield, *Not Quite So Simple*, 122.

54 David Peterson del Mar, *Oregon's Promise: An Interpretive History* (Corvallis: Oregon State University Press, 2003), 222–223.

55 Hatfield, *Not Quite So Simple*, 123–124.

56 Ibid., 125.

57 Cone Lumber Company to Morse, Sept. 13, 1967, WLM Papers, Series B, Box 65, Folder "Forest Resources 4 (Sales)-Log Exports C."

58 William B. Macomber to Morse, Oct. 20, 1967, WLM Papers, ibid.

59 Letter exchanges between John B. Crowell and Morse, Dec. 1, 5, 11, and 18, 1967, WLM Papers, ibid.

60 "Morse Calls Log Hearing," *TO*, Jan. 6, 1968; Gerry Pratt, "Morse Asked to Join In Japan Log Talks," *TO*, Jan. 14, 1968.

61 A. Robert Smith, "Vote-Conscious Morse Now Lumberman's Pal," *TO*, Jan. 18, 1968.

62 "Morse Shift on Logs Hit," *TO*, Jan. 24, 1968.

63 "Morse, Hatfield Blast U.S. Stand on Logs," *TO*, Jan. 24, 1968.

64 "Log Export Impasse," *TO*, Jan. 25, 1968.

65 "Senator Morse Reports, February 1968," WLM Papers, Series B, Box 105, Folder "Metals 1 (Gold) 1968."

66 "Oregon Republicans Need Wayne Morse More Than They Know," *TO*, Oct. 30, 1968.

67 Drukman, 444.

68 "Port of Portland 1977 Ocean Commerce Statistics," Robert W. Packwood Papers, Box 310, Folder "China Trade Briefing Book."

69 Lonsdale, 30, 53.

70 Harry Lonsdale, "U.S. Senate Single-Chair Debate," *C-SPAN* video, Sept. 7, 1990, https://www.youtube.com/watch?v=rUrNOFUlqMU.

71 Schwantes, 489.

72 Mark O. Hatfield, "Lonsdale vs. Hatfield," *TO*, Oct. 14, 1990.

73 Dan Goldy, "The Forestry War of 1990," *Oregon Business*, Jan. 1990.

74 Schwantes, 445, 508.

75 "Oregon Wheat Growers League," *Oregon Wheat*, http://www.owgl.org/about-us/oregon-wheat-growers-league.

76 Richard Baum to WLM, Jan. 29, 1954, WLM Papers, Series A, Box 105, "Oregon Wheat Growers League, 1954–1959."

77 WLM to Jack Smith, Feb. 6, 1958, ibid.; WLM to Andrew Morrow, Dec. 3, 1959, ibid.

78 Joe Bianco, "Beef, Grain Spark Trade," *TO*, Dec. 29, 1963.

79 "From the office of Senator Wayne Morse (D-Ore.), July 13, 1962," WLM Papers, Series B, Box 151, Folder "Trade 1 Fruits 1962."

80 Henry Jackson, Warren Magnuson, Wayne Morse, and Maurine Neuberger to Under Secretary of State George Ball, Jan. 23, 1963, HMJ Papers, Accession 3560-3, Box 97, Folder 8; Ball to HMJ, Feb. 4, 1963, ibid.

81 HMJ to Ernest Falk, Apr. 8, 1963, ibid.; HMJ and WGM to Christian Herter, Apr. 16, 1963, ibid.; Herter to HMJ and WGM, May 3, 1963, ibid.; Herter to HMJ, May 3, 1963, ibid.; Herter to HMJ, July 29, 1963, ibid.

82 HMJ and WGM to Orville Freeman, Aug. 22, 1966, HMJ Papers, Accession 3560-4, Box 54, Folder 8; constituent to HMJ, Nov. 28, 1966, ibid.; L. F. Whiteley to HMJ, Dec. 13, 1966, ibid.

83 F.A. Johnston to HMJ, Mar. 29, 1967, HMJ Papers, Accession 3560-4, Box 54, Folder 8.

84 "Statement of Senator Henry M. Jackson for the Department of Agriculture, Unshu Orange Hearings in Portland, Oregon," Apr. 19, 1967, ibid.

85 "Taboo on Mandarin Oranges May End," *ST*, Apr. 21, 1967; Robert B. McCleary to HMJ, Oct. 3, 1967; Kenneth F. Grimes to HMJ, Dec. 12, 1967; HMJ Papers, Accession 3560-4, Box 54, Folder 8.

86 Joe Bianco, "Beef, Grain Spark Trade," *TO*, Dec. 29, 1963; "S. 2612," Mar. 6, 1964, WLM Papers, Series B, Box 152, Folder "S. 2612"; Ray Powell to WLM, May 18, 1964, WLM Papers, ibid.; WLM to Powell, May 27, 1964, WLM Papers, ibid.; *Congressional Record*, July 28, 1964, WLM Papers, Series B, Box 153, Folder "Trade-1 (Beef) (H.R. 1839) 1964."

87 Dick Wilkinson to WLM, undated 1964 letter; Hallie Daniels to WLM, Sept. 1, 1964; League of Women Voters representative Lucile Chastek to WLM, July 27, 1964; WLM Papers, ibid.

88 *Congressional Record*, Aug. 18, 1964, WLM Papers, ibid.

89 "Closing the Door on Beef," *NYT*, Aug. 15, 1964; Tad Szulc, "Latins, Worried by U.S. Restrictions on Imports, Warn of Repercussions," *NYT*, Sept. 24, 1964.

90 "S. Res. 111," WLM Papers, Series H, Box 58, Folder "S. Res. 111"; "Excerpts from an Address by Senator Wayne Morse (D-Ore.) to the Twelfth Annual Meeting of the Red Angus Association of America, Friday, June 25, 1965," WLM Papers, ibid.

91 "S. 1613," Apr. 24, 1967, WLM Papers, Series H, Box 59, Folder "S. 1613"; Morse to Bob Ward, June 11, 1968, WLM Papers, ibid.; Morse to E.W. Harvey, Aug. 21, 1967, WLM Papers, Series H, Box 59, Folder "S. 2411."

92 Biggs and Foley, 277.

93 Baodi Zhou, "Thomas S. Foley and the Politics of Wheat: U.S. Wheat Trade with Japan, China, and the Soviet Union, 1965–1986," PhD diss, Washington State University, 1999, v–vi.

94 Zhou, 2, 6 fn. 4, 27.

95 Bird, "The Speaker from Spokane", 45; Zhou, 35, 39–40; Lyndon B. Johnson, "Statement by the President upon Signing the Food and Agriculture Act of 1965," Nov. 4, 1965; Gerhard Peters and John T. Woolley, *The American Presidency Project*, http://www.presidency.ucsb.edu/ws/?pid=27348.

96 "Wheat Deal Put into Gear," *SSR*, Jan. 11, 1968; Frank Hewlett, "Wheat Pact with India Authorized," *SSR*, Jan. 28, 1969; Frank Hewlett, "South Korea Purchasing

Wheat, Barley from U.S.," *SSR*, Feb. 13, 1969; "India to Buy White Flour," *SSR*, Apr. 7, 1971; "Sales to Aid Wheat Growers," *WDW*, Apr. 28, 1971.

97   Horn, *Thomas S. Foley, Democratic Representative from Washington*, 10.

98   Zhou, 71.

99   Ibid., v–vi.

100 "Foley Says Food Talks Won't Affect NW Soon," *WDW*, Nov. 20, 1974.

101 Les Blumenthal, "Moos Assays Food Conference," *SSR*, Nov. 22, 1974; "World Seeks Food Aid," *SC*, Feb. 14, 1975; Betsy Trainor, "Butz Criticizes Food Aid Emphasis," *Walla Walla Union Bulletin*, Mar. 16, 1975.

102 Zhou, 85.

103 Richard W. Larsen, "Foley's for '100% Parity' as Goal," *ST*, Apr. 2, 1978.

104 "Foley Says Teng Visit May Bring Trade Gains," undated press release, TSF Papers, Box 412, Folder "Press Files/Press Releases—n.d. (Jan. 1979) Visit of Teng Hsiao-Ping (Deng Shou-ping); Jim Spoerhase, "Foley Envisions China Buying State's Wheat," *SC*, Feb. 5, 1979; Francis G. Crane to TSF, Apr. 12, 1979, TSF Papers, Box 241, Folder "96th Cong., 1st Session/Dept Files/Dept of Agriculture—general, Part 1"; Eddie K. Eng to TSF, Sept. 26, 1979, TSF Papers, ibid.; "Foley Reports on China Talks," Sept. 7, 1979, press release, TSF Papers, Box 412, Folder "Press Files/Press Releases, Sept. 7, 1979—China Talks."

105 WGM to Senator Walter F. George, May 11, 1951; WGM to Dean Acheson, June 18, 1951; WGM Papers, Accession 3181-003, Box 46, Folder 1; Scates, 198–199; David Kludas, "Centennial Exposition of 1959," *Oregon Encyclopedia*, https://oregonencyclopedia.org/articles/centennial_exposition_of_1959/#.W0aINbgnZPY; "Century 21 World's Fair," *Seattle Municipal Archives*, https://www.seattle.gov/cityarchives/exhibits-and-education/digital-document-libraries/century-21-worlds-fair.

106 "S. 4022," Sept. 22, 1972, HMJ Papers, Accession 3560-5, Box 220, Folder 45.

107 "U.S. Participation in the Spokane Expo 1974," Senate Foreign Relations Committee report, HMJ Papers, ibid.

108 "Public Law 92-598, 92nd Congress, S. 4022," Oct. 27, 1972, HMJ Papers, ibid.

109 "Public Law 92-598, 92nd Congress, S. 4022, October 27, 1972," HMJ Papers, Accession 3560-5, Box 220, Folder 45; John Webster, "Tom Foley's Legacy Left an Impact across Northwest," *SSR*, Oct. 20, 2013.

110 Jesse Tinsley, "Then and Now: U.S. Pavilion at Expo," *SSR*, Dec. 11, 2017.

111 Dorothy Rochon Powers, "Expo '74—Spokane's Gift to the Bicentennial," *Mainliner*, Mar. 1974.

112 TSF to media outlets, Mar. 13, 1974, TSF Papers, Box 310, Folder "District Office/Expo '74—Background—Miscellaneous 1972–1975"; TSF to Gens Evensen, Ole Alhard, and Soren Christian Sommerfelt, Apr. 9, 1974, TSF Papers, ibid.

113 "The Littlest Show on Earth," *WS*, undated (probably early 1974).

114 Mack, 129.

115 James P. Sterba, "Expo '74—Pint-Sized World's Fair in Spokane," *International Herald Tribune*, May 16, 1974.

116 Dorothy Powers, "President Praises Spokane, Expo '74," *SSR*, May 5, 1974.

117 Larry Young, "Opening Day Goes Like Clockwork," *SSR*, May 5, 1974.

118 "Spokane Angels May End Up with Expo Bill," *TO*, Dec. 14, 1974.

119 Jim Kershner, "Expo '74: Spokane's World's Fair," *HistoryLink.org*, http://www.historylink.org/File/10791.

CHAPTER 5

1 Irwin, 534.

2 Connally quoted in Irwin, 543.

3 Connally and Nixon quoted in Irwin, 752, fn. 75.

4 Irwin, 574.

5 Ibid., 577.

6 O'Neill quoted in Irwin, 599.

7 Theodore H. White, "The Danger from Japan," *NYT*, July 28, 1985; Chalmers John-son, *MITI and the Japanese Miracle: The Growth of Industrial Policy, 1925–1975* (Stanford, CA: Stanford University Press, 1982); Pat Choate, *Agents of Influence: How Japan's Lobbyists in the United States Manipulate America's Political and Economic System* (New York: Knopf, 1990).

8 Fox Butterfield, "New Hampshire Speech Earns Praise for Trump," *NYT*, Oct. 23, 1987; Michael Kruse, "The True Story of Donald Trump's First Campaign Speech—in 1987," *Politico*, Feb. 5, 2016.

9 Irwin, 559, 595–597.

10 David Sheff, *Game Over: How Nintendo Zapped an American Industry, Captured Your Dollars, and Enslaved Your Children* (New York: Random House, 1993), 14; Jeff Ryan, *Super Mario: How Nintendo Conquered America* (New York: Penguin, 2011), 13.

11 Sheff, 97–98.

12 Ibid., 105–113; Nao Hardy, Miguel Llanos, and Rosemarie Ives, "Overview of Red-mond History," *Redmond Historical Society*, http://www.redmondhistoricalsociety.org/RHS/index.php?option=com_content&view=article&id=567&Itemid=299.

13 Vincent quoted in Sheff, 262, 279–280.

14 Ibid., 404–405.

15 Vincent quoted in Timothy Egan, "Mariners Fans Angered by Vincent's Response," *NYT*, Jan. 25, 1992.

16 Vincent quoted in Tom Farrey, "'Accidental Commissioner' Takes Stand," *Orlando Sentinel* (hereafter *OS*), June 14, 1992.

17 Hughes, *Slade Gorton*, 167; Gorton quoted in Stephen H. Dunphey, "Trade Wars," *ST*, Feb. 27, 1983.

18 Hughes, 181, 289; Patty Murray, "A Tribute to Slade Gorton from Sen. Patty Mur-ray," *ST*, Dec. 11, 2000.

19 Lincoln quoted in Hughes, *Slade Gorton*, 272.

20 "Put Baseball First," *TO*, Jan. 26, 1992.

21 Steven L. Kendall, "The Easy Way or the Hard Way," *NYT*, Mar. 8, 1992.

22 Ryan, 141–142.

23 Memorandum of Conversation, Meeting with Prime Minister Miyazawa of Japan, Jan. 30, 1992, OA/ID 91109-005, Bush Presidential Records, Brent Scowcroft Files, George H. W. Bush Presidential Library (hereafter GHWBL), https://bush-41library.tamu.edu/files/memcons-telcons/1992-01-30--Miyazawa.pdf.

24 Memorandum of Conversation, Meeting with Kozo Watanabe, Minister of Trade and Industry (MITI), May 1, 1992, GHWBL, https://bush41library.tamu.edu/files/memcons-telcons/1992-05-01--Watanabe.pdf.

25 "Remarks at the Signing Ceremony for the Paper Market Access Agreement with Japan," Apr. 23, 1992, Public Papers, GHWBL, https://bush41library.tamu.edu/archives/public-papers/4210.

26 Hughes, *Slade Gorton*, 273.

27 Vincent quoted in Tom Farrey, "'Accidental Commissioner' Takes Stand," *OS*, June 14, 1992.

28 George Vecsey, "Japanese Owner Gets the Shaft," *NYT*, June 1, 1992.

29 Sheff, 406–407.

30 Biggs and Foley, 100.

31 Bart Preecs, "Another Expansion for Electronics Firm," *SSR*, Apr. 13, 1982.

32 Thomas S. Foley to James Chase, undated (ca. Apr. 1985), TSF Papers, Box 133, Folder 3850.

33 Rick Bonino, "Spokane Unveils Splashy Ag Trade Center," *SSR*, Jan. 18, 1989.

34 TSF to Robert Allen Skotheim, Sept. 27, 1985; TSF to Eiji Toyoda, Oct. 17, 1985; TSF Papers, Box 134, Folder 3859.

35 O'Neill quoted in Irwin, 611.

36 Reagan quoted in Irwin, 606–607.

37 Jim Langlois to TSF, Sept. 17, 1985, TSF Papers, Box 41, Folder 98.

38 Booth Gardner to TSF, Oct. 1, 1985, TSF Papers, ibid.

39 Jack Block to TSF, Oct. 14, 1985; Thomas C. Lowinger to TSF, May 1985; Paull H. Shin to TSF, Oct. 22, 1985; Jan Wiley-Gee to TSF, Nov. 5, 1985, all TSF Papers, ibid.

40 T. A. Wilson to TSF, Oct. 4, 1985, TSF Papers, ibid.

41 Strom Thurmond to TSF, Nov. 14, 1985; Jim Wright to TSF, May 13, 1986, TSF Papers, ibid.

42 Tsutomu Hota to TSF, Dec. 26, 1985, TSF Papers, ibid.

43 Bunsai Sato to TSF, May 6, 1986, TSF Papers, ibid.

44 TSF robo letter to constituents, Oct. 11, 1985, TSF Papers, ibid.

45 TSF to Thomas C. Lowinger, Oct. 16, 1985, TSF Papers, ibid.

46 TSF to Thomas A. Marabello, Nov. 25, 1985, TSF Papers, ibid.

47 Jim Sparks, "Washington 'to Lose' in World Trade War," *SSR*, Feb. 15, 1987.

48 Bert Caldwell, "Danger of Protectionist Legislation Stressed," *SSR*, Mar. 6, 1987.

49 Bill Salquist, "'Trade War' May Bypass Spokane," *SSR*, Apr. 1, 1987.

50 Robert G. Baker to TSF, Mar. 6, 1987; William Whitaker to TSF, Apr. 22, 1987; T. R. Brice to TSF, Apr. 23, 1987; Gary Dilley to TSF, Apr. 28, 1987; Edward L. Kelly to TSF, May 22, 1987; all letters from TSF Papers, Box 43, Folder "100th Congress: Legislative—Ways and Means, Trade."

51 "Militant Nationalism," *ST*, Apr. 21, 1987.

52 Eric Pryne and Linda Keene, "State Could Be a Victim of Trade Plan," *ST*, Apr. 29, 1987.

53 Irwin, 619.

54 "Takeshita, Reagan Vow to Support Ailing Dollar," *ST*, Jan. 14, 1988.

55 Foley quoted in Tom Brown, "Japan versus the U.S.?" *ST*, Feb. 28, 1988.

56 TSF robo to constituents, Jan. 11, 1988, TSF Papers, Box 43, Folder "100th Congress: Legislative—Ways & Means, Trade."

57 Brown, "Japan versus the U.S.?" *ST*, Feb. 28, 1988.

58 Yates and Yates, 43, 48.

59 "Boeing to Build Plant at Spokane," *ST*, Oct. 25, 1988; Press release, "Boeing Breaks Ground for New Spokane Facility," Apr. 28, 1989, TSF Papers, Box 416, Folder "Press Files/1989/Boeing"; Becky Kramer, "If Boeing Builds New Jetliner in Washington, Spokane Manufacturers Would Benefit, Leaders Say," *SSR*, Apr. 17, 2018.

60 Vladimir Lukin to TSF, Dec. 7, 1992, TSF Papers, Box 424, Folder; Press files/1993/ Russia-U.S. Technology & Economic Development.

61 Rockne Timm to TSF, Mar. 24, 1993, TSF Papers, Box 184, Folder 5505; TSF to Warren Christopher, Mar. 31, 1993, TSF Papers, ibid.

62 Raymond A. Hanson to TSF, Sept. 24, 1993, TSF Papers, ibid.

63 Rockne Timm to TSF, Sept. 24, 1993, TSF Papers, ibid.

64 TSF to Simon Alberto Consalvi and Warren Christopher, Oct. 5, 1993, TSF Papers, ibid.

65 Biggs and Foley, 77; "Congressmen Seek Ways to Boost Exports," *Pullman Herald*, Jan. 13, 1982; "Foley's Bill: Farm Export Plan Desirable," *SC*, Aug. 10, 1984.

66 Eric Pryne, "For This State, Farm Bill Affects Mostly Wheat, Milk," *ST*, Oct. 23, 1985.

67 Zhou, 95, 97.

68 Ibid., 101.

69 Candace Frasher to TSF, May 9, 1992; TSF to Undersecretary of Agriculture for International Affairs and Commodity Programs Richard Crowder, May 27, 1992; TSF Papers, ibid.

70 Jeff Mapes, "Oregon's First Statesman," *TO*, Aug. 8, 2011.

71 "Inaugural Address of Mark O. Hatfield, Governor of Oregon, to the Regular Session of the Fiftieth Legislative Assembly, January 12, 1959, Salem, Oregon," from Mark O. Hatfield, *Selected Speeches and Other Public Statements, 1959–1967*, Willamette University Archives, Salem, OR.

72 Gerry Pratt, "Hatfield State Plan Demonstrates Drive," *TO*, Feb. 10, 1963.

73 Gordon Dodds and Craig Wollner, *The Silicon Forest: High Tech in the Portland Area 1945 to 1986* (Portland: Oregon Historical Society Press, 1990), 17–19.

74 Ibid., 99–118.

75 Gerry Pratt, "Hatfield Preparing for Visit to Japan," *TO*, Oct. 11, 1964.

76 Gerry Pratt, "Hatfield Heads Party Junketing to Japan," *TO*, Nov. 8, 1964; Gerry Pratt, "Seattle's Sister City Trades with Oregon," *TO*, Nov. 29, 1964; Hatfield quoted in "Market Seen in Orient," *TO*, Dec. 3, 1964.

77 Gerry Pratt, "State's Roving Chief Pays Big Dividends," *TO*, Oct. 17, 1965.

78 "Trade Lanes Across Pacific," *OJ*, Dec. 5, 1964. The Oregon Legislature merged the Commission of Public Docks with the Port of Portland in 1970, keeping the latter name for the whole entity.

79 "Economic Countdown for the Pacific Northwest: Speech of Mark O. Hatfield, Governor, State of Oregon, Before the Oregon-Washington-Idaho Chamber Managers and Officers Conference, February 15, 1965, Cosmopolitan Motor Hotel, Portland, Oregon," Mark O. Hatfield, *Selected Speeches and Other Public Statements, 1959–1967*, Willamette University Archives.

80 "Judge What He Will Do . . . by What He's Done for Oregon", *TO*, Nov. 7, 1966.

81 Brent Walth, "Mark of Distinction," *TO*, Dec. 29, 1996.

82 "Hatfield's Mark," *TO*, Jan. 2, 1997.

83 Bill Keller, "Capital Stew: Successful Shoes Have Run-Ins in Washington," *TO*, Apr. 23, 1978.

84 Jeff Mapes, "Old-time Senate Clout Is Returning to Oregon," *TO*, Jan. 26, 2014.

85 Don Ritchie, *J. Keith Kennedy, Staff Director/Clerk of the Senate Appropriations Committee, Deputy Senate Sergeant At Arms, Oral History Interviews, August 5, 2003–July 22, 2008* (Senate Historical Office, Washington, DC), 23–25.

86 Carl Abbott, *Portland in Three Centuries: The Place and the People* (Corvallis: Oregon State University Press, 2011), 152–153.

87 Carl Abbott, *Portland: Planning, Politics, and Growth in a Twentieth-Century City* (Lincoln: University of Nebraska Press, 1983), 111, 119.

88 Glenn Vanselow, "Port of Portland," in Larry W. Price, ed., *Portland's Changing Landscape* (Portland: Portland State University Foundation, 1987), 164.

89 Vanselow, "Port of Portland," in Price, ed., 165.

90 "Reap Center's Harvest," *TO*, Feb. 21, 1988.

91 Hatfield quoted in Foster Church, "U.S. Agency Balks on Export Office," *TO*, May 15, 1989; "Portland (Oregon) U.S. Export Assistance Center," *Commerce. gov*, https://www.commerce.gov/locations/portland-oregon -us-export-assistance-center#15/45.5161/-122.6749.

92 Steve Nousen, phone interview by author, December 3, 2015.

93 "Pacific Rim Report," *Oregon Business*, Feb. 1987.

94 Nousen interview; Alan K. Ota and Roberta Ulrich, "Reunion with Akihito on Hatfield's Agenda," *TO*, Feb. 7, 1991.

95 Nousen interview; Robert Landauer, "Refugees' Stories Feature an Uncommon Denominator," *TO*, Mar. 17, 1996.

96 Sam Howe Verhovek, "Besmirched 'Deportland' Wrestles with the I.N.S.," *NYT*, Aug. 31, 2000; "Nonstop Destinations from PDX," *I Fly Nonstop*, https://www.ifly-nonstop.com; Andrew Theen, "Daily Flights from Portland to Central Tokyo's Airport Coming in 2020," *TO*, Aug. 19, 2019.

97 Carl Abbott, *Greater Portland: Urban Life and Landscape in the Pacific Northwest* (Philadelphia: University of Pennsylvania Press, 2001), 50.

98 "Hatfield Projects," *TO*, Sept. 29, 1996.

CHAPTER 6

1 Some sections of this chapter were originally published in *Oregon Historical Quarterly*: the author thanks Eliza Canty-Jones for permission to reprint those here. See Christopher Foss, "'I wanted Oregon to Have Something': Governor Victor G. Atiyeh and Oregon-Japan Relations," *Oregon Historical Quarterly* 118:3 (Fall 2017), 338–365.

2 "Governor Victor Atiyeh Oral History: Tape 44, Side 2," *Pacific University Archives Exhibits* (hereafter VAOH), https://exhibits.lib.pacificu.edu/items/show/3395.

3 Richard A. Clucas and Melody Rose, "Oregon in the Nation and the World," in Richard A. Clucas, Mark Henkels, and Brent S. Steel, eds., *Oregon Politics and Government: Progressives versus Conservative Populists* (Lincoln: University of Nebraska Press, 2005), 45; Justin Worland and Philip Elliott, "Republican Allies Warn Trump on Trade," *Time*, July 2, 2018, http://time.com/5328475/donald-trump-trade-republicans; Jared Cowley, "'It Will Impact the World': Gov. Brown on Wheat Loss from Substation Fire," *KGW.com*, July 19, 2018, https://www.kgw. com/article/money/it-will-impact-the-world-gov-brown-on-wheat-loss-from -substation-fire/283-575534125.

4 For recent work on Atiyeh, see Foss, "'I Wanted Oregon to Have Something'"; in addition, Jim Moore, political science professor at Pacific University, is writing an as-yet untitled biography of Atiyeh.

5 Peter Wong, "Former Oregon Governor Vic Atiyeh Dies at 91," *Capital Press* (hereafter *CP*), July 21, 2014.

6 Jeff Mapes, "Former Governor Led Oregon through Trying Times," *TO*, July 21, 2014.

7 John Herbers, "Study Says States Seize Initiative on World Trade," *NYT*, Aug. 5, 1985.

8 Rhodes quoted in McKevitt, *Consuming Japan*, 84–87.

9 Alvin Felzenberg, *Governor Tom Kean: From the New Jersey Statehouse to the 9/11 Commission* (New Brunswick, NJ: Rutgers University Press, 2006), 229–231.

10 Jeff Mapes, "Republican Vic Atiyeh, Who Guided Oregon through Economic Upheaval, Dies at 91," *TO*, July 20, 2014; "In Life," *Victor Atiyeh Collection*, https://exhibits.lib.pacificu.edu/exhibits/show/atiyeh/life; VAOH, Tape 1, Side 1, http://exhibits.lib.pacificu.edu/items/show/3310.

11 VAOH Tape 5, Side 1, https://exhibits.lib.pacificu.edu/items/show/3318.

12 VAOH Tape 6, Side 2, https://exhibits.lib.pacificu.edu/items/show/3321.

13 Abbott, *Greater Portland*, 109; Jewel Lansing, *Portland: People, Politics, and Power, 1851–2001* (Corvallis: Oregon State University Press, 2003), 409; Dodds and Wollner, 22, 36–39.

14 Foss, "'I Wanted Oregon to Have Something,'" 344; Charles K. Johnson, *Standing at the Water's Edge: Bob Straub's Battle for the Soul of Oregon* (Corvallis: Oregon State University Press, 2012), 251–253; Floyd McKay, *Reporting the Oregon Story: How Activists and Visionaries Transformed a State* (Corvallis: Oregon State University Press, 2016), 200.

15 Gerry Thompson, phone interview by author, July 11, 2016; on McCall's remarks see Walth, 428.

16 Thompson interview.

17 Mapes, "Former Governor Led Oregon through Trying Times," *TO*, July 21, 2014.

18 VAOH, Tape 44, Side 1, http://exhibits.lib.pacificu.edu/items/show/3394.

19 "Gubernatorial Debate between Atiyeh and Kulongoski in Eugene, Oregon Video Recording," Pacific University Archives Exhibits (hereafter PUAE), http://exhibits.lib.pacificu.edu/items/show/4845.

20 Victor Atiyeh, "Atiyeh's Re-Election Campaign Speech," *PUAE*, http://exhibits.lib.pacificu.edu/items/show/3846.

21 Foster Church, "Governor's Edge Best in 20 Years," *TO*, Nov. 3, 1982.

22 Marsh, 353.

23 Liu, 82–86.

24 For more on these trends, see Roger Buckley, *US-Japan Alliance Diplomacy 1945–1990* (Cambridge, UK: Cambridge University Press, 1992); William R. Nester, *Power Across the Pacific: A Diplomatic History of American Relations with Japan* (New York: New York University Press, 1996); Andrew C. McKevitt, "'You Are Not Alone!' Anime and the Globalizing of America," *Diplomatic History* 34:5 (Nov. 2010), 893–921.

25 Danforth quoted in Walter LaFeber, *The Clash: A History of U.S.-Japan Relations* (New York: W. W. Norton, 1997), 376.

26 Martin Weinstein, "Trade Problems and U.S.-Japan Security Cooperation," *Washington Quarterly* 11 (Winter 1988), 19–20.

27 Japan Federation of Economic Organizations, "'Japanese Businesses Welcome New Legislation by the State of Oregon to Repeal the Worldwide Unitary Tax System' press release," *PUAE*, http://exhibits.lib.pacificu.edu/items/show/4209.

28 Thompson interview; Mapes, "Former Governor Led Oregon through Trying Times," *TO*, July 21, 2014; Thompson email correspondence with author, Apr. 14, 2017.

29 VAOH, Tape 40, Side 1, http://exhibits.lib.pacificu.edu/items/show/3386.

30 Memo from Gerry Thompson to Victor Atiyeh, June 28, 1984, box ACC 2015.137-ACC 2015.138, folder 2015.64, Victor Atiyeh Papers, Pacific University Archives, Forest Grove, OR (hereafter VAP).

31 Victor Atiyeh, "Speech on Unitary Method of Taxation to Oregon Legislature," *PUAE*, http://exhibits.lib.pacificu.edu/items/show/1138.

32 Clifford B. Alterman and Gary P. Compa, "Unitary Tax Curbs Growth," *TO*, July 27, 1984.

33 Jeff Mapes, "Legislature Votes to Jettison Unitary Tax Law," *TO*, July 31, 1984.

34 Japan Federation of Economic Organizations, "'Japanese Businesses Welcome New Legislation by the State of Oregon to Repeal the Worldwide Unitary Tax System' press release," *PUAE*, http://exhibits.lib.pacificu.edu/items/show/4209.

35 Juniciii Umeda, "Oregon Attracts Japanese Investments; Targeting at High-Tech Manufacturing Firms," *Japan Economic Journal*, Aug. 14, 1984; *PUAE*, https://exhibits.lib.pacificu.edu/items/show/4211.

36 Gerry Thompson to Victor Atiyeh, May 23, 1984, ACC 2015.174, box 1, folder "Economic Development-International Trade," VAP.

37 Gerry Thompson to Victor Atiyeh, June 14, 1984, ibid.

38 VAOH, Tape 40, Side 2, http://exhibits.lib.pacificu.edu/items/show/3387.

39 Sue Hill, "Atiyeh: We Have Inside Track in Japan," *SSJ*, Sept. 11, 1984.

40 Atiyeh speech, Keidanren meeting, Sept. 14, 1984, "Travel binder for Atiyeh's trade missions to Japan and China," *PUAE*, http://exhibits.lib.pacificu.edu/items/show/4212.

41 Memorandum to John Anderson, Sept. 18, 1984, "Travel binder for Atiyeh's trade missions to Japan and China," *PUAE*, http://exhibits.lib.pacificu.edu/items/show/4212.

42 VAOH, Tape 44, Side 2, http://exhibits.lib.pacificu.edu/items/show/3395.

43 Speech by Atiyeh, May 3, 1996, "Welcome Back to Oregon Fuji-TV" dinner at the Governor Hotel in Portland, box Atiyeh Post-Gov Papers D-K, folder "Fuji television 1987–1999," VAP.

44 Hisashi Hieda to Atiyeh, Jan. 12, 2000, ibid.

45 VAOH, Tape 39, Side 1," *PUAE*, http://exhibits.lib.pacificu.edu/items/show/3385.

46 Carlene A. Jackson to Jon Yunker, Apr. 23, 1984, ACC 2015.174, box 1, folder "Economic Development Department," VAP.

47 Thompson interview.

48 "Atiyeh—Skilled Trade Diplomat," *CP*, Oct. 5, 1984.

49 Todd Crowell, "Invasion of the Asian Investors," *Seattle Weekly*, Nov. 27, 1984.

50 VAOH, Tape 41, Side 2, http://exhibits.lib.pacificu.edu/items/show/3389.

51 "KATU-TV transcript on United States trade with Saudi Arabia," *PUAE*, https://exhibits.lib.pacificu.edu/items/show/6032.

52 "KOIN-TV transcript on a rug factory in Saudi Arabia," *PUAE*, https://exhibits.lib.pacificu.edu/items/show/6033.

53 VAOH, Tape 41, Side 2, http://exhibits.lib.pacificu.edu/items/show/3389.

54 "Correspondence from King Fahd of Saudi Arabia," *PUAE*, https://exhibits.lib.pacificu.edu/items/show/4488.

55 "News coverage of Governor Atiyeh's vetoing of bills and trade missions to the Middle East and China video recording," *PUAE*, https://exhibits.lib.pacificu.edu/items/show/4837.

56 "Itinerary and special information for Atiyeh's trade mission to Egypt," *PUAE*, https://exhibits.lib.pacificu.edu/items/show/4182.

57 "KATU-TV transcript on Egyptian economy and trade," *PUAE*, https://exhibits. lib.pacificu.edu/items/show/6036.

58 VAOH, Tape 41, Side 2, http://exhibits.lib.pacificu.edu/items/show/3389.

59 VAOH, ibid.

60 "KOIN-TV transcript on Atiyeh's arrival in Syria," *PUAE*, https://exhibits.lib.pacificu.edu/items/show/5974.

61 Patricia Moir, "Politics, Poverty Hamper Syrian Wheat Talks," *East Oregonian*, Apr. 7, 1984.

62 VAOH, Tape 44, Side 1, https://exhibits.lib.pacificu.edu/items/show/3394.

63 Alan K. Ota, "Atiyeh's Group to Try to Sidestep Politics," *TO*, Mar. 26, 1984.

64 "KOIN-TV transcript on Mideast attempts at self-sufficiency," *PUAE*, https://exhibits.lib.pacificu.edu/items/show/6022.

65 "Atiyeh Declares Mission a Success," *Eugene Register-Guard* (hereafter *ERG*), Mar. 26, 1984.

66 VAOH, Tape 44, Side 1, http://exhibits.lib.pacificu.edu/items/show/3394.

67 "Atiyeh trade mission to the Middle East," *PUAE*, http://exhibits.lib.pacificu.edu/ items/show/4848.

68 VAOH, Tape 44, Side 1, http://exhibits.lib.pacificu.edu/items/show/3394.

69 VAOH, ibid.

70 VAOH, ibid.

71 "Atiyeh trade mission to China, meeting with Premier Zhao, and signing Fujian Province agreement, video recording," *PUAE*, http://exhibits.lib.pacificu.edu/ items/show/4847.

72 "Schedules, correspondence and other material on Atiyeh's trade mission to Hong Kong and Fujian Province," *PUAE*, http://exhibits.lib.pacificu.edu/items/ show/4272.

73 VAOH, Tape 44, Side 2, http://exhibits.lib.pacificu.edu/items/show/3395.

74 *Nomura Newsflash*, Mar. 4, 1985, in "Correspondence leading up to Atiyeh's trade mission to Japan," *PUAE*, http://exhibits.lib.pacificu.edu/items/show/4217.

75 VAOH, Tape 44, Side 2, http://exhibits.lib.pacificu.edu/items/show/3395.

76 Charles Humble, "New Year Best Bet for Cheer," *TO*, Dec. 31, 1985; on Tektronix, see Dodds and Wollner, 158.

77 VAOH, Tape 44, Side 2, https://exhibits.lib.pacificu.edu/items/show/3395.

78 Richard Reeves, "Trader Vic's Visits Prove Profitable," *TO*, Dec. 26, 1985.

79 Victor Atiyeh, "Press release statements on international trade partnerships," *PUAE*, http://exhibits.lib.pacificu.edu/items/show/4146.

80 "Summary of findings from the Keidanren Investment Expansion Mission," *PUAE*, http://exhibits.lib.pacificu.edu/items/show/3818.

81 Jeff Lewis to Gerry Thompson, Apr. 7, 1986, box 5.6, Folder "Gov. S.F. Memoranda and Reports 'Accomplishments and Goals' Covers 1979–1986 (written '86 –87)", VAP.

82 "Port of Portland Update March 1986," ACC 2015.174, box 1, folder "Economic Development-International Trade," VAP.

83 "Correspondence from Mark Hatfield," *PUAE*, http://exhibits.lib.pacificu.edu/ items/show/4494.

84 "Miscellaneous keeper letters from various constituents," *PUAE*, http://exhibits. lib.pacificu.edu/items/show/4485.

85 Ibid.

86 "Remarks by Shosaku Tanaka thanking Atiyeh for his promotion of economic and cultural relations between Oregon and Japan," *PUAE*, http://exhibits.lib.pacificu.edu/items/show/3807.

87 "Vic Worked for State," *TO*, Jan. 9, 1987.

88 "Atiyeh had Misfortune to Lead at Wrong Time," *Klamath Falls Herald and News*, Jan. 5, 1987.

89 "Assessing the Atiyeh years," *ERG*, Jan. 1, 1987.

90 Eric Goranson, "Gresham Officials, Residents Celebrate Fujitsu Plans", *TO*, Aug. 26, 1987.

91 VAOH, Tape 44, Side 2, http://exhibits.lib.pacificu.edu/items/show/3395.

92 Thompson interview.

93 "Atiyeh at JCA senior executive meeting sound recording," *PUAE*, http://exhibits.lib.pacificu.edu/items/show/4856.

94 Judy Rooks, "Northwest Export Business Ridin' High," *TO*, Oct. 4, 1987.

95 Judy Rooks, "Goldschmidt Heads Asian Trade Mission," *TO*, Oct. 16, 1987.

96 Richard Colby and Judy Rooks, "Group Returns from Trade Trip with New Zeal," *TO*, Oct. 29, 1987.

97 VAOH, Tape 45, Side 1, http://exhibits.lib.pacificu.edu/items/show/3396; on the defense industry in California, see "State and Regional Economic Developments in California, Part II," Legislative Analyst's Office, Sept. 1998, http://lao.ca.gov/1998/0998_regional_econ/0998_regional_economic_part2.html.

98 "Japanese Artisans Commit to America Japan Week 1992," Atiyeh Post-Gov Papers, box A-C, folder "America Japan Week 1992," VAP.

99 "Appropriately Honoring a Trade Leader," *TO*, July 19, 2007.

100 "Memoranda and Reports, 'Accomplishments and Goals,' Covers 1979–1986 (written '86 –'87)", MSS 96, box 5.6, VAP.

101 "September 2, 1993, "'Speech from the Sideline' by Mas Tomita," box "Atiyeh Post-Gov Papers D-K," folder "Epson," VAP.

102 Richard Read, "NEC Plant in Hillsboro Will Go on Sales Block," *TO*, Oct. 22, 1999; "Fujitsu Will Shut Gresham Plant," *TO*, Nov. 29, 2001.

103 Andrew C. McKevitt, "Consuming Japan: Cultural Relations and the Globalizing of America, 1973–1993," PhD diss., Temple University, May 2009, 266.

104 Victor Atiyeh, "To the Editor," May 10, 2000, box "Atiyeh Post-Gov Papers D-K," folder "Epson," VAP.

105 Atiyeh to Minoru Ozawa, Aug. 1, 2000, ibid.

106 Richard Read, "Door Opens to Japan," *TO*, June 6, 2004; Richard Read, "Japanese Come Back, Bearing Jobs," *TO*, June 10, 2012.

CONCLUSION

1 In particular, see Emily Rosenberg, *Spreading the American Dream: American Economic and Cultural Expansion, 1890–1945* (New York: Hill and Wang, 1982), 163; David Kennedy, *Freedom from Fear: The American People in Depression and War, 1929–1945* (Oxford: Oxford University Press, 1999), 50, 77.

2 Donald J. Trump, "Inaugural Address," Jan. 20, 2017; Gerhard Peters and John T. Woolley, *The American Presidency Project*, http://www.presidency.ucsb.edu/ws/?pid=120000.

3 Andrew Selsky, "Oregon Agriculture Hit Hard by Us-China Trade War," *TO*, Sept. 26, 2019.

4 Donald J. Trump, "Memorandum on Withdrawal of the United States from the Trans-Pacific Partnership Negotiations and Agreement," Jan. 23, 2017; Gerhard Peters and John T. Woolley, *The American Presidency Project*, http://www.presidency.ucsb.edu/ws/?pid=122516.

5 Heefner, 8.

6 Marsh, 451.

7 Abbott, *Greater Portland*, 111.

8 Dodds and Wollner, 158–179.

9 David Sarasohn, "Memories of Things Repast," *TO*, Dec. 24, 1999; "Monday, July 30, 2018, Fresh Seafood," http://menus.mccormickandschmicks.com/JKCR/JK-CR-Dinner.pdf.

10 Jennifer Bjorhus, "A Third World Order," *TO*, Jan. 2, 2000.

11 James Mayer, "State's Income Inequality Grows, Study Says," *TO*, Jan. 18, 2000.

12 Richard Read, "Failure of WTO Talks Adds Chaos to Trade Disputes," *TO*, Dec. 5, 1999.

13 "Peace Is Light in the Darkness," *TO*, Sept. 23, 2001.

14 Susan Banyas, "What Causes Hatred toward U.S.?" *TO*, Oct. 1, 2001.

15 Richard Read, "Global Anxiety May Hinder Already Depressed Oregon Exports," *TO*, Oct. 7, 2001.

16 M. Lee Pelton, "Universities Must Keep 'Open Borders' to the World," *TO*, Oct. 17, 2001.

17 Cumings, 467–471.

18 Mike Rogoway, "Oregon Businesses Feel the Uncertainty," *TO*, June 17, 2018.

Selected Bibliography

ARCHIVAL COLLECTIONS

Gerald R. Ford Presidential Library, Ann Arbor, MI
  Max L. Friedersdorf Papers
  White House Central File: Congressional Mail File
  White House Central File: Name File
  William E. Timmons Papers
Lyndon B. Johnson Presidential Library, Austin, TX
  Bill Moyers Files
  Congressional Favors File
  Fred Panzer Papers
  John H. Macy Office Files
  Lawrence O'Brien Papers
  LBJ Archives 1931–1968
  LBJ Senate Papers
  White House Central Files: Confidential File
  White House Central Files: Federal Government
  White House Central Files: Name File
Oregon Historical Society, Portland, OR
  Connie Trullinger and Mark A. Chamberlin Papers
  Edith S. Green Papers
  Hatfield Backgrounders
  Hillman Lueddemann Papers
  Interview with Mark Hatfield by Chet Orloff
  J. Keith Kennedy Oral History
Pacific University Archives, Forest Grove, OR
  Digital Exhibits: Victor Atiyeh Collection
  Victor Atiyeh Papers
University of Oregon Special Collections and University Archives,
    Eugene, OR
  Margie Hendriksen Papers
  Wayne L. Morse Papers
University of Washington Special Collections and Archives, Seattle, WA
  Henry M. Jackson Papers
  Warren G. Magnuson Papers

Washington State University Manuscripts, Archives and Special Collections, Pullman, WA
    Thomas S. Foley Papers
Willamette University Archives, Salem, OR
    Robert W. Packwood Papers
    Travis L. Cross Papers

CONGRESSIONAL PUBLICATIONS

Congressional Digest
Congressional Record

DATABASES

C-SPAN
HistoryLink.org
The Oregon Encyclopedia

BACKGROUND INTERVIEWS BY AUTHOR

Walt Evans, interviewed in Portland, OR, September 22, 2015
Tom Getman, phone interview, October 15, 2015
Wes Granberg-Michaelson, phone interview, October 20, 2015
Steve Nousen, phone interview, December 3, 2015
Jack Robertson, phone interview, September 22, 2015
Rick Rolf, interviewed in Portland, OR, November 5, 2015
Gerry Thompson, phone interview, July 11, 2016

PERIODICALS

Atlantic Monthly
Oregon Business
Time

MEMOIRS AND EDITED COLLECTIONS

Abell, Ron. "Ron Abell Memoir 17: Some Personal Observations on the Wayne Morse Re-Election Campaign of 1968." http://www.ronabell.com/uploads/Ron_Abell_ Memoir__14--Personal_Observations_of_the_Wayne_Morse_Re-Election_ Campaign_of_1968.pdf, 2005.
Dimick, Dan. *Wayne Morse: The Record of a Working Senator . . . In Detail: A 1968 Handbook for Morse Workers.* Re-Elect Wayne Morse Committee, 1968.
Gruening, Ernest. *Many Battles: The Autobiography of Ernest Gruening.* New York: Liveright, 1973.
Hatfield, Mark O. *Against the Grain: Reflections of a Rebel Republican.* As told to Diane N. Solomon. Ashland, OR: White Cloud Press, 2001.
Hatfield, Mark O. *Not Quite So Simple.* New York: Harper & Row, 1968.
Lonsdale, Harry. *Running: Politics, Power, and the Press.* Bloomington, IN: 1stBooks Library, 2002.
Reagan, Ronald. *The Reagan Diaries.* New York: HarperCollins Publishers, 2007.

NEWSPAPERS

Albany Democrat-Herald
Associated Press
Bellingham Herald
Bend Bulletin
Bremerton Sun
Capital Press
Daily Astorian
Ellensburg Record
Eugene Register-Guard
Everett Herald
Kitsap County Herald
Los Angeles Times
Moscow-Pullman Daily News
New York Times
Oregonian
Oregon Daily Emerald
Oregon Journal
Portland State University Vanguard
Salem Statesman Journal
Seattle Post-Intelligencer
Seattle Times
Seattle Weekly
Spokane Chronicle
Spokane Spokesman-Review
Tacoma News Tribune
Tri-Cities Herald
Wall Street Journal
Walla Walla Union Bulletin
Washington Post
Washington Star
Wenatchee World
Willamette Week

PUBLISHED ORAL HISTORIES

Atiyeh, Victor (interviewee), "Governor Victor Atiyeh Oral History: Tape 44, Side 2." Pacific University Archives Exhibits, https://exhibits.lib.pacificu.edu/items/show/3395.

Bluemle, Lewis W. Jr. (interviewee) and Joan S. Ash (interviewer). "Interview with Lewis W. Bluemle, Jr." (1998). *Oral History Collection.* Paper 37. http://digitalcommons.ohsu.edu/hca-oralhist/37.

Hatfield, Mark O. (interviewee) and Joan S. Ash (interviewer). "Interview with Mark O. Hatfield" (1998). *Oral History Collection.* Paper 3. http://digitalcommons.ohsu.edu/hca-oralhist/3.

Jacob, M.D. , Stanley W. (interview) and Linda A. Weimer (interviewer). "Interview with Dr. Stanley Jacob" (1998). *Oral History Collection.* Paper 60. http://digitalcommons.ohsu.edu/hca-oralhist/60.

Kendall, Jr., M.D., John W. (interviewee) and Joan Ash (interviewer). "Interview with John W. Kendall, M.D." (1999). *Oral History Collection.* Paper 63. http://digitalcommons.ohsu.edu/hca-oralhist/63.

Koler, Robert D. (interviewee) and Joan Ash (interviewer). "Interview with Robert Koler" (1997). *Oral History Collection.* Paper 11. http://digitalcommons.ohsu.edu/hca-oralhist/11.

Laster, Leonard, M.D., Ruth Ann Laster (interviewees), and Joan Ash (interviewer). "Interview with Leonard and Ruth Ann Laster" (1999). *Oral History Collection.* Paper 65. http://digitalcommons.ohsu.edu/hca-oralhist/65.

Neuberger, Maurine (interviewee), and Clark Hansen (interviewer). "Interview with Maurine Neuberger" (1991). Oregon Legislature Oral History Series.

Pritchard, Joel M., and Anne Kilgannon. *Joel M. Pritchard: An Oral History.* Washington State Oral History Program, Office of the Secretary of State, 2000.

VIDEOS

Gentleman of the Senate: Oregon's Mark Hatfield. Produced by Kevin E. Curry. Portland, OR: Lyon Films, 2014.

The Last Angry Man: Senator Wayne Morse. Produced by Christopher Houser. Portland, OR: Square Deal Productions, 1999.

Tom McCall. Produced by Eric Cain. Portland, OR: Oregon Public Broadcasting, 2013.

Wayne Morse. Produced by Eric Cain. Portland, OR: Oregon Public Broadcasting, 2012.

Wild Wild Country. Directed by Maclain Way and Chapman Way. Los Angeles, CA: Duplass Brothers Productions, 2018.

THESES AND DISSERTATIONS

Baz, Sara Stanley. "Senator Wayne Morse, Liberal Peacemaker: Conflicts of American Imperialism in the Cold War Era." MA thesis, University of Oregon, June 2005.

Bird, Robert Kenton. "The Speaker from Spokane: The Rise and Fall of Tom Foley as a Congressional Leader." PhD diss., Washington State University, Aug. 1999.

Brenes, Michael. "For Right and Might: The Militarization of the Cold War and the Remaking of American Democracy." PhD diss., City University of New York, Feb. 2014.

Casserly, Brian G. "Securing the Sound: The Evolution of Civilian-Military Relations in the Puget Sound Area, 1891–1984." PhD diss., University of Washington, 2007.

Courtney, Mary. "The Significance of the 1968 Packwood-Morse Debate, with Special Emphasis upon Robert Packwood." BA thesis, Linfield College, Mar. 1970.

McKevitt, Andrew C. "Consuming Japan: Cultural Relations and the Globalizing of America, 1973–1993." PhD diss., Temple University, May 2009.

Robson, John Sinclair Petifer. "Henry Jackson, the Jackson-Vanik Amendment and Détente: Ideology, Ideas, and United States Foreign Policy in the Nixon Era." PhD diss., University of Texas at Austin, 1989.

Wilkins, Lillian Claire. "Wayne Morse: An Exploratory Biography." PhD diss., University of Oregon, Mar. 1982.

Zhou, Baodi. "Thomas S. Foley and the Politics of Wheat: U.S. Wheat Trade with Japan, China, and the Soviet Union, 1965–1986." PhD diss., Washington State University, 1999.

ARTICLES AND BOOKS

Abbott, Carl. *Greater Portland: Urban Life and Landscape in the Pacific Northwest.* Philadelphia: University of Pennsylvania Press, 2001.

Abbott, Carl. *Portland: Planning, Politics, and Growth in a Twentieth-Century City.* Lincoln: University of Nebraska Press, 1983.

Abbott, Carl. *Portland in Three Centuries: The Place and the People.* Corvallis: Oregon State University Press, 2011.

Abbott, Carl. "Regional City and Network City: Portland and Seattle in the Twentieth Century." *Western Historical Quarterly* 23:3 (Aug. 1992), 293–322.

Allman, Joseph M. "The 1968 Election in Oregon." *Western Political Quarterly* 22:3 (September 1969): 517–525.

Anderson, Terry H. *The Movement and the Sixties.* New York: Oxford University Press, 1995.

Ayers, Edward L., et al. *All Over the Map: Rethinking American Regions.* Baltimore: Johns Hopkins University Press, 1996.

Balmer, Donald G. "The 1962 Election in Oregon." *Western Political Quarterly* 16:2 (June 1963), 453–459.

Balmer, Donald G. "The 1966 Election in Oregon." *Western Political Quarterly* 20:2 (June 1967), 593–601.

Barber, Benjamin R. *If Mayors Ruled the World: Dysfunctional Nations, Rising Cities.* New Haven: Yale University Press, 2013.

Bhatt, Amy, and Nalini Iyer. *Roots & Reflections: South Asians in the Pacific Northwest.* Seattle: University of Washington Press, 2013.

Bird, Kenton. "Tom Foley's Last Campaign: Why Eastern Washington Voters Ousted the Speaker of the House." *Pacific Northwest Quarterly* 95:1 (Winter 2003/2004), 3–15.

Bloodworth, Jeffrey. *Losing the Center: The Decline of American Liberalism, 1968–1992.* Lexington: University Press of Kentucky, 2013.

Brown, Kate. *Plutopia: Nuclear Families, Atomic Cities, and the Great Soviet and American Plutonium Disasters.* Oxford: Oxford University Press, 2013.

Buenger, Walter. "Texas and the History of American Foreign Policy." *Diplomatic History* 36:3 (June 2012), 495–498.

Caro, Robert A. *The Years of Lyndon Johnson: Master of the Senate.* New York: Alfred A. Knopf, 2002.

Casserly, Brian. "Confronting the U.S. Navy at Bangor, 1973–1982." *Pacific Northwest Quarterly* 95:3 (Summer 2004), 130–139.

Ceplair, Larry. "The Foreign Policy of Senator Wayne Morse." *Oregon Historical Quarterly* 113:1 (Spring 2012), 6–35.

Chang, Kornel. *Pacific Connections: The Making of the U.S.-Canadian Borderlands.* Berkeley: University of California Press, 2012.

Citino, Nathan J. "The Global Frontier: Comparative History and the Frontier-Borderlands Approach in American Foreign Relations." *Diplomatic History* 25:4 (Fall 2001), 677–693.

Clucas, Richard A., Mark Henkels, and Brent S. Steel, eds. *Oregon Politics and Government: Progressives versus Conservative Populists.* Lincoln: University of Nebraska Press, 2005.

Clymer, Adam. *Drawing the Line at the Big Ditch: The Panama Canal Treaties and the Rise of the Right.* Lawrence: University of Kansas Press, 2008.

Cobb, James C., ed. *Globalization and the American South.* Athens: University of Georgia Press, 2005.

Cosens, Barbara, ed. *The Columbia River Treaty Revisited: Transboundary River Governance in the Face of Uncertainty.* Corvallis: Oregon State University Press, 2012.

Craig, C. Campbell, and Fredrik Logevall. *America's Cold War: The Politics of Insecurity.* Cambridge, MA: Harvard University Press, 2009.

Cumings, Bruce. *Dominion from Sea to Sea: Pacific Ascendancy and American Power.* New Haven, CT: Yale University Press, 2009.

Dallek, Robert. *Flawed Giant: Lyndon Johnson and His Times.* New York: Oxford University Press, 1998.

Dodds, Gordon B. *The American Northwest: A History of Oregon and Washington.* Arlington Heights: The Forum Press, 1986.

Dodds, Gordon B. *Oregon: A Bicentennial History.* New York: W. W. Norton, 1977.

Dodds, Gordon B. and Craig E. Wollner. *The Silicon Forest: High Tech in the Portland Area 1945 to 1986.* Portland: Oregon Historical Society Press, 1990.

Drukman, Mason. *Wayne Morse: A Political Biography.* Portland: Oregon Historical Society Press, 1997.

Durbin, Kathie. *Tree Huggers: Victory, Defeat & Renewal in the Northwest Ancient Forest Campaign.* Seattle: Mountaineers Books, 1996.

Durfee, David L., ed. *Patriot's Progress: A Living Military History of the People of Kitsap County, Washington.* Centralia: Gorham Printing, 2009.

Edwards, G. Thomas. "Student Activism at Whitman College and Willamette University, 1965–1971: A Photographic Essay." *Pacific Northwest Quarterly* 99:4 (Fall 2008), 173–180.

Edwards, Laura. "What Constitutes a Region?" *Diplomatic History* 36:3 (June 2012), 483–486.

Eells, Robert, and Bartell Nyberg. *Lonely Walk: The Life of Senator Mark Hatfield.* Chappaqua, NY: Christian Herald Books, 1979.

Eisenberg, Ellen M. *The First to Cry Down Injustice? Western Jews and Japanese Removal during World War II.* Lanham, MD: Lexington Books, 2008.

Federal Elections 82: Election Results for the U.S. Senate and the U.S. House of Representatives. Washington, DC: US Government Printing Office, 1982.

Fellner, Kim. *Wrestling with Starbucks: Conscience, Capital, Cappuccino.* New Brunswick, NJ: Rutgers University Press, 2008.

Fendall, Lon. *Stand Alone or Come Home: Mark Hatfield as an Evangelical and a Progressive.* Newberg, OR: Barclay Press, 2008.

Findlay, John M., and Ken S. Coates, eds. *Parallel Destinies: Canadian-American Relations West of the Rockies.* Seattle: University of Washington Press, 2002.

Findlay, John M., and Bruce Hevly. *Atomic Frontier Days: Hanford and the American West.* Seattle: University of Washington Press, 2011.

Foss, Christopher. "Bringing Home the (Irradiated) Bacon: The Politics of Senator Henry M. Jackson's Support for Nuclear Weapons and Energy during the Cold War." *Pacific Northwest Quarterly* 109:1 (Winter 2017/2018), 3–18.

Foss, Christopher. "'I Wanted Oregon to Have Something': Governor Victor G. Atiyeh and Oregon-Japan Relations." *Oregon Historical Quarterly* 118:3 (Fall 2017), 338–364.

Frank, Dana. *Purchasing Power: Consumer Organizing, Gender, and the Seattle Labor Movement, 1919–1929.* Cambridge: Cambridge University Press, 1994.

Frederickson, Kari. "Confronting the Garrison State: South Carolina in the Early Cold War Era." *Journal of Southern History* 72:2 (May 2006), 349–378.

Frederickson, Kari. "Creating a 'Respectable Area': Southerners and the Cold War." *Diplomatic History* 36:3 (June 2012), 487–490.

Fry, Earl H. *The Expanding Role of State and Local Government in U.S. Foreign Affairs.* New York: Council on Foreign Relations Press, 1998.

Fry, Joseph A. "The Adventures of Lumping, Splitting, and Preparing Matzo Ball Soup." *Diplomatic History* 36:3 (June 2012), 511–514.

Fry, Joseph A. *Debating Vietnam: Fulbright, Stennis, and Their Senate Hearings.* Lanham, MD: Rowman & Littlefield Publishers, 2006.

Fry, Joseph A. *Dixie Looks Abroad: The South and U.S. Foreign Relations, 1789–1973.* Baton Rouge: Louisiana State University Press, 2002.

Fry, Joseph A. "Place Matters: Domestic Regionalism and the Formation of American Foreign Policy." *Diplomatic History* 36:3 (June 2012), 451–482.

Gerber, Michele Stenehjem. *On the Home Front: The Cold War Legacy of the Hanford Nuclear Site.* Lincoln: University of Nebraska Press, 1992.

Gies, Martha. *Up All Night.* Corvallis: Oregon State University Press, 2004.

Gimpel, James G., and Jason E. Schuknecht. *Patchwork Nation: Sectionalism and Political Change in American Politics.* Ann Arbor: University of Michigan Press, 2003.

Goble, Dale D., and Paul W. Hirt, eds. *Northwest Lands, Northwest Peoples: Readings in Environmental History.* Seattle: University of Washington Press, 1999.

Goldman, Robert and Stephen Papson. *Nike Culture: The Sign of the Swoosh.* London: SAGE Publications, 1998.

Grundstein, Margaret. *Naked in the Woods: My Unexpected Years in a Hippie Commune.* Corvallis: Oregon State University Press, 2015.

Harvey, David. "Defense of the Hanford Site during the Early Years of the Cold War." *Pacific Northwest Quarterly* 95:2 (Spring 2004), 82–90.

Heefner, Gretchen. *The Missile Next Door: The Minuteman in the American Heartland.* Cambridge, MA: Harvard University Press, 2012.

Hinckley, Barbara. *Less Than Meets the Eye: Foreign Policy Making and the Myth of the Assertive Congress.* Chicago: University of Chicago Press, 1994.

Hirt, Paul W., ed. *Terra Pacifica: People and Place in the Northwest States and Western Canada.* Pullman: Washington State University Press, 1998.

Hirt, Paul W. *The Wired Northwest: The History of Electric Power, 1870s–1970s.* Lawrence: University Press of Kansas, 2012.

Hobbs, Heidi H. *City Hall Goes Abroad: The Foreign Policy of Local Politics.* Thousand Oaks, CA: SAGE Publications, 1994.

Hoganson, Kristin. "Meat in the Middle: Converging Borderlands in the U.S. Midwest, 1865–1900." *Journal of American History* 98:4 (Jan. 2012), 1025–1051.

Horn, Margo S. *Thomas S. Foley, Democratic Representative from Washington.* Washington, DC: Grossman Publishers, 1972.

Hughes, John C. *Booth Who? A Biography of Booth Gardner.* Washington State Legacy Project, 2010.

Hughes, John C. *John Spellman: Politics Never Broke His Heart.* Washington State Legacy Project, 2013.

Hughes, John C. *Slade Gorton: A Half Century in Politics.* Washington State Legacy Project, 2011.

Irwin, Douglas A. *Clashing Over Commerce: A History of U.S. Trade Policy.* Chicago: University of Chicago Press, 2017.

Jackson, Tim. *Inside Intel: Andy Grove and the Rise of the World's Most Powerful Chip Company.* New York: Dutton, 1997.

Johns, Andrew L. *Vietnam's Second Front: Domestic Politics, the Republican Party, and the War.* Lexington: University Press of Kentucky, 2010.

Johns, Andrew L., ed. *A Companion to Ronald Reagan.* New York: Wiley Blackwell, 2015.

Johns, Andrew L. and Mitchell B. Lerner. *The Cold War at Home and Abroad: Domestic Politics and U.S. Foreign Policy Since 1945.* Lexington: University of Kentucky Press, 2018.

Johnson, Robert David. "Congress and the Cold War." *Journal of Cold War Studies* 3:2 (Spring 2001), 76–100.

Johnson, Robert David. *Congress and the Cold War.* Cambridge: Cambridge University Press, 2005.

Johnson, Robert David, et al. "Domestic Politics & Foreign Policy: A Roundtable." *Passport: The Society for Historians of American Foreign Relations Review* 46:3 (Jan. 2016), 47–64.

Kaufman, Robert G. *Henry M. Jackson: A Life in Politics.* Seattle: University of Washington Press, 2000.

Kennedy, David. *Freedom from Fear: The American People in Depression and War, 1929–1945.* Oxford: Oxford University Press, 1999.

Kershner, Jim. *Carl Maxey: A Fighting Life.* Seattle: University of Washington Press, 2008.

Keys, Barbara. *Reclaiming American Virtue: The Human Rights Revolutions of the 1970s.* Cambridge, MA: Harvard University Press, 2014.

Kirchmeier, Mark. *Packwood: The Public and Private Life from Acclaim to Outrage.* New York: HarperCollins Publishers, 1995.

Kirkendall, Richard S. "The Boeing Company and the Military-Metropolitan-Industrial Complex, 1945–1953." *Pacific Northwest Quarterly* 85 (Oct. 1994), 137–149.

Kresl, Peter Karl, and Gary Gappert, eds. *North American Cities and the Global Economy: Challenges and Opportunities.* Thousand Oaks, CA: SAGE Publications, 1995.

Kropp, James J. *Eden Within Eden: Oregon's Utopian Heritage.* Corvallis: Oregon State University Press, 2009.

LaLande, Jeff. "Oregon's Last Conservative U.S. Senator: Some Light upon the Little-Known Career of Guy Cordon," *Oregon Historical Quarterly* 110:2 (Summer 2009), 228–261.

Lansing, Jewel. *Portland: People, Politics, and Power, 1851–2001.* Corvallis: Oregon State University Press, 2003.

Leopold, Richard W. "The Mississippi Valley and American Foreign Policy, 1890–1941: An Assessment and an Appeal." *Mississippi Valley Historical Review* 37:4 (March 1951), 625–642.

Lerner, Mitchell. "Of Derma and Diplomacy: 'Place Matters' and American Diplomatic History." *Diplomatic History* 36:3 (June 2012), 499–504.

Limerick, Patty. "Fencing in the Past." *Diplomatic History* 36:3 (June 2012), 505–510.

Liu, Wendy. *Connecting Washington and China: The Story of the Washington State China Relations Council.* New York: iUniverse, 2005.

Logevall, Fredrik. *Choosing War: The Lost Chance for Peace and the Escalation of War in Vietnam.* Berkeley: University of California Press, 1999.

Longley, Kyle. *In the Eagle's Shadow: The United States and Latin America.* Wheeling, WV: Harlan Davidson, 2002.

MacColl, E. Kimbark. *The Growth of a City: Power and Politics in Portland, Oregon, 1915 to 1950.* Portland: Georgian Press, 1979.

Mack, Dwayne A. *Black Spokane: The Civil Rights Struggle in the Inland Northwest.* Norman: University of Oklahoma Press, 2014.

MacNeil, Neil, and Richard A. Baker. *The American Senate: An Insider's History.* New York: Oxford University Press, 2013.

Markusen, Ann, et al. *The Rise of the Gunbelt: The Military Remapping of Industrial America.* New York: Oxford University Press, 1991.

Marsh, Tom. *To the Promised Land: A History of Government and Politics in Oregon.* Corvallis: Oregon State University Press, 2012.

Mason, Thomas E. *Governing Oregon: An Inside Look at Politics in One American State.* Dubuque, IA: Kendall/Hunt Publishing Company, 1994.

McKay, Floyd A. *An Editor for Oregon: Charles A. Sprague and the Politics of Change.* Corvallis: Oregon State University Press, 1998.

McKay, Floyd A. *Reporting the Oregon Story: How Activists and Visionaries Transformed a State.* Corvallis: Oregon State University Press, 2016.

McKevitt, Andrew C. *Consuming Japan: Popular Culture and the Globalizing of 1980s America.* Chapel Hill: University of North Carolina Press, 2017.

McKevitt, Andrew C. "'You Are Not Alone!' Anime and the Globalizing of America." *Diplomatic History* 34:5 (November 2010), 893–921.

Memorial Addresses and Other Tributes in the Congress of the United States on the Life and Contributions of Wayne L. Morse, Ninety-third Congress, Second Session. Washington: US Government Printing Office, 1974.

Meyer, David S. *A Winter of Discontent: The Nuclear Freeze and American Politics.* New York: Praeger, 1990.

Milazzo, Paul Charles. *Unlikely Environmentalists: Congress and Clean Water, 1945–1972.* Lawrence: University Press of Kansas, 2006.

Moffat, Riley. *Population History of Western U.S. Cities and Towns, 1850–1990.* Lanham, MD: Scarecrow Press, 1996.

Moore, Stephen T. "Cross-Border Crusades: The Binational Temperance Movement in Washington and British Columbia." *Pacific Northwest Quarterly* 98:3 (Summer 2007), 130–142.

Nash, Gerald D. *The American West Transformed: The Impact of the Second World War.* Bloomington: Indiana University Press, 1985.

Nelson, Garrison. *Committees in the Congress Volume 2: 1947–1992 Committee Histories and Member Assignments.* Washington, DC: Congressional Quarterly, 1994.

Nelson, Kurt R. *Fighting for Paradise: A Military History of the Pacific Northwest.* Yardley, PA: Westholme, 2007.

Nokes, R. Gregory. *Breaking Chains: Slavery on Trial in the Oregon Territory.* Corvallis: Oregon State University Press, 2013.

Nordstrom, Lars, ed. *Swedish Oregon.* Portland: Swedish Roots in Oregon Press, 2008.

Ognibene, Peter. *Scoop: The Life and Politics of Henry M. Jackson.* New York: Stein and Day Publishers, 1975.

"The Peace Politics of Mark Hatfield." *Arms Control Today* 17:3 (April 1987).

Peace, Roger. *A Call to Conscience: The Anti-Contra War Campaign.* Amherst: University of Massachusetts Press, 2012.

Perlstein, Rick. *Nixonland: The Rise of a President and the Fracturing of America.* New York: Scribner, 2008.

Peters, Ronald M., ed. *The Speaker: Leadership in the U.S. House of Representatives.* Washington, DC: Congressional Quarterly, 1995.

Peterson del Mar, David. *Oregon's Promise: An Interpretive History.* Corvallis: Oregon State University Press, 2003.

Price, Larry W., ed. *Portland's Changing Landscape.* Portland: Portland State University Foundation, 1987.

Robbins, William G., ed. *The Great Northwest: The Search for Regional Identity.* Corvallis: Oregon State University Press, 2001.

Robbins, William G. *Hard Times in Paradise: Coos Bay, Oregon.* Seattle: University of Washington Press, 1988.

Robbins, William G. *A Man for All Seasons: Monroe Sweetland and the Liberal Paradox.* Corvallis: Oregon State University Press, 2015.

Robbins, William G. *Oregon: This Storied Land.* Portland: Oregon Historical Society Press, 2005.

Robbins, William G., and Katrine Barber. *Nature's Northwest: The North Pacific Slope in the Twentieth Century.* Tucson: University of Arizona Press, 2011.

Rosati, Jerel A. *The Politics of United States Foreign Policy.* Belmont, CA: Wadsworth Learning, 2004.

Rosenberg, Emily. *Spreading the American Dream: American Economic and Cultural Expansion, 1890–1945.* New York: Hill and Wang, 1982.

Rushing, Wanda. *Memphis and the Paradox of Place: Globalization in the American South.* Chapel Hill: University of North Carolina Press, 2009.

Ryan, Jeff. *Super Mario: How Nintendo Conquered America.* New York: Penguin, 2011.

Sanchez, George. *Becoming Mexican American: Ethnicity, Culture, and Identity in Chicano Los Angeles, 1900–1945.* New York: Oxford University Press, 1993.

Sarathy, Brinda. *Pineros: Latino Labour and the Changing Face of Forestry in the Pacific Northwest.* Vancouver: University of British Columbia Press, 2012.

Scates, Shelby. *Warren G. Magnuson and the Shaping of Twentieth-Century America.* Seattle: University of Washington Press, 1997.

Scheuerman, Richard D., and Alexander C. McGregor. *Harvest Heritage: Agricultural Origins and Heirloom Crops of the Pacific Northwest.* Pullman: Washington State University Press, 2013.

Schmitz, David F. *Thank God They're on Our Side: The United States and Right-Wing Dictatorships, 1921–1965.* Chapel Hill: University of North Carolina Press, 1999.

Schulzinger, Robert D. *A Time for War: The United States and Vietnam, 1941–1975.* New York: Oxford University Press, 1997.

Schwantes, Carlos A. *The Pacific Northwest: An Interpretive History.* 2nd ed. Lincoln: University of Nebraska Press, 1996.

Scott, George W. *Governors of Washington.* Civitas Press, 2012.

Sell, T. M. *Wings of Power: Boeing and the Politics of Growth in the Pacific Northwest.* Seattle: University of Washington Press, 2001.

Senate Foreign Relations Committee. *U.S. Policy with Respect to Mainland China.* Washington, DC: US Government Printing Office, 1966.

Settje, David E. *Faith & War: How Christians Debated the Cold and Vietnam Wars.* New York: New York University Press, 2011.

Shapiro, Ira. *The Last Great Senate: Courage and Statesmanship in Times of Crisis.* New York: Perseus Book Group, 2012.

Sheff, David. *Game Over: How Nintendo Zapped an American Industry, Captured Your Dollars, and Enslaved Your Children.* New York: Random House, 1993.

Sherry, Michael. *In the Shadow of War: The United States Since the 1930s.* New Haven, CT: Yale University Press, 1997.

Siekmeier, James F. "Trailblazer Diplomat: Bolivian Ambassador Victor Andrade Uzquiano's Efforts to Influence U.S. Policy, 1944–1962." *Diplomatic History* 28:3 (June 2004), 385–406.

Simpson, Jeffrey. *Star-Spangled Canadians: Canadians Living the American Dream.* Toronto: HarperCollins, 2000.

Small, Melvin. *At the Water's Edge: American Politics and the Vietnam War.* Chicago: Ivan R. Dee, 2005.

Small, Melvin. *Democracy and Diplomacy: The Impact of Domestic Politics on U.S. Foreign Policy, 1789–1994.* Baltimore: Johns Hopkins University Press, 1996.

Smith, C. Mark. *Community Godfather: How Sam Volpentest Helped Shape the History of Hanford and the Tri-Cities.* Richland, WA: Etcetera Press, 2013.

Smith, Steven S., Jason M. Robert, and Ryan J. Vander Wielen. *The American Congress.* 6th ed. New York: Cambridge University Press, 2009.

Soden, Dale E. *Outsiders in a Promised Land: Religious Activists in Pacific Northwest History.* Corvallis: Oregon State University Press, 2015.

Sprunger, Luke. "'This Is Where We Want to Stay': Tejanos and Latino Community Building in Washington County." *Oregon Historical Quarterly* 116:3 (Fall 2015), 278–309.

Stapilus, Randy. *The Oregon Political Field Guide.* Carlton, OR: Ridenbaugh Press, 2012.

Statistics of the Presidential and Congressional Election of November 6, 1956. Washington, DC: US Government Printing Office, 1958.

Statistics of the Presidential and Congressional Election of November 8, 1960. Washington, DC: US Government Printing Office, 1961.

Statistics of the Presidential and Congressional Election of November 8, 1988. Washington, DC: US Government Printing Office, 1989.

Stratton, David H., ed. *Spokane & The Inland Empire: An Interior Pacific Northwest Anthology.* 2nd ed. Pullman: Washington State University Press, 2005.

Stratton, David H. and George A. Frykman, eds. *The Changing Pacific Northwest: Interpreting the Past.* Pullman: Washington State University Press, 1988.

Swarthout, John M. "The 1956 Election in Oregon." *Western Political Quarterly* 10:1 (March 1957), 142–150.

Swartz, David R. *Moral Minority: The Evangelical Left in an Age of Conservatism.* Philadelphia: University of Pennsylvania Press, 2012.

Thompson, John Herd and Stephen J. Randall, *Canada and the United States: Ambivalent Allies.* Athens: University of Georgia Press, 2008.

Thompson, Roger C. *The Pacific Basin since 1945: A History of the Foreign Relations of the Asian, Australasian, and American Rim States and the Pacific Islands.* London: Longman, 1994.

Toll, William. *The Making of an Ethnic Middle Class: Portland Jewry Over Four Generations.* Albany: State University of New York Press, 1982.

Trombold, John, and Peter Donahue, eds. *Reading Portland: The City in Prose.* Portland: Oregon Historical Society Press, 2006.

Trubowitz, Peter. *Defining the National Interest: Conflict and Change in American Foreign Policy.* Chicago: University of Chicago Press, 1998.

Walth, Brent. *Fire at Eden's Gate: Tom McCall & the Oregon Story.* Portland: Oregon Historical Society Press, 1994.

Wasniewski, Matthew A., ed. *Women in Congress, 1917–2006.* Washington, DC: US Government Printing Office, 2006.

Whaley, Gray. *Oregon and the Collapse of Illahee: U.S. Empire and the Transformation of an Indigenous World, 1792–1859.* Chapel Hill: University of North Carolina Press, 2010.

Woods, Randall, ed. *Vietnam and the American Political Tradition: The Politics of Dissent.* Cambridge: Cambridge University Press, 2003.

Wright, Mary C., ed. *More Voices, New Stories: King County, Washington's First 150 Years.* Seattle: University of Washington Press, 2002.

Wyatt-Brown, Bertram. "Andrew Fry and Regionalism, Honor, and War." *Diplomatic History* 36:3 (June 2012), 491–494.

Xu, Guangqiu. *Congress and the U.S.-China Relationship, 1949–1979.* Akron: University of Akron Press, 2007.

Yates, Richard, and Charity Yates. *Washington State Atlas & Databook, 1990 Edition.* Eugene: Information Press, 1990.

Zeiler, Thomas W. *American Trade and Power in the 1960s.* New York: Columbia University Press, 1992.

Zelizer, Julian E., ed. *The American Congress: The Building of Democracy.* Boston: Houghton Mifflin Company, 2004.

Zelizer, Julian E. *Arsenal of Democracy: The Politics of National Security—From World War II to the War on Terrorism.* New York: Basic Books, 2010.

Zelizer, Julian E. *The Fierce Urgency of Now: Lyndon Johnson, Congress, and the Battle for the Great Society.* New York: Penguin Press, 2015.

Index

Abell, Ron, 88–91

bin Abdul Aziz, King Fahd, 232

Adams, Brock, 11, 36, 46

aerospace, importance to Pacific Northwest, 19, 184, 194, 198, 212, 245. *See also* Boeing

AFL-CIO, 43, 51

agriculture: Arbor Crest Wine Cellars, 201; Atiyeh and, 231–232, 234–235, 237, 241, 246; Foley and, 148, 169–173, 192, 195, 199–201; Grand Coulee Dam, 164; Hatfield and, 110, 205–206, 209; Jackson and, 166–167; Morse and, 154–155, 167–169; pre-World War II economy, 1; Oregon Department of Agriculture, 241, 244; Oregon-Washington Farmers' Union, 79; pre-World War II economy, 1; US Department of Agriculture (USDA), 110, 155, 166, 169–171, 173; US House Agriculture Committee, 10, 139, 154, 169–171, 200–201; US Secretary of Agriculture, 166, 172; US Senate Agriculture Committee, 200; Washington State Agriculture, 171; Washington Wheatgrowers Association, 200. *See also* apples, cattle industry, wheat

aircraft carriers, 2, 21, 36–37, 51

Air Force Academy, 7, 68

Akihito, Emperor, 210–11, 229

Alaska, 21, 81, 157, 220, 257

Alfa Concession, 199

Allen, William, 23–24

aluminum, 6, 55, 191, 260. *See also* Kaiser Aluminum

American Tokyo Kasei, 241

Amin, Idi, 110–111

Anderson, John, 240

Antelope, OR, 122, 216

anti-Americanism, 8, 104, 125

anti-ballistic missile (ABM) system, 39–42

antinuclear activists: ABM system opposition, 39–40; contrast with Jackson, 35; Foley and, 51–52; Hatfield antinuclear positions, 45, 93, 115, 117–118; Nuclear Navy, 37, 42, 44–45, 48

apples, 164–66, 173, 251

Arakawa, Minoru, 185–86, 188–89

Arlington, OR, 112

Arms Control Today, 93

arms reduction, 44–45, 94, 112, 114–115, 118. *See also* SALT

Asia: South Asia generally, 110, 170, 194; Southeast Asia, 98, 100. *See also* China, Japan, North Korea, South Korea, and Vietnam

al-Assad, Hafez, 233, 235

Asotin County, 50

atomic bombs, 6, 28, 30, 141; arsenal, 96; bombings of Hiroshima and Nagasaki, 12, 44, 93

atomic energy: Atomic Energy Commission (AEC), 28–33; Joint Committee on Atomic Energy, 21–22, 28–29, 31

atomic submarines. *See* nuclear submarines

Astoria, 12, 69–70, 72–75, 169, 223; *Daily Astorian*, 70

Atiyeh, Aziz, 220

Atiyeh, Dolores, 243

Atiyeh, Edward, 220

Atiyeh, George, 220

Atiyeh, Linda Asly, 220

Atiyeh, Richard, 220

Atiyeh, Victor: automobile exports and, 208; background, 220–221; elections, 221–224 and international trade generally, 9, 215–216, 219, 256; legacy of

spending, 95, 125–134; international
trade generally, 13, 163, 169, 181,
201–202, 206, 223; on Morse's defeat,
86; Nicaraguan contras, 120; opposition to Iraq War, 124–125; opposition
to Vietnam War, 65, 95–109; Panama
Canal Treaties, 112–114; praise for
Atiyeh's trade efforts, 242; Rajneeshpuram and, 122–24; redefining national security, 8, 13, 65, 67, 93–122,
133–135, 216, 249–250; religious beliefs, 3, 95–97; Senate Appropriations
Committee, 13, 95, 201, 251; Silicon
Forest, 202–203, 210; support for de-
fense interests, 94, 112, 116, 118–121,
216; timber, 101, 153, 156–157, 161–
164, 247; trade with Japan, 156–157,
161, 174, 181, 204–205, 210–213
Hawaii, 37–38, 185, 257
Hawley, Willis, 1, 142, 250
Hendriksen, Margie, 115–117, 121
Herter, Christian, 153, 165–166
Hewlett-Packard, 238
Hickenlooper, Bourke, 30
Hicks, Floyd, 10, 42
Hillsboro, OR, 133, 217, 227–228, 242–
243, 247
Hirohito (Emperor), 204
Ho Chi Minh, 83, 100, 102
Holmes, Robert, 68
Homestead Air Force Base, 53
Honda, 4, 204, 208, 218, 225
Hood Canal, 41
Hood River, 154, 231
Hoover, Herbert, 142, 250
Hota, Tsutomu, 194
Hsu, Ming, 219
Hu, Ping, 238–239
Humphrey, Hubert, 80, 84, 86, 99
hydroelectricity: China, 146; Columbia
River generally, 5, 20; drought, 34;
Grand Coulee and Bonneville Dams,
6, 20, 29; influence of Pacific
Northwest generally, 4; Jackson and,
28; Morse support for, 11, 77;
Washington's geographic advantages,
12
hydrogen bombs, 28
Hyundai, 219

immigration: Atiyeh as child of Syrian
immigrants, 220; Chinese immigrants,
148, 211; economic development of
Pacific Northwest and, 256, 260;
Hatfield as champion of, 211; ICE,
211; Japanese immigrants, 149; Latino
migrants, 14; Northwest as Edenic, 5;
Silicon Forest, 256; Trump and, 254
Import Export Consultants, 149
India, 122–123, 170, 257
Indonesia, 70, 109, 171
Intel, 2, 221
International Herald Tribune, 178
International Trade Commission, 206
Iran, 171, 176
Iraq, 124–125, 134, 163
Israel, 34, 156, 233–234
Ivancie, Frank, 230

Jackson, Helen Hardin, 188
Jackson, Henry "Scoop": anti-commu-
nist, 62, 124, 252; Boeing, 23–27;
China, 144–148, 253; civil rights, 177;
death, 119, 181, 188, 251; elections,
62, 63; Expo '74, 174–175; federal
largesse generally, 8, 64, 67, 95, 201;
Foley and, 10, 49, 51–52, 139;
Hanford Nuclear Reservation 10, 19–
20, 22, 27–36, 249; international
trade, 140, 151–152, 165–167, 187–
188, 253; Johnson and, 139; legacy, 4,
10–11, 47–48, 180, 249–250; Morse
and, 75; Puget Sound, 10, 20–21, 36–
45, 47, 52, 63; supersonic transport,
24–25, 95
Jacob, Stanley, 129–130
Japan: air travel to Tokyo, 210, 212, 225,
245; Akihito visit to Portland, 149;
American protectionism, 152, 183–
184, 186–195; Arakawa and, 185–188;
Atiyeh and, 13–14, 215, 217, 221–231,
239–247; atomic bombs, 6, 12, 93;
automobile imports from, 182–183;
Bank of Tokyo, 228; Bush and, 189–
190; Centennial Exposition, 173–174;
Diet, 150, 194, 204; economic decline,
246–247; Electro Scientific
Equipment, 221; Expo '74, 176; Foley
and agricultural trade, 10, 140, 169–
171, 173, 198–200; Foley and trade
generally, 139, 149, 181, 192–198;